THE WARS OF FI

MW00777139

MODERN WARS IN PERSPECTIVE

General Editors: *H.M. Scott and B.W. Collins*

This ambitious new series offers wide-ranging studies of specific wars, and distinct phases of warfare, from the close of the Middle Ages to the present day. It aims to advance the current integration of military history into the academic mainstream. To that end, the books are not merely traditional campaign narratives, but examine the causes, course and consequences of major conflicts, in their full international political, diplomatic, social and ideological contexts.

ALREADY PUBLISHED

Mexico and the Spanish Conquest
Ross Hassig

The Anglo–Dutch Wars of the Seventeenth Century
J.R. Jones

The War of the Austrian Succession, 1740–1748
M.S. Anderson

The Wars of Frederick the Great
Dennis Showalter

The Wars of Napoleon
Charles J. Esdaile

The Spanish–American War: Conflict in the Caribbean
and the Pacific 1895–1902
Joseph Smith

China at War, 1901–1949
Edward L. Dreyer

The Wars of French Decolonization
Anthony Clayton

THE WARS OF
FREDERICK THE GREAT

DENNIS SHOWALTER

LONGMAN
London and New York

Longman Group Limited,
Longman House, Burnt Mill,
Harlow, Essex CM20 2JE, England
and Associated Companies throughout the world.

Published in the United States of America
by Longman Publishing, New York

© Longman Group Limited 1996

First published 1996

ISBN 0 582 06260 8 CSD
ISBN 0 582 06259 4 PPR

British Library Cataloguing-in-Publication Data

A catalogue record for this book is
available from the British Library

Library of Congress Cataloging-in-Publication Data

Showalter, Dennis E.
  The wars of Frederick the Great / Dennis Showalter.
     p. cm. — (Modern warns in perspective)
  Includes bibliographical references and index.
  ISBN 0–582–06260–8. — ISBN 0–582–06259–4 (pbk.)
  1. Frederick II, King of Prussia, 1712–1786—Military leadership.
  2. Prussia (Germany)—History, Military. 3. Prussia (Germany)—
History—Frederick II, 1740–1786. I. Title. II. Series.
DD403.8.S54   1996
943'.053'092—dc20   95–13124
                                                       CIP

Set by 5 in 10/12 Sabon
Produced by Longman Singapore Publishers (Pte) Ltd.
Printed in Singapore

CONTENTS

LIST OF MAPS

ACKNOWLEDGEMENTS

A book taking a half-dozen years from conceptualization to completion incurs corresponding personal and professional debts. My wife, Clara Anne McKenna, and my children, John and Clara Kathleen, manifested patience beyond the call of love or duty with a husband and father who often seemed over two centuries behind the times. My colleagues and students at Colorado College and the U.S. Air Force Academy, where I served as visiting professor from 1991 to 1993, loyally supported my frequently-arcane enthusiasms. Colorado College was also generous with financial assistance that greatly facilitated the manuscript's preparation.

Longmans deserves special mention both for their enthusiastic support of the project and their willingness to 'take a long day' in the delivery of its original and final versions. Their flexibility contributed much to the manuscript's quality. Series editor Hamish Scott, himself a leading scholar in the field, provided dozens of useful suggestions, and kept dozens more factual errors and questionable interpretations from the cold light that falls on the printed page.

Diane Broderson, Interlibrary Loans Librarian of Colorado College, had an uncanny knack for finding and obtaining even the most obscure sources. Her efforts shortened the completion of this book by months. Susan Ashley, Chair of the History Department, suggested books, verified translations, and provided moral and institutional support particularly welcome in the context of a teaching institution. And Bob McJimsey, himself a scholar of early modern Europe, took time from his own work to find references, listen to half-baked theories, and answer questions that I know to him seemed obvious. His intellectual influence did much to shape in particular my presentation of Britain's policies and behaviours from 1740 to 1763. I thank all of my colleagues and friends for their contributions; the shortcomings remain my responsibility.

One special acknowledgement remains. Sheila Fuller typed the successive drafts of this manuscript from the first longhand text to the final copy. But she has been far more than a typist. Her feeling for style and sense inform every chapter, sometimes every page. Her cocked eye and her "Dennis, are you *sure* that's what you mean to say?" gave the work much of whatever stylistic quality it possesses. Her interest in the subject kept me going at times when my feelings toward Frederick the Great were more hostile than those of Maria Theresa or Empress Elizabeth. The book is dedicated to her, with my appreciation and gratitude.

INTRODUCTION

To open this book at random may seem to step backwards in time. Instead of class, ethnicity, and gender, it focusses on states at war. Instead of the 'longue durée' it concentrates on a quarter-century. Instead of abstract forces it emphasizes the specific decisions of particular men and women. It is written not from the perspective of enlisted men and junior officers, but consorts instead with monarchs, generals, and ministers. And in a final spasm of unfashionableness, the text emphasizes battles and campaigns.

Do these points make *The Wars of Frederick the Great* an exercise in archaeology rather than history? Is the book a valedictory to an approach relegated to the dustbin by modern perspectives and methods? Far from it. Instead this study approaches the eighteenth century on that century's own terms. The social, economic, and political orders of early modern Europe depended on the state system that emerged in the aftermath of the Thirty Years' War. A state's domestic legitimacy depended at bottom on that state's ability to protect its subjects from the direct consequences of war. The enlightened absolutists' concern for social stability and economic development reflected less perception of these as absolute goods than recognition of their necessity for what might best be called a 'security state' – an entity able at the least to defend its interests.

The states of Europe, whatever their size, perceived themselves as power entities existing in the context of, and in relationship to, other power entities. This perception made diplomacy their primary concern, and enhanced the importance of war-making as the logical consequence of a zero-sum game played in a state of anarchy. An Age of Reason perceived conflict as a rational means of arbitrating differences, even among individuals. To concentrate on diplomatic and military interaction is to enter the minds of eighteenth-century decision-makers: to emphasize what they emphasized and analyze what they considered important. In both areas, moreover, truth lies in nuances. To pay attention to the details of negotiating and fighting is to understand behaviours that, considered without such underpinning, often defies the logic beloved of system-makers, whether Marxists, *Annalistes*, or international-relations theorists. *The Wars of Frederick the Great* emphasizes war-*making*: the *behaviour* of the diplomats, the soldiers, and the institutions to which they belonged. The text is informed by the fact that the participants in the events presented frequently had as many hours or minutes to spend making decisions as scholars have months to spend analyzing those decisions. In this sense *The Wars of Frederick the Great* is 'event history'. Yet the negotiations and the treaties, the marches and the fighting, did not exist in a vacuum. *Histoire événementielle* is not merely a euphemism for 'one damn thing after another'. Events establish contexts, and the contexts of the wars that ravaged Europe between 1740 and 1763 continue to influence the continent's history to the present day. With that cosmic generalization, let us begin.

1   MATRICES AND PROBABILITIES

In an era of secular relativism, military history remains dominated by Whigs and Calvinists. The military Whig interprets war as a contest between progress and obscurantism with progress, whether represented by technology, social attitudes, or clear understanding of war's principles, inevitably emerging triumphant. The Calvinist takes that approach one step further by interpreting victory and defeat as judgments on the militarily righteous. The generals, armies, and societies taking the straight and narrow path are admitted to the scholars' Valhalla. Those failing to perceive and act on war's revealed truths are cast into darkness.

WAYS OF WAR IN THE AGE OF REASON

Nowhere are these mind-sets more apparent than in studies of eighteenth-century warfare. For the Whigs the era of Marlborough, Eugene, and Frederick is at best a stepping stone to the 'real' wars that began in 1793. The French Revolution, with its patterns of general mobilization, ideological justification and national aggrandizement, is perceived as establishing norms followed and developed ever since. However sincere the original anti-militarist rhetoric of the revolutionaries may have been, they ultimately developed wholly new patterns of military organization, structured for waging a wholly new kind of war. Henceforth annihilation, political when not social or cultural, became for governments a normative risk of defeat. By the mid-twentieth century, physical annihilation had become established as a possible fate for losers. Whigs seldom present total war as desirable. Its bitter necessity, however, remained virtually unchallenged until the midpoint of the nuclear era. In such a context eighteenth-century conflicts usually appear no more than a series of

1

gavottes, a form of Noh drama whose outcomes were determined by their structures.[1]

Military history's Calvinists have usually contented themselves with depicting the collapse of *ancien régime* armies in the face of a Revolutionary/Napoleonic challenge that pitilessly exposed every flaw of the old ways of war-making. And those flaws are legion. David Chandler describes armed forces consistently unable to execute in the field the strategic and political designs of their governments. Martin van Creveld alleges an arteriosclerotic fortress-and-siege mentality imperfectly camouflaged by false issues of logistics. Geoffrey Parker argues that wars 'eternalized themselves' because strategic thinking was trapped between the rapid growth in the size of armies and the relative inability of states and societies to support those armies. Russell Weigley offers a counterpoint by describing the eighteenth century's obsessive tactical focus: a search for the *fata morgana* of a decisive battle that would in a single day determine a war's outcome by destroying an enemy's army. While states bankrupted themselves pursuing this mirage, Weigley argues, wars remained exercises in futility. Battles only killed more men – they decided nothing in themselves.[2]

Weigley certainly appears at times to argue that only permanent resolution of the sources of intra-state conflict merits definition as decisive. Certainly he overlooks the wider consequences of defeat and victory on the battlefield – especially the negative ones. Steenkirk in 1692, for example, left a French army in possession of the field, but too badly hammered to pursue the campaign's original objective of capturing the fortress of Liège. Frederick the Great's victories at Leuthen and Rossbach did not end the Seven Years War. They did, however, encourage both Prussia's king and Prussia's soldiers to keep the field even in adversity, believing that these triumphs could one day be repeated. Leuthen and Rossbach also encouraged Frederick's enemies to pursue war to the hilt. A state and an army capable of achieving that kind of double triumph seemed too dangerous to be treated as merely another partner in the diplomatic minuet.

---

1 Geoffrey Best, *War and Society in Revolutionary Europe, 1770–1870* (New York, 1986); and John Keegan, *A History of Warfare* (New York, 1994), are well executed and familiar examples of this approach.

2 David Chandler, *The Art of Warfare in the Age of Marlborough* (London, 1976), pp. 19–20; Martin van Creveld, *Supplying War: Logistics from Wallenstein to Patton* (Cambridge, 1977); Geoffrey Parker, *The Military Revolution* (Cambridge, 1988); Russell Weigley, *The Age of Battles: The Quest for Decisive Warfare from Breitenfeld to Waterloo* (Bloomington, Indiana, 1991).

Weigley nevertheless establishes a point vital to any understanding of eighteenth-century warfare. The generals and the statesmen alike sought decisions. Commanders and theorists alike warned against the risks of basing military operations on the possession of certain fortresses, or the establishing of certain supply routes, while neglecting operations in the open field. The elaborate manoeuvring was not an end in itself, but a preliminary to establishing conditions for battle. If those conditions were favourable enough to encourage one's opponent to concede without risking a test, then so much the better![3] In diplomatic contexts the eighteenth century's principled commitment to balance-of-power politics must not be exaggerated. Major and middle-sized powers regularly contemplated and frequently attempted significant aggrandizement at the expense of weaker and declining states. Poland, Sweden, the Ottoman Empire, even Spain, were regularly targets of their neighbours' ambitions.

Pragmatically, even the best of the *ancien régime*'s armed forces could not hope to dominate its adversaries enough to implement the diplomats' grand designs. Only with the untaming of Bellona in the Age of Democratic Revolution could maps be redrawn and destinies reshaped to the degree later generations have considered a norm. To speak of 'limitation' in this context, however, is to misuse that term in the same way Weigley arguably misuses 'decisiveness'. Any conflicts between organized political systems are limited. Even in a nuclear context, war's goals do not include as ideals the complete annihilation of an opposing population and the total destruction of its economic base. At least the adversary's material resources are expected to be at a conqueror's disposal. It is correspondingly appropriate to examine the particular structures that shaped the particular limitations of eighteenth-century conflict.

Intellectual factors played a major role in the process. Every era defines ultimate truth in its own way. The biological determinism of the nineteenth century gave way to the computer printout of the twentieth. The eighteenth century's intellectual life was dominated by a concern for first principles, for integrating social phenomena into an order borrowing its essential rationale from the world of mathematics. It is hardly surprising that military theorists and practical soldiers alike sought to tame that process which is above all the province of confusion, not so much to put the conduct of war and the behaviour of armies under artificial restrictions as to express

---

3 See the analysis of this issue in Jeremy Black, *European Warfare: 1660–1815* (New Haven, Connecticut, 1994).

them in terms comprehensible and acceptable to the societies and systems the military establishments existed to serve. The Thirty Years War marked the end of the temporary ascendancy of the military enterpriser and his *soldateska*. Whatever the financial and moral costs of bringing armies under the control of governments, the alternatives were perceptibly worse. The process generated a certain reciprocity, as soldiers sought to justify their existence to their now-permanent paymasters in universal rather than craft-specific terms. It would be surprising if they had done so in any other way than in terms of *l'esprit géometrique*.[4]

Moving from the metaphysical to the concrete, fortifications did much to structure eighteenth-century ways of war. The complex and expensive systems beginning with the 'Italian trace', and culminating in the exotic designs of Vauban, Coehorn, and their less familiar imitators, seldom became strategic objectives in themselves. Nor were they regarded as impregnable. Even the most skilfully conducted defence was expected to end with a capitulation on terms. Fortresses, however, could not simply be bypassed. Until well into the eighteenth century, undeveloped road networks created a correspondingly large number of choke points that in enemy hands could prove disastrous for an army dependent on its own magazines for supplies and, increasingly, ammunition. Rapid-firing flintlocks required predictable resupply on scales that, if modest by contemporary standards, nevertheless put unheard-of pressure on logistical systems. Moreover, the often-noted requirement of modern fortifications for ever-larger garrisons increased the risks of leaving such positions in the rear of one's own lines of operation. Even the most passive of governors was likely to be able to mount serious threats to weak screening or blockading forces.

In central Europe neither budgets nor terrain would support the kinds of fortress systems familiar in the Low Countries, northern France, and northern Italy. The fortresses of Prussia, Austria, and the lesser German states were more of the traditional model: extended protection for cities like Prague or Dresden, or *points d'appui* like Schweidnetz, Kolberg, or Olmütz. This did not mean that they could be ignored with impunity. The region's relatively limited road network, which by mid-century fell significantly behind the growing size of the region's armies, meant that even an isolated fortress could play

---

4 Thomas F. Arnold, 'The Geometry of Power: War in the Age of the Early Modern Military Revolution, 1500–1800', paper presented at the 1994 meeting of the Society for Military History.

a major role as a choke point. Nor could siege guns be brought up with anything like the speed possible in more developed theatres of war. A related problem involved the difficulty in obtaining the large amounts of construction material necessary for the elaborate system of saps and trenches necessary for a formal eighteenth-century siege. Finally, neither the Russian, Prussian, nor Austrian armies paid much attention to their respective engineer corps. The combined result of these factors, particularly during the Seven Years War, was a general preference for bluff and bombardment: threats from the pages of Grimmelshausen combined with throwing a few hundred rounds over the walls almost at random. A governor willing to ignore both words and deeds could usually count on pinning a significant number of the enemy beneath his walls until they gave up in disgust or a relief force came close enough to invite them to take their chances in the open field.[5]

Fighting meant moving, and moving meant supply. The exact role of logistics in determining the nature of eighteenth-century warfare remains a subject of debate. In typically sweeping fashion, Martin van Creveld denies the tyranny of magazines. Armies, he asserts, lived off the countryside because existing transportation technologies made it impossible to move more than 10 per cent of an army's requirements – non-improvisable essentials like ammunition, uniforms, and medical supplies. The scales of baggage allowed to officers may seem extreme by later standards, but that had more to do with social issues than logistical ones and in absolute terms did little to clog supply lines. Instead van Creveld stipulates that eighteenth-century armies were not particularly good at living off the land compared to their mercenary predecessors and Napoleonic successors. That, however, reflected another organizational problem: a general failure to provide for a field quartermaster system able to feed large bodies of troops under operational conditions.[6]

Van Creveld's numerous critics describe a broad spectrum of technical and institutional factors making it anything but 'relatively simple' to supply an army on the move.[7] Requisitioned grain usually needed to be threshed as well as baked. In supply terms the eighteenth century was at a watershed: conscious enough of the perils of

5 The best general analysis is Christopher Duffy, *The Fortress in the Age of Vauban and Frederick the Great, 1660–1789* (London, 1985).

6 Van Creveld, *Supplying War*, pp. 26 ff.

7 See particularly John A. Lynn, 'The History of Logistics and *Supplying War*', in *Feeding Mars: Logistics in Western Warfare from the Middle Ages to the Present*, ed. J.A. Lynn (Boulder, Colorado, 1993), pp. 9–27.

digestive diseases to take pains in their prevention, but not yet sophisticated in the techniques of food preparation on a large scale under improvised conditions. Ovens as well as wagons significantly constrained the movement of armies. Requisitioned cattle could not simply be butchered on the spot and the meat issued still quivering. Vegetables too required some preparation; raw or half-cooked they were worse than nothing.

Psychological factors played an often-overlooked role in the process of logistics. Eighteenth-century armies were far more contractual than is generally recognized. Soldiers may have enlisted under what amounted to absolute terms of service. In practice they had very solid ideas of their implied rights. Men fed poorly enough to perceive their short commons as a breach of contract might not go so far as to respond by deserting. They could and did, however, develop a broad spectrum of maladies ranging from incapacitating boils to debilitating homesickness: the *nostalgie du pays* dreaded by all armies. It is worth noting that eighteenth-century Europeans were not a healthy lot. Poor diets and outright malnutrition combined with hard physical labour from early years to produce men who were fragile beneath their surface robustness, and correspondingly vulnerable to a broad spectrum of camp diseases. Keeping them fed with a minimum of effort on their part was the kind of obvious insurance policy no sensible commander was likely to ignore.[8]

The pattern of eighteenth-century warfare was also determined by the structure of eighteenth-century armies. These were high-tech forces. Relative to the economic, administrative, and technological infrastructures supporting them, the fleets and armies of the Age of Reason represented as close to total mobilization as developed societies could achieve and sustain. A state-of-the-art ship of the line was among its era's most complex technological artefacts, in the category of a space shuttle rather than an aircraft carrier.

A similar point might be made regarding land warfare. For all its shortcomings in a 'Whig' context, the flintlock musket and socket bayonet that was the dominant weapons system of eighteenth-century armies increased both the offensive and defensive capacities of the infantry to a point where, for the first time since the Roman legions, European battlefields were dominated by a single arm of service. Even at his peak the medieval knight never possessed the flexibility of the Frederician musketeer in his variant forms.

8 Marcel Reinhard, 'Nostalgie et service militaire pendant la Révolution', *Annales historiques de la Révolution française*, XXX (1958), pp. 1–15.

At the same time the flintlock was a system whose optimal use demanded levels of training, discipline, and commitment that created what amounted to a professional outlook. Man and weapon must be able to function as a single entity, in the context of a battlefield experience increasingly remote from even the most violent sectors of civil society. And that was only the initial step. The musketeer could not become so absorbed in the process of loading and firing that he became unresponsive to orders. The eighteenth-century soldier, far from being the automaton of so many later legends, had to combine mechanical skill and mental alertness in ways more familiar to the contemporary tanker or infantryman than to the uniformed civilians of the two world wars.

The other combat arms, cavalry and artillery, faced similar challenges. No longer could cavalry decide an action by riding at will through and over enemy footmen. Timing was everything in a mounted charge. Knowing when to launch one was the product of combinations of experience and insight impossible to calculate precisely, but devastating in their presence – or their absence. Such an attack depended in its initial stages on dash and aggressiveness on the part of all ranks: the much-vaunted, often-derided 'cavalry spirit'. Yet the adrenalin rush needed to be choked off the moment the trumpets sounded 'rally'. Heedless pursuit of a beaten enemy, or the less spectacular but more common pattern of continuing a stalemated mounted mélée, were as high-risk prospects as was excessive caution. Combining the qualities of warrior and soldier in a cavalryman was by no means an automatic process; as late as the Napoleonic Wars the British army had failed to master the trick.

Throughout the eighteenth century artillerymen remained primarily technicians – a circumstance exacerbated by their relatively low status in the army's pecking order. Yet by the Seven Years War the gunners played a crucial ongoing role in any major battle. Not only were they expected to shoot their guns, but to move them and fight for them on a regular basis. The jealously guarded status of the artillery as a 'scientific' branch of service, in short, was being challenged by a new role as a fighting force.[9]

Were these complexities not enough, eighteenth-century armies had to fight with an underdeveloped nervous system. Tactical

---

9 Cf. B.P. Hughes, *Firepower: Weapons Effectiveness on the Battlefield, 1630–1850* (New York, 1974); Chandler, *Art of Warfare in the Age of Marlborough*; and Christopher Duffy, *The Military Experience in the Age of Reason* (London, 1987), especially pp. 104 ff. and 197 ff.

organizations above the regiment were for all practical purposes non-existent. Even brigades were frequently improvised from operation to operation. Higher formations were entirely *ad hoc*. General texts frequently use the words 'division' and 'corps' as convenient shorthands. The terms, however, are sufficiently misleading that the following narrative substitutes 'battle group' and 'task force' as more clearly indicating the nature of the bodies.

The decision not to implement a more comprehensively articulated organizational structure is one of the major uninvestigated negatives of eighteenth-century military history. In part this reflected a point made by Thomas Kuhn: the conditions for a paradigm shift remained unmet. Between the 1650s and the 1750s, for example, armies increased in size rapidly but steadily. There was no sudden explosion of numbers to shatter the limits of existing structures of thought about how those armies might be organized for optimal effectiveness. Both the *mentalité* of the Age of Reason and the wisdom of great captains like Turenne and Montecuccoli favoured command from the top: a single will shaping and directing the campaign and the battle. To a degree this was a response to the later Thirty Years War, when tactical control often tended to disappear within minutes after the shooting started. In more general terms the legacy of Wallenstein still survived, if only as a ghost-memory of the potential risks of over-mighty subordinates. Nor did officer corps dominated by still proud, still economically independent aristocracies offer promising material for elaborate hierarchic systems of command and obedience.[10]

This point was highlighted even in Prussia, where in 1717 King Frederick William had established a Corps of Cadets whose adolescent members were drawn from the ranks of the aristocracy. The King's intention was to integrate these young men into state service even if, as sometimes happened, they had to be enrolled by force. Specific programmes of general and professional education took second place to that goal. The eventual result was to establish a pattern of noblemen's sons attending a state institution.[11] An equally significant, but unintended, consequence was the development of Prussia's officer corps as a collegial community where lieutenants as well as generals could in principle address the King on a footing of comradeship.

10 Thomas Barker, 'Armed Forces and Nobility: Austrian Particulars', in *Army, Aristocracy, Monarchy: Essays on War, Society, and Government in Austria, 1618–1780* (New York, 1982), pp. 37–60, is a useful case study.

11 J.K. Zobel, *Das preussische Kadettenkorps. Militärische Jugenderziehung als Herrschaftsmittel im preussischen Militärsystem* (Frankfurt, 1978).

Another factor retarding the development of articulated organizations was the relative heterogeneity of senior officer corps. One-sixth of Frederick the Great's generals between 1740 and 1763 came from outside Prussia.[12] In countries like France and England, ethnic origins might be more homogeneous but professional competence was a matter of accident. An officer was still expected to master his craft by a mixture of direct experience and force of character. This process worked well enough at regimental levels. Higher achievements were essentially random, both in absolute terms and relative to the system as a whole.[13] Erratic genius can be as dangerous as predictable mediocrity. In the context of multiple unpredictability it was the better part of common sense to limit risks by limiting opportunities for failure – particularly when battle was increasingly perceived as the best way of cutting the Gordian knots of 'forever wars'.

A final element facilitating the acceptance of rigid control involved the symmetrical nature of eighteenth-century armies. At least in western Europe they were trained, armed, and organized in essentially identical fashions. They kept abreast of one another's innovations, not least through the steady movement of middle-ranking officers from service to service. In contrast to forces developed in differing paradigms, symmetrical opponents seldom offer each other obvious windows of opportunity.

The exporting of early modern Europe's military revolution illustrates the latter process, through which rapid victories could be achieved by either side. Braddock's disaster on the Monongahela and Cornwallis's triumph at Mysore were two sides of the same coin.[14] Great power conflict in the first half of the eighteenth century, however, increasingly prefigured a pattern more familiar in 1914. It is possible for an army to defeat its mirror image. But to do so means taking advantage of nuances. It means planning and control as opposed to inspired improvisation. And above all it must be done quickly, by getting inside an enemy's loop of competence and turning his strengths to weaknesses. The alternative is attrition: the kind of drawn-out, exhausting war no early modern state could afford.

---

12 Christopher Duffy, *The Army of Frederick the Great* (New York, 1974), p. 30.

13 Martin van Creveld's phrase, 'the stone age of command', is particularly apt: *Command in War* (Cambridge, Mass., 1985), pp. 52 ff.

14 Parker, *Military Revolution* pp. 115 ff.; Bruce P. Lenman, 'The Transition to European Military Ascendancy in India, 1600–1800', in *Tools of War: Instruments, Ideas, and Institutions of Warfare, 1445–1871* ed. J.A. Lynn (Urbana, Illinois, 1990), pp. 53–73.

An up-to-date army of the mid-eighteenth century significantly resembled its successors in the late twentieth century. Both depended heavily on state-of-the-art technology applied by highly skilled professionals. Both were structured to provide quick victories – not least because neither could absorb large numbers of untrained, unmotivated replacements. And both placed barely acceptable, long-term stress on the systems whose interests they ostensibly exist to enhance.

The tap-root of modern war was money, yet that root was weak and shallow relative to the size of the tree it was expected to nurture.[15] Since the mid-sixteenth century the size of armies had increased significantly. The causes of this phenomenon have recently been debated with vigour and clarity. Geoffrey Parker focuses on the numbers of men required to besiege a fortress defended by the Italian trace, with its complicated system of bastions. These fortresses also required increasing numbers of men as garrisons. Even if individual towns were lightly held, the growing number of modern fortifications tied down such large forces that a state hoping to maintain a field army as well as an aggregate of garrisons found itself constrained to increase its order of battle significantly.[16]

Parker's critics and modifiers assert other reasons as well for the growth in the size of Europe's armies. The demographic and social changes of the early modern period created, particularly in the west, increasing numbers of young men of all social classes who were no longer bound by familiar restrictions and who saw few prospects in familiar surroundings. As traditional bonds of lordship weakened or vanished, so did traditional patterns of security and protection, however meagre these might have been. Far from being the harmonious communities of populist mythology, peasant villages and urban neighbourhoods alike were undergoing a process of complex stratification, with significant distinctions between alpha families, the *coqs du village*, and those on the margins of power and influence. Apart from the expected difficulties of finding steady work, to say nothing of securing an apprenticeship or inheriting a usable plot of land, it required no great leaps of imagination for a young man in the latter category to perceive in his native environment a

15 R. Bonney, *The King's Debts: Finance and Politics in France, 1589–1661* (Oxford, 1981); J. Brewer, *The Sinews of Power: War, Money and the English State, 1688–1789* (London, 1989); and Dietmar Stutzer, 'Das preussische Heer und seine Finanzierung in zeitgenossischer Darstellung 1740–1790', *Militärgeschichtliche Mitteilungen*, XXIV (1978) pp. 23–48.
16 Parker, *Military Revolution*, pp. 24 *passim*.

future so limited that any change might prove for the better – or at least offer possibilities of a new servitude.[17]

Hunger, as always, remained the best recruiting sergeant. Nevertheless the armies of early modern Europe did not lack a steady supply of true volunteers. Military service offered food and clothing. It offered some cash income – an important point in an increasingly comprehensive money economy, however unreliable the paymasters might be in reality. A fortunate few became rich, or improved their social status to degrees all but impossible for civilians. Above all, following the drum promised adventure, a way out of one's presemt surroundings. One 17-year-old Alsatian travelled as far as Aachen to join the Prussian army because of its high reputation. His account, while written from a perspective of age that often confuses positive specific experiences with the general vigour of lost youth, nevertheless described even his recruit days as full of fun and horseplay, passed among men far more interesting than those of his home village.[18]

Such career decisions were frequent enough that in peacetime, at least, outright criminals were enlisted only as a last resort, for the same reasons that they are not sought by modern armies. They made up a disproportionate number of the wilful troublemakers. They were also a constant source of friction in the ranks. Thieves, alcoholics, and brawlers made life far more miserable than it had to be for their better-conducted comrades, and for their officers as well. On the other hand, men who found themselves in trouble with the civil authorities over such issues as land titles or paternity claims readily found homes in any army. Another frequent source of recruits were craftsmen and professionals who had fallen on hard times. Teachers grew tired of beating the same scraps of knowledge into unwilling students. Clerics lost vocations that might have been shaky from the beginning. Textile workers who found their tasks increasing and their compensation declining abandoned hearth and loom for the sake of regular meals and more or less regular pay. 'Travelling people', jugglers, actors, puppeteers, might find themselves in uniform as a consequence of rheumatism, a broken hand, or a simple loss of the touch that made audiences laugh, cry, and throw money. These

---

17 Cf. the survey in Frank Tallett, *War and Society in Early-Modern Europe, 1495–1715* (London, 1992), pp. 69 *passim*; and John Lynn, 'The *Trace Italienne* and the Growth of Armies: The French Case', *Journal of Military History*, LV (1990), 297–330.

18 J.D. Dreyer, *Leben und Thaten eines preussischen Regiments–Tambours* (Breslau, 1870).

latter, in passing, were usually particularly welcomed by officers and men alike as comrades able both to take the bad with the good and to provide laughter and distraction when the going got difficult.[19]

Translated from social to operational terms, the armies of early modern Europe were composed, by and large, of men willing to fight under conditions other than the immediate defence of their own homes. This fact alone gave them a significant edge over the various militias still maintained in the states of Europe. Bringing such men into the ranks was less of a problem than maintaining them there. Financial problems had much to do with the replacement of mercenary and contract forces raised on an *ad hoc* basis by standing armies kept under the control of a central government. A permanent force was both more cost-effective and easier to fit into a state budget.[20] Such forces, however, generated another kind of crisis as states persisted in creating armed forces larger than they could feed, clothe, and pay. Under Louis XIV, for example, the French army's official strength was no fewer than 400,000 men, and perhaps as many as 300,000 actually stood in its ranks. Even the Grand Monarchy, with the most efficient administration in early modern Europe, could not support such numbers except by policies of improvisation. The result was an early version of 'imperial overstretch'. Unable to meet their military needs from their own resources, unwilling in the face of perceived threats to cut their coats according to their cloth, states increasingly resorted to war to support their swollen armed forces.

The limitations of this process in its extreme form are familiar to even the most casual student of the Thirty Years War. Left to their own devices armies destroyed or wasted far more than they actually consumed. These patterns persisted long after the Peace of Westphalia. Even in France, the Sun King's soldiers made up the gap between what the state supplied them and what they needed to survive by ruthless exploitation of the people they had ostensibly been recruited to defend. That pattern may well have been enhanced by a certain desire for revenge against the social system that offered too many of its sons no respectable place.

The initial response involved replacing what John Lynn calls

19 Tallett, *War and Society*, p. 87; Duffy, *Military Experience*, pp. 89–90.

20 Charles Tilly, *Coercion, Capital, and European States, AD 990–1990* (Oxford, 1990), pp. 68 ff.; M.S. Anderson, *War and Society in Europe of the Old Regime 1618–1789* (London, 1988), pp. 99 ff.; John A. Mears, 'The Emergence of the Standing Professional Army in Seventeenth-Century Europe', *Social Science Quarterly* (1969), 106–15.

'the tax of violence' by 'contributions'. These were little more than systematic extortions, ideally from enemy or neutral territory but in emergencies from one's own people as well. They marked a major improvement in both the behaviour of armies and the efficiency of resource mobilization for war. Ultimately, however, contributions were limited in two ways. The first involved a consistent temptation to bleed a territory beyond its capacity to recover beyond subsistence levels. The Seven Years War offers dozens of examples of armies forced to move because even the most efficient, most controlled systems of contribution and requisition had left them sitting in a wasteland. The second shortcoming of the contribution system is more obvious. It could be exercised properly only outside a state's own frontiers. This in turn created an international climate highly favourable to aggressive wars – which required ever-larger armies to wage with any hope of success. The result was a vicious circle, producing the very problem it was originally intended to solve. War could support war in none but the shortest terms. And whether rulers evaluated their vital interests in the context of their dynasty or their state, short-term interests by the end of the seventeenth century were everywhere giving way before long-term planning.[21]

At this point the story once again becomes familiar. At least by the end of the War of the Spanish Succession European states were well on their way towards evolving, in Charles Tilly's words, 'from wasps to locomotives'.[22] 'Extraction', the systematic drawing on a state's legal subjects for the means of making war, involved a mix of coercion and cooperation. What might loosely be called the productive classes of society, peasants as well as landlords, shopkeepers as well as international businessmen, could not be forced to provide taxes beyond certain levels. Resistance was not only confined to the popular uprisings documented in such works as Perez Zagorin's *Rebels and Rulers*.[23] Resistance could also involve a kind of political/social akido – going with the force of the state's claims in order to assert claims on the state.

Nowhere did this process go further than in the Electorate/Kingdom of Brandenburg-Prussia. It is fashionable to depict Prussia as an anomaly, the absolute state developed to the point of distortion. Early modern Prussia is more accurately perceived as an archetype:

---

21 John A. Lynn, 'How War Fed War: The Tax of Violence and Contributions during the *Grand Siècle*', *Journal of Modern History*, LXV (1993), 286–310.

22 Tilly, *Coercion*, p. 96.

23 Perez Zagorin, *Rebels and Rulers, 1500–1660*, 2 vols (Cambridge, 1982).

a state that succeeded, for good and ill, in synthesizing the perceived requirements of its armed forces with the expressed interests of its subjects. It is to this development that we now turn.

PRUSSIA: AN ARMY WITH ITS OWN COUNTRY?

Brandenburg-Prussia began its modern existence in the aftermath of the Thirty Years War as a small state whose territories had been repeatedly ravaged by contending armies and whose ambivalent foreign policies had earned a reputation for unreliability. Its lack of geographic integrity, with provinces scattered almost at random across Germany, was remarkable even by seventeenth-century standards. Economic and geographic determinists have described compensating advantages. The state's Rhenish duchies, Cleves and Mark, possessed significant metallurgical and cloth industries, as well as providing a bridge between north and south Germany. Brandenburg proper lay athwart the Elbe and Oder rivers, the major north–south commercial arteries of central Germany. The province of Prussia, that much-disputed legacy of the Teutonic Knights, furnished a major Baltic trading port in Königsberg and provided a geostrategic sally-port into a region whose growing political instability offered corresponding opportunities for a state able and willing to fish in the troubled Polish and Russian waters.

These potential advantages were scarcely apparent in the strategic and diplomatic climate of the mid-seventeenth century. Far from being considered even a regional power, Brandenburg-Prussia's image was of an oyster without a shell. Sweden, by then a Baltic power with limited continental pretensions, ignored for seven years the provision of the Treaty of Westphalia allocating eastern Pomerania to Brandenburg. When Sweden and Poland went to war in 1655, the Elector of Brandenburg, Frederick William, changed the homage he offered for Prussia from the crown of Poland to the crown of Sweden. He provided a contingent of troops to seal the bargain – a force that repeatedly proved its worth in the swirling, wide-open fighting on the plains of Poland. Diplomacy, however, proved more important than force of arms.

Relations between Hohenzollern Prussia and Habsburg Austria had never been particularly cordial. They were fostered in this particular case by Prussian willingness to support Habsburg retention of the Holy Roman Imperial crown in return for Habsburg endorsement of Frederick William's full sovereignty over the Duchy of Prussia. The Swedes were neither interested in changing Prussia's international status nor susceptible to Habsburg pressure. Poland was another story. A king and a Sejm desperate for vengeance against the heretic Swedes accepted Prussia's sovereignty in return for Brandenburg's military support. The Peace of Oliva in 1660–61 wrote the new order into international law.

Given the relative lack of court cards in the Elector's hand, his achievement was no small triumph. Similar flexibility, not to say opportunism, shaped Frederick William's foreign policy to the end of his reign. In 1672 he allied with the Netherlands against France, then extricated himself from the Dutch collapse. He sent Prussian troops to join the Anglo-Austrian coalition against Louis XIV – but in return for generous subsidies. In 1675 Prussian troops inflicted a major defeat on the Swedes at Fehrbellin, only to be forced to return the resulting territorial gains four years later in the context of a general European peace. When Silesia's Duke George William died in 1675, Vienna ignored a treaty assigning part of his legacy to Brandenburg and annexed the province by main force. A disgruntled Frederick William sought an alliance with France, only to learn that dining with Louis XIV required an extremely long spoon. By the time of the Elector's death in 1688, his army had established a reputation as an effective fighting force. His state, however, was at best just another middle-ranking German principality dependent on the good will of its more powerful neighbours for more than sheer survival.

Even Brandenburg's military reputation had been bought at a price. The state's tax base was too narrow to support the 30,000 men Frederick William considered the minimum necessary force to keep his Electorate playing at the head diplomatic table. Foreign subsidies were useful supplements, but more readily promised than delivered. They were also addictive. Frederick William had no desire to become a permanent client of either France or Austria, nor did he propose to leave his heir with such a dangerously comfortable prospect. Instead, the Great Elector sought on one hand to expand Brandenburg's commercial and industrial capacity, while on the other establishing an administrative structure able to maximize utilization of private resources for public purposes.[24]

His successes were greater in the latter endeavour than the former. Provincial institutions and elites remained important in gov-

---

24 Volker Press, *Kriege und Krisen: Deutschland 1600–1715* (Munich, 1991), puts the Prussian experience in its German context. Cf. as well Ernst Opgenoorth, *Friedrich Wilhelm. Der Grosse Kurfürst von Brandenburg: eine politische Biographie*, 2 vols (Göttingen, 1971–78).

ernment on a local level. Nevertheless, by the end of Frederick William's reign the often-fractious nobility of his far-flung lands had been effectively excluded from a central administration now including many men from outside Brandenburg-Prussia who often held Imperial patents. Aristocratic resistance was met by combinations of carrot and stick, divide and conquer, plus a few judicious imprisonments and an occasional execution *pour décourager les autres.*

The Great Elector's officials were not civilian bureaucrats at heart. A large number of them were noblemen, noblemen *manqués*, or commanders who had internalized the Elector's conviction that Brandenburg needed above all a strong, centrally financed military establishment to maintain its tenuous position in the German and European pecking orders. Revenue-raising was a means, not an end. Anything interfering with the army's efficiency, however marginally, became the legitimate concern of Frederick William's War Commissariat and War Chamber, the two administrative agencies incorporating all of the Electorate's regional War Commissars. Brandenburg-Prussia became increasingly subject to comprehensive social and economic regulation at all levels. Frederick William, of Dutch descent on his mother's side, copied Holland's systems of raising and collecting revenue and enforced them with a rigour unheard of in that more stable structure. Bureaucrats, however, had as yet not discovered how to make three blades of rye grow where two sprouted, or to increase the productivity of hand-loom weavers – even on paper.[25]

The revolution of the Edict of Nantes in 1685 gave Brandenburg's economy a welcome boost. The Elector welcomed Huguenot refugees with open arms. They responded by making significant contributions to their new homeland's commercial and industrial infrastructure. The contributions, however, were chiefly personal: few of the refugees salvaged major investment capital from the *dragonnades*.[26] The Elector's periodic attempts to establish colonies and trading companies

25 Hans Rosenberg, *Bureaucracy, Aristocracy, and Autocracy: The Prussian Experience 1660–1815* (Cambridge, Mass., 1958) remains the standard general account. Cf. as well Edgar Melton, 'The Prussian Junkers, 1600–1786' in *The European Nobilities in the Seventeenth and Eighteenth Centuries*, vol. II, *Northern, Central and Eastern Europe*, ed. H.M. Scott (London, 1994), pp. 71–109; and F.L. Carsten, *A History of the Prussian Junkers* (Aldershot, 1979).

26 H. Erbe, *Die Huguenotten in Deutschland* (Essen, 1937); Meta Kohnke, 'Das Edikt von Potsdam zu seiner Entstehung, Verbreitung, und Überlieferung', *Jahrbuch für Geschichte des Feudalismus*, IX (1985), 241–75.

proved ephemeral, while Brandenburg's navy never expanded beyond a small-ship coastal force.

Frederick William had more success in agriculture. The electoral treasury opened its strong boxes to purchase breeding stock and hybrid seed. The electoral bureaucrats distributed them to peasants and landlords alike. Electoral subsidies and tax remissions encouraged settlement initially of lands abandoned during the Thirty Years War, then in the relatively virgin territories of Prussia and eastern Brandenburg.

When it came to industry, results were more mixed. The Elector was unable to eliminate the complex system of tolls that choked Brandenburg-Prussia's commerce. He did, however, improve the physical network of roads, rivers, and canals. The establishment of a reliable postal service did much to facilitate centralized bureaucratic administration. Wool production increased, in good part due to the army's large-scale requirement for uniforms. Iron and copper were exploited to produce cannon. These and other infant industries were nurtured by a rigorous system of protective tariffs and regulations of production and distribution. Berlin evolved, if not to a world city, then to a neat and tidy small-state capital. If the Great Elector's economic goals remained unfulfilled, Frederick William nevertheless left firm foundations for his state's prosperity.[27]

The Elector's heir, Frederick III, is usually described as more concerned with the trappings of power than with power's substance. His primary concerns were to establish himself as a patron of the arts, and as a king in his own right. By his death he achieved both, the latter in good part because of the continued strong performance of the Prussian army. Frederick indeed may deserve more credit for perspicacity than nationalist and conservative historians allow. He was shrewd enough to leave the army alone, and perceptive enough to maximize its significance as a subsidy/client force, especially during the War of the Spanish Succession.

Under circumstances that significantly diminished the effectiveness of most of the small and middle-sized forces involved, Prussian soldiers and their officers maintained consistent levels of battlefield performance that looked better and better in comparative terms.

---

27 Cf. H. Rochel, *Die Handels-, Zoll-, und Akzisepolitik Brandenburg-Preussens bis 1713* (Berlin, 1911), for details; and Wolfgang Neugebauer, 'Zur neueren Deutung der preussischen Verwaltung im 17. und 18. Jahrhundert. Eine Studie in vergleichender Sicht', *Jahrbuch für die Geschichte Mittel- und Ostdeutschlands*, XXVI (1976), 86–128.

Vienna would in principle allow no kings within the Reich, since that would break a prized – and vital – Habsburg monopoly of the right to create titled nobles. Nevertheless it was worth the price of a royal title to Habsburg Emperor Leopold to keep Prussia's fighting men under his colours – as long as the title itself lay outside the borders of the Holy Roman Empire. Allowing Frederick III to call himself 'King in Prussia' was a significant concession – one generating increased attention to Frederick's behaviour and increased concern for his motives.[28] In that context it was not mere fecklessness that led Elector/King Frederick to believe his new royal dignity was best sustained by display. Elaborate court costumes, handsome public buildings, and collections of the best in modern art represented no obvious challenges to Vienna's position.

Frederick's son and heir, Frederick William I, found equivalent pleasure in soldiers. Although his actual reorganization of the army was limited, it favoured function over form. Uniforms were simplified and household troops reduced to a minimum. Even the King's most often-cited military indulgence, his regiment of 'giant grenadiers', was a useful test bed for new methods of drill and new items of equipment as well as a military hobby.[29]

Frederick William inherited 40,000 men from his father. This, he believed, was a force insufficient for the strategy best suited to Prussia's requirements. Frederick William I perceived Prussia not as a rival to Austria, but as a *fidus Achates*, the second-ranking power of the Holy Roman Empire. As such it was important that it possess freedom of action. Its army, however, was of an awkward size. Too large to ignore or to be treated merely as another subsidy force, it was at the same time too small to be more than a makeweight in the game of great-power politics.

The Prussian King possessed few specific territorial ambitions. Above all he wanted Stettin, principal city of Swedish Pomerania and key to control of the Oder River. Taking advantage of growing Swedish military weakness, playing the complex diplomatic situation of the Great Northern War with a finesse often overlooked in general histories, Frederick William achieved his objective by the Treaty of

28 Linda Frey and Marsha Frey, *Frederick I: The Man and His Times* (New York, 1984), is a recent revisionist study of the Elector/King's reign. Cf. J.P. Spielman, *Leopold I of Austria* (New Brunswick, NJ, 1977); and older but still useful, A. Berney, *König Friedrich I und das Haus Habsburg, 1701–1707* (Munich, 1927).

29 Helmut Schnitter, 'Die "langen Kerls" von Potsdam', *Militärgeschichte*, XXIX (1990), 457–63. Cf. Kurt Zeisler, *Die 'Langen Kerls'. Geschichte des Leib und Garderegiments Friedrich Wilhelm I* (Frankfurt/Berlin, 1993).

Nystad in 1721. Though Stettin had fallen to Prussian arms several years earlier, Frederick William believed in alienating as few of his neighbours as possible. Rather than act unilaterally, he waited for Russia, Sweden's principal enemy, to conclude peace, then sailed comfortably in the wake of Peter the Great to acquire not merely Stettin, but most of Swedish, or western, Pomerania as well.

For the rest of his reign Frederick William played the part of a satiated monarch. Frederick William's pro-Imperial foreign policy was not entirely altruistic. He hoped to profit by his loyalty, obtaining Habsburg support for Hohenzollern claims to the Rhenish duchies of Jülich and Berg. These territories, adjacent to the Prussian territories of Cleves and Mark, had the kind of complex legal history that encouraged hopes and delusions on. all sides. Frederick William was willing to settle for Berg, and the Treaty of Berlin in 1728 promised Austrian support for the acquisition in return for Prussia's guaranteeing the Pragmatic Sanction, the succession of Maria Theresa to Austria's throne on the death of the sonless Charles VI. Moral support, however, was never translated into diplomatic action by an Austrian foreign office increasingly wary of any further Prussian aggrandizement. Frederick William swallowed his disappointment and continued his support of the Habsburgs. He believed Prussia's best interests were served by a stable European situation. Nor did he have any serious desire to cultivate improved relations with a Britain seeking possible alternatives to an Austrian connection that seemed even in the 1730s to offer more risks than advantages.[30]

Keeping Prussia outside of the wars and crises that characterized European diplomacy during his reign was in good part a function of an army large enough and efficient enough to discourage attempts at compelling Prussia to choose sides in any specific situation. In modern-day terms Frederick William sought to transform his army into a deterrent force.

In his mind the first prerequisite of that status was size. Half again as many men under arms as he actually possessed would be good. Twice as many would be better. But how could such a force be recruited and maintained? The Prussian army since the days of the Great Elector had depended on volunteers. Most of them came from Prussian territory; there were always men footloose, desperate,

---

30 For the man and his policies cf. W. Venohr, *Der Soldatenkönig. Revolutionär auf dem Thron* (Frankfurt and Berlin, 1988); Gerhard Oestreich, *Friedrich Wilhelm I: Preussischen Absolutismus, Merkantilismus, Militarismus* (Göttingen, 1977); and Heinz Kathe, *Der 'Soldatenkönig' Friedrich Wilhelm I. 1688–1740. König in Preussen – Eine Biographie* (Cologne 1981).

or adventurous enough to take the King's thaler. Under Frederick William I, however, local sources faced unfamiliar strains. As the army's size increased landlords saw their labour force diminished by recruiting parties. Nor were economic considerations a sole consideration. Seeing the last of a local troublemaker was one thing; losing steady hands to crimps was another.

The King preferred tall, well-built soldiers. Big men could more readily handle and more quickly reload the long-barrelled infantry musket. Linking size and physical fitness was also reasonable in an economic environment where malnutrition was common and a military environment where captains and colonels concerned with keeping their muster rolls reasonably honest might well overlook such minor problems as double hernias. Under pressure to produce not only more but better men, Prussian recruiting parties began to resemble press gangs. Open racketeering was common. A man would be detained, claimed to have enlisted, and be released only on payment of a bribe whose recipient was not always a noncommissioned officer. Prussian recruiters had historically operated in neighbouring states – a common German practice. By the late 1720s even honest officers were embarking on open man-hunts. Hanover came close to declaring war in 1729 over the misdeeds of Prussian agents on its territory. In other states recruiting for the Prussian service became a capital offence, alongside witchcraft and parricide.

The most obvious solution to the army's personnel problem involved tapping Prussia's own manpower resources on a long-term, systematic basis – not to make good high death and desertion rates, but to enlarge the number of men under arms and to improve their physical quality both directly, and by offering enlistment bonuses large enough to attract strong, healthy men who could also command high prices on the civilian labour market.[31]

A model stood ready to hand. Beginning in the reign of Gustavus Adolphus, the Swedish infantry had been recruited by the 'allotment system' under which groups (later pairs) of farms furnished a soldier and provided him with an enlistment bonus and a yearly wage, food, clothing, and either a small plot of land or living space on one of the farms. In peacetime the soldier worked his own land and provided

31 R. Schrötter, 'Die Ergänzung des preussischen Heeres unter dem ersten Könige', *Forschungen zur brandenburgischen und preussischen Geschichte*, XXIII (1910), 403–67; Willerd R. Fann, 'Foreigners in the Prussian Army, 1713–56: Some Statistical and Interpretive Problems', *Central European History*, XXIII (1990), 76–85; and the overview in John Childs, *Armies and Warfare in Europe, 1648–1789* (New York, 1982), pp. 52 ff.

labour for the other farms; in war his neighbours helped his wife and children. If the soldier died or was killed, the group provided a replacement. Russia under Peter the Great introduced a similar system, with every twenty taxable 'hearths' furnishing a recruit and replacing him when necessary, with first landowners and village councils, later state authorities, choosing among serfs made liable for service by the law of 1705.[32]

The Prussian cantonal system introduced in 1733 divided the kingdom into districts based on the number of 'hearths.' Each regiment was assigned a specific district, which was in turn sub-divided into as many 'cantons' as the regiment had companies. All able-bodied men between the ages of 18 and 40 were registered and eligible for enrolment. Since their physical requirements differed significantly, infantry, cavalry, and artillery shared the same districts with minimal competition. Prussia's recruiting policies strongly pre-figured the Selective Service system practised in the United States in the 1950s and 1960s. Whatever the theoretical value of universal service, practical considerations made it impossible. Prussia's subsistence agricultural economy could not stand to lose its most vigorous elements for several of their most productive years. Nor could the army afford to absorb and properly train every eligible man – and experience everywhere in Europe indicated that half-trained men in an infantry firing line were positively dangerous. A process of random selection seemed as irrational to King Frederick William as it did to General Lewis Hershey and the US Congress. Therefore numerous social and economic groups were exempted – or, more properly, occupationally deferred: nobles and businessmen, landowners, apprentices in a broad spectrum of crafts, textile workers, theology students, first-generation agricultural colonists – the list grew with the years, each category having its own rationale.

The familiar argument that this left the burdens of military service entirely on small-scale farm labourers, poor peasants, and urban workers is accurate but misleading, if for no other reason than its applications of nineteenth-century standards to an earlier period. In eighteenth-century Prussia, all owed service to the state. Those who could provide other than physical service were not merely expected but required to do so. The military system of Prussia increasingly expanded to influence the entire life of peasant and townsman

---

32 Cf. Alf Oberg, 'The Swedish Army from Lützen to Narva', in *Sweden's Age of Greatness, 1632–1718*, ed. M. Roberts (New York, 1973), pp. 265–87; and Christopher Duffy, *Russia's Military Way to the West: Origins and Nature of Russian Military Power, 1700–1800* (London, 1981), pp. 38 ff.

alike. Taxes and quarterings, feeding army bases and providing draft animals for military purposes, compulsory labour on the new network of fortresses built throughout Prussia – all contributed to the process of integrating state and subject that Frederick William considered vital for his kingdom's future.

In peacetime Prussia's peasant conscript was by no means an obvious object of pity. While his term of service was not fixed, once the recruit learned his new craft, he could count on being 'given leave' – returned to civilian life and the civilian economy for an average of ten months each year, then recalled for a brief refresher course. Nor was every man who was enrolled conscripted. Between 1727 and the system's abolition in 1813, fewer than half of those registered actually donned uniform – a percentage allowing ample margin for *Bauernschlauheit* in all its variant forms for those seeking to avoid service. As a result most cantonists seem to have been at least tractable, when not willing, soldiers.

From the state's perspective the cantonal system enabled Prussia to maintain a formidable standing army while minimizing the expenses usually accompanying such a force. Given the generous system of leave and the occasional package from home, cantonists might be almost self-supporting. At regimental levels as well the canton system had significant advantages. It provided a manpower pool deep enough to allow selectivity. Compared to their mercenary counterparts, the cantonists were big, well-set-up youngsters, well able physically to meet the demands of both drill and active service. As a class they were steady and reliable. This may have owed something to a Lutheran faith which in its north-east rural German version particularly stressed obedience, subordination, and performance of assigned duties.

The army's piety probably should not be exaggerated. If Prussian troops sang hymns on the march, this reflected not so much religious enthusiasm as the familiarity of the songs. The British armies of World War I used hymns as the basis for many of their parodies less from a sense of class-conscious blasphemy than because these were the tunes everyone knew. More useful in securing the cantonist's compliance was the fact that he was commanded, often literally, by the same men who ordered his civilian destiny. This gave him every practical reason to manifest a positive attitude – particularly since a native shirker or a deserter left more hostages to fortune than did an alien.

While national identification lay far in Prussia's and Germany's future, the cantonal structure did generate significant parish and regional solidarity in the companies and regiments. The presence of cantonists in the ranks also appealed to a sense of feudal obligation far from dead in the officer corps. It was far easier to identify with the welfare of men whose fathers and grandfathers had served yours than with the rootless cosmopolitans brought in at random by the recruiting parties. Intellectually, an increasing number of Prussian officers were influenced by Enlightenment concepts of the dignity and rationality of all men. On a more practical level, even the rawest and most arrogant of subalterns was unlikely to rejoice at the prospect of marching into battle in front of a hundred loaded muskets carried by men who hated him.[33]

One of the most pervasive and misleading myths of Prussian military history is that the army of Frederick William suffered an average loss of 20 per cent of its manpower through desertion and death – the latter usually ascribed to ill-treatment. Willerd Fann has traced the source of this improbably high attrition rate to an error made in the nineteenth century by Max Lehmann, and repeated enough times by enough historians to acquire a life of its own. The uncritical approach also fits nineteenth- and twentieth-century notions of life in the old Prussian army as brutish and nasty enough to be short as well. Fann demonstrates that in fact the overall desertion rate was a modest 1.9 per cent per year. The death rate was even lower – under 1.4 per cent, a percentage comparing quite favourably with admittedly incomplete figures for the equivalent civilian population.[34]

Fann's evidence fits a significant body of anecdotal evidence that service in the army of Frederick William I was by no means an undifferentiated nightmare, particularly for anyone with a minimal attraction to the military life. The duty might be demanding, but the pay was regular and the uniforms unusually durable. The Prussian army's peacetime obsession with desertion was a form of preventive maintenance. Trained soldiers were commodities scarce and valuable enough to be worth preserving. The well-known sanctions – men set to watch one another, generous rewards for contributing to a fugitive's capture, draconian official punishments – acted more as a deterrent system than an actual, applied set of punishments. They were balanced, moreover, by a significant spectrum of positive incentives. Frederick William steadily extended the right of leave, particularly

33 Curt Jany, *Geschichte der preussischen Armee*, 2nd edn rev., 4 vols (Osnabrück, 1967), I, pp. 549 ff.; remains the best source for the system's details.

34 Willerd Fann, 'Peacetime Attrition in the Army of Frederick William I, 1713–1740', *Central European History*, XI (1978), 323–34.

23

during the harvest season. Soldiers were also encouraged to seek employment outside of duty hours, partly to contribute to Prussia's economic development and partly because of the King's conviction that busy hands were, if not happy hands, at least contented ones. Boredom and empty pockets, he believed, contributed as much as direct ill-treatment to desertion.

Nor was the treatment of enlisted men, particularly recruits, casually brutal. Frederick the Great's order of 28 October 1740, recommending that 'physical' means of instruction be used only when appeals to the common soldier's better nature proved in vain, was by no means a tongue-in-cheek document. Prussian recruits were trained slowly and patiently, with a level of individual instruction impossible in the conscript forces of later centuries, with their massive annual intakes. A common practice was to put the fledgeling under the wing of a reliable old soldier who, usually for a share of anything the recruit might possess or receive from home, would provide basic instruction in dress and demeanour. The more arcane details of drill and uniform regulations were left to more senior NCOs, but they too were instructed to deal patiently, if not always gently, with recruits who showed basic good will.

As in any army, a disproportionate amount of punishment fell to a relatively small number: the dull-witted, the loud-mouthed, the sullen, and the vicious. The Prussian army of the eighteenth century resembled the British army of the Peninsular War in that sober and well-conducted men often tended to accept the need for strong sanctions against the others. Collective punishment was not a usual feature of the Prussian army, and that fact also served to reduce sympathy for men whose fate was perceived as a consequence of their own derelictions.[35]

---

35 Duffy, *Army of Frederick the Great*, pp. 57 ff., is a good modern summary emphasizing the negative aspects of Prussian service. Jany, *Preussischen Armee*, vol. I, pp. 700 ff., strikes a positive note. For purposes of comparison, cf. J.A. Houlding, *Fi: for Service: The Training of the British Army, 1715–1795* (Oxford 1981); and Rodney Atwood, *The Hessian Mercenaries from Hessen-Kassel in the American Revolution* (New York, 1980). Without attempting to whitewash Frederician discipline, many vivid accounts of the system's horrors were composed by officers who favoured a discipline based on honour and mutual respect, or soldiers who perceived themselves as having been enlisted by guile or force. Such works as Ulrich Bräker's *Der arme Mann im Tockenburg* (Zürich, 1789: reprint edn Munich, 1965), often cited for the army's routine on the eve of the Seven Years War, are best taken at a certain critical distance. Willerd Fann, 'On the Infantryman's Age in Eighteenth Century Prussia', *Military Affairs*, XLI (1970), 165–70, stresses the rootedness foreigners and old soldiers generally had in their regiments.

In *The Face of Battle* John Keegan repeatedly raises the question why men fight when the common sense of self-preservation urges running away. Even in an eighteenth-century context, when vigorous pursuit of a defeated enemy was an exception, flight was often likelier to be a more dangerous reaction than aggression or passivity: simply remaining in place. *Homo sapiens* appears to have no significant biological inhibitions against killing a submitting fellow human – on the contrary, he is quite capable of enjoying the process. The ultimate purpose of the tactical offensive is not to kill the enemy in place, a costly task, but to force or frighten him into running, and *then* kill him. This latter was the particular function of eighteenth-century cavalry, one which contributed not a little to the long-standing antagonism between the two branches of service. If casualties for an infantry force that stood its ground could be murderous, the results of breaking in the face of an enemy might well prove annihilating – particularly at the end of a hard-fought day, when surrenders of common soldiers were not likely to be observed as strictly as the laws of war demanded. Individual mastery of musket drill, and the offensive approach implied in that mastery, was for over a century a survival mechanism whose utility surpassed the obvious alternative of flight.

Eighteenth-century battle drill, with its blend of complexity and flexibility, functioned as a social bond. Anthropologists may debate whether common movement of major muscles does in fact rouse echoes of primitive hunting groups. Certainly the process as applied to eighteenth-century armies had its own communities and its own status structures. The private soldier who mastered the arcana of military bearing and military movements tended to take pride in the accomplishment. His chances, moreover, for such tangible signs of approval from his superiors as promotion to noncommissioned rank depended essentially on his ability to perform in the context of his new community. These standards were no more artificial than their counterparts in the civilian world, and arguably much more survival-orientated. The well-being of a military community depended essentially on the skill of each of its members. The clumsy, awkward, or unwilling soldier in an eighteenth-century line of battle could endanger his comrades more than himself. A musket held inches out of alignment when firing by ranks could mean a burst eardrum for the man in front of the muzzle blast. A man out of alignment during an advance could be the first link in a chain ending with enemy troopers cutting down an entire battalion.

Eighteenth-century discipline is generally presented as imposed

25

from above, reflecting Frederick the Great's familiar aphorism that the common soldier should fear his officers more than the enemy. But it must also be remembered that for the man in the ranks, mastery of the drill book was a battlefield survival mechanism. Any sympathy for the torment suffered by the inexperienced or the incompetent was likely to be significantly diminished by the knowledge that their clumsiness put their fellow-soldiers at risk. Thus the sanctions imposed by superiors were reinforced, directly or indirectly, by the rank and file.

Many of the Prussian army's apparently footling regulations were also manifestations of the need, learned at great cost in previous centuries, to maintain high levels of cleanliness and sanitation among concentrations of men whose civilian experiences had done little to inculcate appropriate behaviours. Sewing and washing were women's work. Disease could spread like wildfire in concentrations of men who had to be taught such rudiments as the regular use of latrines. Even in garrison conditions, Frederick William's rank and file were as capable as their counterparts of all eras in finding ways to damage themselves. Drink and women were only the most obvious ones.[36]

Underlying these points is a fact often overlooked by modern scholars. The kinds of grass-roots cooperation engendered by team sports, the factory system, and compulsory school attendance were foreign to ordinary people in the Age of Reason. Bowing to the squire or the pastor was given and understood because of their place in the hierarchy. Taking orders from someone of one's own social status and close to one's own age was, however, a much more dubious proposition, particularly among males whose enlistment was often prompted by impatience with conventional social restrictions. Correspondingly, the authority of the non-commissioned officers who supervised the army's daily routines could not be taken for granted, particularly since eighteenth-century tactics denied the NCOs' familiar modern role as junior combat leaders. It had to be sustained and reinforced at every turn in ways even the most bloody-minded rear-ranker could not misunderstand.[37]

Christopher Duffy offers one final, relatively unfamiliar point

36 Duffy, *Military Experience* pp. 96 ff., is a solid general overview of the dynamics of eighteenth-century armies.

37 Cf. Michel Foucault, *Discipline and Punish: The Birth of the Prison*, trs. A. Sheridan (New York, 1979); and Lynn Hunt's provocative *The Family Romance of the French Revolution* (Berkeley, Cal., 1992), pp. 1 ff. I am indebted for these references, and for good advice on the general concept, to my colleague Susan Ashley.

about Prussian army discipline. It was not a dawn-to-dusk, seven-days-a-week system. Soldiers off duty were left to their own devices to a degree unthinkable in even the US and British forces until the 1970s. They could dress as they pleased, seek private employment, or practise the arts of idleness – and they were off duty much of the time. Since most Prussian soldiers spent most of their time in billets, 'civilianization' was as much a concern as in twentieth-century armies with large numbers of men living off-base in private apartments or houses. A good deal of the often-cited problems involved in complying with the regulations governing one's appearance on parade seems to have been a consequence of making up for previous sins of omission and commission in matters of uniform and personal appearance.

All this is not to say that a soldier's lot in Frederician Prussia was a happy one – only that it was bearable, and an acceptable alternative to choices realistically available elsewhere. The Prussian army of Frederick William did not evolve into a military community held together by moral force. Yet its mix of cantonists and mercenaries provided a solid basis for a reasonably competent commander who understood how best to use the composite force at his disposal.

The underlying prerequisite for the army's effective use was, of course, effective administration. This point was particularly important given the theatres of operation in which the Prussian army could most probably expect to conduct large-scale operations. Saxony, Silesia, Bohemia were relatively prosperous countrysides, but hardly ones flowing with milk and honey on scales sufficient to support large armies over several campaigning seasons. To the other three points of the compass, local logistic possibilities were most charitably described as limited. The land could not support war for Frederick William I as it had for Louis XIV.

The Prussian King's response was to organize his state administration to the point where it could skin a ghost for the hide. At its apex initially were the General War Commission, which evolved from an embryonic high command to the focal point for tax and welfare matters; and the General Finance Administration, responsible for administering the extensive royal domains. Internal rivalries led the King to combine them under a variously translated, Teutonically mouth-filling title of 'General Superior Finance, War, and Domains Directory', usually shortened to 'General Directory'. This body combined territorial, functional, and collegial principles in a way impossible to a larger state or a looser hand. Its four departments were responsible both for certain provinces in general and specific functions for the kingdom as a whole, with the minister and his counsellors making collective decisions on specific policies. The provincial estates, already largely vestigial, lost any remaining powers of taxation and were forced to resign most of their administrative functions to provincial agencies of the central government. In their final versions these War and Domain Chambers collected revenue alike from towns and villages, from royal property and general taxes.

The result on one hand was an unprecedented concentration of power. On the other, the rapidly expanding bureaucracy drew most of its rank and file from interest groups able most of the time to temper the wind as it blew on their particular fellows. The result in grass-roots terms is best described as a balancing of discontents. No group was perceived as dominant; the grievances of one body were usually countered by the advantages of another. The system worked, particularly given the growing importance in Prussia of pietism, with its emphasis on responsibility to the collective at the expense of self-aggrandizement.[38]

One overriding question remained: exactly what was the army raised and supplied by the administration intended to do? Given the relative quiescence of Prussian diplomacy in the last fifteen years of Frederick William's reign, the issue seemed almost moot. There seems indeed to have developed a certain institutional pride in meeting the demands of an institution apparently destined to be unused.[39] Frederick William's death in 1740 would create a new paradigm.

FREDERICK THE YOUNG, 1712–40

There is a Frederick the Great for every taste, from the dreamy child driven to pathological misanthropy by a brutal parent to the stern but benevolent 'Old Fritz' who watched over his subjects and his state and became a symbol for Prussia and for Germany. Frederick has been depicted as a lover of war, never more eloquently than by Thomas Babington Macaulay:

---

38 Reinhold Dorwart, *The Administrative Reforms of Frederick William I of Prussia* (Cambridge, Mass., 1953), remains the best English-language survey. Cf. as well Richard L. Gawthrop, *Pietism and the Making of Eighteenth-Century Prussia* (Cambridge, 1993).

39 K.R. Spellmann and K. Spellmann, 'Friedrich Wilhelm I und die Preussische Armee. Versuch einer Psychohistorischen Deutung', *Historische Zeitschrift*, 246 (1988), 549–89, ascribe the King's caution in diplomacy and war-making to his personal pathologies.

On the head of Frederick is all the blood which was shed in a war which raged during many years and in every quarter of the globe – the blood of the column of Fontenoy, the blood of the brave mountaineers who were slaughtered at Culloden. The evils produced by this wickedness were felt in lands where the name of Prussia was unknown; and, in order that he might rob a neighbour whom he had promised to defend, black men fought on the coast of Coromandel, and red men scalped each other by the great lakes of North America.[40]

Frederick has also been described as a ruler who drew his sword with reluctance – seldom more forcefully than by Gerhard Ritter. For him the Seven Years War, 'this final crucial test of the power of [Frederick's] state was elicited not by a headlong urge for conquest but from concern to secure, defend and salvage Prussia's position as a great power'.[41]

Focus on the character and motivations of a single person, even an absolute monarch, risks an obscuring of first principles. Aside from any moral questions, Prussia's geographic vulnerability and economic weakness condemned it to a defensive grand strategy whenever it chose to play an independent role. This point, conceded by the Great Elector, was overtly affirmed by his two successors and ultimately conceded by Frederick the Great as well.[42] But it is precisely states with such a limitation that must pay close attention to the offensive on strategic, operational, and tactical levels. An army thinking only in defensive terms sacrifices both moral and physical initiative. Doomed always to react, it observes, waits, ripostes – and ultimately retreats. Even the argument, based primarily on experiences from 1861 to 1918, that the offensive costs lives to no purpose, can be significantly misleading. Hesitating and over-caution can produce effects similar to those generated by repeatedly testing the speed of a buzz-saw with the bare hand: a series of small-scale

40 Thomas Babington Macaulay, *Life of Frederick the Great* (New York, 1885), p. 32.

41 Gerhard Ritter, *The Sword and the Scepter: The Problem of Militarism in Germany*, vol. I, *The Prussian Tradition 1740–1890*, tr. H. Norden (Coral Gables, Florida, 1969), p. 30.

42 Gregor Schöllgen, 'Sicherheit durch Expansion? Die Aussenpolitischen Lageanalysen der Hohenzollern im 17. und 18. Jahrhundert im Lichte des Kontinuitätsproblems in der Preussischen und Deutschen Geschichte', *Historisches Jahrbuch*, 104 (1984), 22–45.

losses for correspondingly small gains that can rapidly mount to a disastrous total with no positive results.

These truisms had been reinforced significantly in Prussia by the experiences gained in the reign of the Great Elector and King Frederick I. In addition to furnishing contingents for the Empire's wars with the Turks and for the great coalitions against France, Brandenburg's army had fought first Poland, then Sweden in the east. Where the distances were so extensive relative to the forces deployed, defensive-mindedness was a gateway to disaster. Sweden depended for its Baltic empire on the ability of its armies to move fast and strike hard. Even in Poland's decline, its aggressive cavalry could embarrass any but the steadiest infantry. Nor, for that matter, were the experiences of the Prussian contingents who served under the Duke of Marlborough likely to encourage commitment to the concept of 'little war' as ultimately a less costly alternative to decisive action.

In his first comprehensive reflections on foreign policy, composed nine years before he assumed the throne, Frederick argued that Prussia must expand its territory according to a systematic, long-term plan. The state's extreme degree of fragmentation made it impossible in the long run to maintain Frederick William's policies of deterrence, particularly given the lack of common traditions and experiences in the lands currently under the Prussian crown. Prussia could not avoid being drawn into virtually any conflict anywhere in Europe unless it succeeded in rounding off its borders. Frederick regarded West Prussia, the northwestern tip of Pomerania still under Swedish rule, and the Rhenish duchies of Jülich and Berg as primary objectives. It was scarcely accidental that one of these regions was in western Germany, one in east-central Europe, and one in the middle.[43]

Frederick claimed to speak in 'objective' terms – what now might be called think-tank analysis. He correspondingly eschewed both the moral and practical aspects of achieving the objectives mentioned in his letter. Six years later the Crown Prince again discussed Prussia's future. By this time Frederick had patched up his quarrel with his father. He had also become an enthusiast for the military life. Placed in command of an infantry regiment in 1732, the Crown Prince assumed his duties with unexpected energy and success. His troops performed well at the annual manoeuvres. He visited the nearby battlefield of Fehrbellin. He listened to the advice and counsel of his father's senior officers. In 1734 Frederick put theory into practice

---

43 Frederick to K.D. von Natzmer, Feb. 1731, in *Die Werke Friedrichs des Grossen*, ed. G.B. Volz, 10 vols (Berlin, 1912–14), VII, pp. 197 ff.

when he took the field under Prince Eugene of Austria. A dispute over claims to the Polish crown brought Austria and its German allies and clients into war with France. During the summer the rival armies undertook a stately gavotte that decided nothing and left Frederick significantly disillusioned with the elderly Eugene and the way of war he seemed to represent. The Crown Prince came away convinced above all that he could do much better given an opportunity.

For the time being that opportunity seemed far away. Promoted beyond regimental command, Frederick established an independent residence a safe distance from Berlin. At Rheinsberg on the Mecklenburg border, the Prince indulged to the full his taste for books and music. He also praised Frederick William for providing the resources necessary for the wars Frederick expected Prussia to fight in the near future. Whether he was already thinking of acquiring the Austrian province of Silesia is uncertain. It is certain, however, that the Crown Prince was well aware of the advantages of possessing territory whose material and geographic circumstances would definitely raise Prussia from its current ambiguous position as 'an hermaphrodite, being a kingdom in name but an electorate in fact'.[44]

Frederick's belief that Prussia must be either hammer or anvil was enhanced by the events of 1738, when France, Austria, Britain and Holland combined to force Frederick William to accept the claims of a rival house to the long-disputed duchies of Berg and Jülich. To Frederick this incident highlighted Prussia's isolation and affirmed its second-rank status. It also confirmed his commitment to playing an independent diplomatic role. Certainly his father's long-term policy of collaborating with the Austrian Habsburgs had produced no good will negotiable in the context of England's disapproval, or even the form of a rapidly declining Holland.[45]

Left unstated, but probably influential, was Frederick's consciousness of his own youth and inexperience. As Crown Prince his preparation for assuming the throne of Prussia had been at best episodic. Nor was there any guarantee that the powers who had so casually dismissed what Frederick regarded as Prussia's eminently defensible claims in the Rhineland would be any less cavalier in disposing of territory currently under Prussian rule. The diplomatic corps in Berlin was hardly reassuring on that point; none of the

44 The quotation is from *Histoire de mon temps*; the citation is to the German translation in *Werke*, II, pp. 58–9.

45 Leopold von Ranke, *Preussische Geschichte*, vol. II, ed. A. Andreas (Wiesbaden, 1957), pp. 43 ff., remains lucid and useful on the complex details of this issue.

major powers was at particular pains to send high-ranking talent to a backwater in the middle of a potato patch.

Months before his father's death, in short, Frederick appears to have accepted the ultimate necessity for Prussia's expansion by annexation – annexation based not on the dynastic claims that had proved so futile in 1738, but on 'reason of state', the necessity that knows no law. Frederick saw international relations as subject to rational calculation. In *Reflections on the Present Political Condition of Europe*, written in 1738, he described the behaviour of the great powers as essentially consistent, reflecting permanent principles that could be learned and applied in the way a craftsman repairs a clock.[46] The image was a familiar one in the eighteenth-century Enlightenment. The mind-set behind it is even more familiar among people who have spent time on the fringes of power without exercising that power. For crown princes, losers of the last election, and talk-show pundits, belief that incumbents exaggerate the randomness of the process is a virtual article of faith. It might also be suggested that Frederick at the age of 26 could not afford to contemplate seriously the notion that his future path might be a random one, its course shaped if not dictated by the law of unintended consequences. Prussia could not afford such a process. Neither could Frederick. Asserting control was a way of sidestepping his own 3 a.m. fears that he might after all not be up to the task his father's increasingly fragile health would soon place in his hands.

It is in the context of these concerns that Frederick's best-known early work is best understood. *Anti-Machiavel* was published anonymously in 1740. Its author, however, did not long remain a secret – particularly since the text's emphasis on the importance of law and ethics to international relations seemed such in stark contrast to Frederick's actual behaviour in war and peace alike. The Crown Prince was neither cynic nor hypocrite. His challenge to Machiavelli reflected his belief that the Florentine regarded the interests of the ruler as congruent with the interests of the state. Machiavelli, moreover, at least in Frederick's mind, dealt only with the small states of Renaissance Italy. In such a context, power games were unjustified by their costs relative to their benefits. Great-power relations were another matter. These differed in essence from the squabbles of Milan and Pisa – or Dresden and Munich. Only a large, strong state, Frederick argued, could secure the welfare of its subjects and

---

46 'Considérations sur l'état présent du corps politique de l'Europe' in *Œuvres de Frédéric le Grand*, ed. J.D.E. Preuss, 30 vols (Berlin, 1846–56), vol. VIII, pp. 3 ff.

enhance the happiness of mankind. In this context a truly enlightened ruler might well be constrained to make war even against his will. The ultimate welfare of the many could outweigh the immediate desires of the one.[47]

When Frederick assumed the throne on 1 June 1740, he was primed to carry out a *coup* in international affairs. His target was as yet uncertain, and at this point it is correspondingly appropriate to present a few details of the institution Frederick proposed to use as his primary instrument of aggrandizement.[48] The core of the Prussian army when Frederick assumed the throne was its infantry: thirty-one regiments, with a standard wartime strength of about 1,700 men organized into two battalions. During his reign Frederick would add another twenty-four. Most of these were recruited in the new provinces of Silesia and West Prussia. They were called 'fusiliers' in token of the King's opinion that their men were smaller, weaker, and less reliable than units recruited pre-war from the 'old kingdom'. In 1740, four specially designated 'garrison battalions' secured the state's fortresses. In the course of Frederick's wars these second-line troops would be increased to as many as seventeen regiments; a few found themselves taking the field as Prussia's manpower dwindled. Each line and most garrison regiments included two companies of grenadiers – one per battalion in peacetime. As a rule two regiments would combine their four companies of these picked shock troops into a battalion at the start of a war. The composition of these battalions was not usually altered until during a campaign. Some of them achieved what amounted to independent identities during the Seven Years War, and took corresponding pride in their achievements.

In contrast to most of its counterparts the Prussian army of 1740 had no light infantry to speak of – neither regular companies, nor equivalents of the Croats and Scots Highlanders featured in contemporary Austrian and British orders of battle, nor the composite

47 L'Antimachiavel ou Examen du prince de Machiavel, *Œuvres*, vol. VIII, pp. 55 ff. Cf. the analysis in Theodor Schieder, *Friedrich der Grosse. Ein Königtum der Widersprüche* (Frankfurt, 1983), pp. 102 ff.

48 Duffy, *Army of Frederick the Great*, 69 *passim*; and Jany, *Preussische Armee*, vol. II, pp. 3 ff., remain the best sources for details of organization and equipment at the beginning of the King's reign. Martin Guldat, *Grenadiere, Musketiere, Füsiliere. Die Infanterie Friedrichs des Grossen* (Herford, 1986) is solid on the King's foot soldiers. Günter Dorn and Joachim Engelmann, *The Infantry Regiments of Frederick the Great*, tr. E. Force (West Chester, Pennsylvania, 1983); and the *Cavalry Regiments of Frederick the Great*, tr. E. Force (West Chester, Pennsylvania, 1989), offer brief histories of the major formations.

'legions' of foot and horse so favoured by French Marshal Maurice de Saxe. Not for Frederick the swarms of skirmishers like those French irregulars who shredded the British at Fontenoy in 1745 and shielded the assault columns at Lauffeld in 1747. Prussia lacked even the specialist forces of riflemen, snipers and sharpshooters present in most German orders of battle. In 1740 Frederick created the first *Jäger* unit, less a military formation than a corps of guides, no more than sixty strong. Four years later there were only two companies of them. Not until 1760 did the *Jäger* achieve battalion strength, and their operational record was at best spotty.[49]

The King's indifference to skirmishing has been attributed to his distrust of ordinary soldiers' willingness to fight except under direct supervision. It also reflects his conviction that 'little war' in all its forms wasted time – and time was something Prussia did not possess in either strategic or tactical terms. The Prussian army could not afford to wear its enemies down lest it wear down itself as well. Instead, Frederick's concept of war as he assumed the throne emphasized what Mexican revolutionary general Pancho Villa would call the *golpe terrífico*: a single smashing blow, carefully prepared and then delivered with no waste motion.

Prussia's cavalry reflected a similar approach. In 1740 it included no fewer than thirteen heavy regiments, cuirassiers complete with breastplates, and another ten regiments of dragoons, medium cavalry who by this time had lost any trace of their origins as mounted infantry except the bayonets they carried along with their carbines. The normal establishment of dragoon and cuirassier regiments was five squadrons – about 870 officers and men at full field strength, usually one or two hundred fewer in practice. As for light cavalry, Frederick inherited only nine squadrons of hussars, mostly foreigners with evil reputations as undisciplined marauders. In 1741 the King would expand this force to five regiments, initially with the kind of results to be expected from improvisation under eighteenth-century conditions.

The artillery was, if not quite the Prussian army's illegitimate stepchild, certainly held well below the salt. In 1740 its field branch consisted of a single six-company battalion; Frederick formed a second in 1741. They went to war with three basic types of cannon: six-pounders and three-pounders distributed among the infantry as

---

49 Cf. Peter Paret, *Yorck and the Era of Prussian Reform* (Princeton, NJ, 1966), pp. 21 ff.; and Johannes Kunisch, *Der kleine Krieg. Studien zum Heerwesen des Absolutismus* (Wiesbaden, 1973).

close-support pieces, and twelve-pounders for the heavy work of opening the battle and wearing down enemy infantry. Horses and drivers were mobilized only on the outbreak of war as an economy measure – a decision significantly diminishing the artillery's combat effectiveness.

Frederick was not indifferent to artillery as a battlefield weapon even in the early years of his reign. Like so many other generals before and since, however, he initially tended to emphasize mobility over fire-power. A new model of three-pounder regimental gun introduced in 1742 so lacked range and hitting power that in the Second Silesian War the infantry often advanced without them. Frederick responded by ordering the design of heavier guns with improved ballistics. New six-pounders began entering service in 1755. From the beginning of the Seven Years War they became targets for the longer-ranged Austrian artillery. Frederick and most of his generals nevertheless continued to agree on the role of battalion guns for direct fire support, and as rallying points in action. Beginning in 1758, improved three- and six-pounders, longer-ranged than their predecessors, took the field. The Prussian artillery also made increasing use of short-barrelled, high-trajectory howitzers, seven- and ten-pounders whose explosive shells and large charges of small shot often proved invaluable at close quarters.

In the aftermath of the Silesian Wars, Frederick introduced a new heavy piece as well. The Prussian artillery went to war in 1756 with a twelve-pounder designed to sacrifice fire-power for manoeuvrability and deficient in both respects. Most of these unfortunate weapons were lost in early defeats, replaced by older, heavier twelve-pounders stripped from fortresses and mounted on improvised field carriages. This expedient solution also responded to a certain gigantism among Prussia's gunners, who simply felt more comfortable with the heavier pieces. Their *Brummer* performed spectacularly at Leuthen, tearing open Austrian positions and providing significant psychological suppport to an infantry that began the battle with pardonable misgivings at being once more used as cannon fodder. For the rest of the war it was an article of faith among Prussian officers that their men fought better when heavy guns were available.

The steady increase in the proportion of artillery in Prussia's field armies, to as many as six guns per thousand muskets in the final period of the Seven Years War, represented for Frederick a compensation for the decline of his infantry rather than a commitment to the 'long arm'. Heavy guns required a larger number of draft horses and heavy-duty wagons than were commonly available anywhere in

Germany in order to maintain their supply of ammunition – ammunition that could be neither requisitioned nor improvised. The effect of large artillery trains on unpaved roads, even in the dry season, further restricted the army's movements.

Another major brake on the development of artillery in Prussia was its cost. The false starts with the too-light three-, six-, and twelve-pounders and the limited improvement represented by wartime designs meant that cannon were constantly being recalled for the expensive process of recasting. Frederick particularly feared the consequences of being drawn into a wartime arms race with Russia and Austria – a race he insisted Prussia had no chance of winning when a single campaign consumed three times as much gun-power as the state could produce in a year.[50]

Frederick's engineers stood even lower than his gunners in the army's formal and informal hierarchies. This was less a manifestation of social prejudice than of resource allocation. Frederick believed Prussia could not afford to become bogged down in siege operations, and correspondingly refused to develop either the technical skill or the numbers of his pioneers. Prussia's own fortresses were, for the King, more fortified supply bases than links in a systematic chain of defence. Frederick staked his state's future on his field army, on soldiers rather than walls.

Soldiers required captains. Among Frederick's senior subordinates in 1740, one man and his family stood out. Leopold of Anhalt-Dessau had worn Brandenburg colours since the age of 12, winning an enviable reputation in the wars of Louis XIV. He became a confidant of Frederick William I – the closest thing to a friend that monarch possessed, and the one on whom he most relied in military matters.

The crucial feature of Leopold's professional life was his self-image as an infantryman. In an era when the cavalry remained the most prestigious branch of service, Leopold stood by the musketeers. He was in good part responsible for developing the tactical principles that became the basis of Frederician Prussia's drill regulations. His memorandum on military leadership, prepared for the Crown Prince sometime in the 1730s, may never have reached Frederick's hands. Its principles were nevertheless well known in the army. Although not remarkable for his social polish, Leopold insisted on humane discipline, eschewing curses and blows, and on systematic, honest administration ensuring that the common soldier was fed and

50 Frederick II, 'Das militärische Testament von 1768', *Werke*, vol. VI, pp. 225 ff.

clothed according to regulations. Above all, Leopold asserted, men must be led rather than driven. His emphasis on the motivational role of officers and NCOs would stand comparison with many a twentieth-century tract on leadership – as would his insistence that drill was only a means to an end.[51]

By 1740 Leopold had become the 'Old Dessauer'. Not only was he well into his sixties but three of his sons were Prussian generals as well. One would retire in 1750. Another, Prince Leopold Maximilian, died in 1751. Prince Moritz would gain a mixture of fame and notoriety. Prefiguring Rousseau, Leopold brought him up with no formal education. Moritz was neither the complete illiterate of some legends nor the backwoods ruffian of others. He seems rather to have cultivated a rough-hewn persona: a simple field soldier uncorrupted by the niceties of civilization. He also seems to have sustained the role because Frederick found it amusing – most of the time.[52]

Whether child of nature or self-aware poseur, Moritz was typical of his counterparts in being more of a fighter than a commander. We will meet other generals in these pages: the courtly and humane Kurt von Schwerin; Ziethen and Seydlitz, who would bring the Prussian cavalry to achievements unheard of since the Middle Ages; new men like Friedrich von Saldern who would win recognition in the Seven Years War and reshape the Prussian army after 1763. Some were even more exotic. James Keith was Scots by heritage, and won his spurs in Russia before travelling west to improve his fortunes. Henri de la Motte-Fouqué was the scion of Huguenot immigrants. Frederick's senior officer corps at times resembled that mixed bag which Schiller introduces in the opening scenes of *Wallenstein's Camp*. But in contrast to the drama, these real-life generals had in common an ultimate subordination to the man who in peace and war insisted on doing most of their thinking: King Frederick II.

---

51 See F. von Oppeln-Bronikowski, *Der alte Dessauer. Studien seines Lebens und Wirkens* (Potsdam, 1936).

52 M. Preitz, *Prinz Moritz von Dessau im siebenjährigen Krieg* (Munich, 1912), is a narrative history of a man whose career and character invite a scholarly article, if not a short monograph.

2   WARS FOR SILESIA: 1740–45

Frederick's opportunity came in October of 1740 when Charles VI, Emperor of Austria, died suddenly, leaving as his heir a daughter, Maria Theresa. By generally accepted standards the transition should have proceeded smoothly. As early as 1713 the long-sighted Charles had announced a Pragmatic Sanction confirming the unity of the Habsburg family possessions and providing for inheritance in the female line in the absence of a male heir. These provisions, however, did not extend to the Holy Roman Empire. A woman could not succeed to the title of Emperor, and the Imperial dignity was the principal means by which the House of Habsburg elevated itself above its rivals – including a Hohenzollern dynasty that was doing altogether too well for Vienna's comfort.

A PROVINCE OVERRUN

It was correspondingly crucial to make the Habsburgs' Austrian base strong enough to guarantee that Habsburg influence would dominate in electing the next Emperor. For twenty years Charles VI bent every effort to secure both domestic and international approval for the concept of a female succession. In the process he granted concessions to the regional assemblies of his hereditary lands that significantly limited the power of the central government, particularly in matters of taxation. A promising overseas trading company based in Ostend was sacrificed in return for Britain's signature. Italian territories won at significant cost in blood and money were bartered to both local rulers and Spanish Bourbons. For the sake of Russia's *beaux yeux* Austria even accepted an unnecessary war with the Ottoman Empire.

Critics contemporary and academic have accused Charles of bartering Austria's security and future for a collection of parchments that proved no more useful signed than if they had remained blank. Eugene of Savoy, the greatest of the Empire's generals, grumbled that a good army was preferable to even the most comprehensive network of treaties. Charles, however, was by no means a fool. While it would be an exaggeration to credit him with a Grand Design, he perceived a fundamental truth. Austria's welfare, and arguably its existence, depended on an unchallenged succession. Charles recognized the political, economic, and diplomatic sacrifices demanded for this *sine qua non*. He also recognized that eventually these losses could be compensated for, or recovered. An Austria internally stable, benefiting from the modest but steady economic growth that characterized the 1720s and 1730s, was in a position to sustain its treaties, and ultimately perhaps revise them. The alternative course of relying on military strength and domestic centralization was simply not feasible in a system both extended and entropic. Charles may not have been a Richelieu or a Metternich. He was, however, wise enough not to let the best become an enemy of the good.[1]

Then Frederick of Prussia emerged as a wild card. On learning of Charles's death he summoned Schwerin and Foreign Minister Heinrich von Podewils. Referring to Austrian behaviour in the matter of the Berg-Jülich succession, Frederick repudiated any existing agreements with Vienna and declared his intention to obtain Silesia by any means necessary. In later years the King himself explained his actions as the consequence of his possession of a well-trained army, a full treasury, and a desire to establish a reputation. The First Silesian War thus becomes a consequence of youthful high spirits and the opportunity to indulge them – a combination familiar to the skinheads, gang-bangers, and soccer hooligans of the late twentieth century, and still taken at face value in many general histories of the period. Certainly this interpretation receives additional support from Frederick's successful use of overwhelming armed force in the summer of 1740 to resolve a minor territorial dispute with the Bishopric of Liège. Frederick's misogyny may also have played a significant role in his decision. A young queen whose public persona to date had been one of wife and mother offered a well-nigh irresistible psychological temptation to a man contemptuous of women's capacities.[2]

---

1 Charles Ingrao, 'The Pragmatic Sanction and the Theresian Succession: A Reevaluation', in *The Habsburg Dominions under Maria Theresa*, ed. W.J. McGill (Washington, Pennsylvania, 1980), pp. 3–18, is an excellent recent analysis of the subject, from a perspective more critical than that of the present text.

2 Theodor Schieder, 'Macht und Recht. Der Ursprung der Eroberung Schlesiens durch König Friedrich II von Preussen', *Hamburger Wirtschafts-Jahrbuch für Wirtschafts und Gesellschaftspolitik*, XXIV (1979), 235–51 is the best analysis of Frederick's decision. Cf. Gustav B. Volz, 'Das Rheinsberger Protokoll von 29. Oktober 1740', *Forschungen zur brandenburgischen und preussischen Geschichte*, XXVI (1916), 67–93.

It remains a point of debate whether Frederick's action was the result of long-term planning or short-term opportunism. On the one hand he described to one of his entourage the Emperor's death as a trifle and his own behaviour as executing designs long held in mind.[3] On the other, his correspondence for this period contains relatively few references to Silesia in any context. However long its gestation period, Frederick's Silesian land-grab was a calculated high risk for an overwhelmingly valuable prize. Silesia's population was a million and a half; Prussia as it existed could count only three-quarters of a million people more. Silesia's established cloth industry and developing mineral resources were alike attractive to a king strongly influenced by mercantilist economics.

Frederick, moreover, was fully convinced that the Pragmatic Sanction would not long survive Charles's funeral. He expected the Habsburg Empire to be challenged on all of its frontiers, if not entirely dismembered. Nor was Frederick mistaken in his perception. Piedmont had never signed the Pragmatic Sanction, and the state's chief minister had repeatedly dismissed the document as a nullity. The Spanish government had prepared a position paper justifying King Philip's claims to much of the Habsburg inheritance.[4] In such a context the Prussian army, ready to go to war from a standing start, was a trump card in two ways. It could be counted upon to overrun Silesia quickly. It could also be expected to defend the acquisition, particularly in the context of the all-out war Frederick believed to be a certain consequence of Maria Theresa's accession.

The details of Frederick's negotiations with Austria during the late autumn and early winter of 1740 are less important than the military preparations undertaken at the same time. In a state whose army was so highly visible, these were impossible to conceal. The speed and smoothness of Prussia's mobilization was disquieting in a Europe where war's relative stateliness reflected in good part the length of time the armies required to wind up and deliver a punch. Prussia was ready to strike in six weeks. Frederick threw up a diplomatic smokescreen, indicating that Prussian preparations were aimed at seizing the long-disputed duchies of Jülich and Berg. He betook himself to his still-favourite refuge at Rheinsberg. He complained

---

3 Robert B. Asprey, *Frederick the Great: The Magnificent Enigma* (New York, 1986), p. 155.

4 Reed Browning, *The War of the Austrian Succession* (New York, 1993), pp. 37 *passim*.

of ill-health. He deceived no one of importance.[5] Nevertheless, as talk of war increased, Frederick stood mute even in the company of his generals. An old tutor's cautious inquiries on the subject led to a famous exchange. When asked if he could keep a secret, the pedagogue answered 'certainly'. Frederick replied, 'so can I.'[6] If the story is not true, it deserves to be. For the rest of his reign Prussia's head of state would keep his own counsel, for good and bad.

The King's intentions became more or less public on 13 December, when he boarded his travelling coach and started not west, but south. With just over 27,000 troops concentrated on the Silesian border, Frederick planned less for a conquest than for an occupation. Despite its growing economic strength, which by 1740 generated a quarter of the direct tax revenues from the Austrian and Bohemian crownlands, Silesia seemed taken for granted by its overlords. Not for over a century had anyone from a Habsburg ruling house dominated by concern for its southern frontier and its rivalry with France spared the time to tour the region. Silesia's Protestants had religious reasons to welcome a change of rule. Its business community saw wider opportunities under Frederick than in a Habsburg Empire more concerned with milking Silesia than assisting its development. In particular, the provincial capital of Breslau was permeated top to bottom with Prussian sympathizers.[7] The Habsburgs did not depend on local enthusiasm to defend their province. Silesia was dotted with medium-sized fortresses whose garrisons, though not expected to take the field against an invasion, were considered more than able to deny an enemy the use of the country until a relief force could be collected and despatched. From a Prussian perspective, these places were seen as little more than grass-grown parapets commanded by officers with no financial alternative to retirement.

Frederick described his troops as enthusiastic, his officers as ambitious, his generals eager for glory.[8] Reality set in on 18 December, when the weather broke. Neither the men nor the horses of Frederick's expeditionary force were accustomed to climatic adver-

---

5 Asprey, *Frederick the Great*, 159 ff., colourfully describes the climate in Berlin during the last six weeks of peace.

6 *Beyträge zu den Anecdoten und Characterzügen aus dem Leben Friedrichs des Zweiten*, 4 vols (Berlin, 1788–85), III, 60.

7 Hans-Wilhelm Büchsel, 'Oberschlesien im Brennpunkt der Grossen Politik', *Forschungen zur brandenburgischen-preussischen Geschichte*, XLI (1939), 83–102, is a useful overview.

8 Frederick to Podewils, 16 Dec. 1740, in *Politische Correspondenz Friedrichs des Grossen*, 46 vols (Berlin, 1879–1939) (Hereafter cited as *PC*), I, pp. 147–8.

sity. Manoeuvres had regularly been broken off during inclement weather because of Frederick William I's constant emphasis on sparing wear on uniforms and equipment. Now the infantry slogged through knee-deep water while the cavalry wrestled with a pandemic of equine ailments. On top of the elements, the commandant of the fortress of Glogau, barring the direct route to Breslau, refused to play the game as expected. While he did nothing to obstruct the Prussian advance, neither would he surrender like a gentleman. Frederick, who had expected to take Glogau in ten days, refused the risk of a *coup de main*. Instead he left a screening force behind him and pushed towards Breslau.

The Prussians reached the city on 31 December, amidst a whirlwind of prophecy and argument. Breslau retained a significant degree of self-government, and for centuries had resisted the introduction of an Austrian garrison that might mean the end of the city's civil liberties. In any case, what was the use of making a fight? Breslau was not a modern fortified city. Its walls, dating largely from the Middle Ages, were useful as a customs barrier but offered no protection against an army.

Frederick was ready to storm Breslau's walls; instead, the city's citizens opened its gates. When the King denied any intention of introducing a Prussian garrison as long as Breslau kept out the Austrians, all obstacles to an agreement were removed. On 3 January 1741 Frederick and a small escort entered Breslau, to the cheers of its relieved population.

With Breslau in hand the Prussian army quickly overran the rest of the province. Neisse, whose Lutheran commander may have felt he had something to prove, refused to open its gates and withstood a brief bombardment. Glogau and the fortress of Brieg also continued to hold out. By the last week of January, however, Frederick felt comfortable sending the bulk of his expeditionary force into winter quarters in his new province. Returning to Berlin, the King left Schwerin to complete the mopping-up.

Thus far, so good. A campaign mounted in the most unfavourable of seasons had been decided in six weeks with a minimum of bloodshed. Silesia appeared more than content under its new master. Europe's chanceries were suitably impressed with the young Prussian King's energy and determination. War ministries noted with respect the Prussian army's ability to campaign under adverse conditions without significant loss of efficiency. Only one cloud remained on the horizon. Austria refused to accept the *fait accompli*.

Empress Maria Theresa had ascended the throne, as she later

put it, 'without money, without credit, without an army, without experience or knowledge of my own, and finally also without any advice'.[9] Yet she had the inherent wisdom of Machiavelli: a strong state can flog its enemies while a weak one must destroy them. Better than most of her ministers, the young monarch perceived the risks of negotiating with the Prussian King. The Pragmatic Sanction guaranteed the entire Habsburg inheritance. For Austria to break the agreement by surrendering any of its territory was likely to render null and void, *de facto* when not *de jure*, two decades of painful and costly negotiations. As much to the point, Frederick's land-grab challenged the delicate balances of Central Europe and the Holy Roman Empire. Prussia's upstart King must therefore be taught his place by force of arms.

This decision was by no means empty posturing. Austria had not established itself as one of continental Europe's great powers solely through dynastic marriage. In the preceding half-century, Habsburg troops had driven the Bourbons out of Italy and forced the Ottomans from territory Constantinople had ruled for centuries. Under Prince Eugene, the Austrian army had been a major factor in thwarting French ambitions in western Germany and the Low Countries at the turn of the century. Raimondo Montecuccoli was arguably the most-read, most-cited theorist of war during this period. An administrative structure making colonels responsible for their regiments enabled the Habsburgs to tap their empire's resources without the risks of levying new taxes. At least on campaigns, the system also provided reasonable levels of unit efficiency.[10]

Two decades of peace took much of the edge from the Habsburg blade. Prince Eugene in his later years discouraged the development of younger generals who might become potential rivals. At his death Austria lacked a successor as supreme commander. Eugene, moreover, despite his merits as a field soldier, was no administrator. Left to run themselves, the army's systems tended to gridlock. Certainly Austria's military performance on both operational and planning levels in the War of the Polish Succession from 1733 to

---

9 *Kaiserin Maria Theresias Politischen Testament*, ed. J. Kallbrunner and C. Biener (Vienna, 1952), p. 29.

10 Charles Ingrao, *The Habsburg Monarchy, 1684–1815* (Cambridge, 1994), pp. 53–120, is an excellent overview. Derek McKay, *Prince Eugene of Savoy* (London, 1977); and Thomas Barker, *The Military Intellectual and Battle* (Albany, NY, 1975), are the best English-language biographies of Eugene and Montecuccoli respectively.

1735 and during the war with Turkey from 1737 to 1739 had ranged from uninspired to abysmal.[11] At the same time, the initial response to Frederick's invasion of Silesia achieved successes out of all proportion to the forces involved. Habsburg soldiers had learned the nuances of small war against the Ottoman Empire in the hard school of the Danube Basin. The techniques transplanted well to the Silesian-Bohemian frontier. Austrian raiding parties harassed Prussian convoys and outposts. Local notables too public in their change of allegiance found themselves unwilling guests of Austrian commandos, with ample leisure to reconsider their positions on the wrong side of the border. Prussian troopers exhausted their horses and themselves in vain pursuit of an enemy that seemed at times to have bargained with Satan for invisibility.

By the end of February, Frederick was sufficiently concerned to return to Silesia and take personal charge of affairs. Some indication of the Austrian ascendancy in the developing war of outposts came on 27 February, when a detachment of their hussars barely missed capturing the King himself. On a positive note, Glogau finally fell to a Prussian night attack on 9 March. This removed a significant threat to Frederick's rear. Though Neisse still held out, Glogau's fall meant that, if Austria wanted Silesia, the province would have to be retaken on the field of battle.

This did not mean a major concentration of Habsburg resources against the Hohenzollern upstart. By the end of March, about 16,000 Austrians had been assembled in Moravia under Field-Marshal Wilhelm Neipperg. He led a mixed bag. Croats and Serbians from the Military Border rode alongside local volunteers from the Bohemian and Moravian hill country. At the army's core were twelve battalions of infantry and eleven cavalry regiments, most of them with recent combat experience against the Turks.

It was not a force calculated to wage and win a battle of annihilation, but one well structured for what Vienna perceived as a punitive expedition on the Empire's northern marches. Neipperg was the sort of commander often unfairly dismissed as 'a good ordinary general'. He was not particularly inspired but he knew his job well enough, and had no great fear of an opponent hitherto distinguished more by literary gifts than martial performance. Defying recent snows that blocked the main routes into Silesia, Neipperg broke camp at

11 Karl Roider, *The Reluctant Ally: Austria's Policy in the Russo-Turkish War, 1737–1739* (Baton Rouge, 1972), highlights the negative synergy between diplomatic and strategic shortcomings.

the end of March. He caught his opponents still in winter quarters, bypassed the Prussian right, and was on the way to Neisse when deserters informed Frederick what was happening.

The next few days demonstrated the applicability to land warfare of the naval axiom that 'a stern chase is a long chase'. Frederick summoned his troops and marched in pursuit, harried at every turn by the ubiquitous Austrian light cavalry. Neipperg stayed nicely in front. On 5 April he relieved Neisse and crossed the river. The move put him squarely athwart Frederick's main line of communication: the high road to Breslau and Brandenburg.

AUSTRIA'S RESPONSE

With his front now facing his own capital, Frederick had no choice but to fight. Spring blizzards cut visibility to yards and immobilized the cavalry on both sides. Even the Austrian hussars, the best scouts in either army, lost track of a Prussian army that periodically lost touch with itself in the driving snow. But by 10 April the sky was clear, the snow frozen over. The Prussians shook into march formation, starting north about 10 a.m. Shortly afterwards peasants and prisoners confirmed the enemy's presence around the village of Mollwitz. Neipperg was taken unaware, with most of his men cooking their noon meal. Frederick, however, sacrificed any possible advantage of this tactical surprise by ordering his army to form line of battle, instead of attacking at once.

The Prussian deployment took over 90 minutes. The five columns in which the army had marched were required to turn at right angles and form two separate lines of battle. On the drill field it was routine. In the face of the enemy, with depth and space perceptions confused by flat ground, sunlight glaring off the snow, and simple nervous tension, things went less than well. Several units could not be precisely fitted into the fighting lines, and for a while stood forlornly about like pieces left over from assembling a Christmas bicycle. As finally constituted, the first Prussian line included fifteen battalions of infantry, covered on the flanks by twenty squadrons of cavalry. Its commander, Marshal Schwerin, was expected by the King and everyone else to orchestrate the actual fighting. The second line, eleven battalions and nine squadrons under the Prince of Anhalt, was seen as support and reserve.

Counting a few squadrons detailed as baggage guards, gunners, and assorted detachments the Prussians had slightly over 21,000 men. More than 17,000 of them were infantry, the best in the service. Frederick and Schwerin expected to sweep the Austrians from the field by sheer force: not the mystique of cold steel, but the weight of numbers would settle the day. This was by no means a mere theoretical concept. Neipperg's eighteen infantry battalions counted fewer than 11,000 men, many of these ill-trained recruits. The Austrian cavalry, on the other hand, far outnumbered the Prussian – and its eighty-six squadrons included a high proportion of experienced soldiers. Common sense as well as doctrine indicated the wisdom of pitting strength against weakness, driving the Austrian infantry from the field before their cavalry could react.

At 1.30 Frederick gave the order to advance. Years on the parade ground had their results. An Austrian officer later said that the Prussians advanced like moving walls, showing no sign of stopping to fire. That was the mission of the artillery, whose six-pounders accompanied the infantry from position to position, throwing round-shot into the Austrian lines at long and medium ranges.

Neipperg, far from passively awaiting the Prussian onslaught, had intended to make an attack of his own, but the Prussians moved too rapidly. With cannonballs ploughing through his ranks, General Römer, commanding the cavalry of the Austrian left wing, ordered a charge. Outnumbered more than two to one, the Prussian horsemen facing him compounded their problem by receiving the charge at the halt. This behaviour in part reflected the King's decision to stiffen his cavalry by putting battalions of grenadiers at intervals along their line in the style of Gustavus Adolphus a century earlier. In theory, the musketry of these elite troops would shatter any mounted charge, leaving the survivors vulnerable to a counterattack.

Reality proved disastrously different. Instead of a frontal attack, Römer's men enveloped the Prussian flank. The far right of the Prussian line was held by a dragoon regiment that was both poorly commanded and unnerved by its experiences in the war of outposts waged earlier in the winter. But no regiment ever formed for battle was likely to have withstood the storm that burst upon the flank of the 3rd Dragoons. Those of its men not ridden down by the Austrians scattered in all directions. The rest of the cavalry on the Prussian right wing had no time to deploy and meet the new threat. Both Römer and the Prussian wing commander Count Schulenberg died in the swirling mêlée. A battalion of grenadiers left isolated by the rout of their cavalry stood firm, but compounded the confusion by firing in every direction at anything on horseback.

But the gravest challenge to Prussia's cause came from Prussia's

King. Frederick had ridden forward with this wing of the army. When the Austrian thunderbolt struck, he placed himself at the head of the 11th Cuirassiers and sought to rally his broken troopers.[12] But he was one man and one voice, in a situation where only a few could see or hear. Some of the infantry on the Prussian right began firing without orders in an effort to keep the Austrian horse at a distance – firing in the King's direction. A century earlier Sweden's Gustavus Adolphus had ridden to his death in the fog of Lützen, taking with him the hopes of Germany's Protestants. Schwerin took in the situation with an old soldier's eye. The Austrian charge had lost its momentum. The Prussian infantry was standing firm. There was still hope for the battle – if the King could be brought to safety. Schwerin and several of his subordinates urged Frederick to leave the field for the sake of Prussia. By this time the young monarch probably did not need a second suggestion. No man could question his presence in the thickest of the fighting so far. Like Henry Fleming and Pierre Bezuhov, he was nevertheless shocked when everything just kept on, instead of pausing to witness his initiation to battle. Around 4 p.m. Frederick – not yet the Great – left the field on a fresh horse, later to enter Prussian folklore as the 'Mollwitz grey'.

Freed of the King's amateur presence, Schwerin gave his attention to the battle. Neipperg, always the solid book soldier, proposed to complete his cavalry's unauthorized success by sending the Austrian infantry forward. But his men moved slowly enough for the superbly trained Prussian foot to close its ranks and recover its order. Römer's cavalry, itself by this time badly disorganized, drew off to the Austrian left flank. This gave Schwerin his opening. Kurt von Schwerin was an archetype of the Enlightened gentleman as a soldier. As a young man he had studied at Leiden. He preferred the society of literate civilians to the ruder company of the camp. He ate well, drank well, and lived well. His open, generous manners set him apart in an officers' corps whose senior ranks took pride in rough edges. Rivals and critics made no secret of their opinion that Schwerin was a carpet-knight who would collapse under pressure.[13]

Schwerin himself, who had not seen serious combat in twenty years, may have wondered. He blamed himself no little for what had

12 Regimental numbers did not come into use until Frederick's reign, and even then regiments were generally known by titles. These, however, often changed. For the reader's convenience the text therefore accepts the neologism of numbering Prussian regiments.

13 D. Schwerin, *Feldmarschall Schwerin* (Berlin, 1928), remains the best biography of this important figure.

gone wrong that day – not least what appeared to be the lethargic advance of the army's main body. Not until late afternoon were its battalions in line. Schwerin ordered an advance. The Prussians moved forward, their bayonets glinting in the setting sun of a winter day. Their movements were less mechanical and more reflexive than they had been at the start of the fighting. But for these virgin soldiers, the endless hours of conditioning on the drill ground kept them moving to the barking of their officers and sergeants. The light field guns that had bravely stood their ground against the Austrian cavalry moved forward, manhandled by their crews, to support Schwerin's attack first with round shot and then, as the ranges closed, with canister.

The Austrians watched like men hypnotized. Pre-war Prussian drill regulations were based on a four-rank firing line: two kneeling and two standing. Frederick, in the interests of enhancing fire-power, had instead ordered the troops invading Silesia to form three ranks.[14] They had had four months to get used to the new formation. The musketeers responded perfectly to their officers' commands, their volleys rolling from the flanks of each battalion to the centre, then resuming again as if on the drill field.

The increasing confusion endemic to firing on the move made little impression on Austrian battalions outshot, according to their commander, five rounds to two. Neipperg's infantry included large numbers of inexperienced men. Its fire discipline and its fire techniques alike were among the worst in Europe. Its volleys on the day of Mollwitz were slow, irregular, and above all high.[15] Römer's charge had failed to break the Prussians. Now their infantry was coming on like a flame-tipped wall. With or without orders, Austrian musketeers sought to increase their own rate of fire by simply dropping musket balls down the barrel without ramming. The resulting increase in noise and smoke may temporarily have raised Austrian morale. But Prussian spirits were lifted even higher when the reduced muzzle velocity of rounds so loaded inflicted superficial wounds, rather than the incapacitating ones normally characteristic of an eighteenth-century musket at battle ranges.

The Austrians grew so preoccupied with loading and firing that orders to advance went unheeded. As Prussian fire hit home

---

14 Brent Nosworthy, *The Anatomy of Victory: Battle Tactics 1689–1763* (New York, 1990), p. 187.

15 K. Duncker, 'Militärische und politische Aktenstücke zur Geschichte des ersten Schlesischen Krieges', *Mittheilungen des K.K. Kriegs-Archivs* (Vienna, 1887), p. 205.

Neipperg's men instead sought security in masses, bunching thirty or forty men deep. Battalions brought from the second line to fill the gaps behaved in the same way. Instead of the solid wall prescribed by doctrine, the Austrian line of battle soon resembled Tilly's at Breitenfeld: clumps of men, bayonets pointing in all directions, with gaps between them wide enough for whole regiments of cavalry to pass unscathed.

The cavalry of the Austrian right, ordered forward to check the Prussian advance, was equally intimidated by the Prussian musketry. Even when their commander turned his sword on his own recalcitrants, the Austrian troopers remained immobile. It was Neipperg's hard-tried infantry which moved first – one or two men, then a dozen or twenty, discovering urgent private business somewhere to the rear in defiance of threats and commands. Making a virtue of apparent necessity, Neipperg ordered a general retreat as night fell.

An efficient Prussian cavalry would have been in a position to turn the day into a rout with one well-timed charge. Schwerin, however, had no particular confidence in the horsemen who still remained under his control. Glad enough to have escaped disaster, he bivouacked on the field and sent a message of victory to his sovereign.

Writing a quarter of a century later, Frederick blamed his generals and himself for mechanical adherence to regulations, as opposed to common sense. 'If the King', Frederick declared, 'had attacked off the line of march, as Marlborough had done at Höchstatt [Blenheim] in 1704, he would have been in a position to capture or scatter the Austrian infantry bivouacked around Mollwitz.'[16]

Reality was less promising. The Austrian infantry in fact was camped sufficiently far from the village that a thrust at Mollwitz itself would have found no worthwhile objective. Instead, both flanks of Frederick's army would have been exposed to the Austrian cavalry. Perhaps more to the point, the Prussian army faced its first serious action in over a quarter of a century. It was not the worked-in, flexible instrument available to Marlborough. Prussian confidence had, if anything, been diminished by the events of the preceding weeks and months. Performing by the book, following familiar routines, was sensible behaviour for an army's initiation. The process gave the regimental officers and the rank and file a sense that things

---

16 Frederick II, *Geschichte meiner Zeit* in *Die Werke Friedrichs des Grossen*, ed. G.B. Volz, 10 vols (Berlin, 1912–14), II, p. 77.

were proceeding as they ought to proceed – no bad attitude for a first battle.

Both sides had suffered approximately equal losses on the day of Mollwitz – 1,500 dead, about twice as many wounded, a thousand missing or prisoners. The 20 per cent butcher's bill was hardly unusual for the period. But the Prussian victory and the Austrian defeat were alike portentous. The Austrians had lost because of poor coordination. Römer's attack had promise only if followed up by the rest of the army. Neipperg, however, lacked the *coup d'œil* for such a decision. In its absence his subordinates and their rank and file lacked the tactical skill to win the fight by themselves. On the Prussian side, Schwerin proved able to use the time the Austrians gave him. But the real victors of Mollwitz were the Prussian infantrymen – and the system of training that produced them. For the first time in Prussia's history, military experts elsewhere in Europe began taking serious note of that state's military methods.

Meanwhile Frederick had undergone his own private comedy of errors. With a few companions from his personal household, he rode at top speed to the town of Oppeln – to find the gates shut, and a detachment of Austrian hussars in possession! Frederick was saved from capture only by the freebooting behaviour of his enemies. Instead of opening the gates and allowing the royal mouse to enter the trap, the Austrian troopers chose the alternative of sallying out and seeking booty, each for himself. Frederick stood not on the order of his departure, abandoning his fellows in a headlong gallop that brought him by morning, accompanied by a single aide-de-camp, to the nearby village of Löwen.

It was scarcely remarkable that the King spent his first hours of safety pacing up and down, asking God what he had done to deserve such punishment. Even less remarkable was his reaction to the news of the victory. Frederick never quite forgave Schwerin for turning the day's fortunes, keeping the marshal conspicuously at arm's length until his death in battle years later. The horse which saved the King's life, it is more pleasant to note, spent the rest of his days as a pensioner in the royal meadows of Potsdam.[17]

On 11 February, a chastened Frederick rejoined his troops. He drew three conclusions from his first experience of war. One was strategic. The Prussian army had been scattered instead of concentrated, then feinted out of position and forced to fight in circumstances where

---

17 Christopher Duffy, *Frederick the Great: A Military Life* (London, 1985), p. 33.

defeat meant ruin. One was tactical. The deployment in front of Mollwitz had begun too early and taken too long.[18] The last conclusion was institutional. The Prussian cavalry needed overhauling.

'The cavalry', Frederick declared, 'is damnably awful. None of our officers can do a thing with it.'[19] In fact the Prussian cavalry was better than its immediate reputation. The cavalry engaged at Mollwitz had spent the preceding months doing things it had never been expected to do by anyone in the Prussian army, and doing them with corresponding ineffectiveness. Horses and men alike were tired and jittery by the time they faced Römer's attack. They needed no king to remind them of their failure. But for Frederick throwing himself into details, correcting errors for which others could be blamed, was a way of coming to terms with his own behaviour.

The six weeks after Mollwitz were devoted to training and reorganization. By four each morning, the King was inspecting the army's camps. Whatever the weather, battalions and squadrons were put through their paces, sometimes by the King himself. The infantry needed relatively little work. Frederick focused on his cavalry. Mollwitz had shown that leadership was at a discount in a mêlée; neither discipline nor training survived well at close quarters. Instead, Frederick sought to break the enemy at the first shock, before it ever came to hand-strokes. By early June, Prussian cavalry units were manoeuvring at the gallop, and while Frederick recognized the risks of exhausting horses by committing them too early, he insisted that at least the last thirty paces of any attack must be ridden at top speed.[20]

With Schwerin under a cloud, his humane influences gave way to the King's harsher mind-set. The pace of events was frantic enough that dozens of officers – several hundred by some accounts – offered their resignations. All were refused. New men were emerging in the army's command structure. Hans Joachim von Ziethen came from a poor family of Brandenburg nobles. He was an unlikely soldier. Physically unprepossessing, with a weak voice and a weak head for liquor, he impressed no one by his peacetime performance. He could maintain discipline among his subordinates neither by force nor by example. Among his colleagues, Ziethen suffered from 'small man's

18 Frederick, *Œuvres de Frédéric le Grand*, ed. J.D.E. Preuss, 30 vols (Berlin, 1846–56), vol. II, p. 17.

19 Grosser Generalstab, *Die Kriege Friedrichs des Grossen*, Part One, *Der Erste Schlesische Kriege, 1740–1742*, vol. I (Berlin, 1890), p. 419.

20 Christopher Duffy, *The Army of Frederick the Great* (New York, 1974), p. 107.

syndrome': an aggressive nature often exacerbated by the aftermath of drinking bouts. His record to date included two duels, a term of fortress arrest, and a brief cashiering. He managed to reach the rank of major, but few less promising officers took the field in 1740 and none rode with less promising troops.[21]

Ziethen's peacetime performance led him into the hussars the way sand sifts to the toe of a boot. He started in the infantry, transferred to the dragoons and in 1731 was assigned to the hussars. These light cavalrymen made their appearance in Prussia's order of battle as direct copies of the Hungarian originals who had earned such reputations as scouts and raiders. There were only nine squadrons of them in 1740; Frederick used these as the basis for five full regiments. The new formations suffered alike from rapid expansion and poor traditions. They may have worn Hungarian-style uniforms, but bore no more than surface resemblance to their models. Prussia had borders, but not frontiers. Its hussar recruits were not the kind of good horsemen and bold adventurers who set the tone for the Habsburg – and later the French – light regiments. They tended rather to be young men who sought to prove their toughness by challenging regulations and restrictions, with a strong infusion of 'King's hard bargains', throwbacks to the Thirty Years' War from half the states of central Europe.

It was an unpromising mixture, and the hussars had been even more humiliated than their colleagues of the heavy cavalry during the winter fighting in Silesia. The Austrians rode rings around them. If they did not run away at Mollwitz, it was because they had no opportunity to do so. The three squadrons 'engaged' on that day were detailed as baggage guard – and at the first opportunity looted the trains they were sent to protect.

Ziethen and the hussars alike could have gone in one of two ways after Mollwitz: substantial improvement, or permanent relegation to the army's fringe. In the battle's aftermath Ziethen made a decision to quit drinking. Abstention improved his leverage over his temper – and the hussars' current low status made officers and men alike more willing to overlook the still frequent outbursts of a man who day by day showed that he at least knew how to train and command.

Ten weeks after Mollwitz, Ziethen showed that he could fight as well. On 17 May he took six squadrons of his own Red Hussars, the 2nd, on a scout, and surprised a force of Austrian hussars in the

---

21 G. Winter, *Hans Joachim von Ziethen*, 2 vols (Leipzig, 1886), is the most detailed biography.

village of Rothschloss. Ziethen took his men in at the gallop and scattered the Prussians' long-time tormentors to the winds with few casualties. It was a pretty piece of work, archetypical of the later *Husarenstücke* of the Seven Years War. Even the defeated Austrian commander sent Ziethen his congratulations.[22]

PEACE, AND WAR AGAIN

Rothschloss did for the Prussian cavalry, albeit on a smaller scale, what Brandy Station would do for their Union successors in 1863, during the Civil War. It was a portent for the future in a branch of service whose past was anything but distinguished. It was also the summer's operational highlight. Frederick, in a pattern not uncommon to commanders who came close to disaster in a first battle, had no desire to risk a second. Besides, diplomacy bade fair to bring Prussia surer and richer prizes than those to be won under arms. For thirty years after the Treaty of Utrecht in 1713, Europe's greatest maritime power, Britain, and its greatest land power, France, had remained at peace. While this situation persisted, a general war like those that had racked the continent under Louis XIV was impossible despite the existence of sustained tensions that generated both extensive military preparations and lively alliance diplomacy.[23]

At the same time, mutual mistrust among the powers reached new heights by 1740, with every state suspicious of its neighbours' intentions and capacities. The death of Charles VI was a catalyst in other capitals than Berlin. Diplomats had long predicted conflict over the Austrian inheritance, and plans for partitioning the Austrian lands had been discussed in many ministries. Temporarily at least, however, the Franco-Austrian Treaty of 1738 appeared to diminish the likelihood of a European upheaval. Cardinal Fleury, *de facto* ruler of Bourbon France, was sufficiently concerned for the revival of an anti-French coalition, like that which had brought low Louis XIV to guarantee the Pragmatic Sanction, in an effort to keep Austria from seeking British support.[24]

This decision meant that France's traditional middle-ranking Ger-

22 G. von Pelet-Narbonne, *Geschichte der brandenburg-preussischen Reiterei von den Zeiten des Grossen Kurfürsten bis zur Gegenwart*, 2 vols (Berlin, 1905), I, pp. 135 ff.

23 Jeremy Black, *Natural and Necessary Enemies: Anglo-French Relations in the Eighteenth Century* (Athens, Georgia, 1986), pp. 1 ff.

24 Still useful is A.M. Wilson, *French Foreign Policy during the Administration of Cardinal Fleury, 1726–1743* (Cambridge, Mass., 1936).

man allies, Saxony and Bavaria, were left to their own devices, at least temporarily. Bavaria in particular had been a key factor in French foreign policy since the Thirty Years War. In its own right, however, the Wittelsbach monarchy was a Catholic counterweight to Austria in Germany. While the previous quarter-century had witnessed a growing discrepancy between first- and second-rate powers, Bavaria was by no means simply a French stalking horse. Its army had earned a solid reputation in the wars of Louis XIV. Diplomatically it was a state willing in its own interest to challenge Austrian efforts either to enhance the powers of the Holy Roman Empire or to increase its direct prestige in Germany. Franco-Austrian *détente* restricted Bavaria's freedom of action; King Charles Albert nevertheless insisted on the just claims of the House of Wittelsbach to participate in any sharing-out of the Habsburg inheritance.

An enigmatic clause in a pact of mutual succession concluded thirty-five years earlier gave Charles Albert some arguable rights to the throne of Bohemia. What he really sought was the Imperial crown which the Wittelsbachs had so often failed to seize. On the death of Charles VI, the Bavarian king issued a ringing challenge to Louis XV to immortalize his name by establishing a 'just' balance of power in Germany and Europe. Fleury initially temporized. His plans had gone no further than considering theoretical ways of splitting the office of Holy Roman Emperor from the Habsburg monarchy when Prussia invaded Silesia.[25]

Frederick's move forced France's hand. Left to his own devices the Prussian king would have preferred direct negotiations with the Habsburg empress on the basis of *faits accomplis*. In return for Silesia, even for part of it, he offered in the summer of 1741 guarantees of the remaining Austrian possessions in Germany and diplomatic support for Austria's retention of the Imperial dignity, both underwritten by troops and cash. Maria Theresa remained adamant, from a mix of pragmatism and principle. Conceding one land-grab was still regarded as setting a precedent too dangerous to be accepted in the context of Austria's current international position.

Frederick had previously been dubious about the value of a French connection. Support for Prussia's gains would be welcome

25 Bernhard Kroener, 'Von der bewaffneten Neutralität zur militärischen Kooperation. Frankreich und Bayern im Europäischen Mächtekonzert 1648–1745', *Wehrwissenschaftliche Rundschau* VI (1980); and L. Hüttl, 'Die bayerischen Erbansprüche auf Böhmen, Ungarn und Österreich in der Frühen Neuzeit', in *Die böhmischen Länder zwischen Ost und West: Festschrift für Karl Bösl*, ed. Ferdinand Seibt (Munich, 1983), pp. 70–88.

enough, but not at the risk of permanent Habsburg hostility or the price of a general European war. In the aftermath of Mollwitz, however, Frederick was flattered by an increasing level of French attention. Fleury was by now almost 90. His lack of enthusiasm for another in a long series of wars with Austria was overshadowed by a new generation of soldiers and diplomats. Their principal spokesman, Marshal Count Belle-Isle, spoke eloquently of the need to seize the moment and mobilize Germany and Europe against an Austria that was uniquely vulnerable. Britain, the Habsburg Empire's traditional great-power ally, had been engaged since 1739 in a naval and colonial war with Spain, and showed no indication of seeking continental involvement. On the other side of that particular coin, the war hawks argued that France would eventually have to give open support to its Spanish ally. In the fall of 1740 two French squadrons had made their way to the West Indies. Instead of drifting into a naval war against the world's greatest maritime power, was it not preferable to take advantage of Prussia's actions to isolate Britain definitively, then deal with it at leisure?

In Belle-Isle's grand design Prussia was a useful tool, if not quite a cat's-paw. Frederick for his part adopted a policy of 'flight forward'. On 4 June 1741, he signed a secret treaty guaranteeing Prussian possession of Breslau and Lower Silesia in return for Prussian support of any candidate France proposed as Holy Roman Emperor – which meant Bavaria's Charles Albert.

A distinguished contemporary student of eighteenth-century international relations has argued that France in 1741 arguably came closer to dominating Europe than did any modern state prior to Napoleon I.[26] Austria was in shock at the unexpected combination of its current and its historic enemies. Maria Theresa stood alone. Her quondam allies, Britain and the Netherlands, were initially unwilling to commit resources to central Europe in the face of domestic indifference and hostility. This position was concretely demonstrated in July, when King George of England, concerned for the safety of his Electorate of Hanover, signed a convention with France guaranteeing its neutrality in any continental war. Prussia was unstable, eager to participate in the great game but uncertain of the best course.

French primacy was, however, a potential that defied the best efforts of Versailles to transform it to reality. In good part this

---

26 Jeremy Black, 'Mid-Eighteenth-Century Conflicts with Particular Reference to the War of the Polish and Austrian Successions', in *The Origins of War in Early Modern Europe*, ed. J. Black (Edinburgh, 1987), p. 228.

failure was the work of Frederick. He had no desire to see Prussia replace Bavaria as the lead dog in France's German sled. The position might be temporarily rewarding, but was scarcely gratifying to a ruler whose underlying long-term ambition was to make Prussia a first-rank power pursuing an independent foreign policy. He was content enough during the summer of 1741 to allow the French and Bavarian troops to do the bulk of the fighting, while Prussia's forces in Silesia skirmished with Neipperg's rebuilt army and Prussia's diplomats put forth peace feelers to Vienna.

By Autumn the Austrians were willing to talk, *faute de mieux*. French and Bavarian troops, supported by a contingent from Saxony, were meeting little opposition as they drove into the Empire's heartland of Upper Austria. Neipperg's troops represented the best and largest Habsburg force north of Vienna itself. They were needed too badly to set hard bargains on the order of their going. On 9 October 1741, the Convention of Klein-Schnellendorf ceded Lower Silesia to Prussia and allowed Frederick to quarter troops in Upper Silesia. In return, Neipperg's forces marched away unopposed.[27]

In the King's intellectual context of front-loaded wars for negotiated aims, Klein-Schnellendorf was a major triumph. The Convention legitimated part of his Silesian claim *de jure*, authorized the rest *de facto*, and gave Prussia significant freedom of action without flatly betraying its French allies. Frederick's hope, not to say expectation, was that the French would achieve a similarly limited success on a larger scale, then legitimate the Convention as part of a general peace that would leave Prussia the dominant power in Germany. Instead, the Austrians showed that recuperative power which was to characterize the Habsburg army until the dissolution of the Habsburg state in 1918. Their light troops struck north into Bavaria, wreaking havoc on an exposed countryside. The main army, now under the command of Maria Theresa's brother-in-law, Prince Charles of Lorraine, did no serious fighting. It did, however, constitute a force in being that by November threatened the Franco-Bavarian position even from its winter quarters.

With his still-official allies so badly over-extended that overt accusations of bad faith grew louder in Munich and Paris, Frederick saw himself constrained to take the field once more. The moral consequences of being forsworn concerned him less than the diplomatic risks inherent in a too obvious pursuit of specific Prussian interests in

---

27 A. Unzer, *Die Konvention von Klein-Schnellendorf (9 Oktober 1741)* (Frankfurt, 1889), is good for the details.

the context of a coalition. A place among the great powers could not be secured by overt betrayal. The election of Charles Albert as Holy Roman Emperor in January 1742 was another straw in the wind. By combining the Imperial title and French support, Bavaria now seemed in a promising position to assume the role Frederick sought for Prussia.

At the same time Frederick proposed to take up no more of the war than might prove absolutely necessary. Prussian troops had established their own winter bridgeheads deep in the now undefended province of Moravia. Frederick proposed to use these positions as a springboard for a diversion against Vienna. On 18 January 1742, he set out for the theatre of operations. He received a welcome reinforcement on 20 January, when the Saxon government agreed for the sake of unity to place its expeditionary force of 16,000 under his command.

This gave Frederick about 34,000 men – the Saxons, 15,000 of his own Prussians, and a token contingent of 2,900 French. The allied force moved slowly southward in the first two weeks of February. A raiding party under the indefatigable Ziethen advanced to within sight of Vienna, causing a brief panic. But Frederick had no intention of pushing his advantage and striking the Austrian capital. He was more concerned with protecting communications increasingly threatened by Austrian irregulars, supplemented by sorties from the poorly block-aded Habsburg fortress of Brünn in his army's rear. Friction emerged in the allied ranks, the Saxons complaining with regularity and justice about receiving the hardest jobs and the shortest commons.[28]

Frederick combined operational caution with a steady politi-cal pressure, insisting that Maria Theresa cede strategic positions in Bohemia as the price of his withdrawal. He underwrote his demands by sanctioning policies of requisition and plunder that rapidly exhausted Moravia's limited resources. To suggest, as does Christopher Duffy, that this was part of a grand design to reduce Moravia to a 'strategic desert' is to understate the effect of even a well-disciplined eighteenth-century army on local economies and local ecosystems.[29] The supply lines into Saxony, Brandenburg, and even Silesia, were long enough and vulnerable enough that Frederick's expeditionary force was constrained to live more and more from the land. Under the best of circumstances that meant hunger. Given the

---

28 E. Bleich, *Der mährische Feldzug Friedrich II. 1741/42* (Berlin, 1901), is a sound operational overview.

29 Duffy, *Frederick the Great*, p. 39.

season of the year, it meant famine. And contrary to all expectations, the victims refused to remain quiescent. By early spring Moravian peasants were joining uniformed Austrians in an increasingly wearing guerrilla struggle against Frederick's garrison towns and outposts.

With the countryside in flames behind him, Frederick's move of the main Prussian army into north-eastern Bohemia in early April incorporated more hope than strategy. A desire to escape the partisans, an intention of directly supporting the French and Bavarians currently around Prague, were overshadowed by a vague but relevant sense that the army should be doing something other than sitting on its collective haunches. In fact, unknown to Frederick and for the second time in the Silesian War, the initiative had been seized by the Austrians. Stripping her garrisons in Bohemia, the Empress concentrated 30,000 men under Prince Charles of Lorraine with the mission of pursuing and destroying the Prussian invader.

Charles was not an optimal choice for the mission. Even by eighteenth-century standards he was cautious, timid, and defensive-minded. He was also lucky, at least temporarily. Broken terrain combined with a still inefficient Prussian reconnaissance served to conceal his movements completely until 10 May. Even then Frederick did not expect an Austrian attack. He regarded Charles's army as no more than a 'force in being', intended to see him off without a fight. So convinced was Frederick of his own wisdom that he divided his army, moving across Charles's front towards Prague on 15 May with a third of his forces and leaving the remaining two-thirds to follow on the next day. The King compounded his error when he mistook Prince Charles's camps for those of another, far smaller Austrian force reported in the neighbourhood – a classic example of what Napoleon would later call 'making pictures'.

As at Mollwitz, Frederick was saved from disaster by a subordinate. He had left his main body under the command of Prince Leopold Max. This eldest son of the Old Dessauer was an experienced field soldier who knew basic field arithmetic. When, following Frederick on the 16th, he caught sight of the Austrian camp, Leopold counted the rows of tents, did some multiplication, and concluded – accurately – that the main enemy army was in a position to defeat the divided Prussians in detail. Leopold drove his men to the point of exhaustion in a vain effort to close the gap between himself and Frederick. When his troops finally bivouacked, the situation was set for a race between the Austrians, by now aware of their opportunity, and Frederick, by now aware of his peril.

The King broke his camp at 5 a.m. on 17 May and set out on

his own back trail in a desperate effort to reach Leopold before the Austrians could strike. By the time he met the Prince in front of the village of Chotusitz, the Austrians were in sight and advancing. Frederick, memories of Mollwitz on his mind, proposed to use the cavalry of his right wing, thirty-five squadrons, in order to buy time by charging. To their left the King deployed his principal strike force: twenty-three battalions under his personal command, concentrated more or less out of sight in low ground. Another twelve battalions were deployed to *their* left under Leopold. The army's left flank was closed by three dozen cavalry squadrons whose principal mission was to contain their Austrian opposite numbers.

Lieutenant General von Buddenbrock put four cuirassier regiments in the first wave and supported them with two regiments of dragoons. This time the Prussian troopers got in their blow first, riding over and scattering the Austrians in front of them. But Buddenbrock, instead of following up the success of his cuirassiers, halted them in order to reorganize. The dragoons in his second line lost their way and rode into the fire of the advancing Austrian infantry. Once again, Prussian horsemen were standing still when the rallied and reinforced Austrians counterattacked, cuirassiers and dragoons in the front, hussars enveloping the Prussians' flanks. The results were predictable. By 9:30 a.m. Buddenbrock's troopers were out of the action, most of them on their way to the rear.

The Prussian left-flank cavalry had not been idle, but in this sector their zeal exceeded their tactical skill. As the Austrian centre and right advanced, three regiments of cuirassiers charged. Not only did they cut their way right through the Austrians in their sector; elements of the strike force even found themselves in the rear of the entire Austrian army! But the opportunity proved ephemeral to the weakened, disorganized Prussians. Instead of attacking the enemy infantry, troops and squadrons sought the best possible way back to their own side of the field.

That left things squarely up to Frederick's infantry. Leopold's wing of the Prussian foot had initially deployed in the open country west of Chotusitz, then advanced in an effort to hold the village itself. By 9 a.m., a coordinated Austrian attack, well supported by artillery, set Chotusitz afire and forced the Prussians, shaken and disorganized, to withdraw beyond reach of the flames. But fire proved a double-edged weapon. The Austrian infantry lost its way in the smoke. Their cavalry drifted north and east to plunder Leopold's camps. Meanwhile, the two dozen battalions still under Frederick's direct command remained inactive.

The nineteenth-century suggestion that the King planned to use these troops to deliver a decisive attack once the Austrians had worn themselves out bears all the earmarks of hindsight influenced by the General Staff.[30] Chotusitz was the King's first real exercise of field command; at Mollwitz he had played no more than a squadron officer's role. Frederick would not have been the first nor the last general confused by the dynamics of a battlefield where realities were far more opaque than the reconstructions of the historians. Not until half-past ten did he make a decision. It was the right one. The Prussians marched out of their concealed positions onto the plateau of Chotusitz, did a half-wheel, and opened fire into the exposed Austrian flank. The Austrian infantry wavered. Charles, perceiving a possible threat to his line of retreat, decided to settle for what seemed a draw and ordered his subordinates to disengage.

Frederick was more than satisfied with the day's results. This time he not only was on the field for the final outcome; he also commanded the attack that settled the issue. The philosopher had become, in his own mind at least, a soldier. Anything that had gone wrong with the day was someone else's fault – specifically Leopold's. Frederick criticized him, with no particular justice, for the haphazard way the Prussians fought the battle. With perhaps better reason, the King also condemned Leopold's decision to occupy Chotusitz.

In truth Chotusitz had been less an encounter battle than a battle of increments. Like Union general George McClellan at Antietam in 1862, Frederick had fought in separate segments. First one, then a second cavalry attack were followed by Leopold's fight for Chotusitz, then by Frederick's manoeuvre, itself more decisive morally than physically. The victory was correspondingly incomplete, characterized by an absence of pursuit. 'I don't want to beat them too badly,' Frederick replied when a staff officer urged him to follow the disorganized Austrians. In 1754 he noted in a conversation that both his cavalry and his infantry had been too disorganized to do much more that day without falling into disorder.[31] But it seems legitimate to suggest as well that Frederick himself had not developed the capacity to ignore adrenalin surges that is sometimes described as the 'killer instinct'. The tendency to relax as the

30 O. Herrmann, 'Von Mollwitz bis Chotusitz. Ein Beitrag zur Taktik Friedrichs des Grossen', *Forschungen zur brandenburgischen und preussischen Geschichte*, VII (1894), pp. 340 ff.

31 G.F. Schmettau, *Lebensgeschichte des Grafen von Schmettau*, 2 vols (Berlin, 1806), II, 222; C. Rousset (ed.), *Le Comte de Gisors 1732–1758* (Paris, 1868), p. 106.

Austrians retreated must have been overwhelming – particularly when inaction offered seemingly promising diplomatic fruits.

Charles, his officers and men, were proud of their own achievements. The Austrians had lost more than 6,000 men and a dozen guns, but fought well enough to deter Frederick from trying conclusions soon again. Instead the King moved what remained of his army into the entrenched camp of Kuttenberg, using it once again as a force in being. The military threat was minimal: the Austrians had no difficulty shifting most of Charles's army against the Franco-Bavarian forces concentrated near Prague. Politically, however, the continued Prussian presence in Moravia was decisive.

Eighteenth-century coalitions were notoriously unstable, prone to fission based on self-interest. As early as January the French foreign minister had noted that France was suffering because it was constrained to consider its allies. Frederick was correspondingly suspicious of French intentions and French good will. His troops were tired; his treasury was depleted.[32] The Austrian government for its part was once more ready to negotiate. For the present Silesia was definitely lost. Even had Charles won a decisive tactical victory at Chotusitz, the overall strategic situation prohibited sending him north-east towards Breslau while Prague and Vienna lay under the allies' shadow. The province's eventual recovery remained an Austrian goal, but would have to depend on combinations of war and statesmanship impossible to calculate under existing conditions. Britain was anxious for peace between Prussia and Austria – not least because its foreign office hoped to induce Prussia's king eventually to support an anti-French coalition. King George's Hanoverian policies had been unpopular enough to bring to power a new government, more or less committed to the support of Maria Theresa. From a British perspective this meant concentrating against the main enemy. French policies and behaviour seemed far more threatening to British interests than Frederick's ambitions in central Europe – ambitions which, the past year and a half suggested to London, were modest in themselves and pursued without excessive zeal.[33]

---

32 Frederick II to C.F. Jordan, 13 June 1742, *Œuvres*, XVII, pp. 226–7.
33 For British policies and their background, cf. Black, *Natural and Necessary Enemies*, p. 37 *passim*; H.M. Scott, '"The True Principles of the Revolution": The Duke of Newcastle and the Idea of the Old System', in *Knights Errant and True Englishmen: British Foreign Policy, 1660–1800*, ed. J. Black (Edinburgh, 1989), pp. 55–91, esp. 63 ff.; and Manfred Schlenke, *England und das friderizianische Preussen 1740–1763* (Munich, 1963).

British attention in the 1740s was increasingly turning overseas, towards North America, the West Indies, and India. Nevertheless, a majority of its statesmen remained committed to the idea that the greatest threat to Europe's freedom and stability was the appetite of France for more. They also remained committed to an image of Britain as the natural focal point of anti-French coalitions. The British government offered subsidies to a Habsburg Empire whose treasury was badly depleted. It offered troops: a British contingent to be sent to the Netherlands, the Habsburg province most exposed to a French offensive. And it offered assistance in bringing the Dutch Republic into the war. These initiatives were enough to encourage serious negotiations between Vienna and Berlin. Preliminary terms were concluded in June 1742. A month later Prussia formally left the war in return for Silesia, except for a few frontier areas with no strategic importance.

Frederick perceived no likely long-term consequences of his initiative. Central Europe's boundaries had changed time and again over a century. Prussia was a quintessentially artificial creation, the product of treaties rather than history. There seemed no reason not to rejoice in a province acquired so cheaply. And if Prussia's monarch was not yet exactly a great captain, he could with some justice call himself a warrior king. When Voltaire chided him for defeating the Austrians at a place with the awkward name of Chotusitz, Frederick cheerfully answered that the victory rhymed well enough with Mollwitz![34] In any case, the double-headed triumph exceeded anything achieved by his father.

Philip V of Spain had taken advantage of the Prussian occupation of Silesia to assert an almost equally shadowy set of claims to the Habsburg possessions in Italy. The military and financial drain on Austria was exacerbated by the ambiguous position of Piedmont's King Charles Albert. France seemed more vulnerable since the Peace of Breslau had left a French army isolated in Bohemia. Unfortunately the Austrians' continued success at raids and manoeuvres neither created favourable conditions for a decisive battle nor bled the French to death from a thousand cuts. At the turn of the year the French were able to evade their opponents and withdraw into Bavaria.

Fleury died in January 1743, and Louis XV announced his intention to control French policy personally. By that time France was ready to end the fighting, at least in Central Europe. France needed to focus its resources – specifically against a British empire

---

34 Quoted in Duffy, *Frederick the Great*, p. 45.

that was emerging as France's real enemy.[35] Since Fleury had insisted on acting as the auxiliary of Charles Albert, legally speaking France was not at war with Austria. The price of peace was correspondingly obvious: leaving the new Holy Roman Emperor to his devices and his fate. This prospect was anything but appealing. Apart from its costs in prestige, Bavaria was not an asset to be despised whether as client or stalking horse. Particularly in the context of Frederick's demonstrated unreliability, Louis and his advisers by no means felt comfortable in coldly sacrificing France's long-time *fidus Achates*.

Nor could France guarantee that such a sacrifice would be accepted. In 1743 a contingent of British troops marched into Hanover, joining a small Austrian force and a *mélange* of Hanoverian and other German auxiliary troops to complete the 'Pragmatic Army'. Led by King George II in person, it won a neat tactical victory at Dettingen, in Bavaria, on 27 June, and continued to constitute a significant independent threat to France's eastern frontier.[36]

The Pragmatic Army was not an end in itself. In the summer and autumn of 1743 Prussia was courted by an unexpected suitor. Britain's position on the Continent seemed less secure in London than it appeared in Paris. Public and political opinion saw limited promise in an expensive continental alliance whose primary purpose seemed to involve restoring or enhancing the Habsburg position in central Europe. The British foreign office was correspondingly interested in recruiting Prussia to the coalition. Diplomatic folk wisdom insisted that the lesser German princes were more committed to their private interests than to any concept of the general good of the Holy Roman Empire. If foreigners truly began at Calais, Frederick might be bought cheaply. In any case Britain's ultimate purpose was less to fight France to a finish than to encourage it to back down by creating diplomatic conditions replicating those of the War of the Spanish Succession: France against the rest of Europe. In that context the gesture of Prussia's side-switching would be more important than any actual military contributions Frederick's army might make to a new coalition.

Britain's hopes for success in the Prussian quarter were encouraged by its achievements elsewhere. A tentative agreement with Charles Albert that would have resulted in his renouncing all claims

---

35 Browning, *War of the Austrian Succession*, pp. 129 *passim*.

36 Wolfgang Handrick, *Die Pragmatische Armee 1741–1743* (Oldenburg, 1990), is a model case study of the origins, nature, and performance of this polyglot force.

to Austrian territory in return for Bavaria's elevation to a kingdom, plus a generous British subsidy, collapsed because of domestic opposition. The negotiations, however, highlighted both the relative weakness of France's position and the growing importance of English money in diplomatic negotiations. Any doubts on the latter point were removed in September 1743, when Austria very reluctantly agreed to the Treaty of Worms, conceding territory in Italy in return for Piedmontese military support against France – the whole arrangement smoothed by British subsidies to both parties.[37]

A familiar German proverb advises the customer never to calculate the bill without consulting the waiter. Maria Theresa's renunciation of Silesia was anything but permanent. Apart from personal and dynastic factors, the economic potential of the province became increasingly attractive once it came under Prussian rule. Frederick, moreover, posed the kind of internal challenge to the Holy Roman Empire that could not be safely ignored. The Empress who concluded a letter to one of her generals with the admonition to 'live long and strike hard' had revitalized her heritage in the middle of a war. The watchword in Vienna had not yet become 'Prussia must be destroyed'. Nevertheless, Austria's diplomats and Austria's generals agreed that the upstart state and its provincial king must be shown their subordinate places in the European order as expeditiously as possible. No amount of English money was likely to alter this mind-set.[38]

Frederick was also revising his thinking in the context of events. The continued presence of Austrian troops on Bavarian soil led him to the reasonable – and accurate – conclusion that Austria proposed to avenge itself for Charles Albert's presumption in assuming the Imperial title by annexing enough Bavarian territory to prevent any similar challenges in the future. Common sense suggested that Prussia was equally unlikely to be left to enjoy undisturbed the profits of its king's Silesian venture.

Frederick's seizure of Silesia had set other forces in motion as well. For a quarter-century Russia's attitude towards Prussia had

37 Basil Williams, 'Carteret and the So-called Treaty of Hanau', *English Historical Review* XLIX (1934), 684–7; Gustav Otruba, 'Die Bedeutung englischer Subsidien und Antizipationen für die Finanzen Österreichs 1701–1748', *Vierteljahrschrift fur Sozial- und Wirtschaftsgeschichte*, LI (1964), 192–234.

38 Charles Ingrao makes a strong case that geopolitical considerations, albeit imperfectly perceived, influenced Austrian policies as much as did dynastic issues. 'Habsburg Strategy and Geopolitics during the Eighteenth Century', in *East Central European Society and War in the Pre-Revolutionary Eighteenth Century*, ed. G. Rothenberg *et al.* (Boulder, CO, 1982), pp. 49–66.

been essentially benevolent. Prussia was regarded in St Petersburg as a useful make-weight in Germany, one conditioned by its own weaknesses to support a *status quo* in eastern Europe that depended on a weak Poland – also a Russian interest. Even as Crown Prince, Frederick had accepted the advantages of an alliance with Russia, and put great hopes on a limited treaty concluded with St Petersburg in 1740.

Russia renewed that alliance in March 1743, but more as a reaction to French plans for a Grand Coalition of Baltic powers against Russia than from any positive affirmation of Prussian policies *vis-à-vis* Austria. Not until November could Russian diplomats be brought to guarantee Frederick's Silesian acquisition. Mollwitz and Chotusitz had created new perspectives. Russia now perceived itself confronted by a militarily strong, internally stable kingdom, one offering an essentially different challenge than the maladroit state of Poland. This Prussia was also available *in potentia* for anti-Russian alliances. From the perspective of St Petersburg, the most desirable response was to put Prussia back in its place, to restore 'the old and legitimate order of Europe'.

This did not mean immediate, direct military intervention against Prussia. But Chancellor A. P. Bestuzhev constantly warned his sovereign against the risks of Prussian expansionism. 'The more the power of the King of Prussia grows', he wrote, 'the greater the danger for us becomes' – particularly because Frederick himself was an incalculable quantity, a loose cannon whose impact was disproportionately greater in an age when diplomacy was conducted within restricted parameters. Bestuzhev saw Frederick as able to threaten Russian security not only from his own power base, but from a Sweden whose heir had recently married the Prussian King's sister, and from Russia's ancient foe Turkey as well.

Bestuzhev's was only a single manifestation of a pattern of Russian anxiety over perceived weaknesses that went so far as to call Prussia the potential key to a pan-European coalition that, once finished with Austria, would turn its envious eyes on Russia! In order to reduce Prussia to its previous circumstances of dependence on Russia, Bestuzhev recommended eventual partition. Not only should Silesia be returned to Austria, he argued; East Prussia would be assigned to Poland – with Russia, naturally, receiving compensation in the areas of Smolensk and Pskov. That this could be achieved only at the price of a general war did not greatly disturb an Austrian government which for its part lost no opportunities to stress to St Petersburg Prussia's insatiable appetites. These were described as extending far into Courland and Lithuania – a fantasy to be sure, but one reinforcing the anxieties of a government even less certain than Prussia of its exact place in Europe's order.[39]

Frederick was well aware of a Russian hostility that seemed to him completely irrational. He did not, however, fear direct Russian intervention – particularly since Russia seemed at the moment to have its hands full in coping with a new Swedish war. The King's ambitions were by no means as vaulting as those ascribed to him by Bestuzhev. At the moment they extended no further than seeking to extend Prussia's influence in Germany by championing the position of its lesser states against what Frederick described as the hegemonical ambitions of the Habsburg court. His initiatives came to nothing, partly because of the Prussian King's image as a stalking horse for French ambitions, and partly because Frederick himself inspired little confidence among his fellow-sovereigns. He had shown no unusual capacities as either statesman or general, and his character was most often described in negative terms.

The best Frederick could manage was a shadow 'Union of Frankfurt': Prussia, Hesse-Kassel, the Palatinate, and Bavaria linked in the context of developments in Vienna. However unpopular the Treaty of Worms, it freed Austria to concentrate its efforts against France and Bavaria, – efforts that proved successful enough to arouse Frederick's fear. His concerns were enhanced by what he viewed as a significant omission in the Worms document. The treaty guaranteed the Pragmatic Sanction, but said nothing whatever about Silesia. Instead, British officials seeking to smooth ruffled Habsburg feathers regularly spoke of Austrian concessions as temporary. That Great Britain would have provided more than verbal support for an Austrian effort to recover the lost province is extremely doubtful.[40] Frederick, however, saw himself as unable to accept the risks of passivity. In August 1744 the Prussian army would take the field once more, in the process marching over the treaty of 1742.

---

39 Cf. Walter Mediger, *Moskaus Weg nach Europa. Der Aufstieg Russlands zur Europäischer Machtstaat im Zeitalter Friedrichs des Grossen* (Braunschweig, 1952); p. 258 *passim*; and Paul Karge, *Die russisch-österreichischen Allianz von 1747 und ihre Vorgeschichte* (Göttingen, 1886), pp. 102 ff., for the quotations.

40 Jeremy Black, 'British Foreign Policy and the War of the Austrian Succession, A Research Priority', *Canadian Journal of History*, XXI (1986), 313–31; and P.G.M. Dickson, 'English Negotiations with Austria 1737–1752', in *Essays in Eighteenth Century History Presented to Dame Lucy Sutherland*, ed. A. Whiteman *et al.* (Oxford, 1973), pp. 81–112.

THE PRUSSIAN ARMY TAKES STOCK

The end of the First Silesian War had brought reappraisal in Prussia in military as well as diplomatic spheres. The army had done well enough in its first real test, but there was still room for improvement. As a soldier Frederick would ultimately prove more traditionalist than innovator. The King was also more consistently willing than any of his contemporaries to seek decisions through offensive operations. And in the eighteenth century, this meant that the infantry must sooner or later go forward and do the ultimate dirty work of war: close with the enemy, force him off his ground, and kill him, or facilitate his being killed by someone else.

Frederick's 'Instruction' of 20 June 1742 formed the basis for the comprehensive Infantry Drill Regulations of 1743.[41] This document made the three-rank formation introduced on an *ad hoc* basis in Silesia regulation for the entire army. The ranks themselves were tight. Until 1748, regulations prescribed that the right arm of each man fit behind the left arm of his next in rank – a position impossible to maintain away from the drill ground and still load a musket.

These dense formations had a certain tactical utility. Controlling long lines of men, much less moving them forward into enemy fire, could not be done entirely by force and threats. Even during manoeuvres, it was considered noteworthy when colonels and company officers were able to move a line of twenty or more battalions forward a few thousand paces without losing direction and touch. Once such a line halted for any reason, moreover, experience indicated that it was extremely difficult to start it moving again. This had less than is commonly supposed to do with the absence of patriotism and enthusiasm in the Prussian army. The noise level of a modern battlefield rendered it extremely difficult to pass commands along a line of advance – to say nothing of the effect of fear and excitement on the concentration of captains and subalterns. The results generally resembled those achieved in the party game of passing a story round a circle in whispers: compounded confusion.

The problem of control was further exacerbated because the tactical and the administrative organizations of a Prussian battalion rarely coincided. Instead of forming for action by companies, the unit of administration, a battalion was closed up and divided into eight platoons of essentially equal strength commanded by subalterns. The

---

41 Frederick II, 'Instruction für die Infanterie', June 20, 1742, *Œuvres*, XXX, pp. 121 ff.

platoons in turn were grouped by twos into divisions, usually led by captains. The resulting juggling of command assignments meant that soldiers often went into battle led by officers they barely knew, and more to the point, officers whose voices they were unlikely to recognize. Wise peacetime instructors correspondingly stressed method over haste. However ponderous Prussian tactical movements might seem initially, experience indicated that they were also precise. No time needed to be lost in repetition, in catching up, in restoring dress or alignment distance sacrificed to the search for speed.

The infantry's fire tactics further complicated its tactical situation. The battalions which marched into Silesia in 1740 had been intensively trained in 'platoon fire'. This system, developed around the turn of the eighteenth century, theoretically enabled infantry formations to maintain continuous fire while preserving a reserve of loaded weapons. The eight platoons of a battalion delivered their volleys in a complicated order that proved far more difficult to sustain in battle than on the drill grounds.

In practice, platoon fire tended to collapse into 'rolling fire', a polite term for every man reloading and pulling the trigger as fast as he could on his own hook, with officers unable to halt the process in the general din. Paradoxically, the carefully inculcated small-arms drill designed to make every move virtually automatic significantly inhibited controlling them once begun. The musketeer in battle was caught up in a mechanical process that gave some purpose to his presence and also dulled, because of its complexity, the desire to run away. Distracting him from it by any means short of striking up his gun muzzle was difficult at best.

When infantry was expected to combine movement with fire, the challenge grew even more complex. Individual musketeers were taught how to reload on the move. The drill regulations prescribed as well a collective method for 'fire while advancing'. Successive platoons took three long strides forward, fired, then reloaded while the rest of the battalion closed on them 'with short and slow steps'. Results in battle were too often similar to those achieved by the hypothetical individual unable to chew gum and walk simultaneously. A battalion playing this martial version of 'Captain, May I', with its giant steps and baby steps, was likely to disrupt itself by its own evolutions long before the enemy's muskets or artillery could do it any significant damage – to say nothing of the probable impact of a well-timed cavalry charge on a line of battle practising these complicated gymnastics.

Mollwitz and Chotusitz suggested an alternate way of looking at the problem. Both had arguably been decided morally rather than physically. The steady advance of the Prussian infantry had in one case panicked their Austrian opponents into breaking formation, and in the other convinced the Austrian commander that it was time to quit the field and fight another day. Intimidation – enhanced by proper timing – had apparently counted for more than fire-power.

A general with more combat experience than Frederick might well have been pardoned for assuming that the bayonet, or more accurately the threat of the bayonet, was the true mistress of the battlefield. The 1740s witnessed a general revival of interest in the potential of infantry shock action. Partly, this reflected a new interest in classical military history; in particular, an appreciation of the use Macedonia's phalanx had made of the *sarissa*, and Rome's legions of the combination of *pilum* and *gladius*. Partly, it manifested growing concern for the cost of battles which required firing lines to exchange volleys at point-blank range. The effect resembled pushing two candles into a blow-torch and seeing which melted more quickly. Thousands of essentially irreplaceable, highly trained infantry were slaughtered, and for results that too often proved marginal. Some distinguished contemporary field soldiers like Marshal de Saxe also believed that fire action was significantly overrated. At worst it made noise without doing damage; at best it broke wills before it killed men. The key to victory, as argued by Saxe and his epigoni, lay not in overwhelming an enemy where he stood, but in destroying the cohesion of his formations by convincing each individual in the opposing ranks that survival was better assured through flight than by fighting.[42]

The revised Prussian infantry drill regulations of 1743 sustained the new conventional wisdom by proclaiming that no enemy could stand before a charge properly delivered. Various forms of platoon fire were retained in the drill manual for their value against cavalry or the light troops of the Austrian army, the *Grenzer*. But on the outbreak of the Second Silesian War in 1744, the King asserted that his infantry had to do only two things in battle: form line quickly and precisely, then keep advancing when ordered.[43]

---

42 Maurice de Saxe, *Reveries on the Art of War*, T.R. Phillips (Harrisburg, Pennsylvania, 1944).

43 Duffy, *Army of Frederick the Great*, 82 ff.; Chandler, *The Art of Warfare in the Age of Marlborough*, (London, 1976), pp. 128 ff.; and Nosworthy, *Anatomy of Victory*, pp. 183 ff., are the best contemporary analyses in English of Prussian infantry tactics at this period.

Frederick had not fallen a complete victim to the mystique of cold steel that was to obsess so many generals in a later century. He insisted it was against all expectation that any enemy would withstand a determined and steady advance. But if he did, a volley at twenty paces, or better yet ten, should change his mind – particularly if the Prussian 'battalion guns' had done their work.

The Prussian army, like most of its counterparts, assigned each of its infantry and grenadier battalions two or three light cannon at the beginning of a campaign. They were commanded by NCOs and crewed by a mix of artillerymen and men detailed from the infantry. The latter were usually men their own officers were glad to be rid of. But the battalion guns' mission was more important than their personnel suggested. Eighteenth-century artillery legitimately tended to be regarded as a stationary arm. Yet even a few cannon in the right place at the right time could achieve much.

Prussia's battalion guns, like the 'accompanying guns' of World War I and the infantry guns of the World War II Wehrmacht, were to engage targets of opportunity and provide direct fire support for their battalions. In practice, their employment often tended to be along the lines of the apocryphal British battalion commander's order to his machine-gun officer: 'Take the damned things off to a flank and hide them!' While technical ignorance and caste pride played roles, the underlying problem of the battalion guns was their weight. Keeping pace with a steady infantry advance ranged from difficult to impossible, whether the guns were limbered up or manhandled from position to position.

Despite this problem the regimental pieces performed generally well at Mollwitz – well enough to encourage Frederick to consider them for a larger role in the army's tactical doctrine. In the summer of 1741, the King proposed introducing a new design of regimental gun. This would be a light three-pounder, weighing under 500 pounds and drawn by only three horses. Sacrifices of range and killing power would be compensated by improved mobility and increased rate of fire. Despite some criticism from his senior officers the King persisted. By the summer of 1742, most Prussian regiments had received their new guns. If they worked as planned, they would be able to 'shoot in' the infantry to a point where the musketeers could deliver the final, decisive volleys.

Heavier artillery played at this stage a minor role in Frederick's approach to war. The King expected his 'battery pieces', mostly twelve-pounders, to do little more than stay in position on the battlefield, preferably massed on the flanks, and fire for effect. In theory, heavy guns might also be distributed among the regiments to enhance the infantry's fire-power. In general, however, the worth of these cumbersome pieces in the kind of fast-paced, offensive battle Frederick proposed was more than dubious. The artillery was still an auxiliary arm. It was to the cavalry that Frederick turned when he sought quantum improvement in the Prussian army's operational efficiency.[44]

'Giants on elephants who could neither ride nor fight.' So Frederick characterized the horsemen he inherited from his father. Though the King's memory was significantly coloured by the events of Mollwitz, in truth Prussia's cavalry had arguably been as much a military stepchild as its gunners. This was in sharp contrast to Europe's other armies. France and Austria, Britain and Sweden, even the United Netherlands, regarded their mounted forces as a battle-winning instrument, and worked to develop the efficiency of officers, troopers, and horses alike. Frederick William I disagreed. Throughout his career he insisted that infantry – good infantry, the kind he proposed to develop – could see off even superior numbers of cavalry by a combination of steadiness and fire-power.

As in so many other cases, Frederick William's mind-set reflected economic considerations. Cavalry was an expensive arm, particularly its heavier branches. Horses were expensive, and correspondingly the royal sympathy. Cavalry officers by and large shared their master's perspective. They were aristocrats, but poor aristocrats. A *Rittergut*'s horses were working animals. Few *Junker* kept large private stables; a broken leg in the hunting field, glanders, thrush, or any of a dozen equine ailments was a cause of deep concern. It was scarcely to be wondered that captains and majors took tender care of their troop horses, braiding ribbons into their manes, keeping them safely stabled in bad weather, and insisting on a kind of conditioning that produced overfed, glossy-coated beasts suitable enough for short bursts of intense activity, but ill-adapted to the demands of a long campaign.

The troopers suffered almost as much as their mounts. In theory, personnel should have been the Prussian cavalry's strong point. Its heavy regiments in particular, the cuirassiers and dragoons, included a high proportion of Prussian subjects. Many of them were volunteers from the more prosperous peasant holdings, and correspondingly familiar with horses. In practice, however, these men had the same

44 Hans Bleckwenn, 'Zur Handhabung der Geschütz bei der friderizianischen Feldartillerie', *Zeitschrift für Heereskunde*, XXIX (1965), 96–105, is a good overview.

problems that the Union Army's cavalry faced in the first three years of the American Civil War. They knew just enough about horses to be dangerous, and nothing at all about cavalry service. Institutional reluctance to exhaust the animals meant that in most regiments standards of horsemastership did not rise above the farm-boy level. Some troopers could not even tighten saddle girths properly under field conditions. As for skill at arms, Frederick William I's faith in fire-power meant that his cavalry spent a good deal of its limited mounted drill practising firing pistols and carbines from the saddle – an exercise of marginal utility at best, given the accuracy of short-barrelled flintlocks.[45]

Frederick followed up his post-Mollwitz innovations by beginning with the physical. His father had valued big men on big horses – the larger the better. Frederick reduced the minimum height for both a cuirassier and a dragoon to 5 feet five inches. Their mounts were to be no larger than 15 3/4 hands for cuirassiers, 15 1/2 hands for dragoons. While Holstein continued to be a favourite source for heavy cavalry horses, Frisian cold-bloods increasingly gave way to native-bred mounts from Neumark and East Prussia.

New men received new instructions. Each recruit was given thorough training on foot to develop his carriage and discipline before he ever touched a horse. Riding drill began bareback, with the intention of teaching the new troopers to control their mount by body movements instead of merely sawing on the reins, farmer-style. Once the recruit graduated to a saddle, he found himself on a new design whose shorter stirrups meant that a standing rider cleared his horse's back by a hands-breadth. The resulting leverage gave added force to a sword's cut or thrust – and the sword, it was stressed from the first, was the cavalryman's primary weapon. Cuirassiers and dragoons now carried heavy, straight blades primarily designed for thrusting. This fit Frederick's aim of developing his heavy cavalry as a shock instrument. Curved sabres, he argued, invited the degeneration of cavalry combat into a series of man-to-man duels, indecisive by themselves and taking far too long to determine anything collectively. A thrusting sword was, in fact, a do-or-die weapon.

Individual horsemanship and skill at arms were only the bases of Frederick's overall design for his cavalry. Existing Prussian doctrine prescribed mounted attacks to be ridden at a slow trot. This concept

---

45 W. Unger, *Wie ritt Seydlitz?* (Berlin, 1906), presents the details of mounted service in Prussia at this period. Cf., as well, Christopher Duffy, *The Military Experience in the Age of Reason* (London, 1987), pp. 115 ff.

incorporated wisdom overlooked by its numerous critics. A steady pace preserved formation and spared horses; a cavalry charge that got out of hand was a proven recipe for tactical disaster. A slow, determined attack, moreover, could have the effect of inhibiting enemy horse or foot, encouraging those quick glances over the shoulder that so often prefigured retreat at the moment of impact. On the other hand, cavalry that moved *too* slowly made themselves vulnerable to a counter-charge by a more daring adversary. Gustavus Adolphus and Charles XII of Sweden had taught their squadrons to charge home at the gallop, sword in hand. Initially, as previously mentioned, Frederick's goals were more modest: his troopers were to begin the gallop only in the thirty paces before an enemy. In 1742 the distance was increased to 100 paces. Not until July 1744 was the gallop ordered for 200 paces' distance, and even then the horses were to be given their heads only in the final moments.

Frederick's emphasis on cavalry shock in the mid-1740s paralleled his approach to infantry tactics. His avowed intention was to break the enemy before a mêlée could begin. If the Prussian squadrons and regiments stayed in close formation, the adversary would be swept away by the shock alone. Even more important, the successful attackers would remain in hand, under control of their officers, ready for further participation in the battle.[46]

SECOND ROUND FOR SILESIA

That there would be a next battle was increasingly apparent. Instead of behaving, as Frederick had expected, like a rational actor and accepting its loss of Silesia, Austria between 1742 and 1744 made one of the eighteenth century's more remarkable diplomatic and military comebacks. Cumbersome administrations and limited powers made it difficult for a state actually at war to make anything but minor improvements in its capacities. Austria not merely survived but actually flourished – at least, relative to initial performances.

Maria Theresa herself inspired much of her state's recovery. Her dramatic appearances before the Hungarian estates in Magyar costume, on one occasion with the infant Joseph in her arms, were gestures to inspire poets. More significant were the constitutional

46 Cf. particularly Frederick II, 'Reglement für Cavallerie und Dragoner, was bei den Exerciten geändert wird', 17 June 1742; 'Disposition pour la cavalerie', July 1744; and 'Disposition, wie sich die Officiere von der Cavallerie, und zwar die Generale sowohl als die Commandeurs der Escadrons, in einem Treffen gegen den Feind zu verhalten haben', *Œuvres*, XXX, pp. 111 ff., 143 ff., 135 ff.

concessions the Empress offered in return for the support of the Magyar magnates. While the actual results in terms of troops and money provided fell far short of the rhetoric and the promises, the enthusiastic public acceptance of Maria Theresa as Queen of Hungary showed the powers that the Habsburg lion was not yet entirely toothless.

Nor did Maria Theresa depend entirely on public charm and private compromises. In the aftermath of the Prussian and French withdrawals from Bohemia in 1742, the Empress ignored her local commander's promise of no reprisals. Anyone who even accepted an honour from her enemies was barred from her service. Overt collaborators faced loss of property, high fines, long prison sentences – even death or mutilation.[47] Such measures were not unknown in the eighteenth century. They were nevertheless considered extreme in the environment of 'live and let live' that was considered by civilians the desirable norm of warfare. Times were changing, and Frederick of Prussia was not the only one ready to rewrite the rules.

By early 1744 Maria Theresa had also reorganized her command and policy teams. One of the administration's brightest young men, Count Wenzel Anton von Kaunitz, was promoted to be *de facto* governor of the Austrian Netherlands.[48] Military appointments were similarly shifted, with a certain pattern of successful and energetic officers being assigned to Bohemia and Moravia: the Prussian sector. In December 1743, the Empress capped her comeback by ordering an alliance with Saxony – a defensive alliance on paper, but one that nevertheless heightened tension in Berlin.

There is irony in the fact that Austria's military plans for 1744 focused not on Silesia's recovery, but on offensives in Italy and along the Rhine. Nevertheless, 'the wicked flee when no man pursueth'. Particularly in the context of emerging Russian hostility Frederick saw no point in clinging to temporary realities. Diplomatically, France was willing to renew its alliance with Prussia in the hope that Austria would respond by shifting forces to the Silesian/Bohemian sector. Operationally, Austria's new Saxon connection gave Frederick a broader spectrum of options than he had enjoyed in 1740. The Electorate had supported Prussia in 1740 with no rewards for its exertion. Its resources exhausted, Saxony proposed to remain neutral in any second round between its powerful neighbours. Frederick had

47 Browning, *War of the Austrian Succession*, p. 127.

48 W.J. McGill, 'The Roots of Policy: Kaunitz in Italy and the Netherlands 1742–1746', *Central European History*, I (1968), 131–49.

other ideas. The direct routes of advance into Bohemia from Silesia possessed too many logistical problems for a large force. Saxon terrain was easier, and a flank march through Saxony offered the possibility of a strategic surprise. For Frederick the decision was obvious: his columns headed for the Saxon frontier.

Violations of neutrality were hardly unfamiliar phenomena in eighteenth-century warfare; it was nevertheless unusual for a middle-sized power cavalierly to invade the territory of another middle-sized power. The Saxon government and the Saxon army, alike taken by surprise, offered no resistance to a Prussian force that took pains to do as little damage as possible along its route of advance. The Austrians, their attention concentrated on the Low Countries, could do no more than harass the Prussian columns once they entered Bohemia. By early September Frederick was in position in front of Prague.

The second city of the Habsburg monarchy was so large that its effective fortification was a fiscal impossibility and its effective defence correspondingly difficult. The governor put up a *baroud d'honneur*, forcing the Prussian siege gunners to knock a practicable breach in his ramshackle walls before he surrendered on 16 September. Frederick, by now under heavy pressure from his French allies to thrust into the Danube valley through southern Bohemia, left the city three days later. By 1 October the Prussians were across the Vltava River (Moldau River) – and then Frederick received two unpleasant surprises. Saxony had decided after all that it was a state and not a highway. Its army was moving south, and not alone. On 2 October Frederick learned that Austria's main field army was also somewhere in Bohemia. More than that, neither his spies nor his scouts were able to say.

Frederick initially expected a repetition of events in 1741. He had 62,000 men and was confident of his army's ability to decide the campaign in the open field. Charles of Lorraine, or more accurately his new adviser, the canny veteran Field-Marshal O.F. von Traun, had no intention of giving the King that opportunity. The Austrians waited for the Saxons and threatened Frederick's communications with Prague as the weather turned colder and wetter. On 22 September the Saxons arrived, giving Charles a disposable force of 74,000 men. The next night the Austro-Saxon force moved to within 6 miles of Frederick's main position and established a position later known as the Camp of Marschowitz. Frederick marched towards the enemy, and on 25 September made a personal reconnaissance. Nature and artifice, he concluded, combined to make the camp too strong to be taken by direct assault by men and animals already on short commons. That same day the Prussians started their march back to Prague, leaving a number of isolated garrisons to be snapped up by the Austrians.

With Saxony hostile Frederick had no hope of surviving a winter in Prague. The Prussians headed north-east, suffering heavy losses from desertion and disease. Frederick crossed the Elbe at Neu-Kolin on 8 and 9 November, and sent his exhausted troops into winter quarters in the part of Bohemia he had hoped to secure by going to war. If the King initially assumed the Austrians would fight, he now made an opposite assumption about their passivity. Instead, ten days later the allies crossed the Elbe, destroyed an isolated Prussian battalion, and sent Frederick in a headlong run for the Silesian passes. By now winter had set in, with drifting snow blocking the increasingly narrow roads. Stragglers froze to death, or were snapped up by the Croats and hussars who hung on the flanks and rear of an army that was on the point of disintegration by the time it crossed the frontier.

Frederick's losses in this near-disaster remain a subject of confusion. The Austrians boasted of receiving almost 17,000 deserters. Other reliable sources estimate that fewer than 40,000 Prussians returned to Silesia, and half of those died of disease or were unfit for further service.[49] Silesia was overrun by stragglers and marauders, which did nothing to enhance acceptance of Prussian rule. Officers openly questioned, when they did not deride, their King's generalship. Frederick later described his own mistakes in detail. He blamed himself in particular for not consolidating his position around Prague, and for failing to establish secure lines of supply into Prussia.[50] The latter omission was particularly important. Bohemia in 1744 was not Silesia in 1740. If its aristocracy might not have been uniformly loyal in principle, Maria Theresa had made enough examples, and Austria's recovery was by now sufficiently evident that few magnates seriously contemplated a change of masters. Bohemia's noblemen exercised a degree of control over peasants and townsmen that kept Frederick's army from obtaining supplies by purchase and requisition. Foraging was once again inhibited by the Austrian light troops, who forced the Prussians to send out such large forces that they themselves ate most of what they obtained. Once the retreat began, hardship made men

49 Duffy, *Frederick the Great*, p. 56; G.L. Mamlocke, *Friedrichs der Grossen Korrespondenz mit Ärzten* (Stuttgart, 1907), p. 12.

50 Frederick II, *Œuvres*, III, p. 76.

increasingly difficult to control by officers and NCOs themselves cold, hungry, and exhausted.

At the same time, and to a degree unusual for him, Frederick credited his Austrian counterparts with having outsmarted him. Years afterward, the King was fond of saying that Traun had been one of his schoolmasters in the art of war.[51] What lessons had he derived from the campaign of 1744? One, certainly, was to put no trust in the durability of his army under stress. There is a curious element in the historiography of eighteenth-century armies. Their brittleness has been so often proclaimed that their resilience in the face of actual adversity has been overlooked. The mercenaries and professionals of the eighteenth century responded to defeat and privation with approximately the same levels of endurance and resilience as their nineteenth-century successors.[52] The differences can be accounted for as much by the higher feasibility of desertion and surrender in the earlier period compared to the total wars of later centuries.

It is not necessary to overdraw the comparison to accept the argument that in any era armies over-marched, under-fed, and out-manoeuvred are prone to dissolution. Why, then, have eighteenth-century soldiers had such a disproportionately unfavourable press in this regard? Some of the answer appears to involve the eloquence with which Frederick in later years stressed the importance of discipline in controlling the rabble that he stated and implied filled his ranks. That mind-set appears to have been in good part the result of his Bohemian experiences in 1744. Frederick was enough of his father's son to take the discipline of the army he inherited in good part for granted. Nothing in his earlier experiences, even the flight of his cavalry at Mollwitz, had challenged the assumption that Prussian troops knew how to endure. But after 1744 the King would never again believe in the good will of the men he led.

Frederick's second conclusion was operational. His career as a general had thus far been characterized by successful battles and sieges, but unsuccessful campaigns. In the manoeuvre warfare of the eighteenth century, Frederick was still what chess players call a *patzer*. Even the Austrians' second string could show him up. It was scarcely remarkable that Prussia's still-young monarch, in calculating the results of his Bohemian fiasco, came away more convinced than ever that battle offered greater promise than finesse.

51 C.J. Ligne, *Mémoires et lettres du Prince de Ligne* (Paris, 1923), p. 158.

52 A good example is the brilliant French withdrawal from Prague in December of 1742 best described in Albert, duc de Broglie, *Frédéric II et Louis XV, 1742–44*, 2 vols (Paris, 1885), I, pp. 105 ff.

Implementing that decision meant not only rebuilding but revitalizing his badly attenuated army. Disgruntled officers were silenced, at least temporarily, with a judicious blend of promotions, cash grants, and royal back-patting. But the regiments that had marched to destruction in Bohemia were Frederick's best. Their cadres of veterans were not easily replaced even by the most determined efforts of recruiters and drill sergeants. With Prussia's credit on the international money market at a low point and its usefulness as an ally openly questioned in Paris and Munich, Frederick needed a victory as badly as any member of his house ever needed one.

War is like baccarat. A good rule of thumb is to bet against the man who has to win; he seldom does. Frederick did everything possible to guarantee his wager for the spring of 1745. He approached Britain with the hope of securing its good offices in Vienna. He urged France to mount a major offensive in the western theatre of operations. Austria was not to be moved. In December 1744 Maria Theresa dispensed Silesians from any allegiance previously given to Frederick. In January 1745, Charles of Bavaria died. The Austrian foreign office promptly began negotiations with his successor — negotiations that by April took Bavaria out of the war on highly favourable terms amounting to *status quo ante bellum*.[53] A month earlier Saxony, resentful of Frederick's disregard of its sovereignty, fearful of Prussian ascendancy in central Europe, and eager for Dutch and British subsidies, had agreed to join a Quadruple Alliance against the upstart power.

From Maria Theresa's perspective, her new German alliances made the recovery of Silesia essential. Instead of being able to browse on Saxon or Bavarian provinces, Austria could now hope for territorial compensation only at Prussia's expense. Frederick for his part decided to fight on his own ground, however recently acquired. In April he established his field headquarters in Silesia near Glatz. The Prussian concentration took longer than Frederick had hoped. By the last week of May, he had approximately 60,000 men in place — 42,000 infantry and just under 17,000 cavalry, plus artillery and engineers.

He faced an enemy equal in strength and not inferior in quality. Forty thousand Austrians under Prince Charles were supported by 19,000 Saxons. Frederick's first intention was to draw the allies out of the Bohemian mountains, onto flat ground where Prussian tactical superiority was most likely to be decisive. A carefully orchestrated

53 Browning, *War of the Austrian Succession*, p. 203.

campaign of disinformation, featuring double agents, rumour mills, and feigned retreats, encouraged Charles to chance his fortune against a foe who seemed on the run. On 3 June, the Saxons and Austrians left the security of the *Riesengebirge* and advanced to the village of Hohenfriedberg. There they established an administrative camp, one without field fortifications. Frederick had kept his main forces well concealed, and the usually efficient Austrian light cavalry this time remained inactive. The King decided to risk attacking an enemy whose confidence invited a challenge.

Frederick's original plan was to make a night march that would put his forces in position first to break the allies' left flank, then roll up the rest of their army from east to west. The initial manoeuvre succeeded brilliantly. Despite the fact that the infantry had to march through fields rather than on roads needed for the artillery, they kept their ranks and kept their silence. A fist or a boot from the man next to him awaited the unfortunate private who sneezed too loudly, or attempted to soothe his nerves with a forbidden pipe. Straggling was at a minimum. Cantonists or mercenaries, Prussian-born or the outcasts of half central Europe, Frederick's rank and file were soldiers enough to gauge their personal chances of survival if the manoeuvre failed.

After a brief rest the Prussians moved forward into a breaking dawn and into an unexpected situation. The allies' camps extended further east than Frederick believed. Instead of open country, the leading Prussian elements ran into high ground occupied by strong detachments of enemy infantry. On hearing this news Frederick accelerated the march of his main body. It crossed the Streigau River just in time to encounter a large force of Saxon and Austrian cavalry.

The Prussian troopers on Frederick's right had the advantage of numbers and terrain – they were in a position to charge down slope. But their discipline held only until the first shock. The cavalry action degenerated into a swirling mass of single combats, with every Prussian squadron in the vicinity being sucked into the vortex. A missed thrust or a clumsy slash could be a death warrant. Quarter was neither asked nor given by Prussians eager to establish the honour of their arm of service, and inspired by the King's alleged encouragement to take no Saxon prisoners.[54]

---

[54] This was at least the understanding of the front-line squadrons: J.A.F. Logan-Logejus, *Meine Erlebnisse als Reiteroffizier unter dem Grossen König in den Jahren 1741–1759* (Breslau, 1934), pp. 91 ff.

As the rival cavalries decimated each other, infantry began reaching the field. The Saxons, who had been camped on the allied left, took up their main position in a zone of broken ground. It was ideal country for light troops, and offered solid defensive terrain for the Saxon line battalions, particularly as their regimental guns moved into supporting positions. This was the moment of Leopold of Anhalt-Dessau. Pulling nine battalions off the line of march, he formed them into fighting lines and led them forward. Other units rallied to the initiative, and by the time the 'Young Dessauer's' attack developed, he was at the head of twenty-one battalions. In accordance with their new regulations, the Prussians advanced with their muskets at the shoulder. Linesmen and grenadiers, the bluecoats moved forward, through the canister of the Saxon guns, through the Saxon musketry, until they delivered their first volleys almost literally in the whites of their enemy's eyes.

The psychological and physical force of the Prussian attack was not enough to break the Saxon infantry immediately. Instead of running the Elector's battalions, mercenaries and *Landeskinder* kept up the fight for almost two hours, meeting the Prussian volleys with their own, falling back from obstacle to obstacle, making the Dessauer's men pay for every yard won. Casualties were heavy on both sides. Not until 7 a.m. did what remained of the Saxons retreat, after waiting in vain for support from Austrian allies who spent most of the time bought by the Saxons shaking out of their tents and into fighting formation.

The Saxon withdrawal also marked the end of Frederick's original plan. Both the cavalry of his right and the infantry who had driven the Saxons were fought out: too tired and disorganized to be brought readily into play for the next round. Frederick therefore ordered his main body, that part of it not drawn into Leopold's fight, to turn left and attack the Austrians where they stood. Confused orders left one brigade dangling, unsupported in open ground. The Austrians, however, did nothing, remaining in place as eighteen battalions of Prussian infantry, covered on their left by nine cavalry regiments, fell into line of battle and advanced, drums pounding an obbligato to the cannon fire.

For a few minutes Habsburg fortunes appeared to have turned. Ten squadrons of Prussian cuirassiers were temporarily cut off from their main body when a bridge behind them collapsed. But before the Austrians could do more than engage them, Ziethen's scouts discovered a ford. The unconventional hussar led his own regiment and the 12th Dragoons to the support of the beleaguered 'heavies'. Five more regiments followed, splashing across the river with the aplomb of men much longer accustomed to such unexpected behaviour. The shock of their charge was enough – just enough – to see off Austrian horsemen already disorganized from their encounter with the first two Prussian waves.

That left only the Austrian infantry. Like their Saxon counterparts the whitecoats stood their ground, exchanging volleys with the Prussians at what sometimes seemed musket-barrel range. The issue on that part of the field was still in doubt when a wandering regiment of Prussian dragoons entered the scene and charged into the history books. Instead of being drawn into the cavalry battle on the Prussian left, the Bayreuth Dragoons, the 5th, had followed its infantry's advance, finally drawing up behind a gap that opened in the first line. The senior officer on the spot, Prince Ferdinand of Brunswick, pointed out a line of Austrian grenadiers whose fire was checking, though not halting, the advance.

Responsibility for what happened next was claimed and debated as long as the old Prussian army existed. No one knows exactly who ordered the charge. But around 8:15 a.m. the *Bayreuther* went forward, first at a trot, then a gallop. With no time to form square, the grenadiers delivered an ineffective volley before they were ridden down and the victorious dragoons crashed into the main Austrian body. Deployed in line with no horsemen of their own at hand to take the shock, the Austrians stood their ground for a few minutes, then broke and ran for their lives.[55] In less than a half hour the Bayreuth Dragoons took no fewer than sixty-seven colors – a far greater tribute to the force of their charge than the five guns that could not be withdrawn, or the 2,500 prisoners who compared their maximum foot speed to the pace of a running horse and sensibly threw down their arms. The regiment's own losses were less than a hundred.

By 9 a.m. it might have been said that the fighting was over because no enemy was left. At least none remained on the field of battle. Frederick's troops advanced no more than a few hundred yards, then halted. Even had the King wished to follow up his victory, he lacked the organized forces to do so. His cavalry was scattered; his infantry exhausted. When the butcher's bill was in, more than 4,700 Prussians were dead or wounded. Three times as many allied troops had fallen – an unusual disproportion in eighteenth-century warfare.

---

55 M.E. Kröger, *Friedrich der Grosse und General Chasot* (Bresen, 1893), pp. 37 ff., has a vivid description of the charge by the man who, as a lieutenant, led the first wave.

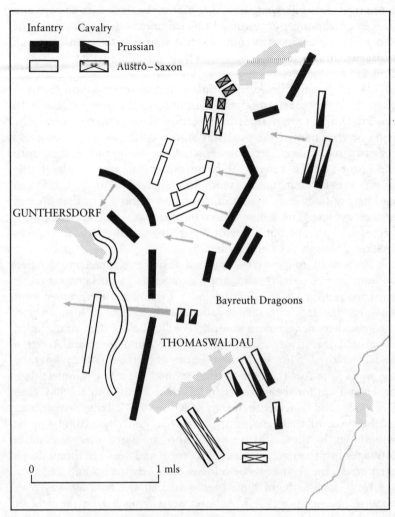

GUNTHERSDORF

Bayreuth Dragoons

THOMASWALDAU

0   1 mls

1. Battle of Hohenfriedberg, 4 June 1745

The list of trophies so impressed the king that on the day after the battle he ordered the captured standards set up in his headquarters, as though he wished to assure himself they were real.[56]

56 Rudolf Keibel, *Die Schlacht von Hohenfriedberg* (Berlin, 1899); and A. Hoffmann, *Der Tag von Hohenfriedberg und Streigau* (Oppeln, 1903), successfully combine narrative and anecdote.

Hohenfriedberg is frequently described as the first appearance of Frederick's most familiar contribution to eighteenth-century tactics: the oblique order of battle. The concept of concentrating against an enemy flank was hardly original to the King of Prussia. From Epamonides to Marlborough commanders had sought to weigh one wing of their army, advance that wing in order to defeat the relatively weaker enemy, then envelop and roll up his line of battle. Raimondo Montecuccoli had advised that an army's best troops be posted on its flanks, with the flank having the advantage in strength and quality taking the initiative. In France, Folard and the Marquis de Feuquières had made similar recommendations.[57]

Frederick, familiar with the works of all three theoreticians, admired the concept. Translating it into action, however, posed significant problems. On the most fundamental level extending a line of battle meant attenuating it. Just how strong did a reinforced wing have to be in order to break through an enemy before that enemy could exploit the accompanying weaknesses in one's own positions? Once that conundrum was resolved, successful implementation of the oblique order seemed to require an obliging enemy – one, that is, careless enough or stupid enough not only to leave a flank unprotected, but to remain unresponsive in the face of a direct threat. Assuming normal, or even low-normal, competence on the part of opposing commanders, the obvious response to an oblique-order attack involved refusing the threatened wing. This forced the enemy to extend his movements, perhaps to a point where his over-extended line would snap or the enveloping force's manoeuvring capacities and powers of initiative would be exhausted. In this context examination of Frederick's tactics at Hohenfriedberg suggest less the first, tentative application of the oblique order than an attempt to execute the more traditional manoeuvres of a night march and a flank attack. Once the fighting started, Frederick virtually ceased to command anything.

The chorus of praise for Hohenfriedberg raised throughout military Europe generated a certain *post facto* tendency to confuse fighting power with virtuosity. Frederick's night march was a stroke bold in conception and brilliant in execution. It was, however, an operational rather than a tactical move, one meant to surprise an enemy as opposed to getting inside his battlefield reaction time.

---

57 For background, cf. Robert L. Quimby, *The Background of Napoleonic Warfare* (New York, 1957), pp. 15 *passim*: and Jean Colin, *L'Infanterie au XVIIIe siècle. La tactique* (Paris, 1907).

In execution, Hohenfriedberg resembled Chotusitz: a series of separate actions, with each part of the Prussian army fighting its own uncoordinated battle. Reinforcements were drawn into the fighting instead of being committed by the higher commanders. The decisive charge of the Bayreuth Dragoons owed as much to serendipity as to initiative. No particular reason existed why the regiment should have been where it was at 8 a.m. on 4 June, as opposed to being in half a dozen other locations. Hohenfriedberg, moreover, was lost as well as won. The Saxons' and Austrians' mutual failure to support each other allowed the Prussians time to recover from their own tactical lapses and win a victory significant enough to give its name to one of Germany's greatest marches.

A PROVINCE SECURED

Significant – but not decisive. That fact escaped Frederick in the summer of 1745. The Prussian army's failure to launch a tactical pursuit after Hohenfriedberg was followed by weeks of inaction: more or less aimless marches into and through Bohemia, designed to spare Prussia's resources and exhaust Austria's while Maria Theresa made up her mind to negotiate peace.[58] But Vienna remained silent as the regrouped Austro-Saxon army kept Frederick under observation and Habsburg light troops demonstrated once again their mastery of 'little war'. Ziethen's hussars exhausted themselves and their animals chasing raiding parties that struck, drew blood, and disappeared into the countryside. A couple of wagons burned here, a foraging party sniped into inactivity somewhere else, a patrol that disappeared without trace – this was the stuff of Frederick's summer campaign. In late September his army went into camp a few miles from the Bohemian town of Soor, expecting no more than the usual debilitating harassment before returning to Silesia and winter quarters. Instead, on 29 September Frederick found the shoe of Hohenfriedberg on the other foot when the allies caught the Prussian army in its blankets.

Frederick's camp had been laid out administratively rather than tactically. In particular, the Prussians neglected to occupy or to picket the high ground on their right, the ground commanding their intended line of march back to Silesia. Prince Charles replicated, and indeed bettered, Frederick's march of three months earlier by executing a

---

58 Frederick II, *Œuvres*, III, 120, is an example of the King's stressing of logistical factors in his conduct of operations.

night march through tangled woods and a quick seizure of the heights just before daybreak. But there the parallels ceased. The ground in front of the allies was obscured by a heavy dawn mist, and Charles was not the man to send his army forward against an enemy he could not see. The allies held their ground as belated warnings of their presence reached the Prussian King. As Frederick and Leopold reconnoitred the scene, the Prussians took arms and fell into rank by regiments and brigades. Between 6 and 8 a.m. they marched out of their camp and took position. Frederick's plan was simple, a product of circumstances rather than intention. He proposed to throw the bulk of his army against the Austrian-occupied heights on his right, leaving the centre and left to contain the Austrians as best they might. Indeed, fighting a general battle was an invitation to disaster. Casualties and sickness, desertions and detachments, had reduced the numbers around Frederick to 22,000. The Austro-Saxons had twice as many, and only a decisive hammer-blow seemed likely to keep the Prussians from a high risk of disaster.

The ground fog cleared at 8 a.m. The Prussians finished their deployment in clear sunlight under an Austrian cannonade that began as soon as the gunners could see their targets. Frederick's principal objective, called by locals the Graner-Koppe, was heavily defended by ten battalions of infantry, the equivalent of four more of grenadiers, forty-five squadrons of some of the allies' best cavalry. Frederick sent six regiments of cuirassiers and dragoons against their allied counterparts. The Prussian army's continued weakness in tactical reconnaissance flared again when the leading squadrons rode into a steep-sided gully near the foot of the Graner-Koppe. But solid, flexible discipline at troop and squadron level kept the cuirassiers from bunching into an uncontrolled mass. Improved horsemastership had left them mounts strong enough, even at the end of a campaign, to carry their armour-plated riders up the gully's far slope. And fighting man's luck favoured the Prussians with an opponent who failed to seize the opportunity. The allied cavalry were under orders to hold the Graner-Koppe. Its officers, from generals to subalterns, took their mission literally. Instead of charging the Prussians as their leading elements emerged, the Austro-Saxons took them under pistol and carbine fire at long range – a tactic made obsolete a century earlier by Gustavus Adolphus. Despite fighting at an almost two-to-one disadvantage, the Prussians managed to clear the front for their infantry in some of the most desperate infighting of Frederick's wars.

Whether this tactical victory would bear wider fruit was initially doubtful. The first Prussian wave, six battalions strong, was decimated by Austrian artillery fire and thrown back in a sharp, nicely timed counterattack of the Austrian grenadiers. The Prussians were not helped by advancing with shouldered muskets – their enemies were in no way intimidated. But unlike so many defeated eighteenth-century forces, these did not break. Instead, most of the survivors passed through the second line, five battalions strong, rallied, and provided enough bulk to carry the next attack up the slopes of the Graner-Koppe and over the Austrian guns. At the same time the Prussian left and centre advanced on the initiative of the local commanders. Prince Charles, rather than risk a mêlée, drew off. Seventy-five hundred of his men were dead, wounded, or captured; Prussian casualties totalled 4,000.[59]

This time, at least according to his memory, Frederick tried to mount a pursuit, but his cavalry were too tired and disorganized to do more than cheer the victory. Once again Frederick, 'in the soup up to [his] ears', had been saved by the regimental-level fighting qualities of his officers and men – and by the presence of an obliging enemy, too timid to push advantages or seize opportunities.[60] Even though not lacking insight at the top and courage in the ranks, the Austro-Saxon army's defects at the tactical level had snatched defeat from victory's jaws.

Frederick believed the war was over. He was convinced that however intransigent Austria's Empress might remain, her generals would convince her that Prussia was unbeatable in the open field. Instead, Maria Theresa became even more determined to put Prussia in its proper place by force of arms. In pursuit of that aim the Empress sought peace with France and alliance with Russia. She ignored British warnings that continued subsidies might depend on peace with Prussia. And she instructed Prince Charles to prepare something highly unusual in eighteenth-century warfare: a winter campaign, this time mounted from Saxony instead of Bohemia, and aiming for Brandenburg instead of Silesia.

Frederick, informed of Austria's intentions by a Swedish diplomat, responded with a pre-emptive strike. Two armies, each around 20,000 strong, one built around the victors of Soor and the other assembled from various garrisons and security forces by the Old

---

59 Hans Stabenau, *Die Schlacht bei Soor* (Frankfurt, 1901), is a good general account.

60 J. Richter (ed.), *Die Briefe Friedrichs des Grossen an seinen vormaligen Kammerdiener Fredersdorf* (Berlin, 1926), p. 58.

Dessauer, drove into Saxony in late November. While Frederick's troops did some effective outpost fighting, it was Leopold who won the brief campaign's only major battle at Kesselsdorf, outside of Dresden, on 15 December. The action is best remembered for the Old Dessauer's preliminary prayer: 'Oh Lord, if you will not grant us victory this day, then don't give it to those bastards on the other side! In Jesus' name, march!'

His tactics were as simple as his theology. Initially, the Prussians faced an exposed Saxon flank. Instead of seizing his opportunity, the Dessauer marched his men to their enemy's front and sent them straight ahead. Few besides Frederick could have made it work, but 'Old Fuzzy' was beloved by the musketeers he had trained for so many years. His battalions advanced in parade-ground order, seemingly ignoring the murderous effect of Saxon artillery undisturbed by Prussian counter-battery fire. As the Prussians drew closer despite heavy losses, the Saxons counterattacked only to be met and ridden down by Prussian cavalry. The survivors stood not upon the order of their going. Two hours after the first shots were fired, the Dessauer held the field. Five thousand of the 31,000 men he led into the fight were casualties. His enemy's losses were somewhere between a third and a half of an army the same size. Small wonder that the Saxon capital fell without a fight.[61]

Kesselsdorf was a convincing argument for an Austrian government already under heavy pressure from Britain to end its war with Frederick or risk losing British financial and diplomatic support. From London's perspective France was Europe's real enemy. The strength of its army had been demonstrated in May at Fontenoy, where England's best troops had been shattered by the wild charge of France's Irish Brigade. French support for the Jacobite uprising of 1745 indicated that the government of Louis XV was ready to suborn revolution for the sake of victory.[62] In that context Frederick of Prussia appeared positively benign: his seizure of Silesia was no more than a land-grab in a time-hallowed context.

Austria too had reasons for grounding its arms. On 25 December 1745, the Second Silesian War officially ended with the Peace of Dresden. On paper, the Prussian victory seemed complete. Maria

---

61 Many of these were deserters as opposed to battle casualties. Cf. Walter von Bremen, *Die Schlacht bei Kesselsdorf am 15. Dezember 1745* (Berlin, 1888); and von Lindenau, 'Die Schlacht bei Kesselsdorf', *Militär-Wochenblatt, Beiheft* XI (1904), 465–503.

62 F. McLynn, *France and the Jacobite Rising of 1745* (Edinburgh, 1981).

Theresa recognized Frederick's sovereignty over Silesia in return for Prussian recognition of Francis as Holy Roman Emperor: territory for titles, in by now familiar Habsburg fashion. This time, however, Austria was not acting entirely from a position of weakness. The Electorate of Bavaria was in the process of undergoing its own version of a diplomatic revolution. Four years of pursuing an Imperial crown had left the state and the country totally exhausted. The treasury was on the edge of bankruptcy and the tax base stressed to its outermost limits. The army had fought well enough. It had also suffered irreplaceable wastage rates, and could no longer compete with the sheer numbers available to its enemies – and its allies. What was the value of the title 'Holy Roman Emperor' if its wearer was no more than a French puppet?[63]

Since the spring of 1745 Charles Albert's successor, Maxmilian Joseph, had sought alliance with Austria. Maria Theresa's initial price was Bavarian entry into the war against Prussia – enough of a movement from frying pan to fire that the Elector's government balked. The Peace of Dresden broke the deadlock. In June 1746, Bavaria signed a treaty with Austria and a subsidy agreement with Britain and the Netherlands. Five thousand Bavarian troops joined the polyglot allied force in the Low Countries. Their presence made possible Austria's capacity to turn against its traditional enemy, France.[64] By the end of the year, Maria Theresa's troops had recovered most of northern Italy. Austria was, however, able to do no more than sustain a stalemate in the Netherlands. The Dutch government was at the end of its financial and emotional resources. Given Britain's increasing reluctance to finance continental operations on the scale required to match French efforts and achievements, the opening of peace talks in early 1748 was a logical, if not quite an inevitable, step.[65]

It was a step taken without the direct involvement of a Prussia whose King seemed, at least for the moment, satisfied with his gains. Any grievances Frederick might have felt at being excluded from the nuts and bolts of negotiation were balanced by the inclusion

63 P.C. Hartmann, *Karl Albrecht. Karl VII. Glücklicher Kurfürst, Unglücklicher Kaiser* (Regensburg, 1985), is a good account of Bavaria's downfall through overstretch.

64 Wolfgang Handrich, 'Der bayerische Löwe im Dienste des österreichischen Adlers. Das kurfürstliche Auxiliärkorps in den Niederlanden 1746–1749', *Militärgeschichtliche Mitteilungen* L (1991), 25–60.

65 Browning, *War of the Austrian Succession*, pp. 327 *passim*, is by far the best overview of the negotiations and their antecedents.

in the final Peace of Aix-la-Chapelle of a guarantee of Prussia's possession of Silesia. This clause gave international sanction to Frederick's seizure of Silesia – no small concession even in an age of flexible frontiers. It also signalled beyond question Prussia's status as a major Continental power. How long that status would endure remained open to question.

3 BREATHING SPACE AND RENEWALS

Few diplomats and fewer generals believed that the Peace of Dresden was more than a footnote to international relations. France and Britain continued their struggle for three more years. Far from being conducted in the pattern of limited war, the last stages of the conflict included a projected French invasion of England and a Jacobite insurrection sufficiently nearly run, both militarily and politically, to encourage Britain's Hanoverian government to seek peace rather than risk another round of escalation. On 18 October 1748, the Treaty of Aix-la-Chapelle silenced the guns, but serious underlying tensions remained. The question of pre-eminence in colonial trade was as yet unresolved. Imperial rivalries, in India and above all in North America, were assuming lives of their own, becoming correspondingly difficult for home governments to ignore. Good will and time would be needed to avert a renewed outbreak of fighting between Europe's two great commercial states – fighting unlikely to be confined to the high seas and overseas.

PLANNING THE NEXT ROUND

From a more limited perspective, Austria had not done as badly as might have been anticipated at several points during the 1740s.[1] The loss of Silesia was the largest territorial amputation suffered by a major power to date in the century. Maria Theresa emerged from the war, however, as mistress in her own house, with a domestic public image as yet unequalled by any European ruler. The death of Charles of Bavaria had removed the only real rival to Habsburg claims on the Imperial crown. Nor was France likely to risk its already strained resources in another conflict with Austria over control of a throne and a title that seemed increasingly honorific. Given the emergence

---

1 Adolf Beer, 'Zur Geschichte des Friedens von Aachen 1748', *Aus österreichische Geschichte*, XLVII (1871), 1–195, remains reliable on this subject despite its age.

of Prussia as a major military and diplomatic factor in Germany, France had far greater prospects in the role of honest broker – or, more bluntly, a court of last resort for the small- and middle-sized states against rival Habsburg and Hohenzollern pretensions. What had been denied to the arson squads of Louis XIV seventy-five years earlier might be granted to a great-grandson able to remember the outcome of the fabled wager between the north wind and the sun as to who could first make a traveller remove his coat.

More important than any objective analysis of Austria's position, however, was the perception of relative decline that infused the Habsburg decision-making system as the War of the Austrian Succession drew to a close. In March 1749, a 'secret conference' of the crown's most senior counsellors was held in Vienna for the purpose of determining the future course of Austria's foreign policy. In the aftermath of this meeting Wenzel Kaunitz submitted a lengthy memorandum arguing for the structural causes of war in *ancien régime* Europe.[2] Using France as an example, Kaunitz argued that an increasingly militarized aristocracy regarded the *general* phenomenon of war as a means of advancing its *private* goals in state and society. Given the legal, political, and economic position of the aristocracy, long-term peace was unlikely no matter who the leading personalities of the French government might be at a given moment.

This built-in belligerent tendency posed a corresponding challenge to Austria – particularly in the context of Prussia's sharp rise in status. Kaunitz described Frederick's kingdom unflatteringly as 'the greatest, most dangerous, and least reconcilable enemy of the House of Austria'. The corresponding problem involved not only defending the Habsburg throne against Prussian aggression, but also weakening and limiting the latter state's capacity to disturb an already fragile European order.

Traditionally, Austria had met continental challenges by seeking cooperation with the maritime powers Holland and, above all, Britain. Holland, however, by now lacked both the military strength and the political cohesion to be worth while as a major ally. As for Britain, its connection with Austria was a classic example of a marriage of convenience, prefiguring the Grand Alliance of World War II far

---

2 Denkschrift des Grafen Kaunitz zur mächtepolitischen Konstellation nach dem Aachener Frieden von 1748', eds R. Pommerin and L. Schilling, in *Expansion und Gleichgewicht. Studien zur europäischen Mächtepolitik des Ancien Régime*, ed. J. Kunisch (Berlin, 1986), pp. 165–239.

more than representing conscious mutual commitment to a balance of power. Commercial and economic links between the systems were all but non-existent. Neither British ministers nor British representatives had much empathy with the Catholic autocracy of Maria Theresa. Nor did Austria suddenly develop vogues for British fashion, British literature, or British cooking. Few travellers visited each other's countries, and fewer of those brought back favourable reports. During the late war Britain had proved, at least from Austria's perspective, niggardly with funds and troops alike, particularly when central European issues were at stake.[3] It required no great leap of imagination for Kaunitz to argue that the British government was hardly likely to provide 'direct and serious cooperation' in any future Austrian attempt to recover Silesia.

In that context, Kaunitz argued, Austria faced two choices. It could accept Silesia's loss and the corresponding likelihood that Prussia would continue to challenge Austria's primacy in Germany. Or the Habsburg Empire could seek 'one way or another' the support of France against Prussian pretensions. From Kaunitz's perspective, the latter approach would not only facilitate rectification of a badly unbalanced German situation. It would also make the best possible use of an inherently aggressive French social structure. The French wanted to fight. Well and good. Let them fight next time for a cause that would benefit not only Austria, but Europe as a whole: the reduction of the House of Brandenburg to its original state as a small, very secondary power.

Kaunitz's hostility to Prussia had a central European, as well as a Habsburg perspective. Could anyone believe that Silesia represented Frederick's last territorial demand – particularly given the unstable frontiers of Russia, Sweden and Poland? What would be the consequences for Russia should Frederick, whether on his own initiative or encouraged by France, involve himself in a Russo-Swedish war? These were anything but rhetorical questions. Russia had sought to intervene in the Second Silesian War after Prussia's declaration of war on Saxony, France's ally. Frederick overran Saxony before the Russians could begin mobilizing an expeditionary force. But the next year Empress Elizabeth had asked her council of state to evaluate the best means of preventing – or pre-empting – a Prussian attack on Russia. The answer to her question was an

---

3 Jeremy Black, 'When "Natural Allies" Fall Out: Anglo-Austrian Relations, 1725–1740', *Mitteilungen des Österreichischen Staatsarchivs*, XXXVI (1983), 120–49.

alliance with Austria. In its final version, like an earlier agreement of 1726, the agreement's ostensible main target was the Ottoman Empire. A secret clause, however, promised mutual support in case of a Prussian attack. A Russian corps of observation, financed largely by British subsidies, had been stationed on Prussia's Lithuanian border for eighteen months as a deterrent to Prussian reintervention in the war after the Peace of Dresden. In February 1748, another Russian auxiliary corps, again paid for by Britain, had reached Nuremberg when the fighting ended.[4]

However much Kaunitz regretted the importance of 'personal factors', a euphemism for the Empress and her ever-changing corps of advisers, in the making of Russian policy, he continued to regard the Russo-Austrian alliance as 'deserving of the greatest care in its preservation'. Give Austria time to rebuild its military strength and make good its financial losses. Then have a Russian army of 60,000 or 70,000 men invade Frederick's eastern provinces. Then have France and Spain support the operation, directly or by benevolent neutrality. Then bring down as many other enemies as possible around the King of Prussia's ears, whether by financial subsidies or the promise of territorial compensation. The result would be in fact what Frederick had vainly hoped to achieve in the First Silesian War: a diplomatic and military victory so decisive, so overwhelming, that Frederick – or his successor – would make and keep peace on any terms set by Kaunitz's Grand Alliance.

The Austrian diplomat's vision possessed at this stage an essentially Platonic character: a thing laid up in heaven, whose realization depended on an unusual synthesis of favourable circumstances. As a theory such a diplomatic environment would have been highly unlikely to encourage a proto-Nietzschean breaking of the sword even in a ruler strongly inclined towards peace with his immediate neighbours. But as early as 1743 Frederick had declared that central to the smallest state or to the largest was a will to expansion that no prince would abandon until his resources were exhausted. This was a basic rule of European politics. Any prince who ignored it would find his neighbours becoming relatively stronger, while the moderate's apparent virtue meant in reality only the corresponding weakening of his state.[5]

4 Eva Mahrer, 'Die englisch-russischen Beziehungen während des Österreichischen Erbfolgekrieges', PhD dissertation (Vienna, 1972).

5 Reinhold Koser, *Geschichte Friedrichs des Grossen*, 4 vols (Stuttgart, 1921), I, pp. 401–2.

Ambition was as important as calculation to the still youthful monarch. In 1741 he had described himself as loving war for the sake of glory. Similar expressions continued to sprinkle his correspondence for the next fifteen years. In his political testament of 1752, the Prussian King declared himself in full agreement with Machiavelli; that a disinterested power could not survive in a network of ambitious neighbours. Far from regarding this as an abstract principle, Frederick recommended Saxony, Mecklenburg, Ansbach-Bayreuth, and the Swedish portion of Pomerania as among the eventually suitable extensions of Prussian territory.[6]

Nor did Frederick write and think in a vacuum. Like a new player in a long-running poker game, Prussia's diplomatic styles, its strengths and weaknesses, were carefully scrutinized by the other players. If some French *philosophes* continued to interpret Frederick as an ascetic and enlightened counterpoint to their own Louis XV, most of the foreign ambassadors in Berlin entertained entirely opposite opinions. Frederick's misanthropy, his unwillingness to listen to others or take them seriously, his confidence in his own judgment, were particularly unlikely to endear him to men whose careers depended on persuading foreign monarchs. Quite apart from the frontiers redrawn by Prussian bayonets, Frederick's manoeuvrings on the diplomatic stage between 1740 and 1745 had given him a reputation as too clever by half that was no less potent for not being entirely deserved. The King's belief that Prussia lacked the resources to fight anything but short and lively wars was an explanation but not an excuse. While alliances were taken lightly in eighteenth-century Europe, Frederick's record of leaving his cohorts in the lurch no fewer than three times in five years during the Silesian Wars through armistices or separate treaties marked him out as a man more willing to take advantage of systems than support them.

Frederick in his own way represented as much a threat to an increasingly unstable set of power relationships as did Maria Theresa's Austria. It was no accident that the Prussian King concentrated increasingly after the Peace of Dresden on building an integrated, front-loaded military system. Eighteenth-century armies tended towards homogeneity. Military systems were far less isolated than in later centuries. Doctrines and personnel circulated freely. Superiority correspondingly depended on organization and administration, training and leadership.

---

6 'Politisches Testament Friedrichs des Grossen (1752)', in *Politische Testamente der Hohenzollern*, ed. R. Dietrich (Munich, 1981), pp. 198 ff.

Frederick was the first grand strategist to engage himself directly and systematically in these areas. War's nuts and bolts had historically been the province of the base-born or the unimaginative. Frederick on the other hand recognized, perhaps more clearly even than his nineteenth-century successors, that few plans survive direct contact with an enemy. This was all the more reason why the first contact had to be the decisive one.

At least since the French and American Revolutions, it has become a virtual article of military faith, particularly in the English-speaking world, that armies reach the peak of their efficiency towards the end of a war. Anglo-American cultural memories are dominated by the Union victory parade through Washington in 1865, by the final British offensive in the fall of 1918, by the world-striding US war machine of 1945. Any idea of peacetime conditions as establishing legitimate norms of efficiency is dismissed as the work of reactionaries anxious to return to 'real soldiering' and forget the unpleasant lessons of combat.

Frederick the Great saw Prussia's strategic needs as demanding an essentially different approach. In 1752 he declared that a commander's principal tasks were the same in war as during peacetime: supervising the *kleine Dienst* of drill and administration, improving the officer corps, and planning the next campaign. These responsibilities grew even heavier in the aftermath of a successful war. Constant example and tireless industry were needed to bring both the army and its supporting institutions back to peak levels of efficiency.[7]

Frederick sought the attainable rather than the ideal. He did not create new military forms, but developed those he inherited to their logical limits. As a product of the Age of Reason, Frederick the Great believed it possible to forge an army like a samurai sword – a tempered instrument, to be drawn, used, and sheathed at the will of its master for the ends of the state.

MEN AND WEAPONS: PRUSSIA'S MILITARY INFRASTRUCTURE

The integration of military and political leadership in the person of the King facilitated the integration of Prussian society into the state's war-making potential. Five years' experience had completely convinced Frederick that Prussian grand strategy must be based on winning immediate, decisive victories. Prussia's army could not main-

---

7 'Politisches Testament Friedrichs des Grossen (1752)', in Dietrich, *Politische Testamente*, pp. 222 *passim*.

tain itself indefinitely against enemies similarly organized, equipped, and trained. Its edge, no matter how carefully honed, could not survive the murderous casualties of flintlock battlefields. This in turn argued for the wisdom, indeed the necessity, of creating a comprehensive system of support for the state's armed forces.

Frederick's predecessors had consistently sought to enhance Prussia's financial capacities by measures resembling those of a private household: increasing public income, limiting public expenses, and depositing the resulting surplus in a series of specially designated war chests. Between 1740 and 1756, an astounding 83 per cent of the Prussian state's revenue was devoted directly to military expenses. Frederick was correspondingly able to finance the Silesian Wars from current income, supplemented by judicious dipping into the treasury. During the Seven Years War, the steady increase in expenses would combine with the growing disruption of the economy through enemy raids, friendly conscription officers, and disturbed patterns of trade and marketing to make Prussia increasingly dependent on external financial sources. British subsidies, debased currency, and annual 'contributions' levied on occupied or newly acquired territories did much to keep Prussia in a war it could less and less afford to abandon – like a gambler on a losing streak, desperately seeking to recover an original bet.[8] This, however, reflected expedience rather than principle. Frederick never accepted the concept of war supporting war on a permanent basis. Conquests always had their limitations; the best way to double one's money was still to fold it and place it under the mattress. Frederick's clearest statement on the theme came in his 'Political Testament' of 1768. Incomes well administered, expenditures well regulated, made for a rich and powerful prince and a contented and prosperous people.[9]

The second area Frederick recognized as vital for the effective use of armed force was the economy. The King saw three levels of significance. At the most basic, Frederick perceived the impossibility of systematic fund-raising from an impoverished population. More

8 Adelheid Simisch, 'Die Grundzüge der preussischen Wirtschaftspolitik im 18. Jahrhundert', in *Die Wirtschaftspolitik des preussischen Staates in der Provinz Südpreussen 1793–1806/07* (Berlin, 1983), pp. 36–51, is a good modern overview. Cf. as well Reinhold Koser, 'Der preussische Staatsschatz von 1740 bis 1756, *Forschungen zur brandenburgischen und preussischen Geschichte*, IV (1891), pp. 529–51; and 'Die preussischen Finanzen im Siebenjährigen Kreig', *ibid.*, XIII (1900), pp. 153–217, 329–75.

9 'Politisches Testament Friedrichs des Grossen (1768)', in Dietrich, *Politische Testamente*, pp. 257 *passim*.

generally, a prosperous economy offered greater surpluses, and wider opportunities for tapping those surpluses without damage to the structure as a whole. Finally, economic development was a major means of fulfilling Prussia's developing social contract, whose general terms involved the exchange of loyalty for security, and at least the promise of prosperity.

In this context the Prussian army was not merely a consumer, but a customer as well. Peasants and craftsmen alike found army purchasing agents a welcome source of steady profits. Food, forage, uniforms, vehicles, gunpowder, small arms and cannon – the army needed everything, and in large quantities. Fortress construction provided financial opportunities for everyone from contractors to day labourers. If clerks and bookkeepers found 'working for the King of Prussia' to be a synonym for long hours and short commons, skilled workers could have an opposite experience.

On a higher level, Frederick throughout his reign supported the foundation of Prussian factories to prevent the export of scarce capital for military purchases, to ensure the constant delivery of high quality material to the armed forces, and increasingly to have a surplus for export. The development of wool and linen manufacture was particularly important for an army whose uniforms for most of this period were of significantly higher quality than those of neighbouring states. The royal wool factory in Berlin, founded in 1714, employed as many as 5,000 workers and counted as the greatest cloth producer in Germany. Although linen was less important than wool in military procurement, army contracts nevertheless helped Silesia's linen industry reach a take-off point that eventually made it as important to Prussia's economy as the mines of Peru were to Spain. Prussian cloth did more than cover soldiers' nakedness. It provided increasing supplies of increasingly cheap goods for the general population. It also became a major export item. For decades the Russian army was uniformed with cloth made across the Prussian border – a major positive factor in Prussia's balance of payments.[10]

Bernhard Kroener has cogently argued the importance of technology, broadly defined, in eighteenth-century warfare. 'Know-how', generally and in the specific fields of arms production; the capacity of factories and workshops; the relative degree of dependence on foreign

10 Adelheid Simisch, 'Armee, Wirtschaft, Gesellschaft. Preussens Kampf auf der "inneren Linie",' in *Europa im Zeitalter Friedrichs des Grossen, Wirtschaft, Gesellschaft, Kriege*, ed. B. Kroener (Munich, 1989), pp. 41 ff.; Carl Hinrichs, *Die Wollindustrie in Preussen unter Friedrich Wilhelm I* (Berlin 1933).

imports; the accurate calculation of material wastage and preparation for its replacement; the systematic organization of production and logistic systems – all of these were crucial links in a chain whose culmination in flintlock muskets and smooth bore cannon was no less significant than its twentieth-century successors, main battle tanks and ICBMs.[11]

Frederick William I began the modern Prussian arms industry shortly after beginning his reign, by founding a powder mill and a small arms factory in Spandau. Having these key institutions under his eye provided comfort to a ruler addicted to direct control. Geography and demographics, however, counted for as much as ego gratification. Brandenburg's primitive road system made the transport of bulk goods impossible except by water, and Berlin lay in the centre of a network of navigable rivers increasingly connected by canals. Deliveries from Holland came through Hamburg and the Elbe. Swedish iron ore came through Stettin and the Oder. The still limited domestic shipments of copper and iron similarly depended on canals and rivers. The Berlin arsenal and the artillery workshops lay directly on the Spree River, facilitating unloading. In human terms, Berlin was the largest city in Prussia, with the largest number of skilled craftsmen. Its garrison also offered ample supplies of muscle power when necessary.[12]

Despite Frederick William's drive for autarky, Prussia's defence industry remained heavily dependent on imports. Sulphur and saltpetre for gunpowder, iron for musket barrels – even wood for gun stocks and flints for gun-locks were in large part foreign products. The private firm of Splitgerber and Daun, founded in 1712, was responsible for their purchasing. The firm won the confidence of Frederick William I by its scrupulous honesty and painstaking attention to detail. By the end of the Soldier King's reign it possessed what amounted to a monopoly. It operated mines, smithies, and forges under lease. It established Prussia's first modern musket factory, and in the process introduced an early form of the assembly line. Frederick William's original plan to establish a single factory foundered on the absence of enough water power for such a large enterprise.

---

11 Bernhard Kroener, 'Wirtschaft und Rüstung der europäischen Grossmächte im Siebenjährigen Krieg. Überegungen zu einem vergleichenden Ansatz', in *Friedrich der Grosse und das Militärwesen seiner Zeit*, ed. Militärgeschichtliches Forschungsamt (Herford, 1987) pp. 176–92.

12 Paul Rehfeld, 'Die preussische Rüstungsindustrie unter Friedrich den Grossen', *Forschungen zur brandenburgischen und preussischen Geschichte*, LV (1944), 1–31.

Instead, Splitgerber and Daun's engineers built two workshops. The barrels were made in Spandau. Then, in Potsdam. barrels, locks, and stocks were assembled into finished products. Tolerances, it must be said, were so wide that one can hardly speak of commonality. Nevertheless, shortly after its foundation the new institution achieved production runs of 300 muskets a week.

The risks of the enterprise were borne entirely by the firm, and those risks were considerable. Frederick William's concern for economy kept him from utilizing the factory's full capacity. His son was simply reluctant to pay his bills. As late as 1751 the firm was still trying to close an account whose muskets had been delivered in 1745! Nor was Frederick exactly obsessed with increasing the stock of weapons on hand. Despite the large material losses of the Silesian War, he took his time about ordering replacements. In 1747 Splitgerber and Daun were obliged to dismiss over a third of their 200 skilled craftsmen – who were not easy to replace when in 1753 Frederick suddenly decided to place new orders for infantry muskets.

Cannon production faced similar problems. Frederick's desire to improve the quality of his artillery has been noted previously. Existing manufacturing facilities, however, were not easily restructured. Between Frederick's theories and the weapons actually delivered yawned a wide gap. The copper for the new bronze cannon desired by the King was available from Prussian resources. The tin was obtainable from England, at a price. Obsolete barrels could be melted down and recast. Unfortunately, Prussia's gun factories proved unequal to the technological challenge. In 1756, for example, over thirty new barrels from the Berlin arsenal had to be recast because of obvious defects. The responsible master was thrown into gaol, but released when the King could not find a qualified replacement. In the end it came to a compromise: the founder agreed to recast the defective barrels at his own expense. Nor was this an isolated case. The chief gun-founder of the Breslau arsenal proved even less equal to his task. Repeated sojourns in prison did nothing to improve the quality of his cannon; finally he was dismissed permanently. Not until 1757 did the Prussian government succeed in recruiting for Berlin a Dutch cannon founder who introduced the state-of-the-art method of casting solid moulds, then boring them to the required calibre. The remoteness of Breslau apparently worked against luring a master founder with equivalent skills to that provincial city.

Despite these ongoing problems, about 1,500 artillery pieces of all kinds were cast in Prussian arsenals between 1741 and 1762.

The popularity of these weapons among their users remained limited enough that cast-iron guns from Sweden, imported again by Splitgerber and Daun, were consistently welcome additions to the Prussian fortress artillery. Indeed, the government was sufficiently impressed by 1754 to authorize its Stockholm embassy to 'discover' by espionage the Swedish techniques for casting reliable iron cannon – an effort that ultimately proved vain. The only alternatives were to continue importing Swedish weapons, or to recruit foreign experts qualified in the technique. Frederick's efforts in the latter sphere proved fruitless.

Lead for small-arms ammunition was initially imported from England. This posed an especially difficult problem given Prussian doctrine, with its emphasis on rapid infantry fire. Flints as well wore down rapidly at three or four rounds per minute, even in peacetime when 'dry-firing' – snapping the lock on an empty pan – was a familiar practice. The Spandau/Potsdam factory, however, was able eventually to replace the losses of the Silesian Wars and subsequently keep pace with peacetime demands. Not until well into the Seven Years War would Frederick be constrained to turn to the Netherlands and the small German states to keep his infantry under arms.

As for powder, Frederick William's original mill was able to produce 3,000 hundredweight annually, by working in two shifts. This proved insufficient. As early as 1746 Frederick ordered the works expanded, and the annual production capacity increased to 5,000 hundredweight. Frederick also sought to increase domestic supplies of saltpetre. In 1748, on the King's order, the Berlin Academy of Sciences offered a prize for the best method of artificially producing saltpetre. Unfortunately – cynics might say typically – the winning method, submitted by a doctor, proved unsuitable for large-scale application. Here as well Prussia remained dependent on foreign imports. During the Seven Years War, French and Austrian agents would wage a buyers' war with Splitgerber and Daun, particularly in the Netherlands, attempting to cut off Prussian supplies. Their failure reflected their own lack of system rather than any particularly Prussian skill in countering the campaign.[13]

13 Kroener, 'Wirtschaft und Rüstung', pp. 128 ff, summarizes the development of Prussia's 'military-industrial complex'. Wilhelm Treue, 'David Splitgerber (1683–1764). Ein Unternehmer im preussischen Merkantilstaat', *Vierteljahresheft für Sozial- und Wirtschaftsgeschichte*, XLI (1954), 253–67; and *Wirtschafts- und Technikgeschichte Preussens* (Berlin, 1984), pp. 86–91, are brief accounts of Splitgerber and Daun's tempestuous relationship with the Prussian government.

Kroener's essay also correctly stresses the lack of anything resembling an armaments programme in the modern sense during the early years of Frederick's reign. Even the period immediately preceding the Seven Years War was characterized by improvisation and catch-up, rather than the systematic implementation of policy. Frederick continued to depend on Splitgerber and Daun as Prussia's military factotum – a circumstance the business house increasingly used to its own advantage, becoming one of Prussia's greatest banking and commercial enterprises by the end of the Seven Years War. In a more general sense the years from 1745 to 1756 were characterized by the increasing integration of Prussia's economy into the state's war-making function. Prussian society was adapting as well to the characteristic Frederician military system. The organization of the economy, the merchants and craftsmen, as part of a warfare state carried with it an implied bargain: protection in exchange for service. This in turn created a corresponding need to find soldiers elsewhere: specifically, from the 80 per cent of Prussia's population that lived on and from the land.

As shown in Chapter 1, the cantonal system combined several advantages for the state. It provided something like a reserve force – an important point given the time it required to train an effective eighteenth-century infantryman. It kept costs to a minimum, since the soldier was on leave the greater part of the year. It diminished the risks of desertion, since the cantonist usually had a good deal to lose by abandoning his identity as a subject-soldier. In this context it is worth stressing that desertion from the Prussian army, as from all Continental armies in the eighteenth century, tended to be a temporary phenomenon. It might be motivated by brutality, but other common causes were boredom and a desire for challenge. In particular, the professional soldier of the Age of Reason, however miserable he might have been in reality, usually had a self-image as a bold adventurer and a free spirit.[14] The swords carried even by infantrymen may have been tactically useless pieces of ironmongery, but they symbolized the common soldiers' link to a higher class and a higher calling.

In such a context, desertion did not usually signify a desire to return home and live out a peaceful existence studying the southern profile of a north-bound ox. The deserter might well spend some time

14 F.C. Laukhard, *Magister C.F. Laukhards Leben und Schicksale von ihm selbst beschrieben*, 13th edn, 2 vols (Stuttgart, 1930), I, pp. 248–9, is a good example of this attitude.

on the road or as a casual labourer, but eventually he was likely to find himself in uniform again, this time under Saxon colours, or perhaps in one of the German regiments of the King of France. He might well return to the Prussian army for a taste of 'real soldiering' after a spell in one of the municipal guards of the Imperial free cities.[15] Such a process seldom involved more planning than was necessary to choose a garrison and a regiment reasonably distanced from one's originals, plus the precaution of a new *nom de guerre*. Company officers and NCOs were seldom interested in probing too deeply into the past of a volunteer – even if that volunteer might show surprising familiarity with Prussian drill movements.

Desertion, in other words, tended to be less a social or political statement than a means of changing employment in a system where the enlistment contracts were entirely one-sided. Even from the state's perspective desertion's costs were financial rather than moral, involving the expenses of recruiting a replacement, plus outlays for any clothing and equipment that might have disappeared with the absconder.

Given the limited alternative prospects, cantonists were far more likely to remain with their regiments than to make the decisive break into the more or less peripatetic world of the mercenary. By mid-century the Prussian cantonist had positive as well as negative reasons for maintaining his ties with the army. Neither soldier nor peasant, he walked a fine line in a dual existence. His landlord and his company commander, if not necessarily the same individual, might well be brothers or cousins. Prussia's landed gentry, itself suffering the enhanced financial and personal burdens of state service, tended to respond by increasing demands on their peasants. Patterns of army discipline and army administration applied unreflectively to a Junker estate could intensify difficult circumstances to the point of unbearability. Yet the conscript was by no means a victim. At its worst, the cantonal system made it possible to plan individual futures. Individuals and families were freed from the pressures of haphazard, uncontrolled domestic recruiting. Perhaps more to the point, each man enrolled on the list of his cantonal regiment passed for the rest of his life under the Prussian code of military justice. His landlord exercised only an employer's authority over him, even when he returned on extended leave.

15 Christopher Duffy, *The Army of Frederick the Great* (New York, 1974), p. 68.

Psychologically as well as legally, soldiers increasingly provided an alternative element in a structure of authoritarian serfdom that had been developing since the sixteenth century. This was carried into everyday life by the requirement that men on leave wear to work some piece of uniform, in order to identify themselves as soldiers. The favoured item seems to have been the buttoned gaiters. They were practical for field work, relatively cheap to replace, and not a common item of civilian dress. The requirement itself, however, is suggestive. It was hardly a safeguard against desertion. Not only could any distinctive item of clothing be quickly discarded; no deserter was likely merely to start walking towards the nearest frontier in the middle of the day. When a cantonist chose to disappear, the process involved secreting food and money, acquiring new clothes so as to throw off descriptions, and a whole spectrum of similar preparations for what could easily become a capital offence even in peacetime. Hans Bleckwenn argues instead that the wearing of a visible item of uniform was meant as a tangible sign of royal authority in an environment where everyday life still reflected the Junker aphorism: 'The King reigns when he does our will.' Neither lord nor bailiff could strike a man of the King with legal impunity.

This context helps explain the ready acceptance of a regulation of 1743 requiring all cantonists to wear full uniform when attending church on Sunday. As a social result, colour appeared once a week in the otherwise drab villages of Pomerania and the Mark. Boys were given regimental neck-cloths and hat tassels on confirmation as a mark of maturity. Nor were the young women completely indifferent to the martial figures cut by actual or potential swains.

The social impact of the cantonal system must not be exaggerated. Frederician Prussia did not develop a 'new class' of young men 'empowered' by military service. Patriarchal patterns of deference and obedience enforced with fists and sticks continued to prevail in northeast Germany until well into the twentieth century. Nevertheless, for the aggressive and the fortunate subject, military service in Frederician Prussia offered both a degree of protection and an opportunity to play both ends against the middle. Privates on leave could and did appeal to the military authorities, even the crown itself, against the abuses of local landlords. Issues of marriage and inheritance could be taken outside the village hierarchy. As the Prussian aristocracy became more completely integrated into the state system, a corresponding number of loopholes shrank or disappeared. However, a significant element in the popular militarism so often described as characterizing Prussia even in the eighteenth century seems to have been the capacity army

103

service conferred on common soldiers to challenge the oppressively deferential society in which they lived.[16]

The landed nobility as well profited from the Frederician military system. Eighteenth century Brandenburg-Prussia lacked really powerful families like England's Newcastles and Bedfords. It lacked as well the large, consolidated estates that sustained these families and their cadet branches. For a caste at once proud and practical, privileged access to officers' commissions was arguably less important than a system making officers directly responsible for the administration of their companies. In contrast to most Continental armies, the Prussian military administration rigorously supervised the ultimate condition of men, animals, and equipment. Simply pocketing government-allocated funds was a correspondingly likely path to incarceration in one of Prussia's numerous fortresses or the arguably worse punishment of cashiering, which meant loss of one's place at the public trough. Given the large size of the average Junker family and the close, complex kinship ties binding them, one man's disgrace could affect the prospects of a large number of relatives. On the other hand, the state had only praise for a captain able to manage his company funds well enough to make both a good showing on parade and a certain surplus for himself. Although Prussia's landed aristocracy had its share of incompetents, it incorporated relatively few fools. The wastrel younger son, the estate owner dependent on his bailiff for all major decisions, had no place in a Junker mythology that produced few Oblomovs. By the time a man was made captain and received a company of his own, he was usually a sound military administrator on a rule-of-thumb, common-sense basis. And properly run, a Prussian company was as valuable an income property as a small estate.

Integration of the nobility into the army involved more than

16 Hans Bleckwenn, 'Bauernfreiheit durch Wehrpflicht – ein neueres Bild der altpreussischen Armee', in *Friedrich der Grosse und das Militärwesen seiner Zeit*, pp. 55–72; and 'Montierung und Ausrüstung der Preussischen Armee in der Mitte des 18. Jahrhunderts', in *Europa im Zeitalter Friedrichs des Grossen*, pp. 302 ff., offers convincing modifications of the standard interpretations best presented in Otto Büsch, *Militärsystem und Sozialleben im alten Preussen*, rev. edn (Frankfurt, 1981). Cf. also Klaus Schweiger, 'Militär und Bürgertum. Zur gesellschaftlichen Prägkraft des preussischen Militärsystems in 18. Jahrhundert', *Preussen in der deutschen Geschichte*, ed. D. Blasius (Königstein, 1980), pp. 179–99; and Manfred Messerschmidt, 'Preussens Militär in seinem gesellschaftlichen Umfeld', *Preussen im Rückblick*, ed. H.J. Puhle and H-U. Wehler, *Geschichte und Gesellschaft, Sondernummer*, VI (1983), 46–53.

economics. Initially, service in the officer corps had been a decidedly mixed blessing for a gentry both unaccustomed to compulsion and, by comparison to its French, Polish, and Magyar counterparts, significantly lacking both martial and belligerent traditions. Between the fifteenth and seventeenth centuries, the Prussian Junkers had become farmers rather than fighters, readily amenable to new political allegiances as long as they could collect their rents and sell their grain. By the mid-1700s, however, a consensus had developed, at least within the Brandenburg aristocracy, that military service did indeed confer negotiable social status. The cantonal system helped nurture a sense of feudal obligation that had almost disappeared after two centuries of profit-motivated serfdom. It was far easier to identify with men whose fathers and grandfathers had served yours than with rootless cosmopolitans brought in at random by the recruiting officers.

On the other hand, cooption did not mean homogeneity. The Prussian officer corps at mid-century was a significantly mixed bag. Younger sons of nameless *Krautjunker* stood side by side with scions of emerging military dynasties like the Kleists and the Bülows. Descendants of Huguenot immigrants, professionals and adventurers from everywhere in central Europe, added tones and seasonings out of proportion to their numbers. Nor did the officer corps possess a dominant style of behaviour. *Haudegen* from the days of Frederick William's *Tabakskollegium* and hard livers like Seydlitz were juxtaposed to a steadily increasing number of young men influenced, however vaguely, by Enlightenment concepts of dignity and reason. Given the absence of anything resembling systematic professional education, it was correspondingly important for Frederick to develop from this mixed bag a corps of officers able at least to apply and implement his concept of war.[17]

'TRAIN AS YOU PROPOSE TO FIGHT': PRUSSIA'S MILITARY EVOLUTION BETWEEN 1745 AND 1756

In 1748 the King completed a manuscript he called 'General Principles of War Applied to the Tactics and the Discipline of Prussian Soldiers'.[18] Initially Frederick kept the work a virtual secret, revealing

17 Edgar Melton, 'The Prussian Junkers, 1600–1786', in *The European Nobilities in the Seventeenth and Eighteenth Centuries*, vol. II, *Northern Central and Eastern Europe*, ed. H.M. Scott (London, 1994).

18 Frederick II, 'Les Principes généraux de la guerre, appliqués à la tactique et à la discipline des troupes prussiennes', 2 April 1748, *Œuvres de Frédéric le Grand*, ed. J.D.E. Preuss, 30 vols (Berlin, 1846–56), XXVIII, pp. 1 ff.

it only to his younger brother. Not until 1753 was a German translation authorized, and then it was issued only to generals. The work is unique. No other army had a similar set of guidelines for senior officers. Its French and Austrian counterparts spent disproportionate amounts of energy discussing tactical and organizational details. Frederick's first concerns involved maintaining the army's structure. The first section of 'General Principles' stressed Prussia's combination of rigid discipline and institutional instability – the latter reflecting, according to Frederick, the large number of mercenaries in the ranks. Since economic and demographic factors alike militated against drawing more recruits from Prussian subjects, officers must remain consistently alert for signs of disintegration – specifically, desertion in the face of the enemy or under demanding operational conditions.

The next dozen sections of the manual presented what would later be described as 'school solutions' for developing a plan of campaign and for keeping an army supplied in the field. Frederick laid an almost Roman stress on the importance of organizing camps. The capacity to move quickly from tent to field could prove decisive, particularly given the high quality of the French and Austrian light troops, and the correspondingly enhanced capacities of their armies for surprise attacks.

The final fourteen 'articles' of 'General Principles' analyzed the conduct of military operations. After surveying the problem of obtaining effective theatre intelligence, Frederick discussed technical problems involved in 'little wars' against light troops and irregulars. He considered the factors involved in crossing and defending rivers. The core of this part of the manual, however, involved Frederick's thoughts on battle. Most subsequent discussions of this subject have been structured by the twenty-year, nineteenth-century *Federkrieg* between civilian scholar Hans Delbrück and the historians of the Prussian General Staff.[19] The ink spilled over the question of Frederick's view of war has obscured a critical point. Frederick the Great was neither an 'attritionist' nor an 'annihilationist'. Both approaches tend to make war an abstraction, an end in itself. For Frederick war was a means to an end. The King's study of military history and military art confirmed his belief that warfare, like any other human activity, could be controlled by talent and shaped by

---

19 By far the best analysis of this issue is Arden Bucholz, *Hans Delbrück and the German Military Establishment: War Images in Conflict* (Iowa City, 1985).

genius. Yet at the same time Frederick was no pre-Romantic, seeing himself specifically blessed by Mars and Bellona. His concept of genius was archetypically eighteenth-century in depending on an infinite capacity for taking pains. War might be the province of chaos, but careful preparation could limit the chaotic effects. Such preparation, the King believed, was best applied at war's cutting edge: the battlefield. Battles, Frederick argued, determined the destiny of states, and war must be the province of quick decisions. Operationally, speed was the best means of getting out of an unfavourable situation and turning the tables on an enemy. Strategically, anything but quick wars would wear down both the Prussian army and the infrastructure supporting it.

Frederick at this stage of his career was to some extent the victim of a double bind. Prussia still lacked the human and material resources to sustain the great power status its King claimed. The state's crucial force multiplier was its army. On the other hand, discipline, training, and tactics were factors that could be duplicated, eventually if not easily, by Prussia's rivals. In general terms Frederick's response was to keep the Prussian army ahead of the game by two processes. One involved refining and improving existing war-fighting skills. The other involved enhancing the Prussian army's operational capacities.[20]

In the 'General Principles', Frederick insisted that it was in fact possible to fight outnumbered and win, even against long odds. This simple assertion seemed at the time a condition virtually contrary to fact. For over a century battles between modern armies had tended increasingly to be decided by tactical attrition. Flintlock muskets and mobile artillery had combined to transform the face of battle by exponentially increasing battle's casualty rates. At Blenheim, a British brigade of 2,400 soldiers lost a third of its men to a single French volley. Four decades later, at Fontenoy, five British battalions, about 2,500 men, inflicted more than 600 casualties at the first fire. These ratios tended to decrease in the course of an action as fatigue and fear took their tolls. The best available evidence, however, suggests that eighteenth-century infantry could hit mass targets like an enemy firing line with around 20 per cent of the shots fired at normal battle ranges.[21]

---

20 Cf. Johannes Kunisch, 'Friedrich der Grosse als Feldherr', in *Friedrich der Grosse in seiner Zeit*, ed. O. Hauser (Cologne, 1987), pp. 193–212.

21 B.P. Hughes, *Firepower: Weapons Effectiveness on the Battlefield, 1630–1850* (New York, 1974), pp. 81 ff.

The principal consequence of this fact was a pattern of each side wearing down the other until fleeting opportunity to decide the issue emerged from the grapple. Even the best generals, the men with the *coup d'œil* and insight of Marlborough and Prince Eugene, found it difficult to shape the course of an action once it began. In that context superior force was, if not an absolute precondition of victory, a factor no general could ignore with impunity. Frederick was flying in the face of conventional wisdom when he informed his senior officers that numerical inferiority offered precisely the most favourable opportunity for employing 'my oblique order'. Hold back one wing, the King asserted, and reinforce the other. By using the stronger wing to attack and envelop the enemy's flank the issue would be decided quickly, before the enemy's numbers could be brought to bear in the crucial sector.

Frederick's writing at this period of his career reflects a concept familiar in the armed forces of the nineteenth and twentieth centuries: the use of tactical and operational methods to solve strategic and grand-strategic problems. Frederick had increasingly used flanking manoeuvres in the Silesian Wars, most notably at Hohenfriedberg. He had not, however, developed a comprehensive operational approach that would enhance the odds of a successful flank attack regardless of any specific advantages of terrain, position, or surprise. In post-war manoeuvres Frederick began experimenting systematically with the technique used at Hohenfriedberg: holding back one wing while attacking and enveloping the enemy with the other. The concept initially proved impractical, both from the difficulties involved in wheeling a long infantry line inward, and because of the tendency for the army's parts to lose contact, opening a potentially fatal gap between the wings.

A theoretically possible approach to solving the latter problem would have involved enhancing the cohesion and independence of the army's component elements – a divisional system *manqué*, or something prefiguring the modern brigade group. Frederick trusted neither his senior officers nor his own still embryonic ideas sufficiently to pursue that approach. Instead he deployed his infantry line *en échelon* by battalions, each slightly ahead of its neighbour on one side, slightly behind its neighbour on the other. Battalions deployed in this way were able to rotate on their own respective axes, instead of playing a military version of crack-the-whip. With distances properly calculated, once all the echelonned units had completed their wheel, the result was a single, orderly line. Under combat conditions, deployment *en échelon* generated a third advantage as well. The enemy found it difficult, at least in the initial period of the Seven Years War, to see any system in the Prussian movements – until what seemed virtual chaos suddenly shook out into fighting formations.

Echelon deployment was the cutting edge of the oblique order. The manoeuvre's necessary preliminary was the 'march by lines'. That process began with a Prussian field army deploying in front of any enemy position in the standard eighteenth-century fashion of two lines of infantry battalions, as at Mollwitz. Instead of advancing to their front, however, each line executed a quarter-wheel by sections or divisions, and formed a column of march. With well-trained troops the process could take as little as 2 minutes. The next step involved marching across the enemy front at an angle leading closer to the chosen flank. Once in position, all that was required was a second quarter-wheel to confront a presumably bemused foe with two lines of battle ready to strike and roll up his flank.

Optimal execution of these manoeuvres required opposing generals sufficiently baffled by the techniques to delay their response, and opposing armies sufficiently inflexible to risk throwing themselves into irretrievable disorder by making sudden alterations in their own deployment. Those considerations apart, Frederick's oblique order depended heavily on three points established by Brent Nosworthy. First, it required officers with a high level of training under common conditions. From colonels to subalterns, each officer had to know what was required of him in order to form a battalion from line to column, maintain its place in the column, then redeploy either normally or *en échelon* for the final attack, all without waiting for detailed sets of orders for each movement. At the risk of some exaggeration, the antecedents of the Prussian/German army's historic emphasis on *Auftragstaktik* had one of its tap-roots in Frederick's oblique order.

The second and third prerequisites for Frederick's oblique order were so closely related that they can be discussed together. They included the ability to march in step, and in closed formation. Systematic drill was hardly a Prussian invention. Its introduction into European armies could be traced back a century and a half, to the work of Maurice of Nassau. That drill, however, concentrated on what later generations would call the manual of arms and the school of the soldier. Recruits were taught how to handle their firearms and instructed in a few basic body positions. They were also trained to march in ranks, a process that essentially involved following the man to one's front. Cadenced marching, each man stepping out on the same foot at the same time, had been a lost craft since the decline of the Roman legions. As late as 1732 it was not a feature of any European army. Maurice de Saxe in *My Reveries* commented on the potential value of marching in step. Leopold of Anhalt-Dessau apparently reached a similar conclusion about the same time. De Saxe seemed to believe that the primary value of the process was operational. Cadenced marching, especially to the music of a properly composed military band, was ultimately less fatiguing than what later generations of soldiers would call 'route step'. The Dessauer for his part perceived the aesthetic and disciplinary value of teaching men to march in a common fashion, in the same way as they handled their weapons. Frederick William I was quick to affirm the idea. Cadenced marching became a feature of Prussian drill sometime in the 1730s, arguably, as well, one of the key elements making that drill more demanding for the ordinary soldier than any of its European counterparts.

It was Frederick, however, who systematically utilized for tactical purposes the Prussian army's ability to march in step. Battalions formed in columns and marching in cadence could move more quickly and – more to the point – in closer formation than their unreformed counterparts. Uncadenced marching required open ranks, lest heavily burdened men stumble into one another and reduce the formation to chaos. Formations able to march in step could close up the files, a practice that in turn facilitated the transmission of signals and orders by drumbeat as opposed to by messenger. The drum corps of a Frederician battalion evolved in the interval between 1745 and 1756 into a forerunner of the modern signal platoon, regulating march and drill movements and transmitting standard commands.

The oblique order had another apparent prerequisite as well. Once begun the attack must be kept moving. During the Second Silesian War at Hohenfriedberg, then again at Kesseldorf, Prussian infantry had successfully broken Saxon opponents by the speed and cohesion of their advance rather than by the impact of their volleys. The effect of this experience on Frederick's thinking must not be overstated. The Saxon army was hardly regarded as a first-rate force by either its allies or its enemies. The emphasis in Prussian infantry doctrine and training between 1745 and 1756 on movement at the expense of fire reflected rather the King's growing confidence in his ability so to manage all three arms in battle that his foot soldiers could normally count on striking an enemy in overwhelming force at its most vulnerable point. In this context it was important above all that the momentum of an advance be sustained, that no battalion stop to fire without orders – which, Frederick expected, it would never be necessary to issue.[22]

Military analyst Maurice Tugwell has identified two kinds of adaptation in military institutions. The most common is reactive adaptation, required as new or unexpected circumstances challenge existing doctrines and practices. The second, innovative adaptation, is so rare that Tugwell describes it as the product of genius.[23] It was the latter that characterized Prussian training in the aftermath of the Silesian Wars. The importance of rapid deployment to Frederick's tactical system led the King to devote increasing amounts of time on the drill ground and the manoeuvre field to developing techniques of 'perpendicular' deployment, with a battalion deploying to the front of its line of advance as opposed to marching parallel to an enemy. The *traversierschritt*, the deployment *en tiroir* or by square movements, 'Rosch's method' – these and other complex evolutions were tested and modified, discarded and combined, in the years prior to the Seven Years War. Scholars have since tended to interpret them as essentially training tools, designed to instil discipline in the soldiers and inculcate alertness in the officers, but never intended for use in actual battle. Brent Nosworthy argues that Frederick was both too much the utilitarian and too much the believer in the direct value of peacetime training in war to put instructional effort into a dead end. Frederick accepted the desirability of deploying an entire army by the perpendicular method. Here, however, he faced two obstacles. One was material: the growing presence of artillery on the mid-eighteenth-century battlefield. Battalions in column, one behind the other, particularly given the close Prussian formations, were sufficiently vulnerable to round shot that deployment within artillery range was an excessive risk. The other obstacle was institutional. Perpendicular deployment of more than a few battalions at the same time multiplied possibilities of confusion, particularly at brigade level. The correct position of each battalion relative to the others was seldom obvious, in contrast to the traditional method of forming line by each battalion simply following the one ahead of it. Frederick's colonels and brigadiers, in the King's mind and probably objectively as well, did not yet possess the grounding in

22 Brent Nosworthy, *The Anatomy of Victory: Battle Tactics 1689–1763* (New York, 1990), pp. 192 ff. Cf. Frederick II, 'Instruction für die General-Majors von der Infanterie', 14 Aug. 1748, *Œuvres*, XXX, pp. 165 ff.

23 *Armies in Low Intensity Conflict: A Comparative Analysis*, ed. D.A. Charteris and M. Tugwell (London, 1989), p. 1.

common principles that would enable them to be trusted to exercise the initiative necessary for the manoeuvre to succeed, not so much while under fire as in those minutes before battle when the conditions for victory were being established.

Probably the most effective, and apparently the most common, method of moving from line to column tested between 1748 and 1756 was called the 'deploy'. The two battalions of a regiment marched forward side by side in columns of platoons. When the leading files reached the point of deployment, a cannon shot gave the signal for the battalions to form columns of divisions, each two platoons. On a second cannon shot, one battalion would face right, the other left, and the 'divisions' would execute an oblique march to their place in line, the rear division of each battalion forming its exterior flank. 'Right face' and 'right dress' completed the process.[24]

The new method was effective, enabling lines of battle to be formed in less than 15 minutes under manoeuvre conditions. It was also simple enough to be executed just before the shooting started, when even the bravest and least reflective officers were likely to be victims of distraction – the 'pucker factor' of later military generations. Frederick did not propose to depart from the linear system characteristic of the century. On the other hand, he perceived the utility of a system that enabled individual battalions to form line quickly and safely. He also perceived the advantage of being able to shift from line to column and back again. By 1756, standing orders provided for battalions to form columns even on the battlefield in the face of obstacles: ponds, swamps, sunken roads, copses. The usual pattern involved the two battalions of a regiment advancing in line side by side. To form columns, the centre platoon of each battalion remained in place. The other seven turned left or right, then marched obliquely to the rear, fell in, and faced front.

The point of Frederick's tactical processes by 1756 was that they seemed most effective at battalion and regimental level. Spans of attention and control were concentrated at those echelons of com-

---

24 Nosworthy, *Anatomy of Victory*, pp. 213 *passim*. Among many accounts of the genesis and nature of the oblique order, Nosworthy's stands out for its appropriate emphasis on the tactical skill required for the movement's implementation. Cf. also *Die taktische Schülung der preussischen Armee durch König Friedrich den Grossen während der Friedenszeit 1745 bis 1756, Kriegsgeschichtliche Einzelschriften*, ed. Grosser Generalstab, vols 28–30 (Berlin, 1900), esp. pp. 440 ff. This work suffers from the present-mindedness common to its genre, tending in particular to exaggerate the King's distrust of fire action.

mand. Peacetime infantry garrisons were distributed by regiment outside the larger centres like Berlin/Potsdam and Magdeburg. Colonels were correspondingly likely to have time to devote to perfecting techniques of deployment, counter-march, and square formation to a degree impossible in the *ad hoc* larger formations created for the purpose of manoeuvres.

The regimental focus of Prussian organization meant therefore that in practice the Prussian army of 1756 still deployed for battle by the traditional 'processional' method of each battalion following the one in front of it in a column of advance. When a cannon shot signalled 'halt', regimental officers made a final check of depths and intervals. A second shot was the signal for each battalion to face left or right by platoons, forming a continuous line.

Normal Prussian deployment during the Frederician era was in two parallel lines, 300 paces apart, with battalions in closed order — a little less than 2 feet between each man. A space of seven or eight paces between each battalion served to allow deployment of the regimental guns. The army's grenadiers were still usually separated from their parent regiments and organized into four-company composite battalions. These were normally deployed on the flanks of the first line, not as its extension but *en potence*, at an obtuse angle to it. The grenadiers, in other words, formed the outer sides of what amounted to a large oblong square. In the context of the oblique order, they minimized the risk of a successful enemy cavalry charge from rolling up the Prussian line of battle. They also served a less heroic but equally obvious function: preventing defeated Prussian cavalry from falling back into the infantry lines for protection and throwing the musketeers into confusion, as at Mollwitz.[25]

The evolution of Prussian infantry formations into a grand tactical square served as well to liberate the cavalry. Reference has already been made to the improvements in that arm of service during the Silesian Wars. The decade of peace after 1745 offered an opportunity to institutionalize concepts and techniques that had emerged, some of them more or less by accident, on the battlefields of Silesia. In the course of the Silesian Wars, Ziethen had solidified his reputation as the beau-ideal of a hussar in the eastern European mode. He shone in action — light cavalry action, when the most important command was, 'Follow me!' Peacetime, however, eclipsed his talent to a significant

25 Nosworthy, *Anatomy of Victory*, pp. 288 ff.; Duffy, *Army of Frederick the Great*, pp. 82 ff.

degree. He challenged Frederick's approach to war openly by denying any capacity to evaluate hypothetical situations. *Coup d'œil*, Ziethen argued, was his peculiar gift: 'I need facts . . . then I know what to do.'[26] Nor did Ziethen have much patience for the painstakingly structured manoeuvres characteristic of the Prussian army after 1745. His interest wandered. He made mistakes – mistakes exacerbated by the fact that the hard-won wartime strengths of Prussia's hussars in scouting and patrolling were not the kinds of things on which Frederick was concentrating.

Above all, the King continued to stress horsemanship and horsemastership. In 1748 Frederick prescribed the normal length of a mounted attack as 700 yards: 300 at a trot, 400 at a gallop. By 1755, the manoeuvre standard was 1,800 yards, the last third delivered at a gallop. That final phase was itself divided into three parts. The first was a gallop in formation. In the second, beginning seventy or eighty paces from the enemy, the troopers spurred forward while checking their horses with the bridle. Only in the last twenty paces from contact did each trooper give full rein to his horse and press forward without regard to alignment or position, the rear ranks driving into the front one to increase the force of the initial shock.[27]

Such a protracted, controlled operation depended on horses in top-flight condition ridden by men as familiar with their mounts as with the regulations prescribing their use. Even more than the infantry, Prussian cavalry drill required high levels of understanding in the rank and file. A trooper who followed procedures mechanically, without a sense of the why behind the what and the how, was a positive menace in the kind of charge Frederick described.

As the attack at a disciplined gallop became an increasing norm in the Prussian cavalry, that arm of the service grew increasingly homogenized. When cavalry charged each other at a trot, the larger force, the bigger men, and the heavier horses had a built-in physical advantage. Light cavalry simply could not develop enough momentum to offset their limited mass. As a result the light horse was limited to the 'little war' of scouting, patrolling, and skirmishing – a role excluding it from the prestige accruing to the squadrons of the line. Between the Second Silesian War and the Seven Years

---

26 D. Thiebault, *Mes Souvenirs de vingt ans de séjour à Berlin*, 3rd edn, vol. III (Paris, 1813), p. 298, cited in Duffy, *Army of Frederick the Great*, p. 100.

27 Frederick II, 'Instruction für die General-Majors von der Cavallerie', 14 Aug. 1748, *Œuvres*, XXX, pp. 179 ff.; C.F. Warnerey, *Remarks on Cavalry*, tr. G.E. Koehler (London, 1798), p. 46.

War, however, Frederick's hussars began adding a new string to their bows, assiduously practising the charge at the gallop, making up in panache and swordsmanship what they lacked in bulk. By 1756 the Prussian army's hussar regiments had become significant battlefield instruments. And as the hussars amalgamated functionally with the army's heavy cavalry, they brought with them some of the dash and swagger that had been missing among the sons of middle-ranking peasants who formed the bulk of the mounted arm's rank and file.

The Prussian cavalry during the years prior to the outbreak of the Seven Years War developed and refined another tactical method as well. This involved using cavalry columns to attack enemy infantry and artillery as yet unshaken by fire. It was a development of the more or less serendipitous charge of the Bayreuth Dragoons at Hohenfriedberg, when the regiment attacked in column because it lacked the space and time to form in line.[28] Frederick encouraged testing the technique during manoeuvres. In that context the Prussian manoeuvres' growing reputation for artificiality stood the army in good stead. Foreign observers either did not notice the new evolutions, or dismissed them as parade-ground eccentricities that would be abandoned when the ammunition was live. At regiment and squadron levels, moreover, the Prussian insistence on prompt and precise execution of orders worked to limit the kinds of questions and explanations that might lead potential enemies to conclude that one or another evolution was meant after all to be taken seriously.

By now even the most patient reader might well inquire as to the purpose of this excursion into the arcanae of eighteenth-century tactics. The minute, almost footling, nature of the material presented makes the discussion important. In eighteenth-century warfare, with armies raised, organized, armed, and equipped essentially alike, with genius at command levels discounted by an Age of Reason stressing calculation rather than inspiration, advantage depended on nuances. Nuances in turn needed careful, systematic development before the process of institutionalization could begin.[29] In Prussia it was General Hans Karl von Winterfeldt who took the lead in making what was still largely a collection of regiments into an army. Son of a poor Pomeranian family, he had been one of Frederick's entourage in

28 Nosworthy, *Anatomy of Victory*, p. 172.
29 'Politisches Testament Friedrichs des Grossen (1752)', Dietrich, pp. 222 *passim*. This is also a major theme of Frederick's 'Pensées et règles générales pour la guerre', 10 Nov. 1755, *Œuvres*, XXVIII, pp. 115 ff.

the campaign of 1734 when the Crown Prince took the field as
an apprentice with Prince Eugene. He served with distinction as a
field officer in the Silesian Wars. By 1745 Winterfeldt had become
Frederick's military confidant, the first among a rising generation of
officers who would replace the Old Dessauer and his compatriots
at the head of Prussia's armies. Contemporary critics attributed to
him enough influence to compel Frederick to go to war in 1756.
More modestly but no less inaccurately, General Staff historians a
century later enrolled Winterfeldt as one of *their* spiritual ancestors.
Christopher Duffy describes him more accurately as a 'military factotum', a general-of-all-work for a king too busy to supervise directly
every detail of an increasingly complex system.

Winterfeldt was above all a systemizer. Like Frederick, he
accepted the importance of decisive battles for the Prussian way
of war. Like the King as well, he insisted upon the importance
of peacetime practice as the key to quick victories. Winterfeldt
possessed the capacity to supervise the details of drill and manoeuvres
without losing sight of the concepts that animated the structure. He
also deserves credit as at least the godfather of Prussia's military
intelligence system, culling diplomats' reports for relevant material
while developing an independent network of informants. These latter
were observers rather than spies; their reports usually involved items
of public knowledge in the states under scrutiny. Nevertheless, in an
era when ambassadors were increasingly losing touch with military
affairs while newspapers and periodicals considered such matters
outside their scope, Winterfeldt was able to provide his king with an
increasingly comprehensive body of information on Prussia's potential
rivals.[30]

THE DIPLOMATIC REVOLUTION OF 1756

Prussia needed every advantage it could obtain by any means at all.
On the surface, Europe's by now traditional diplomatic alignments
seemed undisturbed in the years after 1748. Bestuzhev's continued

30 Wolfgang Petter, 'Hans Karl von Winterfeldt als General der friderizianischen
Armee', in *Persönlichkeiten im Umkreis Friedrichs des Grossen*, ed. J. Kunisch
(Cologne, 1988), pp. 59–88, is a recent overview of this significant figure. Cf. A.
Janson, *Hans Karl von Winterfeldt, des Grossen Königs Generalstabschef* (Berlin,
1913); K.A. Varnhagen von Ense, *Leben des Generals Hans Karl von Winterfeldt*
(Berlin, 1836). The quotation is from Duffy, *Army of Frederick the Great*, p. 166.

hostility to Prussia's existence, to say nothing of its pretensions, led him to cultivate a commonality of interest with Austria – but by the 1750s, Austria was exercising a moderating influence over Russia's diplomatic rhetoric and behaviour. Kaunitz, by now the rising star of Austria's diplomatic corps, particularly warned against reacting to Prussia's rise by over-enthusiastically embracing the other claimant to great-power status. France, he argued, was likely to prefer holding Russia at arm's length – and France was the crucial variable in Kaunitz's calculations. He had emerged from the negotiations at Aix-la-Chapelle convinced that the structure of power relationships developed in western Europe since the 1660s corresponded neither to military and economic realities nor to Austria's strategic requirements. Holland had accepted second-rank status. Britain, confident of its naval power and its financial strength, increasingly regarded the Habsburg Empire as a larger version of a German client state, whose armed forces and good will were for sale at the right price. In particular, the British government had shown no more interest in restoring Silesia to Austrian rule than its successors in later centuries would take in the political fates of other central European states with unpronounceable names.

France was a different story. Relatively and absolutely, Kaunitz argued, France's strength had declined significantly since the days of the Sun King. Its diplomats now accepted a place in a plural international order, without offering the hegemonical challenges of an earlier era. The dynastic concerns of previous Habsburg emperors meant less to Kaunitz, a man of the Enlightenment, than did the prospects of encouraging a 'natural' process of French expansion outside Europe. By initiating a process of stressing common interests and compromises in western Germany and northern Italy, Kaunitz hoped to improve Franco-Austrian relations to a point where Versailles might be brought to consider abandoning a Prussian connection that to date had produced far more kicks than ha'pence.

This policy, Kaunitz argued, did not necessarily involve a breach with either of the maritime powers. Increasing Dutch readiness to trim their sails to French winds in the previous decade, combined with increasing reluctance to fund military expenses on the scale demanded by modern war, in any case had diminished Holland's potential as an ally. As for Britain, its increasing concern for colonial interests and its corresponding lack of concern for Continental aggrandizement, increasingly served to define France as a natural enemy. This fact affected Austria, however, only so long as the Habsburg–Bourbon rivalry remained alive. Defuse that, and circumstances changed essentially. During the War of Austrian Succession it had become plain that neither public nor political opinion in Britain regarded the Austrian connection as valuable except insofar as it was directed against France. France for its part had shown a steady decline in commitment to policies of Continental aggrandizement since the death of Louis XIV. The consolidation of Austrian power in northern Italy and the southern Netherlands had essentially created a trip-wire that all but eliminated the opportunities for salami-slicing that had so attracted the Sun King.[31]

From Kaunitz's perspective the prospects were dazzling. An Austro-French *rapprochement*, even one short of a formal alliance, would not only strengthen the Habsburg Empire's position on the Continent. It would put Vienna in the position to play a role as more or less 'honest broker' between London and Paris. Even if that role failed to materialize, there seemed small likelihood of Austria's being drawn into future Anglo–French conflicts over trade and colonies – as long as those conflicts did not spread to Europe itself. And Austria would be in a position to deter British adventures on the Continent by virtue of its French connection.

'Let others make wars,' a familiar proverb runs. 'You, happy Austria, marry.' For Kaunitz, a diplomatic union with France was as good as a dynastic marriage. Appointed ambassador to Versailles in 1750, the Austrian statesman bent every effort to convince his French counterparts that the traditional rivalry between Habsburg and Valois/Bourbon had been overtaken by events. On the whole, however, neither Louis XV nor his advisers were overly impressed. Prussia's military performance in the Silesian Wars had established it as a useful ally in the tradition of France's German clients: successor to Bavaria as the chief rival to Austrian hegemony over Germany. And no matter how quiescent French policies in central Europe might have become, the diplomats at Versailles saw no reason simply to resign their position in the region for the sake of an unprecedented relationship with a state with no history whatever of wishing well to France. In 1753, Kaunitz was recalled to Vienna.[32]

31 'Denkschrift des Grafen Kaunitz', in *Expansion und Gleichgewicht*, pp. 207 ff.

32 Max Braubach, *Versailles und Wien von Ludwig XIV bis Kaunitz. Die Vorstadien der diplomatischen Revolution im 18. Jahrhundert* (Bonn, 1952). Cf. W.J. McGill, 'The Political Education of Wenzel Anton von Kaunitz-Rittenberg', PhD dissertation, Harvard University, 1960; and 'The Roots of Policy: Kaunitz in Vienna and Versailles', *Journal of Modern History*, XLII (1971), 228–44; and Grete Klingenstein, *Der Aufstieg des Hauses Kaunitz* (Göttingen, 1975).

His mission might have failed, but his star was still rising. The return to Austria's capital meant not disgrace, but promotion to the higher post of State-Chancellor – with correspondingly greater authority to persuade France of the wisdom of his new order. Kaunitz received help from an unexpected but logical quarter. Strongly influenced by the Francophobic Duke of Newcastle, the British government concluded subsidy treaties with two German states previously regarded as outside Britain's direct sphere of influence – Bavaria in 1750, Saxony in 1751. At the same time, local disputes between the French and British colonies in North America increasingly involved the respective mother countries.

From a French perspective Newcastle was actively provoking another confrontation. From an Austrian viewpoint British policies were equally unfortunate – or fortunate, as the case may be. Newcastle's immediate goal was to revitalize the Anglo-Austrian alliance – specifically by supporting the election of Maria Theresa's son Joseph as King of the Romans, and therefore heir-designate to the Empire. From Austria's perspective such a friend made enemies superfluous. The so-called Imperial Election Scheme upset every small court in Germany, forcing Austria to expend – in its eyes unnecessarily – a disproportionate amount of diplomatic capital to soothe ruffled feathers.

For Kaunitz the opportunity was golden. The shrewd Austrian continued to sustain British hopes. Indeed, like any competent diplomat he went so far as to test Newcastle's willingness to participate with Austria and Russia in an anti-Prussian coalition. At the same time he continued stressing to Versailles both the probable consequences of English diplomacy and the willingness of Austria to establish an entirely new diplomatic paradigm.[33]

By 1754 the French government was on the horns of a dilemma. To the steadily increasing tensions in North America was added growing friction in India as aggressive French merchant adventurers challenged the position of the Honourable East India Company. France, with half a century's bitter experience behind it, did not want a colonial war. For that matter neither did Newcastle. But under

---

33 Reed Browning, *The Duke of Newcastle* (New Haven, Conn., 1975), pp. 159 ff.; and more specifically, 'The Duke of Newcastle and the Imperial Election Plan, 1749–1754', *Journal of British Studies*, I (1967), 28–47; and 'The British Orientation of Austrian Foreign Policy, 1749–1754', *Central European History*, I (1968), 299–323.

increasing pressure from a parliamentary opposition using the 'American Question' as its focus, Newcastle despatched a small expedition under Sir Edward Braddock with orders to attack the French in the Ohio Valley. The French responded by despatching reinforcements to Canada. War was not quite inevitable even after Braddock's defeat, and even after the Royal Navy began systematically seizing French merchantmen on the open seas. But ample *justification* for war lay in the hands of both parties.[34]

Newcastle deemed it correspondingly necessary to look to Britain's Continental connection. The distraction of France and the securing of Hanover were alike too important to be left to chance. In particular, British diplomats were interested in the probable behaviour of Prussia. Initiatives for an alliance at the very end of the War of the Austrian Succession had failed. In the war's aftermath Frederick was dismissed as too unpredictable and too self-interested to be worth the wooing – particularly in view of his perceived designs on the Electorate of Hanover. For all the hostility of the parliamentary opposition and certain City of London financial interests to that connection, the severing of Anglo-Hanoverian relations was not a feasible option as long as Hanoverian monarchs ruled England.[35]

Britain's general intention was to deter Prussia by an agreement with Russia. Anglo-Russian relations were historically cordial. The Royal Navy depended heavily on the Baltic for naval stores at reasonable cost, while Russia's ambitions in Poland and the Ottoman Empire brought it into regular conflict with Britain's rival, France. An even more fruitful source of cooperation between London and St Petersburg was finance. The Russian government was in perpetual need of money, and correspondingly ready to court British statesmen and British bankers. Britain for its part was able to play the role of the 'lover who is embraced', criticizing the extent of Russia's requests and highlighting the risks of concluding alliance or subsidy treaties in peacetime, while remaining confident that the faithful Muscovite suitor would remain in the diplomatic anteroom clutching his wilting bouquet.[36]

34 Patrice Higgonet, 'The Origins of the Seven Years War', *Journal of Modern History*, XL (1968), 57–90; T.R. Clayton, 'The Duke of Newcastle, the Earl of Halifax, and the American Origins of the Seven Years War', *The Historical Journal*, XXIV (1981), 571–603.

35 On this issue generally, see most recently Uriel Dann, *Hanover and England, 1740–1760: Diplomacy and Survival* (Leicester, 1991), pp. 67 ff.

36 D.B. Horn, *Sir Charles Hanbury Williams and European Diplomacy, 1747–1758* (London, 1930), pp. 179 ff.

This comfortable situation began changing in 1753, when the Hanoverian governing council took alarm at what it regarded as threatening Prussian troop movements on the Electorate's frontier. Its recommendations that Britain pursue both improved relations with Austria and a subsidy treaty with Russia were accepted by the British cabinet with a surprising degree of equanimity.[37] The former reached a quick dead end. By this time Kaunitz was too committed to his vision to accept its abandonment without the kinds of comprehensive, long-term, positive guarantees no British government was prepared to consider seriously. Kaunitz made a particular point of requesting British adherence to the Russo-Austrian treaty of 1746, with its provision for common action against a Prussian attack. For Newcastle this was no more than handing Austria a loaded gun with a hair trigger. The immediate goal of his diplomacy was to deter a Prussian threat to Hanover, not to commit England's financial and military resources to a general war in central Europe.

Instead, Britain's minister to St Petersburg pursued negotiations for over a year in the teeth of Frederick's repeated denials of any ill intentions towards Hanover. This policy was in part a response to the Prussian King's too often demonstrated mendacity. Partly, too, it reflected British desire to tap and channel Russia's resources for its own purposes. The continued hostility to standing armies had become by the mid-eighteenth century a social, economic, and political given for any British government. At the outbreak of every war forces had to be created anew at corresponding costs in money, lives, and defeats. Since the Restoration, Parliament had accepted these sacrifices as a fair price for English liberty. In particular, the efforts of the Duke of Cumberland in the years after the Peace of Aix-la-Chapelle to improve the discipline and efficiency of the regiments retained under arms had led not only Tories but also oppositional Whigs to attack a policy they regarded as designed to transform the army into a tool of despotism.

British governments had traditionally coped with their own military shortcomings by subsidizing – which meant leasing – armed forces on the Continent. Holland and Denmark, middle-sized German states like Hesse-Kassel and Brunswick, even Prussia itself, had signed English treaties and taken English sterling. By the mid-eighteenth

37 W. Mediger, 'Great Britain, Hanover, and the Rise of Prussia', in *Studies in Diplomatic History: Essays in memory of David Bayne Horn*, ed. R.M. Hatton and M.S. Anderson (Hamden, Conn. 1970), pp. 199–213.

century, however, the limits of this policy were becoming clearer than its advantages. The military potential of even middle-sized states with efficient armies had diminished significantly relative to the major powers, France, Austria, and Prussia. To compete effectively with these states in the future, Britain would most likely have either to enlarge its own army or rely on what amounted to a mosaic of client troops whose cohesion was likely to be far less than optimal.[38]

Russia appeared as a potential source of effective, homogeneous expeditionary forces whose size would be limited only by the depth of Britain's purse. From London's perspective Russia's economic weaknesses made the British offer impossible to refuse. To modify a phrase often attributed to George Bernard Shaw, everyone knew what the Tsaritsa Elizabeth was; all that remained was to fix the price. The long-drawn-out negotiations (the Anglo-Russian treaty was not signed until 30 September 1755) reflected, however, a good deal more than haggling over details of payment and force structures. Russia in the mid-eighteenth century faced two tiers of enemies. One included its by now traditional foes: Poland, Sweden, and Turkey. The second incorporated the Continental great powers. The France of Louis XV had devoted a good deal of attention to establishing an anti-Russia *cordon sanitaire* in east-central Europe, as much because of its economic and political interests in Sweden and Poland as from any direct fear of Russia. Austria too posed a challenge. Although the two states had collaborated effectively in the 1730s against the Ottomans, Austria's behaviour in the latter stages of that war and during the peace negotiations that followed clearly indicated the limits of Vienna's support for St Petersburg's ambitions in the Near East.

Russia's strategic problems were further exacerbated by geography and economics. The Tsarist Empire had the longest and most exposed borders in Europe. Defensive doctrines in the eighteenth-century context were necessarily manpower-intensive. For all its size, however, the Russian army had the lowest force to space ratio of any of the great powers. The poverty of the state and its inefficient administration worked against increasing the size of the armed forces to any significant degree. Too often even the men under arms enjoyed that status only in principle. As late as 1757 recruits were drilled

---

38 Lois G. Schwoerer, *'No Standing Armies!' The Antiarmy Ideology in Seventeenth-Century England* (Baltimore, 1974); and D.B. Horn, 'The Cabinet Controversy on Subsidy Treaties in Time of Peace, 1749–1750', *English Historical Review*, XLV (1930), 463–6.

with wooden guns while men in the field with their regiments waited for sickness or casualties to make muskets available. Horses were pastured rather than grain-fed, and the thin steppe grass that predominated in much of the Empire did not produce animals capable of either load-bearing or exertion.

In this general context, hindsight suggests the wisdom of a quiescent foreign policy. Elizabeth and her advisers, however, reasoned that Russia could not expect to maintain its integrity by standing pat: it was necessary to go forward. Such a policy made Prussia both an end and a means. From Bestuzhev's perspective not only was Prussia a potential major addition to both tiers of Russia's enemies; its defeat meant the opportunity for territorial gains to be absorbed into Russia or exchanged with Russia's other neighbours. It also meant leverage – first, to diminish if not demolish France's eastern position by increasing Russia's power; secondly, to deal with Austria itself in a final round.

The English subsidy treaty was the ball bearing on which the entire scheme turned. British funds would not only stabilize the Russian treasury. They would also make possible the concentration of a strong army close to Prussia's frontier, ready to attack at will – and, just perhaps, that will would emanate from St Petersburg.

By the spring of 1755 Kaunitz as well was paying increased attention to Russia's possible courses of action. As the Anglo-French skirmishes in North America escalated towards full-scale war, Kaunitz saw himself pushed towards a decision. Initially he spoke of upholding the Anglo-Austrian alliance – at least so long as the war was restricted to the high seas and the colonies. Such a situation indeed filled Kaunitz's original concept of Austria as a potential mediator between the maritime parties, an honest broker with no significant interests at stake. Should, however, the British press for an extension of war to the Continent, their most logical demands would involve an Austrian concentration against France. Kaunitz for his part insisted that the next Continental war must begin by doing everything possible to break Prussia's power immediately, once and for all.

How best to square that particular circle increasingly preoccupied the Austrian chancellor. He found his answer, or at least part of it, on the Neva River, in the Anglo-Russian subsidy negotiations. A hundred thousand Russian troops in British pay on Prussia's frontier could well become a prima facie *casus belli* for Frederick. Even if the Prussian monarch stepped out of his self-defined role and awaited developments, Kaunitz still believed – at least in the first six or seven months of 1755 – that Russia's east European ambitions might serve as a lever bringing England into an anti-Prussia combination, if not as a participant then at least as an accepting bystander.[39]

By the summer of 1755 this concept was being moved into the realm of fantasy by a series of British decisions. In July Britain and France severed diplomatic relations. With war a virtual certainty, Newcastle took stock and concluded that Austria was likely to prove no better than a broken reed. Kaunitz continued to assert good will, but refused to support words with troop movements into the Austrian Netherlands. Calls for neutrality, when not alliance with France, were emerging across the spectrum of Dutch politics. The treaty with Russia was still *in potentia*, and no one seriously expected the Tsarist Empire to spring to arms at Britain's whistle with the well-practised facility of a Hesse-Kassel.

On the surface Britain seemed effectively caught in Kaunitz's rip-tide. There remained, however, an alternate path. Its gate was opened by Frederick. The Prussian King, while aware of the general outlines of Kaunitz's grand design, initially seems not to have been particularly disturbed by what he regarded as a pipe dream of Austria as ringmaster of an improbable coalition. He was more concerned with the concrete risks posed to Prussia by an existing treaty: the Austro-Russian agreement of 1746. Prussia's spies had secured a copy of that document, and Frederick was aware of the clauses aimed at his state.[40] He was even more aware of Russia's overt hostility, and of Kaunitz's increasing efforts to secure alliances with the middle-sized German states. The King's trump card was Prussia's French connection – a relationship which Frederick comfortably regarded as depending on France's vital interests, specifically its enduring rivalry with Austria, rather than any Prussian behaviour. In 1752 he described France and Prussia as having married 'sisters', Lorraine and Silesia respectively. 'The connection', Frederick declared, 'obliges them to pursue the same policy.'[41] To extend the image of brothers-in-law, any particular disputes, such as those caused by Frederick's

---

39 Cf. also Herbert H. Kaplan, *Russia and the Outbreak of the Seven Years' War* (Berkeley, Cal., 1968); Michael J. Müller, 'Russland und der Siebenjährigen Krieg. Beitrag zur einer Kontroverse', in *Jahrbuch für die Geschichte Osteuropas*, NF, XXVIII (1980), 198–219; and Reiner Pommerin, 'Bündnispolitik und Mächtesystem: Österreich und der Aufstieg Russlands im 18. Jahrhundert', in *Expansion und Gleichgewicht*, pp. 113–64. John H.L. Keep, *Soldiers of the Tsar: Army and Society in Russia, 1462–1784* (Oxford, 1985), pp. 143 *passim*, is excellent on military issues for this period.

40 Frederick to Maltzahn, 1 Feb. 1753, *PC*, IX, 328–29.

41 'Politisches Testament Friedrichs des Grossen (1752)', Dietrich, p. 186.

behaviour in the Silesian Wars, would be ultimately cancelled by family ties. But the King, as misanthropic as he was misogynistic, overlooked a crucial element in the equation. Brothers-in-law who neither like nor trust each other may nevertheless be kept together by the positive actions of their wives. Lorraine and Silesia had no connection beyond their one-time status as Habsburg provinces.

Frederick did not trust entirely to the automatic workings of the traditional balance of power. While avoiding risk to his French connection by becoming too openly friendly with Britain, he nevertheless did his best to cultivate at least stable relations with that state. At the same time he encouraged France to think of Prussia as a possible mediator in future difficulties. The outbreak of war between the maritime powers in North America brought Frederick's concern to a simmer, as he feared the expansion of the conflict to Europe.[42] British negotiations with Russia brought the simmer to a boil. Russia's growing hostility to Prussia had previously been compensated by Russia's shortage of funds, and the consequent difficulty of keeping a strike force close to the frontier and ready to march. British gold bade fair to solve that problem.

In the summer of 1755 Frederick began launching a series of trial balloons whose messages expressed his interest in discussing the current crisis – perhaps even neutralizing Germany in the war that by now seemed certain. Newcastle was prompt to respond. With the Russian negotiations moving at a snail's pace, an agreement with Prussia offered several promising alternatives. With Germany neutralized under Prussian auspices, Hanover's security would be assured. Britain could fight the war from its strengths: sea power and its capacity to project and support small expeditionary forces outside of Europe. Such an agreement would have favourable domestic repercussions as well, by freeing the government from the political burdens that accompanied hiring foreigners to do England's fighting in Europe. An Anglo-Prussian *rapprochement*, Newcastle realized, would not come free or cheaply. The subsidy, however, could be defended as an exchange between equals. And a payment as a symbol of common interests, made to a monarch of Frederick's status and capacity, seemed somehow far less ignoble than the same amount of money disbursed among dwarf states for purposes as obvious as they were self-serving.

Newcastle saw no immediate reason to choose between Prussia and Russia. England's treasury, he reasoned, could keep both powers

---

42 Frederick II to Knyphausen, 18 Feb. 1755, *PC*, XI, 60.

contented. Properly managed, subsidies to St Petersburg would give Britain significant, if not necessarily decisive, leverage in Russia's councils. Frederick's subsidized guarantees would secure Hanover. In any case, the costs were likely to be far less than those involved in preparing for a Continental war almost no one in either government or opposition wanted. In August, Newcastle authorized opening direct negotiations with Prussia.

Frederick wanted English money and feared English control. On one level he found flattering Newcastle's repeated assertions that the peace of Germany depended on his behaviour. The King, however, was reluctant to promise anything without some sense of the outcome of the Anglo-Russian negotiations. Frederick was also deeply reluctant to do anything that might risk an open breach with France. He had earlier suggested to Versailles that Prussia might take the initiative in mediating the Anglo-French conflict, and was increasingly disturbed by what he regarded as weak and vacillating French policies. Nevertheless, Frederick did not prepare to cut his ties to Paris without first preparing alternate connections.

To some degree French indecision in the first months of 1755 reflected French distaste at the prospect of war with Britain on any terms. The local force ratios in North America were increasingly and irreversibly unfavourable. To sustain itself at war, French Canada required regular infusions of men and supplies, whose delivery the French navy was in no position to guarantee. During the last war the British had been able to keep control of the sea against France and Spain combined. Now France stood alone. There existed, of course, the possibility of winning the war by extending it, by attacking British clients and commerce on the Continent. Frederick himself suggested the advantages of overrunning Hanover in a *coup de main*. Such counsels appeared to Paris, however, akin to encouraging suicide from fear of death. The French preferred to negotiate their way out of the contretemps. But despite Newcastle's previously discussed fear of a general war, he could not convince a divided cabinet and an increasingly critical Parliament of the wisdom of settling colonial disputes by defusing conflict instead of escalating it.

By the summer of 1755, in short, France faced a truth best expressed by American humorist Finley Peter Dunne: if someone wants to fight you, you've got to oblige them. But that did not mean a head-down rush to war. France had little confidence in its existing diplomatic situation. The United Provinces, to be sure, were not the formidable opponent of an earlier era. Indeed, a strong faction of the 'political nation' of Holland favoured alliance with France. The worth of such a relationship, however, was questionable. The Dutch army was inefficient; the navy in a state of institutional and literal decay; the treasury empty. Across the Pyrenees Spain was preoccupied with an extensive domestic reform programme, and had no intention whatever of being drawn into another costly war with England. As for Prussia, Frederick's behaviour in the Silesian Wars had generated strong convictions in Paris that a state having him as an ally scarcely needed enemies.

One major possibility remained. A direct approach to Vienna with the goal of preventing Austria's military cooperation with England was diplomatically impossible in the light of previous French rejections of Kaunitz's overtures. Instead, the French sent signals of good will through the Elector of Mainz. Kaunitz got the message. Fundamental differences between the two states remained. France wished to maintain peace on the Continent, the better to wage war in North America and on the high seas. Kaunitz for his part saw the alliance as a major step towards reshaping Europe's balance of power by unleashing an European war against Prussia. Kaunitz was also attempting to play two chess games simultaneously, keeping negotiations with France completely separate from Austria's prior agreements with Russia. As wheels spun within wheels, the Austro-French negotiations remained static in the autumn and winter of 1755.[43]

Meanwhile the British government applied a mixture of carrot and stick to the King of Prussia. Frederick's resident secretary in London was informed in November of the details of the Anglo-Russian treaty. Verbal reassurances as to the agreement's defensive nature were cold comfort to Frederick, especially in the context of a simultaneous British offer to settle all outstanding disputes with Prussia. Frederick found himself confronting not only the prospects of long-term disaster should the Austro-French negotiations actually come to fruition; but the vision of immediate catastrophe should Russia slip its leash with the aid of Britain's money. In January 1756, Prussia and Britain signed the Convention of Westminster,

---

43 Richard Waddington, *Louis XV et le renversement des alliances: préliminaires de la Guerre de Sept Ans* (Paris, 1896), is the account long standard. It may profitably be supplemented by R.N. Middleton, 'French Policy and Prussia after the Peace of Aix-la-Chapelle: A Study of the Pre-History of the Diplomatic Revolution of 1756', PhD dissertation, Columbia University, 1958; and Walter G. Rödel, 'Eine geheime französische Initiative als Auslöser für das Renversement des Alliances?' in *Expansion und Gleichgewicht*, 97–112.

guaranteeing each other's possessions and agreeing to cooperate in resisting the entry of 'foreign' troops into Germany – including the armed forces of existing allies![44]

Not for the first time in his career Frederick made a decision based as much on wishes as calculations. His contempt for Russia and its empress led him to exaggerate Muscovite venality. In his own mind Frederick was convinced that judicious application of enough pounds sterling would encourage the court of St Petersburg to abandon its hostile intentions towards Prussia. As for France, Frederick seems to have believed – and certainly tried to convince the French – that the Convention of Westminster was ultimately to the advantage of a government now freed to concentrate its military efforts overseas. Frederick, indeed, had successfully argued for excluding the Austrian Netherlands from the treaty's provisions, thereby allowing a potential theatre for war-making on the Continent should Louis or his ministers believe that policy wise.

The King's attempts to influence French behaviour had sudden and dramatic effects – all of them opposed to Frederick's hopes. The crucial issue involved style rather than substance. The French had remained suspicious of Kaunitz, continuing to demand concrete Austrian support for a 'forward policy' in Germany as a condition of more general agreements. They had also taken some pains to mend fences with a Prussia that successive foreign ministers had tended to take for granted as having nowhere to turn save Paris. But when the French ambassador informed Frederick of his instructions to renew the Franco-Prussian alliance, he in turn received from the King a draft of the Convention of Westminster and was told that the document was in the process of being signed in London! An outraged French government denounced Prussia for concluding such an agreement while Britain was waging war against France. Frederick responded by declaring his behaviour within the limits of international law, and by arguing that France was unwilling to consider the positive possibilities of the Convention.

Viewed from the perspective of two centuries, France and Prussia seem to have deserved each other.[45] Neither party was much con-

44 Karl W. Schweizer, *Frederick the Great, William Pitt, and Lord Bute: The Anglo-Prussian Alliance, 1756–1763* (New York, 1991), is now the standard work on this complex relationship.

45 Stephan Skalweit, *Frankreich und Friedrich der Grosse. Der Aufstieg Preussens in der öffentliche Meinung des 'ancien régime'* (Bonn, 1952), surveys the relationship between Frederick's policies and his image.

cerned with communication. Both assumed a level of necessity in their relationships that became an article of faith rather than a subject for consideration. For the French, however, Frederick's behaviour was an unpardonable slight. At a time when French foreign policy seemed everywhere in retreat, its one major ally had abandoned it in a publicly insulting fashion. For men who remembered the efforts of Louis XIV to secure France's rights of intervention in Germany, the Convention's neutralization clauses added injury to insult. Powerful the Prussian army might be; nevertheless, the Prussian state had no right to determine French policy in this sphere of vital interest.

In February the French Council of State declared its refusal to renew the Franco-Prussian alliance. Six weeks earlier France had once again refused to accept Kaunitz's proposals for joint action against Frederick. Now Versailles began seriously and openly considering the Austrian offers. Suddenly it was Kaunitz who began hanging back in the breeching. He understood all too clearly that Britain was France's chief concern, and had no desire to see Austria's newly restored economic and military power squandered in the Low Countries or Hanover. Moreover, the French government, however offended it might have been by Frederick's repeated bad faith, strongly opposed the total destruction of Prussia – an act whose obvious result would be Austrian hegemony in Germany.

The result of this mutual caution was a defensive alliance signed on 1 May 1756. France and Austria promised each other 24,000 men in case of a third-party attack – with the specific exclusion of Britain. Austria, however, did guarantee neutrality in an Anglo-French war, and support should an ally of Britain attack France. No one entertained any doubts as to the ally Kaunitz had in mind! Nor did any of the negotiators expect the respective military contributions to remain at the token levels specified in the treaties.

Like a good sports trade, the initial results satisfied both parties. Britain's long-time Dutch ally became more determined than ever to maintain neutrality in the face of the coming continental explosion. Nor did Louis's ministers expect Prussia to trigger what amounted to a dead man's switch by challenging France and Austria simultaneously. France, in short, might reasonably consider its Continental front secure, especially since the Bourbon monarchs of Spain and Italy were expected to adhere to the treaty without protest – if also without enthusiasm.

Austria for its part had added a key piece – perhaps the key piece – to the Chinese puzzle Kaunitz had been constructing for the better part of a decade. France had backed away from its traditional German allies and claims. Prussia stood alone. Yet the Austrian chancellor wanted more. He regarded French money and French soldiers as crucial to the success of his anti-Prussian alliance. Through the summer of 1756 he sought direct French cooperation in a war with Prussia. When the French balked, Kaunitz refused to take action on his own. Instead, Micawber-like, he expected something to turn up. Given the powder trails laid everywhere in Europe, disappointment was unlikely.

The first match was struck in St Petersburg. Since the days of Peter the Great, successive governments had simultaneously sought to expand its territory in the west and worried about its ability to defend its holdings. More specifically, Russia's diplomats now feared the possible consequences of a Swedish-Prussian alliance. Sweden, while long declined from its position as the terror of the Baltic, was still a military and above all a naval power to be reckoned with. And lest the connection seem far-fetched, the Queen of Sweden was Frederick's sister. While no one ever accused the King of Prussia of exactly cultivating family ties, Frederick had justified war for Silesia with even thinner diplomatic gruel. Nor could the Polish wild card be discounted. For all Russia's growing influence in the Sejm, the unpredictability of the commonwealth's magnates remained proverbial.[46]

To date Frederick had shown little interest in an east he regarded as barbaric. The King's upbringing, interests, and diplomacy all combined to suggest a continued western focus for Prussia's policies. But his attacks on Silesia and Saxony indicated a high level of unreliability and an even higher level of unpredictability. Should Prussia in fact turn east in search of friends – itself not unlikely in view of the Austro-French negotiations – and become the primary power in central Europe, Russia was an all-too-logical second objective. Even unaware of the western powers' nearness to an agreement, Russian diplomats spoke to their Austrian counterparts in November 1755 of joint action for the recovery of Silesia. This position was helped by golden bullets; Vienna was almost as generous with bribes as with promises.[47]

---

46 Klaus Zernack, 'Preussen-Polen-Russland', in *Preussen und das Ausland*, ed. O. Büsch (Berlin, 1982), pp. 106–25; and 'Das preussische Königtum und die Polnische Republik im europäischen Mächtesystem des 18. Jahrhunderts (1701–1763)', *Jahrbuch für die Geschichte Mittel- und Ostdeutschland* XXX (1981), 4–20.

47 Pommerin, 'Bündnispolitik und Mächtesystem', pp. 141–2.

The Westminster Convention translated policy decisions into diplomatic action. From Russia's perspective Britain had behaved badly by seeking to hire a second Continental gunfighter. Instead of being a potential ally against Prussia, perfidious Albion was now in a position to choose its partner. Court intrigues facilitated dissension. Vice-Chancellor Voronozov is frequently and reasonably described as pro-French. He was also anti-Bestuzhev, and took full advantage of Westminster's terms to undermine his Anglophile rival. Tsaritsa Elizabeth, herself perhaps a bit bored with her long-time adviser, withdrew her countenance as well from the British ambassador. By March, Russia was openly planning for a full-scale war against Prussia, with Austrian and French assistance.[48] The army began to mobilize, filling out existing regiments and creating new ones. Once more, however, Kaunitz insisted on caution. He spoke of financial weakness and the need for French subsidies. At the back of his mind remained the question whether even in combination the Russian and Austrian armies could smash their formidable Prussian rival quickly enough and decisively enough to prevent Kaunitz's grand design from falling victim to the axiom that even the best plans never survive a second contact with a competent enemy. He argued strongly for delaying the attack another year, until all the military and diplomatic dominoes could be set in place, with only a touch necessary to initiate and complete the process.[49]

Kaunitz's caution was also the product of diplomatic *Schadenfreude*. He believed that Frederick was trapped badly enough to trigger a war from sheer desperation, giving Austria the high moral ground to go along with all the other carefully structured advantages. Frederick did exactly that, and his exact motives have ever since remained a subject for debate. The 'Patriotic/Realist' school describes a man without alternatives. To borrow contemporary strategic jargon, Prussia faced a rapidly closing window of opportunity. Simply to await developments was an invitation to disaster, particularly given Russia's long-term and comprehensive fears of a strong Prussia on its western frontier. However antagonistic France might be in principle to the partition of Prussia, Versailles was hardly likely to do more than protest vigorously – and briefly – should its new partners reduce Prussia to a badly carved rump. With Russian troops

48 L.J. Oliva, *Misalliance: A Study of French Policy in Russia during the Seven Years' War* (New York, 1964), pp. 14 ff.; Kaplan, *Russia and the Outbreak of the Seven Years' War* pp. 47 ff.
49 Pommerin, 'Bündnispolitik und Mächtesystem', p. 144.

concentrating in the Baltic and Austrian forces moving into Bohemia, Frederick faced the loss of that strategic/operational initiative he regarded as vital for the decisive battles on which Prussia's diplomacy ultimately depended.[50]

Certainly the Russian preparations were hardly a model of disciplined efficiency. Elizabeth's generals were appointed to represent and embody Imperial authority, not to take decisive initiatives. While the hardihood of the rank and file was already proverbial, like their Japanese successors in the twentieth century Russian privates could not live on a handful of flour a day. They stood, moreover, at the far end of fragile supply lines that led back to a country whose administration was scarcely able to sustain any systematic activity.[51] As for the Austrians, their mobilization orders did not go out until mid-July, and implementation lagged significantly behind instructions. 'A day late and a thaler short' might well have served as a motto for Habsburg regimental flags even after the improvements of the previous decades.

Nor was Frederick himself exactly a diplomatic ewe lamb. His previously mentioned generalizations on possible territorial acquisitions for Prussia in Germany were increasingly focusing on Saxony. Whether he desired to annex the state or exploit it remains obscure. His pre-war correspondence mentions the potential pleasure of destroying Saxony. His wartime treatment of the Saxons pre-empted any but the longest-term prospects for their successful integration into Prussia. Whatever his ultimate intentions, Frederick's aggressive designs were concretized by one of history's first strategic net assessments. Winterfeldt had not only considered for several years the military elements of an invasion. He had travelled through Saxony, evaluating first-hand routes, terrain, and fortifications. His conclusion was that the operation was feasible, and likely to be easy if the King acted quickly.[52]

The psychological effects of Winterfeldt's information and recommendations were significant less for their optimism than for their

---

50 Winfred Baumgart, 'Der Ausbruch des Siebenjährigen Krieges. Zum gegenwärtigen Forschungsstand', *Militärgeschichtliche Mitteilungen*, XI (1972), 157–65, is extended in Theodore Schieder, *Friedrich der Grosse. Ein Königtum der Widersprüche* (Frankfurt, 1983), pp. 170 ff.

51 John L.M. Keep, 'Die russische Armee im Siebenjährigen Krieg', in *Europa im Zeitalter Friedrichs des Grossen*, pp. 132–69, focuses strongly on logistics and administration.

52 Christopher Duffy, *Frederick the Great: A Military Life* (London, 1985), p. 87.

concreteness. Frederick's critics and admirers agreed that the King, at least at this stage of his career, was not a man to await events. Mere preference to being a windscreen instead of a bug was not, however, sufficient by itself to motivate action. Frederick might consider the Russians barbarians and the Austrians incompetent. Such chest-beating was little more than a tension reliever. And the King of Prussia had tensions enough by the summer of 1756.

The British minister to Berlin, Andrew Mitchell, was a solid choice on Whitehall's part. He compensated for his legal training by being a man of wide, almost catholic, interests ranging from Roman philosophy to contemporary art. Mitchell indeed was probably the best conversationalist at Frederick's court, and the King was more inclined to loosen his tongue in the Briton's presence than anywhere else. Following the policy of his government, Mitchell consistently urged restraint. The last thing Britain wanted or needed at the moment was a large-scale Continental war.[53] Frederick initially responded reassuringly. Britain's desires, however, were running an increasingly distant second to the King's own concerns. Always inclined to action rather than passivity, Frederick was increasingly obsessed by the sight of the coalition taking shape around him.

The obvious tool of an active policy was the Prussian army. Frederick's correspondence in the summer of 1756 reflects a clear shift from diplomatic to military priorities. Cantonists were recalled, supplies collected, generals brought back from cures or summoned from their estates to join their regiments. By late June Frederick openly declared war possible at any moment. A month later the King informed Mitchell that if Maria Theresa would provide assurance that she would keep the peace through the next year, Prussia would respond in kind. Whether he was being disingenuous is open to question. Certainly, when the Empress temporized, Frederick attempted to tighten the screws by declaring his knowledge of the Austro-Russian alliance and its plans for war with Prussia – information reinforced by a series of specific reports from his ambassador to Holland.

The answer Frederick received from Vienna could best be described as dusty. It was a flat denial of any offensive alliance against Prussia. Whether Frederick expected by now anything more is unlikely. Most likely the King was seeking to demonstrate his good will to Mitchell, and through him to London. Frederick made

---

53 Patrick F. Doran, *Andrew Mitchell and Prussian Diplomatic Relations during the Seven Years' War* (New York, 1986), pp. 50 *passim*.

no secret of the importance he attached to British participation in re-establishing a balance of power he regarded as having been destroyed by Austria's machinations. In his own mind, however, the King was ready to act unilaterally. Better to compel fate, he argued, than await its decisions.[54]

How best to translate this aphorism into policy decisions and troop movements? In the 'Political Testament' of 1752, Frederick made the case that in any future war Saxony was the most obvious immediate objective.[55] Geographically, it was a dagger pointed at Prussia's heart. Berlin and Potsdam lay exposed to attack across a close and vulnerable frontier. The Elbe River could be used to transport supplies for an invading army into the heart of Brandenburg. Saxony had important dynastic links with Vienna and Versailles – the Dauphin of France was married to a Saxon princess. Nor was the Saxon army a foe to be dismissed. It had shown to good advantage in the Second Silesian War, and might reasonably be expected to perform well in a new conflict. Finally, the Elector of Saxony was also King of Poland. Whatever the weaknesses of the latter dignity, it offered at least some opportunities for stirring up trouble on Prussia's eastern frontier.

Saxony, then, was the King's target of choice. It was a decision he made alone. Frederick's ambassadors and senior administrators uniformly advised caution. Frederick's brother, Prince Henry, soon to prove an able commander in his own right, saw no clear reasons for invading Saxony. Even some of Frederick's field officers doubted both the wisdom and the morality of the King's decision – though the retrospective reservations expressed in their memoirs may well be in part the product of hindsight generated during the next seven years. In any case only one opinion mattered in Prussia.

54 Robert B. Asprey *Frederick the Great: The Magnificent Enigma* (New York, 1986), pp. 417 *passim*, vividly conveys the atmosphere in Berlin and Potsdam at this period.
55 'Politisches Testament Friedrichs des Grossen (1752)', Dietrich, pp. 199–200.

4   PRUSSIA ASCENDANT

Initially the campaign seemed a walkover. As a flank column under Ferdinand of Brunswick drove through Leipzig, Frederick's main body struck for Dresden. On 9 September the Prussians marched into an undefended capital. The Saxon army, hopelessly outnumbered, had withdrawn south-east, to the fortified camp of Pirna on the Elbe River. The position was naturally strong, and the Saxons had taken pains to improve it with a complex network of field defences. Given a fair field and a bit of luck, the 19,000-strong garrison had solid prospects of holding until relieved by an Austrian counterattack or, failing that, acting as a 'risk army', encouraging Frederick to negotiate peace rather than pay the price of victory.

BLITZKRIEG WITHOUT VICTORY: SEPTEMBER 1756–APRIL 1757

Frederick was suitably deterred – not least because he found himself a victim of his own wishful thinking. The King's increasing focus on war preparations during the summer had led him to make a picture. In this scenario Austria might declare war, but would not be in a position to initiate serious military operations until the spring of 1757. Instead, the Austrian government sent over 30,000 men into Bohemia within weeks of the Prussian initiative. The Prussian King was correspondingly unwilling to translate his strategic surprise into an operational context by accepting battle on the Saxons' terms. Instead, during the second half of September he shifted the focal point of his campaign to Bohemia. Frederick's decision reflected the fact that the Saxons, ignoring Austrian encouragement, showed no signs of attempting a breakout from Pirna. On the other hand, Prussian intelligence and reconnaissance reports indicated that the Austrian concentration in Bohemia was proceeding slowly enough to encourage seeking battle. The open terrain of north-central Bohemia, moreover, offered far wider opportunities for the Prussian army to display its tactical virtuosity than did the Pirna entrenchments. On 30 September Frederick led 28,000 men forward through the Bohemian mountains. The next day they encountered the Austrians around the town of Lobositz.

Frederick, confused by heavy fog and some more wishful thinking, believed he faced no more than a rearguard. In fact, 34,000 Austrian troops were deployed in the complex, broken terrain surrounding the town. Their commander, Field-Marshal Maxmilian von Browne, was one of the most famous scions of the 'wild geese' – those Catholic Irish who after the Battle of the Boyne had taken service with foreign armies rather than swear loyalty to 'Dutch Billy'. Browne's father initially served the French, but the Duke of Marlborough facilitated his transfer to the Habsburg army in 1707. The son followed his father, demonstrating and refining his capacities in Italy, on the Rhine, and not least in Bohemia during the campaigns of 1740–42.[1]

Browne was not afraid of a fight, but regarded his primary mission as facilitating a Saxon withdrawal. He had sent a flying column of 9,000 men north-west in a vain attempt to encourage the Saxons to emerge from their redoubts and join him. Failing that, Browne proposed to engage the Prussians on ground of his choosing. Operationally the Austrian deployment at Lobositz provided a good fall-back position should the Saxons after all decide to abandon Pirna. Tactically, the complex terrain offered excellent possibilities for a defensive position calculated to ensnare a general with Frederick's aggressive cast of mind. Institutionally the Austrian army was prepared to take advantage of both opportunities.

Military reform in the Habsburg monarchy began during the Silesian Wars and took top priority in the years after the treaties of Dresden and Aix-la-Chapelle. Silesia's loss deprived Austria of its single most productive province. It put Frederick's army within easy striking distance of the Bohemian lands that were the monarchy's second major source of revenue. Whether for offence or defence, Austria needed a new model army. But to support such a force required major administrative reforms as well. For a century the Habsburgs had financed their wars by merging fund-raising from crown estates, self-interested aristocrats, and wealthy allies. Now Maria Theresa was proposing an army with a peacetime establishment of no fewer than 160,000 men. Such a force could not be sustained on an *ad hoc* basis.

---

1 Christopher Duffy, *The Wild Goose and the Eagle: A Life of Marshal von Browne* (London, 1967).

The man most responsible for the reform of Austria's military and administration was Friedrich Wilhelm von Haugwitz, a native Silesian who smarted at the thought of his homeland under Prussian rule. He overhauled the tax system, originally expecting the various provincial estates to double their contributions, commit themselves for a decade at a time and turn over the money they collected to crown administrators. The clergy and the nobility would pay systematic, if not objectively fair, shares. Reality proved less obliging, particularly in Hungary. Nevertheless, the crown income significantly increased after 1748. Exact figures are difficult to determine from available evidence. More relevant for present purposes was the steady increase in military expenditures, from 11 million florins in 1740 to 21,600,000 in 1756.[2]

Money will not always buy good soldiers, but Austria came close. In 1746 the General War Commissary was made totally responsible for supply, freeing the Court War Council to focus on plans and training. In 1748 the latter body received a new president, Field-Marshal Leopold Daun. Under his supervision all three combat arms received new, comprehensive regulations influenced, but by no means shaped, by Prussian models. Officer training improved with the establishment in 1752 of the Wiener Neustadt Military Academy, designed to provide systematic instruction to cadets instead of leaving the matter entirely in the hands of the regiments. Senior officers were more difficult to teach new tricks, but the Field Service Regulations of 1749 offered at least the framework of a beginning. Maria Theresa sought as well to improve the social standing of an officer corps still retaining many images developed in the days of Wallenstein. The Empress even modified the Byzantine etiquette of her court to allow officers in uniform to do no more than bend the knee three times on entering and leaving her presence.

These changes by no means produced a Cadmean crop of educated and observant warriors. Their Prussian counterparts considered Austrians from ensign to marshal lacking in professional dedication, eschewing study for pleasure. The rank and file were dismissed as possessing neither the discipline nor the cohesion of their Prussian counterparts, not least because of the random system of recruiting that persisted throughout most of the period under consideration. The 'German' regiments which were the heart of the army were allowed to recruit in the Holy Roman Empire as well as in the Hereditary Lands.

---

2 Definitive on Austrian finance policy in this period is P.G.M. Dickson, *Finance and Government under Maria Theresia 1740–1780*, 2 vols (Oxford, 1987).

The results were decidedly mixed, though most of the volunteers seem to have been 'true' ones influenced by promises of glory and promotion and bounties that, however small they might be when all the deductions and stoppages were made, nevertheless could look like a fortune to a peasant or craftsman suitably primed by alcohol. When volunteers were in short supply the estates of Austria and Bohemia provided conscripts. In sharp contrast to the Prussian system, these men were rounded up by local authorities on the basis of who was most expendable. Since service was for life, the morale of these men can be easily imagined. Not until 1757 were men allowed to enlist 'for six years or the duration of the war', and these *Kapitulanten* remained a valuable source of more or less willing soldiers.

The 'German' regiments were the army's backbone, but its half-dozen Hungarian infantry regiments were not to be despised as fighting men, particularly at close quarters. Another half-dozen regiments had their depots in the Austrian Netherlands, and established solid records in the Seven Years War as assault troops. Then there were the irregulars, the 'Croats' as they were known everywhere in Europe, actually a mixed ethnic bag better described by their official title of *Grenzer*, or borderers. Almost 90,000 of them, a quarter or more of the army, saw service in the Seven Years War, and added to their laurels both as skirmishers and in pitched battles, where increasingly they bore the first shock of combat and usually bore away glory to match.

The Austrian cavalry, unlike its Prussian rivals, was recruited in essentially the same fashion as the infantry. Its heavy regiments, the cuirassiers and dragoons, were slower than their counterparts in the foot to assimilate Daun's new approach to war-fighting. In neither dash nor cohesion did they match the Prussians under Seydeitz and Ziethen, and their standards of horsemastership were at best mediocre. The hussars remained expert in the 'little war', but their discipline and interior economy hovered somewhere between irregulars and troops of the line. Only in emergencies were they used as battle cavalry.

The Austrian army's approach to drill and discipline differed little in principle from that of the Prussian. Recruits were expected to be initiated into their new life gradually, treated with patience instead of blows and hard words. Efforts to build formal barracks usually foundered on economic grounds. As a result, Austrian soldiers were commonly billeted on the civilian population and enjoyed, again like the Prussians, considerable freedom when off duty. Discipline on duty was far milder than in Prussia. Daun and the Empress gradually forbade most of the grosser informal sanctions, like kicking a man or beating him with a stick around the face and head. Capital offences too were more frequently tempered with mercy – sometimes granted by the Empress herself. The Field Service Regulations of 1749 criticized officers who saw themselves as of different clay from the rank and file. An increasing number of officers of all ranks accepted at least the concept that the private soldier too could possess higher feelings and a sense of honour.[3]

This probably had as much to do with the heritage of an earlier mercenary/entrepreneurial era as with the spread of Enlightened ideals. Nevertheless, foreign observers, particularly British, tended to have more respect for Austrian than Prussian approaches to managing men: 'By education and temper, proper to form a good soldier, and superior to any other' not raised by some species of enthusiasm.[4] At Lobositz, and in the months and years to follow, the Austrian army would prove that Frederick's days of easy victories were over.

Browne had about 34,000 troops under his immediate command. He outnumbered the Prussians in infantry, but was somewhat inferior in guns and cavalry. The Austrian general proposed to compensate for his weaknesses by taking advantage of a Prussian doctrine, the tactical offensive, and a Prussian shortcoming, battlefield reconnaissance. Browne deployed a strong advance guard in the open, with the mission of checking and disrupting the initial Prussian advance. Browne's intention was to lure the Prussians into a series of small killing grounds in front of a main position established behind a network of swamps and wet meadows. Unable either to deploy or to coordinate its advance, the enemy infantry would be correspondingly vulnerable to Austrian cavalry and artillery that could focus their respective shock effects while remaining protected from their Prussian counterparts by the complex terrain reinforced by Austrian field defences.

---

3 The best overview of this subject is Johann Christopher Allmayer-Beck, 'Wandlunz im Heerwesen zur Zeit Maria Theresias', *Schriften des Heeresgeschichtlichen Museums in Wien*, vol. III, *Maria Theresia. Beiträge zur Geschichte des Heerwesens ihrer Zeit* (Vienna, 1967), 7–24; Cf. Christopher Duffy, *The Army of Maria Theresa* (Newton Abbot, 1977), especially pp. 24 ff. Also useful are Jürg Zimmermann, 'Militärverwaltung und Heeresaufbringungen in Österreich bis 1806', *Deutsche Militärgeschichte, 1648–1939*, I, part III (Munich, 1983); and Manfred Rauchensteiner, 'Menschenführung im kaiserlichen Heer von Maria Theresia bis Erzherzog Carl', in *Menschenführung im Heer*, ed. Militärgeschichtliches Forschungsamt (Herford, 1982), pp. 15–40.

4 Quoted in Duffy, *Army of Maria Theresa*, p. 62.

If everything went well Browne hoped to win the battle without bringing the bulk of his force into action at all. Such a victory by economy-of-force would not by itself end the campaign. It would, however, extend the chance of relieving the Saxons. It would check the Prussian advance on Prague. And, not least, it would diminish the myths of Prussian invincibility that still hovered like a miasma over the Austrian camps.

Initially, Browne's trap worked perfectly. His artillery wreaked particular havoc on the Prussian infantry as it formed line and advanced. Neither the rank and file nor their commanders had experienced – or at least remembered – anything similar. Before the campaign Marshal Schwerin was contemptuous: 'The Austrian artillery', he declared, 'caused more noise than actual execution, and was capable of inspiring fear only among cowards, recruits, and born yellow-bellies.'[5] In fact, that maligned arm of service had undergone a particularly remarkable resurgence under its new *Generaldirektor*, Prince Josef Wenzel Liechtenstein. Since his appointment Liechtenstein had regularized administration, improved morale, and developed a tactical system based on concentrating the heavier guns under the army commander, as opposed to the traditional system dispersing them along the front by ones and twos.

It was a 'central battery' of this type, a dozen twelve-pounders, that made a liar out of Schwerin on 1 October. Ulrich Bräker, that most unheroic Swiss mercenary in the ranks of the 13th Infantry, spoke of cannon-balls 'snatching men out of the ranks as if they were pieces of straw'.[6] Another musketeer had his face 'spattered with earth and brains and fragments of skull', and his musket smashed in his hands by a cannon-ball.[7] But the Prussian infantry kept advancing, and their own twelve-pounders quickly came into action in support. The Austrians, however, showed no serious signs of either breaking or withdrawing, putting Frederick into a corresponding quandary. Did he face a rearguard, or did Browne propose to make a fight of it? The King sent eight squadrons of cuirassiers into the valley to test the Austrian intentions. The hapless troopers promptly rode into heavy musket and cannon fire from previously concealed Austrian

5 D. Schwerin, *Feldmarschall Schwerin* (Berlin, 1928), p. 255.

6 Ulrich Bräker, *Der arme Mann in Tockenburg* (Zurich, 1789; reprint edn Munich, 1965), p. 152.

7 Quoted in Christopher Duffy, *Frederick the Great: A Military Life* (London, 1985), p. 104.

positions, then were driven back in confusion to their starting lines by a well-timed cavalry charge.

At this point Prussian tactical doctrine clashed with common tactical sense. Frederick's dawn move had been an ill-advised reconnaissance in force – not an attack. But his cavalry was trained to respond to the defeat of a first charge by mounting a second one without waiting for orders. As the cuirassiers had advanced, the rest of the Prussian cavalry, forty-three squadrons of cuirassiers, dragoons, and a single regiment of hussars, moved through its own infantry and shook into formation. As the Austrian heavy guns found their range the fresh Prussian troopers attacked, joined by the now rallied squadrons of the first wave.

The sight would have impressed Murat. The results resembled a horsed version of Operation Goodwood, the British attack in Normandy in July, 1944. The Austrian infantry in the path of the charge got out of the way before being overridden. Within minutes the Prussians came to a standstill in a network of ditches and swamps swept from end to end by Austrian fire. Horses weakened from the unaccustomed rigours of field operations and an equally unaccustomed lack of fodder were unable to pull themselves out of the marshes and up the sides of the gullies. To dismount and lead the increasingly panicked animals to drier and higher ground was an open invitation to disaster in the face of the still unbroken enemy cavalry. An Austrian counterattack, fresh men on fresh horses, pushed the increasingly disorganized Prussian troopers backwards until they drew bridle and rallied behind their own infantry. They took no further part in the day's fighting.

Meanwhile the Prussian infantry had been drawn into another of Browne's killing grounds. The right flank of the Austrian forward positions was defined and anchored by the Lobosch hill, whose volcanic core rose 1,300 feet above the valley. Frederick ordered the position cleared at 7 a.m. Hours later the issue was still in doubt. Browne had garrisoned the Lobosch with the pick of his light infantry: 2,000 Croat *Grenzer* and irregulars. The steep hillside, broken everywhere by vineyards and sunken roads, was ideally suited for the style of fighting at which these men excelled, and correspondingly disadvantageous to Prussian lines and Prussian volleys. It was bite and run: hit, retire, reform, and strike from a new direction. By early afternoon no fewer than eleven Prussian battalions had been drawn by ones and twos onto the slopes of Lobosch. Platoon volleys gave way to individual fire as the musketeers learned that the best way of keeping the *Grenzer* from picking them off at close quarters was to put as much lead as possible into anything remotely resembling a

141

target. But that process cost ammunition. As cartridge boxes emptied, men turned to the dead and wounded for replenishment. With that source exhausted, majors and colonels began sending appeals for help to the royal headquarters.

Frederick's initial response was to order his uncommitted battalions to strip their men of half their cartridges – thirty rounds apiece – for the benefit of the men engaged on the Lobosch. He then left the field, for reasons he never sought to explain. Perhaps his decision was influenced by a change in the weather. The emerging sun had clearly revealed the deployment of the main Austrian army – and just as clearly shown how badly the Prussians were entangled in their enemy's forward positions. The King's abandonment of responsibility contrasted sharply and negatively with his behaviour at Mollwitz fifteen years earlier. Saving the royal person in the midst of a stricken field was one thing. Riding away from a battle whose outcome remained very much in doubt was something else.

Once again Prussia's *Landser* pulled the royal chestnuts out of an Austrian fire. Before retiring Frederick ordered the commander of the troops on the Lobosch hill to make one last attack. The Prussians, bayonets fixed, went forward with the fury of frustration. The Croats were by this time themselves low in ammunition, with many of their officers down. They had earned their pay and more. According to Austrian doctrine regular troops should have been available to support the light infantry, but no senior officer within reach was willing to take the initiative of marching to the flash of Frederick's bayonets. The Croats stood to the killing for a few minutes, then ran.

At the same time the infantry of the Prussian centre followed the route taken earlier by their cavalry, down the valley and into the town of Lobositz itself. Two battalions of grenadiers, supported by a few howitzers, forced their way from house to house in a hand-to-hand brawl of musket butts and bayonets. The Austrian infantry put up a heroic fight, but Browne had never intended to stake his campaign on a single throw of the dice. He had bloodied the Prussians, taught them some manners. It was time to go. The garrison of Lobositz withdrew, covered by the smoke of burning houses. Browne took personal command of the cavalry rearguard. But the Prussians had had such a near-run thing, and were so disorganized by victory, that from senior officers down to the greenest rear-rank private, no one felt the urge to do more than draw a deep breath, give thanks for his own survival, and begin the search for water, and for missing comrades.

As had so often been the case in the Silesian Wars, losses were close to equal – 2,900 Austrians and just over 3,000 Prussians. But the muskets of the Croats and the sabres of the dragoons and cuirassiers had wreaked havoc at close quarters: half again as many Prussians as Austrians had been killed outright. Many more were soon to die of wounds. The only trophies of the day consisted of the battlefield itself and three knocked-out cannon. Throughout the day Browne had handled his command on his terms. The Prussians were correspondingly shaken. Desertion rates spiked in the battle's aftermath – though this may have reflected an unusual level of disorganization, particularly among the battalions which fought on the Lobosch, as much as any decline in morale.[8]

Frederick received word of the victory late in the afternoon. He was disconcerted, not to say embarrassed. In his correspondence the King praised the performance of his troops, and conceded that he himself had initially misjudged the tactical situation by assuming that the Austrians were in retreat[9]. But Frederick also recognized the root of his discomfiture: consistent underestimation of his enemy. Expecting to carry the field at a single blow, building on the victories of the Second Silesian War and on the undeniable improvement of his army's training and doctrine in the succeeding decade, he had expected to run a physical and moral steamroller over the Austrians. Like Napoleon in 1809 and the Israelis in 1973, he discovered instead that 'these animals had learned something'. Frederick found himself fighting on his enemy's terms against a combined-arms army. The Austrian cavalry had long been recognized as a dangerous battle force. Now the artillery and infantry had improved to points where they too were dangerous adversaries.

Not only had Frederick's tactical nose been bloodied at Lobositz. Browne's detached task force rapped the King's knuckles by reaching the Elbe River opposite Pirna before the Prussian blockading force took effective notice of its new enemy's appearance! Frederick promptly betook himself to the new trouble spot, only to learn that the Saxons had once again proved an obliging enemy. Most of the Saxon army managed to cross the Elbe, but the effort cost most of their organization and all of their energy. The Austrian column

---

8 A. Dopsch, *Das Treffen bei Lobositz* (Graz, 1982), is the best modern account, written from an Austrian perspective. H. Granier, *die Schlacht bei Lobositz am 1. Oktober 1756* (Breslau, 1890), narrates the Prussian side.

9 Frederick to Schwerin and to Prince Moritz of Anhalt-Dessau, 2 Oct. 1756, *PC*, XIII, 479 ff., 482–3.

was too weak to break *through* to the Saxons. The Saxons were too demoralized to break *out* to the Austrians. Instead, the Saxon commander sued for terms on 14 October.

The Saxon army's surrender produced one of the Prussian King's more controversial decisions of the entire Seven Years War. Frederick allowed the Saxon officers to go where they wished, but incorporated the rank and file in his own army. The prisoners were paraded. The oath of allegiance was read. Anyone refusing to swear risked a beating or worse at the hands of his soon-to-be comrades in Prussian uniforms. Not surprisingly, most of the Saxon troops complied. Not surprisingly, few of them took their oaths seriously.

Poor administration and poor man-management counted as much here as did any dynastic or state loyalties. The Saxons were integrated into Prussian service not individually, as replacements and reinforcements, but by regiments. On the surface this decision made sense. It avoided the risk of diluting 'old Prussian' units with numbers of potential malcontents possessing a pre-existing group identity. German states had for generations provided mercenary and auxiliary troops in organized regiments that by and large fought well regardless of their paymasters. Frederick's situation, however, proved anomalous. The Prussian officer cadres of the ten 'Saxon' regiments that emerged from the capitulation of Pirna were selected negatively rather than positively. At senior levels they included disproportionate numbers of men whom their former units were eager to spare: the brutal, the stupid, the antagonistic, the too ambitious. These men provided but poor examples to the newly commissioned ensigns who filled the lower appointments.

The problem was compounded when Frederick took his army into winter quarters immediately after its reorganization. Administratively, this meant that regiments were scattered about in villages and hut camps instead of being concentrated in larger bodies like Union and Confederate armies during the American Civil War. By custom and tradition, moreover, winter was accepted as a time to relax: drill season began with the spring. The results in the ex-Saxon regiments were that the officers established little or no contact with their men, while the latter had ample time to plan futures in new settings.[10]

Desertion rates reached heights unusual even by Prussian standards in the winter of 1756/57. Significantly, instead of merely van-

---

10 Cf. Horst Hoehne, *Die Einstellung der sächsischen Regimenter in die preussische Armee 1756* (Halle, 1926), and Curt Jany, *Geschichte der preussischen Armee*, 2nd edn rev., 4 vols (Osnabrück, 1967) II, pp. 371 *passim*.

ishing, numbers of the native Saxons entered the Austrian army, serving in auxiliary units under their own officers. In part this reflected Frederick's emerging policy of treating Saxony not as a defeated enemy, but as a conquered province to be exploited at will. In addition to constant direct levies on the Electorate's material resources of food, forage, clothing, and men, the Saxon economy was ultimately squeezed to the tune of 48 million thalers – almost a third of the entire cost of the Seven Years War. Such sacrifices were anything but voluntary. The Prussians pursued systematic policies of hostage-taking and *dragonnades* that by the war's end had brought Saxony to the edge of ruin, and long before that had badly tarnished Prussia's international reputation as a state governed by law rather than whim or expedience.[11]

The overrunning of Saxony presented Frederick with a problem of strategy as well as image. Any military advantages gained by his surprise attack had been largely nullified by his later behaviour during the campaign. In shuttling from Pirna to Lobositz and back again, the Prussian King had neither impressed nor intimidated his foes, actual or potential. Nineteenth-century military historian Hans Delbrück highlighted this point in his iconoclastic *The Strategy of Pericles Interpreted through the Strategy of Frederick the Great* (1890). In this work Delbrück described Frederick as wasting a campaigning season in which he had the capacity to concentrate forces in the Bohemian theatre that exceeded by 50 per cent those available to Austria. Instead of seeking battle *à la* Napoleon, however, Prussia's great king went tamely into winter quarters!

Delbrück, of course, was offering 'a methodological parody'. Far from criticizing Frederick, the historian interpreted him as a general of his times, practising a 'strategy of attrition' like the rest of his counterparts. The outraged responses of the 'official' historians of the General Staff to this presumed attack on Prussia's soldier-king are even more tendentious. Frederick emerges from *their* pages as using the campaign of 1756 to 'position the chess figures' in preparation for a truly decisive campaign the next spring.[12]

11 Saxony's harrowing is discussed in Hubert C. Johnson, *Frederick the Great and his Officials* (New Haven, Conn., 1975), pp. 169 ff.

12 Hans Delbrück, *Die Strategie des Perikles erläutert durch die Strategie Friedrichs des Grossen* (Berlin, 1890); Grossen Generalstab, *Die Kriege Friedrichs des Grossen*, Part III, *Der Siebenjährige Kriege, 1756–1763*, 12 vols (Berlin, 1901–13), II, pp. 150 ff; Reinhold Koser, 'Zur Geschichte des preussischen Feldzugsplanes von Frühjahr 1757', *Historische Zeitschrift*, LVII (1904), 71–4.

Both positions suffer from the same form of hindsight. Delbrück sought to establish Frederick as a strategist of attrition. The General Staff insisted that the King prefigured Napoleon and Moltke the Elder in seeking to annihilate his enemies, Frederick's strategy was political.[13] He had never believed in the reality, much less the viability, of Austria's Grand Coalition. He believed he could mobilize significant support among the lesser German states, expecting them to sympathize with Prussia against what Frederick perceived as Austria's ambition to develop from a primary power to a hegemon over the territories of the Holy Roman Empire. But his treatment of Saxony and its exiled ruler quickly diminished that possibility to the vanishing point. Frederick miscalculated even more spectacularly Prussia's position at Versailles. In the aftermath of Lobositz and Pirna he was confident that he could restore good relations with France. Frederick and his advisers consistently discounted or underestimated the dynastic links between Dresden and Versailles.[14] Even on his own terms Frederick lacked perspective. His continental focus worked against understanding the depth of Anglo-French antagonism over commercial and imperial issues. The Prussian king correspondingly failed to comprehend the extent of French hostility to Prussia's signing the Convention of Westminster no matter what might be the agreement's actual results. These obstacles were not inherently insurmountable, but in the autumn of 1756 Frederick did far too little to overcome them. His diplomatic needs by now took second place to his military priorities. Prussia's ruler was acting as its commander-in-chief.

Frederick had increasingly good reasons for concentrating on the battlefield. Whatever Frederick's impression of his victories, Prussia's operational performance did not act as a magnet or a deterrent. In January 1757, the Imperial Diet expelled Prussia from the Empire and declared war against it. Elements at the French court favoured developing the treaty with Austria into an offensive alliance, particularly after the successful expedition against Minorca in June 1756 suggested that the Royal Navy might be less formidable than its reputation. Frederick's ambassador to Versailles reported that in the

---

13 Otto Hintze, 'Delbrück, Clausewitz und die Strategie Friedrichs des Grossen', *Forschungen zur brandenburgischen und preussischen Geschichte*, XXXIII (1920), 131–77, is a balanced analysis of this complex issue.

14 A point noted by Mitchell the English envoy even before the invasion of Saxony. Patrick Doran, *Andrew Mitchell and Prussian Diplomatic Relations during the Seven Year's War* (New York, 1986), pp. 104–5.

coming spring France was preparing to send large forces to Bohemia, and to the lower Rhine as well.

England was meanwhile proving significantly reluctant to furnish or finance an army on the Continent, particularly in the context of Hanover's increasingly frantic insistence on preserving neutrality at any cost.[15] Even worse news was coming from Russia. Empress Elizabeth had supported Saxony to the tune of 100,000 roubles in the immediate aftermath of Frederick's invasion. Through the autumn and winter of 1756, she was reluctant to proceed further – not least because of health problems that threw the Russian court into a frenzy. But Elizabeth's recovery boded ill for a Prussian state and a Prussian king she despised alike.

More by default than by design, then, Frederick confronted the necessity of a spring campaign in 1757. The coming year, he informed his sister Wilhelmina, would decide his fate and that of Prussia as well. He left instructions that should he be killed or captured the war was to continue. Anything he said or wrote as a prisoner should be ignored. No ransom was to be offered for his release.

Melodrama or determination? Historians continue to differ as to the mind-set inspiring these orders. Probably Frederick acted in response to the unstable cocktail of emotions, impulses, and reason that inspire most human behaviour. For all his self-proclaimed rationalism, Prussia's monarch remained fond of the *beau geste*. In more practical terms, Frederick's injunctions may have represented a form of New Year's resolution. Twice now, at Mollwitz and again at Lobositz, he had left an undecided battle rather than risk putting the crown in danger. Perhaps Frederick sought here to put into effect his determination not to confuse his own physical welfare with the well-being of the state whose servant he had so often proclaimed himself.

Frederick's bravado had some solid basis in grand-strategic realities. The French government was taking its time both diplomatically and militarily. Not until May 1757 did France formally agree to send troops to the Rhine and subsidize the forces raised by the Holy Roman Empire. Those, moreover, were proverbially deficient in administration and command, likely to prove a handicap in battle, certain to contribute nothing to a rapid enemy concentration on Prussia's western flank. The Austrians for their part also suffered from divided counsels. The *Hofkriegsrath* was more concerned

---

15 R. Meyer, *Die Neutralitätsverhandlungen des Kurfürstentums Hannover beim Ausbruch des siebenjährigen Krieger* (Kiel, 1912).

with supply depots than plans of campaign, and more interested in good weather for the marches than with the probable results of those manoeuvres. Personal feuds and jealousies influenced command appointments and operational planning. This relative insouciance reflected a mind-set, fairly widespread in Austrian military and diplomatic circles, best expressed by Marshal Browne. He described Frederick's conduct as 'rather calculated to make a great stir than to lend to solid advantages . . . . [He] never has a fixed plan, and the least small maneuver is sufficient to throw him off and make him change his mind'.[16]

THE SHOCK OF VICTORY, THE AGONY OF DEFEAT: PRAGUE AND KOLIN

Browne's opinion underlay, if it did not underwrite, the Austrian plan of campaign as it finally emerged. One army, about 90,000 strong, was to attack Saxony. A smaller force of 10,000 or 11,000 irregulars and light troops would harass southern Silesia from Moravia. The plan, expected to take full advantage of Frederick's perceived strategic and professional weaknesses, was not without its merits. Should the King concentrate against the Archduke, he risked the overrunning of Silesia. He would move east at the risk of getting caught between the Austrian armies. And if he did nothing, paralysed by events, his prize new province would be ravaged by Croats and hussars while Archduke Charles manoeuvred for a killing thrust at his outnumbered enemy. There was, however, one crucial prerequisite: Browne's evaluation of Frederick had to be accurate. The Prussian army must remain on the defensive, its commander mesmerized by Austrian finesse.

Initially the Austrian decision seemed justified. Diplomats, spies, and cavalry patrols gave Frederick by March a reasonable idea of his enemies' general intention. He expected an Austrian attack into Saxony and Lusatia, more or less in cooperation with a French-Imperial offensive across the Rhine. His proposed response was to keep his army concentrated in Saxony and, taking advantage of interior lines, strike at whichever enemy first came into operational range. Only then would Prussia shift to the strategic counter-offensive.[17] The King's plan met sharp criticism from his two principal subordinates. Schwerin, one of the Prussian army's best battle captains, and

16 Quoted in Duffy, *The Wild Goose and the Eagle*, p. 240.
17 Duffy, *Frederick the Great*, pp. 111 ff., is the best modern summary of Frederick's intentions and their matrix.

Winterfeldt, the consummate staff planner, found common ground in advocating an early offensive into Bohemia. Neither man talked of a decisive battle, but rather of a thrust with the quintessential eighteenth-century objective of destroying supply centres. Winterfeldt in particular warned of the risks inherent in allowing the Austrians to begin their operations undisturbed in the context of a growing French build-up along the Rhine. A spoiling attack against the painfully collected stores of food and forage in Bohemia might well impel the Austrian government to conclude a separate peace – or at least encourage the Austrian commanders to spend another campaigning season in minor operations.

By early April Frederick had assimilated and expanded the recommendations of his generals in the context of Prussia's overall war effort. Reports from Versailles and from the Rhine valley confirmed the slowness of French preparations. Russian movements were correspondingly dilatory. Frederick saw a 'window of opportunity' – six weeks more or less – for dealing with the Austrians. He proposed to abandon his original proposals, and instead invade Bohemia on a broad front with the seemingly overwhelming force of 115,000 men. The advance would begin in four columns. Prince Moritz of Dessau, with 19,300 men, would break out of the Zwickau-Chemnitz area and move down the Eger valley. The main army, 40,000 men and eighty guns, would follow the Elbe's west bank. These two forces would eventually combine, as would the army's other half: 20,000 men under August Wilhelm, Duke of Bevern, advancing out of Lusatia, and a fourth column of 34,000 under Schwerin advancing from Silesia. These latter forces would join near the Austrian supply centre at Jung-Bunzlau, seize it, and march to meet Frederick somewhere around Leitmeritz, in the centre of northern Bohemia.

The plan bears enough resemblance to that implemented in 1866 by Moltke the Elder for it to be easy to understand the insistence of nineteenth-century General Staff historians that Frederick had chosen an early version of the concept of marching quickly and separately, then uniting to fight a decisive battle in the enemy's heartland. Indeed, Schwerin's eloquently expressed reluctance to accept the risks of coordinating marches at such great distances over difficult terrain might be said to have prefigured the attitude of Prussian General Karl von Steinmetz in 1866. It is, however, significant that Frederick never stated the precise goal of his invasion. Was it to destroy the Austrian field army? To give it a mere bloody nose and turn to confront the French? Or perhaps did the King hope to achieve a *political* victory, demonstrating to the Austrian government his ability to overrun their

149

territory, discomfit their troops, and seize their supplies at will, all despite any Grand Alliance?

The final point was particularly relevant. Prussia's logistic system had never been designed to support such large numbers of men in such relatively limited zones of operation. Frederick had exacerbated his problems by ordering an advance before the spring grass had begun its growth. This meant that his supply trains were carrying fodder for the horses as well as rations and ammunition for the men. Without the tons of stores collected by the Austrians, Frederick's advance could be no more than a short-term lunge. Supplied by the Austrian magazines, his army would have a broad spectrum of operational prospects – broad enough, perhaps, to encourage second thoughts in Vienna about the wisdom of continuing the war no matter what the French and Russians might decide to do.

Prussian security was impeccable. Not only did the King keep his plans virtually to himself; he established a network of outposts and pickets that, for one of the few times in the war, prevented any significant information on the Prussian operational dispositions from reaching Austrian headquarters. All that crossed the lines were reports of to-and-fro marching and the construction of field fortifications virtually at random. For Browne, by now seriously ill with tuberculosis, this merely confirmed his previous low estimation of Frederick's strategic capacity. The Austro-Irishman paid little attention to contrary warnings, like that from the Elector of Saxony asserting Frederick's intention to invade Bohemia with no fewer than 160,000 men in five columns! Plans for an attack on Saxony were likewise abandoned. Instead, Browne deployed his available forces in a cordon: 24,000 on the upper Eger facing Moritz of Dessau; 36,000 under Browne himself between Prague and the Eger; 28,000 more near the Lusatian border at Regensburg; and a final 24,000 around Königgrätz to check any direct move from Silesia.

On a map these dispositions fit the cutting description attributed to Napoleon: more suitable for stopping smuggling than executing a campaign. Browne was admittedly reluctant to take the field and begin consuming his carefully assembled stocks of food and forage. He remained confident that Frederick did not intend to cross the Bohemian frontier, and even more confident that if the Prussians did invade the Austrian army would see them off as the first stage of a coordinated allied offensive. In December Browne had boasted that he was willing to confront the Prussian King at five-to-one odds in a campaign of manoeuvre: 'I could keep a single march in front of him without fear of being seriously troubled'.[18] This optimism was almost certainly overstated – perhaps it may be attributed to the periodic euphoria that can accompany the later stages of untreated tuberculosis. Browne was not, however, merely seeking to impress. He believed himself a match and better for Frederick in the open field. Browne still saw himself as the professional, Frederick as the amateur – 'a Prince who may possess some great qualities, but in no way be considered a great captain'.[19]

Based on Lobositz, Browne might even have been justified in his ability to embarrass Frederick. But by the time the Prussian columns actually crossed the border, Browne's health had reached the breaking point. He proved unable to coordinate the half-hearted efforts of his subordinates to check the Prussian advance. Frederick and Moritz joined forces on 25 April. The same day Browne made contact with Schwerin's advance guards. The Austrians fell back. Frederick, instead of waiting for his forces to unite as originally planned, ordered a pursuit. His task force would advance directly on Prague. Schwerin and Bevern were to cross the Elbe east of the city, cut off the Austrian line of retreat, then swing west to join Frederick for the siege and capture of Prague.

The next step, according to the King, would involve sending Prussian forces into the Empire to teach France and the Princes their diplomatic manners. Again, this suggests Frederick's orientation towards a political victory. Whether Austria officially withdrew from the war after the projected loss of Prague or merely remained operationally quiescent during the rest of the campaigning season was less important than intimidating it at the policy level.[20]

By 1 May, Frederick's army was no more than a day's march from Prague. The previous day Archduke Charles had assumed command of the Austrians. Browne urged the necessity of fighting Frederick even at unfavourable odds, before Schwerin's force could move within supporting distance. Whatever the theoretical wisdom

---

18 Quoted in Duffy, *The Wild Goose and the Eagle*, pp. 240–1.
19 *Ibid*.
20 Hans Delbrück, 'Über den Feldzugsplan Friedrichs des Grossen im Jahre 1757', *Militär-Wochenblatt*, 1889, *Beiheft*, 281–98, focuses on the military dimensions of Frederick's strategy at the expense of its political dimensions. Cf. also Alfred Boehm-Tettelbach, 'Der böhmische Feldzug Friedrichs des Grossen 1757 im Lichte Schlieffensche Kritik,' in *Schriften den Kriegsgeschichtliche Abteilung im Historischen Seminar den Friedrich-Wilhelms-Universität Berlin*, vol. X, ed. W. Elzc (Berlin, 1936), pp. 20–30; and Carl Grawe, 'Die Entwicklung des preussischen Feldzugsplanes im Frühjahr 1757', PhD dissertation, Berlin, 1903.

of Browne's position, by this time his physical and emotional state inspired little confidence in his judgment. A council of war agreed on the wisdom of retreating across the Moldau River, leaving a strong garrison in Prague itself. The bulk of the army, 60,000 men, would take up defensive positions in the broken ground east of the city, a 'force in being'.

Once again the Austrian decision made conventional sense. Prague, the northern counterpart to Vienna and Budapest, was too important a city, and its magazines were far too large, simply to be abandoned. As in many eighteenth-century economic centres, Prague's population had outgrown its fortifications to a point rendering a drawn-out investment unlikely. On the other hand, the city's very size would strain Prussian capacities even to establish a successful blockade. Frederick could not afford to leave such a position in his rear. Opening a formal siege in the presence of a large Austrian field army was virtually suicidal. Even a drawn battle, moreover, was likely to compel a Prussian retreat because of supply problems. Frederick, in short, had to win. All the Archduke Charles needed to do was not to lose.

Frederick perceived the gravity of his situation clearly enough. Leaving 30,000 men to screen Prague, he took 24,000 men and fifty heavy guns across the Moldau against the Archduke. To have any chance in a pitched battle the King needed Schwerin's troops, but Schwerin had failed to receive previous orders to expedite his advance. Ubiquitous Austrian patrols made short work of Prussian despatch riders and the old marshal, more battle captain than strategist, was not the man to make haste on his own initiative. A royal 'rocket' delivered on the night of 5 May led him to break camp and move out, accepting the risks of desertion and confusion accompanying an improvised march in darkness. At around 6 a.m. on 6 May, Schwerin's forward elements began swinging into line on the left of Frederick's advance. The combined Prussian force totalled 64,000 men.

Two days earlier Frederick had boasted to the British envoy accompanying the army that he was about to wage 'a Battle of Pharsalia' between Germany North and Germany South, the House of Brandenburg and the House of Austria.[21] That battle had been made possible in large part because of Archduke Charles's hypnotized concentration on the enemy in front of him, to the virtual exclusion

---

21 Andrew Mitchell, *Memoirs and Papers of Sir Andrew Mitchell, KB*, 2 vols., ed. A. Bisset (London, 1850), vol. I, p. 325.

of Schwerin. Browne's repeated advice to strike Frederick before the two Prussian forces could unite had been dismissed by an Archduke reluctant to abandon an excellent defensive position and risk a form of war that was not an Austrian strong point. Charles had more than 60,000 men, all the advantages of local ground, and Prague as a fall-back position. The odds seemed favourable even after Schwerin's timely arrival gave the Prussians a marginal numerical superiority.

Frederick for his part was much less sanguine than his rhetoric suggested. The force he left behind at Prague was disproportionally large merely to mask a fortress, and too weak to cut off the westward march of a presumably defeated foe. Thirty thousand men were, however, about right for a *point d'appui* and eventual rearguard should bad come to worst in the test of battle. Another indication of the King's state of mind was the stomach trouble that plagued him on the night of the 5th and 6th. The constant vomiting suggests that taut nerves played at least a partial role in the royal attack of 'colic'. The King's health, moreover, seems to have promptly improved with the news of Schwerin's arrival.

In contrast to the day of Lobositz, the morning of 6 June dawned clear enough for Frederick to conclude that the strong Austrian positions blocked a frontal attack. The King, his stomach still not up to a hard ride, sent Schwerin and Winterfeldt eastward to look for a more promising avenue of approach. They found it on the Austrian right, where high ground gradually sloped into meadows. The ground might be soft but at least it was open. Frederick at once ordered his army to advance south-south-east with the aim of overrunning the Austrian flank and rolling up the entire enemy army before it could react.

The Austrians were taken more or less by surprise as the Prussian army, keeping just out of artillery range, kept right on marching across the Austrian front instead of wheeling into line of battle as expected. Christopher Duffy credits Browne with being 'probably the first' to realize that the Prussians were undertaking a flanking manoeuvre.[22] But the movement was clear enough to attract general attention on the Austrian side – particularly as Prussian vanguards began bogging down in the mix of wood-lots, fish ponds, and bottom land making up the terrain that had looked so promising from the generals' end of a telescope.

The Prussian march began around seven a.m. Three hours later the army was not even approximately positioned for the attack

---

22 Duffy, *The Wild Goose and the Eagle*, p. 249.

Frederick intended. It says much about the continued tactical limitations of the Austrian army that Charles reacted to the situation rather than initiating a counter-move of his own. Austrian guns shifted position and took the Prussians under fire. Austrian reserves, cavalry and light troops, then infantry, shifted into position to block the Prussian advance. In response, Winterfeldt pushed the infantry of the vanguard forward – to the dissatisfaction of Frederick who feared becoming engaged by bits and pieces, as at Lobositz. When he complained to Schwerin, the Marshal responded with a homely aphorism: 'fresh eggs are good eggs'. Instead of slowing Winterfeldt, Schwerin ordered cavalry forward in support. Twenty squadrons of cuirassiers drove back one line of Austrian horsemen, then gave way to a counter-charge. In turn, Prussian dragoons and hussars from the reserve crashed into the Austrians. One colonel who had seen a full share of close-quarter combat called it 'a real mêlée, as it can be seen in battle paintings'.[23]

Like most such combats the direct results were indecisive, with victory depending on individual perception, and perception restricted to a few feet in any direction. But even with the Austrian horse otherwise engaged, the Prussian infantry faced a fighting line increasingly ominous in both numbers and capacity. Musketeers were reinforced first by regimental artillery, then by two heavy twelve-pounders brought from the reserve by Browne himself. Meanwhile Winterfeldt and Schwerin pushed fourteen battalions through the soft ground towards the Austrian-occupied plateau. Following accepted tactical doctrine they advanced with shouldered muskets, expecting to compensate for fire-power with speed and intimidation. The heavy guns that Prussian doctrine prescribed should support such an attack were, however, unavailable, stalled on the crowded road that was the main line of advance.

Themselves unchallenged, the Austrians swept the Prussian lines with a murderous fire of round-shot, canister and musketry. The leading regiments took casualties approaching 50 per cent. Nevertheless, muskets still at the shoulder, they got to within 200 or 300 paces of the Austrian lines when the attack finally stalled. Winterfeldt, as brave a soldier as he was a sound administrator, took a ball in the neck. A few men turned and ran, heedless of any threats from NCOs and file-closers. The Austrians poured an even hotter fire on the stationary and shrinking Prussian line, then pushed

23 Carl von Warnerey, *Campagnes de Frédéric II Roi de Prusse, de 1756 à 1762* (Amsterdam, 1788), p. 109.

forward as their foes gave ground. Three colours were lost and, as these rallying points vanished, even the stoutest among Frederick's hard-tried infantry began looking over their shoulders.

One could not yet speak of a Prussian retreat – rather of a steady backward shuffle, a step at a time. It was then that Schwerin intervened. He saw his own proprietary regiment, the 24th, beginning to waver. Riding forward, the Marshal seized a battalion flag and shouted, 'Come on, my children!' Minutes later he was shredded by a blast of canister. His regiment, and with it the entire Prussian line, broke for the rear.

At that moment, around 10:30 a.m., the battle's outcome rested on a knife-edge. Browne perceived a golden opportunity for a decisive counterattack. 'Show them you're no cowards,' he had earlier encouraged the men of his wing. Now the Austrians' blood was up, their grenadiers leading a hot pursuit of a flying foe. Browne was organizing support when a round shot shattered his leg. Leaderless, his men swept onward with no objective until checked by Prussian reserves. It was Browne's last fight, and perhaps his best. He died on 26 June – a man his state could ill spare.

Ironically, Browne's successful charge had helped open a wide gap between the improvised flank guard that checked and broke Schwerin's attack and the main Austrian army, facing north. Frederick, still periodically turning aside to throw up, perceived opportunity in catastrophe. So did a clutch of majors and colonels commanding the battalions of Schwerin's second line. Instead of following blindly the tracks of their defeated predecessors towards the Austrian right, the Prussians swung hard to the left, largely on field-officer initiative. Several generals accompanied the movement, but the crucial *coup d'œil* provided by a colonel who led his battalion of the 12th Infantry through an abandoned Austrian camp, found an open Austrian flank, and began rolling up the main enemy line from its left. Two more regiments followed, then most of the rest of Schwerin's task force.

Frederick, often praised for ordering this movement, is more accurately credited with supporting it by not interfering. The front-line Austrian battalions, already heavily engaged that day, began to bunch around their flags and to leak men. The general commanding the second line in the threatened sector refused to move without orders – and suddenly Archduke Charles was stricken by a pain in the throat so acute it rendered him senseless as well as mute.

The hypothesis that the illness was psychosomatic is as tantalizing as it is unprovable. What is certain is that with Browne and the

155

Archduke both *hors de combat*, the Austrian army was deprived of any higher control. It was Ziethen who applied the final touch. The veteran hussar had helped restore order on the Prussian left after Schwerin's death. Then he brought up twenty-four fresh squadrons and led them in a headlong charge against the Austrian cavalry to his front. Briefly checked, the Prussians came again, the hussars' pistols cracking through the dust and smoke. Suddenly their foes drew rein, the first line carrying away the second in a rout no one was ever really able to explain and leaving Ziethen free to turn against the whitecoats' infantry.

Threatened on both flanks, the Austrians fell back. They made the Prussians pay for every foot of ground, taking advantage of features of the local terrain to check time and again attacks made in battalion or regimental strength, but never seriously coordinated. Prince Henry of Prussia, the King's younger brother, made his mark that day by dismounting to lead a hesitant regiment across a stream running deeply and swiftly enough to deter prompt rank-and-file heroics. Henry, not a tall man, had to be rescued in mid-stream by his infantrymen, but the sight of the drenched prince waving his sword and shouting encouragement inspired emulation as well as amusement. By 3 p.m. the Austrians were in full retreat along the high road to Prague. Henry and Frederick, each in his own way, urged pursuit. The Prussians were too tired, too disorganized, to respond.

Frederick boasted that night to Wilhelmina of having completely defeated the Austrian army, and the victory at Prague did speak volumes for the qualities of the Prussian military system. To drive an army of equal strength from a prepared position is no mean feat, even with the tactical force multipliers of the twentieth century. Yet how many more such triumphs could Frederick's army sustain before conquering itself to ruin? It had lost more than 14,000 men. Schwerin was dead. Winterfeldt was gravely wounded. Four other generals had fallen. As much to the point, the infantry's reputation for invincibility had been shaken if not destroyed. The regiments which had broken under Austrian fire were counted among the best of the 'Old Prussian' formations. Was their behaviour a portent or an accident? Was the pre-war doctrine of attacking without firing a recipe for wartime disaster? Tactically and operationally, moreover, the Prussians had fought a fragmented battle. Schwerin's attacks had been made with whatever units were on hand at the moment. A good part of the army's right wing never came into action at all. Keith's corps, ordered on the day of the battle to cut the Austrian line of retreat, failed to bridge the Moldau and was unable to ford it. Was the Prussian command system viable only when the King was visibly present and at the top of his form?

Such thoughts may have influenced the sobriety with which Frederick ultimately reacted to the victory. His next step was towards the city of Prague. Its capture, Frederick believed, would end the war as a demoralized Austria sued for terms. But how best to compel surrender? A *coup de main* seemed out of the question. Prague was simply too large to be successfully stormed even if Frederick's army could afford to risk the losses accompanying such an operation. On the other hand, a city with a population of over 70,000, swollen by as many as 50,000 freshly defeated and presumably demoralized soldiers, could hardly be in possession of the kind of morale that fuels defiance. Frederick blockaded Prague and sent north to Saxony for a battering train: a dozen heavy mortars, twenty heavy twelve-pounders, ten twenty-four-pounders.

It took almost a month for the guns and their ammunition to arrive: by boat to Leitmeritz, then overland to Prague. In the interim Frederick's army licked its wounds and absorbed its replacements. The King learned as well that far from considering peace with Prussia, Maria Theresa's foreign office had convinced France to pledge never to abandon the war until Austria had recovered all of Silesia. A deserter reported that Prague held food for two months, and a large city could usually yield additional supplies if warehouses and shops were closely scrutinized by a determined governor. Prussia had no time to waste. Instead of using his heavy artillery to support a formal siege, Frederick decided to compel Prague's surrender by a general bombardment.

The Prussian batteries opened fire on the night of 29 May. Frederick expected fire to supplement the shelling. Two days of heavy rains gave the garrison and the citizens time to organize bucket brigades. Prague absorbed the mortar bombs and cannon-balls like a sponge – actually in some cases, as walls throughout the city sported new decorations of cannon-balls and shell splinters.[24] In effect, the Prussians ran out of ammunition before the Austrians ran out of buildings. Nine days after the first rounds were fired, Frederick ordered the bombardment suspended while his guns still had something left to shoot.

By then he faced a new challenge – and a new opportunity. While Frederick sought a political triumph at Prague, the Austrians

24 Christopher Duffy, *The Fortress in the Age of Vauban and Frederick the Great, 1660–1789* (London, 1985), p. 120.

concentrated an army in eastern Bohemia. Its commander was Marshal Daun, who had contributed so much to the military reforms of the 1740s. As a field soldier he had established something of a reputation as a cool headed subordinate during the Silesian War, but possessed no record of achievement in independent command. Initially Frederick regarded Daun so lightly that he assigned the Duke of Bevern, with no more than 19,000 men, to keep the Austrian under observation. Daun might not have been an inspiring figure, but he was steady. At his worst he gave the impression of being in charge, something the Austrian army had lacked since Browne fell ill. Detached forces throughout Bohemia, new formations from deeper in the Habsburg Empire, fugitives and stragglers, Saxon deserters, rallied to his camp. By early June Daun had 55,000 men under arms and direct orders from Kaunitz to relieve Prague. On 12 June he began marching eastward. Bevern, who had besieged Frederick with requests for reinforcements, promptly informed royal headquarters that the Austrians were on the move.

Frederick wasted little time. On 13 June he set out to join Bevern, whose force by now amounted to about 25,000 men. The King took only 10,000 men with him. He did not believe Bevern's report of Daun's strength. In any case Frederick, far from seeking a pitched battle, seems initially to have hoped to manoeuvre Daun out of Bohemia – and out of range of the city of Prague. Once deprived of any hope of relief, he reasoned, the garrison would surrender and Bohemia fall into his hands without further ado.

Once again Frederick's focus on political objectives shaped his approach to operational circumstances. Daun did not prevent Frederick from joining forces with Bevern on 14 June. Instead of acting to shape the tactical situation, the Prussian king kept his army in camp for the next two days while the Austrians manoeuvred themselves into position for the battle Daun regarded as certain. Frederick's strategic position made it impossible simply to march to Daun's positions and then march back again. Daun chose, not by coincidence, a ridge-line familiar to many of his subordinates from pre-war manoeuvres. Both his flanks were anchored on high ground difficult to approach from the front; the left was further secured by a chain of lakes and ponds. In the centre of the Austrian line, where natural obstacles were weakest, Daun deployed the best of his infantry, supported by the bulk of his 19,000 cavalry. All things considered, the Austrian marshal had reason to be pleased.

Frederick too intended to fight despite suffering an unexpected consequence of his hussars' evolution into battle cavalry. In the dry June heat, dust clouds exposed the general outline of enemy movements, but patrols brought in no precise information either on Austrian dispositions or Austrian intentions. The King was, however, not particularly concerned. Even in the aftermath of Prague he was confident in the ability of his infantry to drive any enemy out of any position, no matter how well chosen and how carefully prepared.

At 6 a.m. on 18 June, the Prussian army broke camp. Lacking both maps and reconnaissance reports, Frederick repeatedly climbed buildings to survey the Austrian positions. On the basis of what he saw and what he did not see, the King decided to repeat the tactics that had brought victory at Prague: march directly across the Austrian front and attack their right wing at a point where, so far as he could discern, the ground appeared to slope downwards, offering easy access to the enemy positions.[25]

Frederick's leading element was a task force of seven battalions, grenadiers and linesmen, under one of the army's noted hardest fighters, Major-General Johann von Hülsen. Hülsen, not much troubled with either imagination or intelligence, was as brave a battle captain as the army possessed: just the man to get well stuck into the Austrians in the battle's opening round and set them up for a killing blow. His mission was to march along the high road paralleling the Austrian front until he reached the village of Krzeczhorz, then shift right, clear the heights behind the village, and take position facing west, against the presumably exposed Austrian flank. Nine more battalions under Joachim von Tresckow would follow Hülsen in close support. The rest of the infantry, swinging into line alongside or behind the leading elements, was to be held back, eventually going in behind Hülsen and Tresckow. A hundred squadrons of cuirassiers and dragoons would deploy behind the main body to exploit the expected envelopment. Ziethen, with fifty squadrons of hussars, was assigned to cover the movement's open left flank.

Whether this was an early attempt to implement the oblique order or a less pretentious flank attack in a more traditional style will forever remain uncertain. Fog, friction, and the Austrians began putting spokes in Frederick's wheel from the battle's beginning. The rudimentary internal articulation of the Prussian army, with no permanent tactical unit above the regiment, did nothing to facilitate

25 Peter Broucek, *Der Geburtstag der Monarchie. Die Schlacht bei Kolin 1757* (Vienna, 1982), is an excellent modern analysis from an Austrian perspective; D. Goslich, *Die Schlacht bei Kolin 18. Juni 1757* (Berlin, 1911); and M. Hoen, *Die Schlacht bei Kolin am 18. Juni 1757* (Vienna, 1911), remain useful as well.

159

implementation of a relatively complex order of march and battle. Hülsen did not move until around noon. It took his infantry another hour, at the hottest part of a blistering summer day, to get into position. On their way they came under a galling fire from Croats in Krzeczhorz. The Austrian light troops inflicted few casualties. Nevertheless, for the first time the King seems to have wondered whether the reports of the Austrian strength he had so cavalierly ignored were in fact accurate. Instead of pushing forward he decided to halt the bulk of his army and await developments in Hülsen's sector.

Leaving the initiative to subordinates proved costly. Ziethen swung his troopers eastward, scattered the mixed bag of Croats and hussars in his sector, then settled down to wait for the infantry. Not until 2 p.m. did Hülsen's battalions begin their advance. Muskets shouldered and bands playing, they made a brave sight and a perfect target. Taking heavy losses from Austrian artillery, the Prussians moved through the burning village and climbed the ridge behind, only to find themselves facing not an unguarded flank but a full half-dozen regiments, moved into position by Daun from his reserves while the Prussians were step-dancing on the road below.

Shortly before 3 p.m. Frederick ordered the rest of his infantry forward. Instead of following Hülsen directly, however, the King set a new objective. Now his troops were to make directly for an oak grove just behind Krzeczhorz that seemed to mark the Austrian right flank. About this time events and motives on the Prussian side become confusing. Instead of executing a flank march in column, the leading battalions under Prince Moritz of Dessau formed line of battle and started up Krzeczhorz ridge – into the teeth of the main Austrian positions!

Frederick later accused Moritz of first so delaying his advance that he lost all touch with Hülsen, then of changing the nature and direction of his attack on his own initiative. The charge is dubious on its face. Frederick's generals were so conditioned to await their master's orders that they found it difficult to take the initiative even in emergencies. Moritz in particular was not a man to go off cavalierly on his own responsibility. The immediate tactical situation in the Prince's sector suggested neither an obvious emergency requiring a response nor an obvious opportunity suggesting a bold stroke. Frederick seems instead to have changed his mind shortly after issuing his initial orders. Instead of a flank march he now proposed to make a frontal attack all along Daun's line. Moritz was sufficiently surprised by this apparently unmotivated alteration of plans that he ignored repeated direct commands. Not until Frederick shouted 'Form front' into his face did the Prince comply, and only then with the mournful aside that the battle was lost.[26]

Frederick was thinking more deeply than his subordinate realized. The King's decision was probably motivated by dust clouds – clouds suggesting a further shift of Austrian reserves eastward, towards Hülsen's sector. The earlier brief doubts about the actual size of the Austrian army might well have been consciously suppressed as a manifestation of anxiety – particularly in the context of Frederick's behaviour at Lobositz. Instead, the King seems to have been taken by the idea that it was now possible to sweep over Krzeczhorz ridge – a relatively low elevation – on a broad front against a weakened enemy.[27] Move quickly enough and the Austrians might even be caught in march formation, before they had time to deploy against Hülsen. This point probably explains Frederick's rage at Moritz, whose lack of comprehension threatened the entire plan.

Frederick's *coup d'œil* and powers of decision stand to his credit. But the Prussian army was not the kind of instrument that could change focus and direction at a hand's turn. Like the Red Army of World War II, it was best in executing a predetermined plan. Frederick, moreover, had pickled a rod for his own back by giving his subordinates an unusually detailed pre-battle briefing. No one on the day of Kolin could complain of not knowing the King's intentions, and that fact gave the army's movements an added dynamic that proved difficult to alter.

Even had Moritz immediately grasped and responded to Frederick's new intentions, another fundamental obstacle confronted the Prussians. Daun's army was much larger than the King believed. The Marshal had not been constrained to strip his front to secure his flank. By the time Prince Moritz's nine battalions shook into fighting lines, Krzeczhorz ridge was full of whitecoats. Frederick's changes of mind had left his artillery well and truly out of the information loop, and out of the fight as well. Habsburg heavy guns once again took a murderous toll in the absence of any effective counter-battery fire. The musketeers, hot, thirsty, and frustrated by repeated delays, attacked with correspondingly lowered enthusiasm.

Nor was support forthcoming from elsewhere in the Prussian order of battle. Major-General C. H. von Manstein, commanding the

26 M. Duncker, *Aus der Zeit Friedrichs des Grossen und Friedrich Wilhelm III* (Leipzig, 1876), p. 76.
27 Hoen, *Die Schlacht bei Kolin*, pp. 380 ff., is a convincing reconstruction of events at this crucial and confusing period of the battle.

task force following Moritz's in the line of march, had been taking increasingly heavy casualties from Croat sharpshooters in the grain fields along the high road. The Prussian army had no specialized light infantry to keep these pests at a respectful distance, and their fire grew correspondingly galling. Here again Frederick describes a grand design frustrated by a subordinate. By his account, between 3 and 3:30 p.m. Manstein launched an unauthorized attack against orders, and became so heavily engaged with the Austrians to his immediate front that the King was forced to support him with the last of the army's available infantry. Other more credible evidence describes Manstein attacking in response to an order, delivered in passing by a royal aide-de-camp, to clear the skirmishers from his flank.[28]

Mistaking this for a royal command – probably because it matched his own immediate wishes – Manstein deployed first one of his battalions, then all five of them. He drove the Croats out of the village of Chozenitz easily enough that he pushed onward up the Przerovsky hill. Manstein may have been unwilling to relinquish pursuit of a fleeing enemy. He may have absorbed enough of Frederick's opinions on Austrian strength to believe he faced no more than a weak screening force. In any case, within a few minutes he was caught in a full-scale battle that eventually sucked in most of the remaining Prussian infantry.

Manstein's decision to press the attack in this sector seems to have matched the wishes of the King. Frederick certainly lent his physical presence to Manstein's front. He certainly did not order Manstein to withdraw. Perhaps the King reasoned that the cursed Austrians had to be vulnerable somewhere. Perhaps too the thought crossed the King's mind that if Manstein's attack failed, he might make a readier scapegoat than the formidably well-connected Prince Moritz. Whatever Frederick's reasons for supporting his subordinate, Manstein was no more able to make headway against the Austrians in his sector than was Moritz in his. Infantry battalions marching forward with shouldered muskets were shot to pieces by Austrian field and heavy guns long before coming to volley range. One lieutenant vividly recalled the hailstone rattling of canister balls against the fixed bayonets pointing skyward.[29] As the decimated battalions closed ranks, more and more formations from the second

28 Duffy, *Frederick the Great*, p. 127.
29 C.W. von Prittwitz und Gaffron, *Unter der Fahne des Herzogs von Bevern* (Berlin, 1935), p. 131.

lines were pushed forward to fill the gaps. By around 4 p.m. there was only a single assault line in this part of the front, too weak and disorganized to accomplish much on its own despite some support by the army's heavy artillery, which had finally come into battery along the road.

With stalemate on the west and in the centre of the field, both commanders began looking eastward. By mid-afternoon, Daun had been able to mass enough of his reserves against Hülsen to risk a counterattack. A task force under Lieutenant-General Starhemberg went forward against the oak grove behind Krzeczhorz, driving the Prussians before them with volleys whose precision impressed even the enemy. Other Austrian formations followed, only to be charged and broken by a Prussian heavy cavalry brigade, the 1st Dragoons and the 2nd and 8th Cuirassiers. Major-General Siegfried von Krosigk led the charge in person, then was hit by a canister round. The 8th's young colonel, Friedrich von Seydlitz, kept the attack going, scattering two regiments of cavalry and badly disorganizing several of the infantry regiments that had made life so difficult for Moritz's and Hülsen's battalions. But he had only three regiments, not a dozen. Rather than risk the annihilation of by now exhausted men on half-foundered horses, Seydlitz ordered 'recall' sounded and led his troopers back to their own lines.

For the rest of the afternoon, Frederick and his subordinates sought to turn a local victory into a general success. An increasingly desperate monarch took sword in hand to inspire Manstein's men – albeit in his own distinctive fashion. His shout of 'Bastards! Do you want to live forever,' and the alleged reply: 'Fritz, we've earned our fifty cents for today!' both suggest the close-gripped nature of the fighting. With his infantry pinned in place, Frederick turned to the cavalry. He ordered Major-General P. E. Penavaire to take his four cuirassier regiments up the ridge south-west of Krzeczhorz village and into the heart of the Austrian position. Supporting him would be some of Ziethen's hussars and the army's last infantry reserves: eight battalions under the Duke of Bevern.

Bevern never received his orders: the messenger's horse was shot from under him. Ziethen, as we shall see, had his own problems. Penavaire pushed his isolated attack but high ground, a steep hill, and the musketry of the ubiquitous Croats kept the charge from developing any force. A prompt Austrian counterattack drove the Prussian troopers from the field despite Frederick's best efforts to rally them.

The Austrians were by this time also in dire straits all along the front. Their ammunition was so low that musketeers were scavenging the cartridge boxes of their dead and wounded. In one regiment the drummers cut off the tops of their drums to improvise buckets, carrying what rounds there were to the men in the ranks. The Prussian army had a last opportunity. As Penavaire's charge was breaking the Duke of Bevern finally reached the field. His battalions, taking heavy losses from Austrian guns seeking a fresh target, formed the heart of a final attack on Krzeczhorz ridge. Sometime around 7 p.m. the Prussians broke through the desperately fighting Austrian infantry for what surely seemed the last time on that blood-soaked June day.

But the victory that seemed in Frederick's grasp proved just as ephemeral. Austrian cavalry followed the trumpets calling them away from their pursuit of Penavaire, to fall instead on the flank and rear of the Prussians. Other Austrian troopers, Daun's last reserves, charged from the direction of the oak groves. Army legend credited the attack's ferocity to the dragoon regiment de Ligne, whose young troopers were determined to avenge Daun's alleged reference to them as 'bare cheeks' (*blancs becs*). To the end of their existence the Windischgrätz Dragoons, as they later became, remained clean-shaven as a point of honour.

Their battering charge decided the day at Kolin. Frederick had no reserves on hand. In despair he rallied a detachment to charge an Austrian battery, only to be deterred by an aide who asked if His Majesty intended to take the guns by himself. As the day waned, what was left of the Prussian infantry withdrew from the fighting line on its own initiative. Detachments made their way to the high road and from there straggled in any direction that promised relief from Austrian sabres and round shot. Hülsen's brigade, or what was left of it, covered the retreat as it had opened the battle. Ziethen's light horsemen, who had spent the day being held in check by the cavalry of the Austrian right wing, did not even learn of the main army's defeat until well into the evening. His frustrated men on their tired horses finally left the field around 9 p.m. They were just enough of a force to discourage pursuit from opponents quite willing to call the day's honours even.

Daun was not the man to drive his subordinates forward. The Austrian marshal had reasons to feel proud and reasons to feel intimidated. Kolin had been a soldiers' battle from first to last, and Frederick's veterans had come too close on too many occasions to eking out a victory against long odds to give Daun any immediate sense that a crowning mercy lay within his grasp. Austrian casualties totalled around 9,000, including 1,300 dead. From squadrons and battalions upwards the victors were almost as disorganized as the vanquished. Small wonder, then, that Daun let his men bivouac on the ground they had paid so much to hold and win.

By the next morning, available evidence might have galvanized another type of general into action on the premise of 'better late than never'. Almost 14,000 Prussians were dead, wounded, or in Austrian captivity. Forty-five guns, half the army's artillery, remained on the battlefield. Twenty-two captured flags were further tokens of victory. For Daun, however, the risks of attempting to destroy Frederick's remnants were far outweighed by the political advantages to be gained by his victory. The Austrian army celebrated with drums and trumpets – under the cynical eyes of their captives, at least some of whom wondered what all the fuss was about.[30] Daun also promptly informed Vienna of the day's events. Maria Theresa responded by proclaiming 19 June as the founding date of the Military Order of Maria Theresa and awarding Daun its Grand Cross. Nor were the ordinary soldiers quite forgotten. The dragoon regiment that led the decisive charge received no fewer than four standards from the hands of its grateful sovereign.

From the perspective of later centuries all this seems time-wasting preening – like the rooster that never won a fight because in the middle he stopped to crow. Eighteenth-century warfare, however, particularly in the context of an alliance, was as much a matter of *gloire* and *vertu* as of casualties suffered and provinces won or lost. Particularly in the context of its new relationship with France, the Habsburg army needed to demonstrate its positive role in the alliance. Victory and its accompanying ceremonies, recognizing the Austrian achievement, was a matter of grand strategy and high politics as well as military operations.

Frederick himself was left in no doubt as to the identity of the loser. He spent the first hours after the battle aimlessly drawing circles in the dirt, then abandoned his surviving soldiers and returned to his original headquarters at Prague. There he informed Prince Henry that he needed rest and could no longer do anything. Henry was charged with bringing what remained of the army out of danger. Administratively at least, the Prince was not handicapped by numbers. Some of the infantry battalions were down to a third of their authorized strength, and a steady trickle of deserters added to the losses from battle.

30 von Prittwitz und Gaffron, *Unter der Fahne*, p. 150.

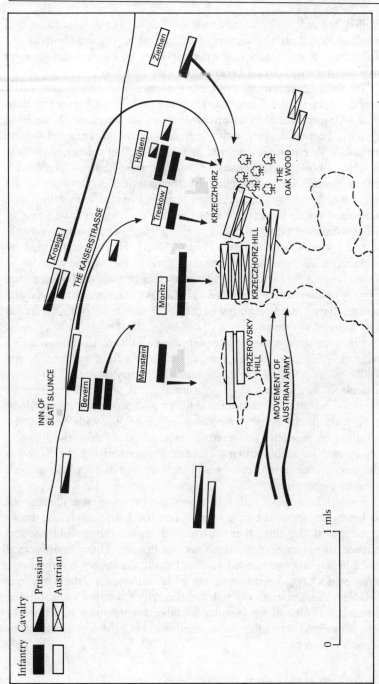

2. Battle of Kolin, 18 June 1757

The King and his army were faced with the same fact: they had been outfought by an enemy they had come to despise. Frederick took the field with too few men. Neither he nor his subordinate commanders paid sufficient attention to compensating by the coordination and timing which were alternate potential strong points in the Prussian system. Admittedly, the advantage of ground had been with the Austrians, whose infantry fought with a grim determination that surprised their adversaries. But from the royal marquee to the bivouacs of the humblest musketeers, the Prussians were haunted by what might have been – a little good fortune, a bit of extra effort, a dash of initiative here and there might have brought Kolin into the column of Frederick's victories. Now the King found himself a long way from home, with an army battered to a pulp and his conduct of the battle being widely and sharply criticized by his senior officers.[31] Like Lee after Gettysburg, he drew conclusions. On 20 June he raised the blockade of Prague and fell back into northern Bohemia. This meant resigning the initiative, but Frederick correctly reasoned that Daun was not likely to abandon a lifetime's conditioning as a consequence of a single afternoon.

FRANCE TAKES THE FIELD

Europe's general political constellation seemed far more threatening to Prussia than anything Daun could contrive by himself. Frederick expressed desperate wishes to Mitchell that his country might either negotiate with Turkey to enter the war or despatch a naval squadron to the Baltic as a strategic wild card, lest the common cause fall to ruin.[32] There was a terrible irony in this line-trolling. Neither England nor Hanover had done much of consequence during the winter of 1756/57 to prepare for war on the Continent. In principle England was supposed to pay for about 45,000 north German troops, the bulk of them Brunswickers, Hessians, and Hanoverians. But funds from London came slowly. Hanover's ministers were reluctant to cooperate in planning a campaign that seemed all too likely to turn their state into a battleground. As late as February the Hanoverian cabinet sought to negotiate neutral status in Vienna. Nor was George II the man to galvanize his Continental subjects. In his capacity

---

31 Cf. the accounts in Mitchell, *Memoirs and Papers*, vol. I, pp 352 ff.; and Heinrich de Catt, *Unterhaltungen mit Friedrich dem Grossen*, ed. R. Koser (Leipzig, 1884), p. 237.
32 Frederick to Mitchell, 11 June 1757; *PC*, XV, 161 ff.

as Elector of Hanover, he too hoped to secure the neutrality of states with which as King of England he was at war! The complex negotiations accompanying this complex situation might even have borne fruit had France not demanded a set of guarantees that, taken together, would have turned Hanover into a highway and a supply depot for the French. As King and Elector, George found the terms unacceptable. Eventually he browbeat his ministers into line, but Hanover was ever a grudging participant in future events.[33]

Meanwhile the French had concentrated 135 battalions and 143 squadrons along the lower Rhine. This force, approximately 100,000 strong, included contingents from the Austrian Netherlands and the German 'circles' of the lower Rhine. It had a two-to-one numerical superiority over its opponents even on paper – and the opposing order of battle was still essentially theoretical: a few Prussian battalions in the Rhine provinces, plus the 'Army of Observation', about 50,000 strong, established under British auspices but with some of its German battalions still in England.

The French army of the Seven Years War has usually been judged in the terms attributed to one of its officers after the débâcle of Rossbach. 'Sir', he allegedly said to his Prussian captor, '*you* are an army. *We* are a traveling whorehouse!'[34] The men in the ranks would have greeted such an aphorism with a mixture of amusement and anger. Any whores they saw under campaign conditions were likely to be either too high-priced for a private's purse, or too unattractive to tempt any but the most frustrated. The French regular army drew its soldiers from two sources: volunteers and militiamen. The militia was in principle a reserve force, recruited in rural areas by casting lots among unmarried men between the ages of 18 and 40. Service was for six or seven years, though in peacetime militia units were only assembled for brief periods of training. The hook – and a major source of anxiety and grievance – came with the militia's legal requirement to provide both organized formations and individual replacements for the active army in time of war. Almost half of the recruits furnished during the War of the Spanish Succession were

---

33 Uriel Dann, *Hanover and England, 1740–1760: Diplomacy and Survival* (Leicester, 1991), pp. 83 ff., is the best modern account of these events.

34 André Corvisier, *L'Armée française de la fin du XVIIe siècle au ministère de Choiseul*, 2 vols (Paris, 1964), is the definitive general account. Lee Kennett, *The French Armies in the Seven Years' War: A Study in Military Organization and Administration* (Durham, NC, 1967), is by far the best treatment of the subject in English.

militiamen. During the Seven Years War that figure was reduced to a fifth. Even the smaller number was enough to generate protests from rural communities – particularly since militia service offered none of the advantages that donning uniform gave to a Prussian cantonist.

The randomness of the selection process generated the most hostility. That the course of a man's life should be decided by the single misfortune of drawing a '*mauvais numéro*' seemed the height of unfairness alike to villages and to the attorneys they increasingly retained to fight the cases of their sons. The hiring of substitutes, though legally prohibited, was an increasingly common practice on both an individual and a communal basis.

In this context it was hardly remarkable that the government and the army alike preferred to fill the regiments with volunteers. The more or less traditional denigration of these men as the dregs of France has been significantly modified by the work of André Corvisier. He shows that a relatively broad spectrum of French society stood in the army's ranks. About a third of the soldiers were townsmen, drawn from communities of 2,000 or larger. The overwhelming majority, around 85 per cent, came from the lower orders: peasants, day labourers, and craftsmen.

The recruiting process was heavily psychological. To a certain degree general example was important. Men from the northern and eastern provinces, where standing garrisons were larger and more numerous, provided a disproportionate number of recruits. Familiarity was important in other ways as well. Although French regiments frequently bore provincial titles or had other forms of regional heritage, they were not recruited from specific districts in the manner of Prussia's cantonal units. Officers, however, did often possess local connections. A captain or subaltern going home on leave might well be requested to return with the proverbial 'few good men', to be attracted by the traditional device of free drinks dispensed by NCOs in new uniforms promising advancement and adventure under the eye of a leading citizen.

Age was also a factor. In contrast to Prussia's, over three-quarters of the French regulars were under 35; half the infantrymen had not reached their twenty-fifth birthday. This highlights the French army's status as an outlet for men seeking to avoid traditional forms of control, whether of family, commune, or church. The army's authority, while it could be harsh, had the merit of being abstract. Once a man had learned the rules, written and unwritten, he was left to his own devices to a degree surprising to observers conditioned to the comprehensive patterns of military control developed in later centuries. And while the pay and benefits may have been unimpressive even by contemporary standards, they were seen as preferable to life on society's margins by many a young man seeking to kick over patriarchal traces without submerging himself in France's underclass.

The latter point highlights the role of economics in stimulating enlistment. Hunger was a consistently useful recruiting sergeant, but arguably even more important was the bonus paid to volunteers. The legal maximum of 60 *livres* was frequently exceeded; during the Seven Years War a tall, well-set-up man could count on negotiating successfully for around 500 *livres*. This was a tidy sum, four or five times a farm labourer's annual salary, which not every recruit spent on cheap liquor and expensive women. It offered the basis for a reasonable nest egg. Lent at interest to friends and relatives, it multiplied even more rapidly.

Corvisier gives high marks as well to emotional displacement as a motivation of enlistment. Widowers and orphans, disappointed suitors, men unable to find a stable pattern of life even after a geographic move or two, were likely to see the army as a source of identity and structure. This pattern was particularly significant in a society emphasizing the collective as a means of support and survival. 'Anomie' is a nineteenth-century term, but the Frenchman uprooted, even voluntarily, from familiar surroundings was likely to become all too familiar with its effects. A common pattern involved moving from a farming village to a town in search of wider opportunities; then, when horizons continued to prove narrow, seeking out the recruiting officer.

An overwhelming majority of the men in the line regiments were French subjects – not least because a fifth of the infantry was composed of foreign regiments in French service. The Swiss formations did their own recruiting, usually confining it to the cantons except in extreme emergencies. German, Irish, and other foreign units tended to accept almost anyone. With foreigners as concentrated as this, a French regiment was likely to be a good deal less polyglot than one of its Prussian counterparts.

Taken collectively, then, the French soldiers of the mid-eighteenth century can legitimately be described as having good to excellent potential, particularly at the beginning of a war. Most of them had joined the army as a positive choice: a way of improving their lots and stations in life, or at least of avoiding conventional forms of servitude. Patriotism in a conventional sense was a less significant motivator in a context that had not seen French identity seriously threatened for a century. But pride of craft – what Corvisier calls 'vocation' – could motivate these men to fight furiously and rally quickly, given anything like a fair field and no favour.

Securing those circumstances was, however, a complex process. The France of Louis XV enjoyed a significantly greater degree of stability than its predecessor. The worst of the religious conflicts involving Huguenots and Jansenists were over. In contrast to the turmoil of the Fronde, Louis enjoyed a peaceful minority. His bureaucrats had developed and refined patterns, originated under the Sun King, of cooperating within local elites and working within local systems of patronage and clientage.

This did not make France a consensus society fully responsive to its government's will. Louis XV himself was the target of an assassination attempt in 1758. The *philosophes'* challenge to conventional wisdoms inspired increasing respect even among their targets in the church and the nobility. Shortly before the Seven Years War the antagonism between Jansenists and Jesuits flared anew, abating only with the Jesuits' expulsion in 1762. The *parlements'* self-proclaimed role as guardians of liberty and watchdogs over absolutism led to increasingly bitter conflicts with an administration seeking to sustain and enhance its war-fighting capacities.

From the army's perspective the principal consequences of these domestic tensions were financial. The absolute share of the French budget devoted to military spending remains difficult to establish, but certainly amounted to well over half of a public budget whose statistics were as dubious as its collection processes were haphazard. Even before the Seven Years War, the French government suffered from a chronic shortage of disposable income. Private financiers and international connections alike proved inadequate to meet the state's needs. By 1760 the King himself would send his silver to the mint, and French officials were seeking to float a loan in England at 11.5 per cent![35]

One result of this process was an increasing dependance on the private pockets and the individual connections of the army's officers. Paying soldiers was considered a personal obligation, a matter of honour as well as common sense. When the army's treasury was empty, colonels frequently stepped into the breach. Enlistment bounties were often provided by regimental proprietors. Such generosity, however, expected recompense through a pattern of substantial gifts and grants

---

[35] James C. Riley, *The Seven Years' War and the Old Regime in France: The Economic and Financial Toll* (Princeton, NJ, 1986), covers the general economic impact of the war.

to senior officers, and by a general climate of outright fraud among officers and civilian administrators. The French army, in short, leaked money at every pore.

A random approach to financing encouraged haphazard behaviour in other crucial areas as well. Like Prussia, like all of the major states of Europe, France depended heavily on private businessmen, manufacturers, and contractors to keep its armed forces fed and equipped. The French system faced an overwhelming challenge simply because of the size of the armed forces for which it was expected to provide. From central agencies like that responsible for providing bread to the entire military establishment to individual contractors with the field armies, *ad hoc* combinations of purchase and requisition were used to sustain operations. Forage, a product difficult to provide at a reasonable rate of profit, was the responsibility of a government corporation whose work was supplemented during the growing season by army foraging parties.

The problem was further exacerbated in campaigns beyond French borders. Politically, France could not afford to alienate the lesser German rulers and their Austrian patron by excessive economic demands. Pragmatically, devastating a region along lines made familiar in the Thirty Years War only created problems when later operational necessity dictated moving through the same area. The challenge lay in taking just enough to keep the complex and fragile local economies characterizing mid-century Germany from collapsing. In practice, the peasants, merchants, and officials on the spot usually managed to take the measure of French foragers and requisitioning officers. Any shortfalls were borne, naturally enough, by the rank, file, and horses.

The nature of the contracting system in France also rendered difficult its incorporation into a centralized, state-directed administration. A military establishment still preoccupied with its great deeds under Louis XIV provided no significant impetus for reform. The contractors themselves were a deeply rooted part of the French establishment. Here were no 'new men', no freshly converted Jews or bourgeois outsiders, but third- and fourth-generation families, whose daughters were married into the aristocracy and whose sons held public office – and who knew, more to the point, where France's political bodies were buried. Nor was the relationship entirely one-sided. The government was able to take a long day in compensating men and firms whose fortunes were too closely linked with those of the state to facilitate ending the symbiosis. Much of the payment, moreover, was in government paper that had to be discounted as high as 60 per cent to be freely negotiable. One might, in short, speak of a 'military-supply complex' in terms applicable to the military-industrial complexes of a later century. Both cases were characterized by a set of relationships whose ongoing nature had less and less to do with their original purpose, but a great deal more to do with the survival, if not always the flourishing, of the participants![36]

The French army's command was shaped by the same factors that structured its administration. Lee Kennett accurately describes the officers as 'amateurs'[37] That term, however, is best understood in its eighteenth-century sense, as reflecting a cultivated taste for a certain activity. Officers at all levels everywhere in Europe obtained appointment and advancement less on a basis of objective qualifications, schools attended or subjects studied, than on the basis of character. This in turn was generally ascribed to 'breeding' – what Martin van Creveld aptly calls a combination of genetic descent and social position, to which experience and achievement were usually added as one grew older.[38]

This approach to military leadership was facilitated by the fact that most of the knowledge necessary to conduct war in the eighteenth century was either highly specialized within the system (such as supply and siege-craft), or part of the general body of knowledge, like geography and rhetoric. It represented no dangerous level of obscurantism to argue that such skills were best acquired by experience.

The general run of regimental officers were overwhelmingly drawn from the nobility – specifically the nobility 'of the sword'. Over 90 per cent were *hommes de particule*, with the non-aristocratic minority being heavily concentrated in the artillery, the engineers, and the administrative services. While the higher ranks were dominated by scions of the great families who had made the move from the provinces to Versailles in the preceding century, the company officers were drawn overwhelmingly from the ranks of the provincial

36 Kennett, *The French Armies*, pp. 99 *passim*, is an excellent survey; C–N. Dublanchy, *Une Intendance d'armée au XVIIe siècle. Étude sur les services administratifs à l'armée de Soubise pendant la Guerre de Sept Ans, d'après la correspondance et les papiers inédits de l'intendant François-Marie Gayot* (Paris, 1908), is a complementary case study.

37 Kennett, *The French Armies*, p. 72; cf. Emile G. Léonard, *L'Armée et ses problèmes au XVIIIe siècle* (Paris, 1958), pp. 1 ff.

38 Martin van Creveld, *The Training of Officers: From Military Professionalism to Irrelevance* (New York, 1990), p. 19.

aristocracy. Some were 'hobereaux' with nothing but a sword and a family name. Others belonged to families that had sustained roots in the countryside and preserved traditions of service to the crown. A third group, probably larger at this period than in later years, but no more visible, were the men of non-noble birth who were able by one means or another to obtain a line commission. The outbreak of war offered particular opportunities for a man with money who was willing to spend it recruiting and maintaining a company. Far, however, from asserting a separate status within their regiments, these base-born individuals were likely to assimilate to their social superiors in every way possible – even to assuming social rank to which they had no legal claim. The life styles of the 'ordinary' regiments of infantry were usually simple enough to facilitate this process. Under conditions of active service, moreover, a man of courage in battle who proved a good comrade in camp was unlikely to face too many embarrassing questions about his pedigree.

This did not mean that the army lacked social consciousness. The officer corps as a body consistently resisted any limitation of noble control. But the Ségur Ordinance of 1781, which required prospective candidates for commissions to prove four generations of nobility, was more than an aristocratic reaction to specific events. Instead, it reflected a generation of resistance on the part of the officer corps to admitting the sons of middle-class families with roots in business or law that had recently gained titles of nobility.[39]

It is easy in retrospect to exaggerate the immediate negative effects of restricting bourgeois access to military commissions in *ancien régime* Europe. The relative weakness of nationalism and patriotism as motives for entering military service, particularly compared to later centuries, meant that an officer's career was likely to be chosen without much consideration for the general welfare. The absence of any significant preliminary military education meant that the prospective officer did in fact depend heavily on the informal socializing of childhood and adolescent milieux. Families with traditions

39 Cf. David D. Bien, 'La Réaction aristocratique avant 1789: l'exemple de l'armée', *Annales: Economies, Sociétés, Civilisations*, XXIX (1974), 23–48, 505–34; and 'The Army in the French Enlightenment: Reform, Reaction, and Revolution', *Past and Present*, LXXXV (1979), 69–98; and Bernhard R. Kroener, 'Militärischer Professionalismus und soziale Karriere der französischen Adel in den europäischen Kriegen 1740–1763', in *Europa im Zeitalter Friedrichs des Grossen, Wirtschaft, Gesellschaft, Kriege*, ed. B. Kroener (Munich, 1989), pp. 99–132.

of linen-draping and paper-shuffling were correspondingly unlikely to produce promising young warriors except by accident.

The exclusionist mind-set of the French officer corps was therefore in good part a response to a perception that the young men who might join their ranks unless otherwise kept out were more concerned with the social advantages of a commission than with its military requirements. Compared to Prussia, even to Habsburg Austria, French *bien-pensant* opinion at mid-century was strongly and increasingly anti-military.[40] From Pascal and Molière to Voltaire and Diderot, the intellectuals of the Enlightenment denounced the false values, the artificial glamour, and the evil results of war. To men taking their way of life seriously as a calling, if not yet as a profession, the tendency to close ranks to outsiders of any kind grew increasingly strong. It was one thing to look the other way for a comrade willing to alter a past and a life style for the sake of admission to the club. It was quite another to accept even the risk of being overrun by a generation of youths whose commitment to the idea of soldiering was at least questionable, and whose internalization of its values was likely to be incomplete.

The French army, in short, was led by men who saw their position in terms of a life style and a way of life, and who learned its details by osmosis. The result, to reformers like the Duc de Broglie, was 'total ignorance, from the second lieutenant to the lieutenant general, of the duties of their post and all the details that concern it'.[41] This opinion is generally supported by scholars with nineteenth- and twentieth-century notions of the value of education and the evil of social exclusiveness. In fact the French officer corps as a body was as reasonably competent by the standards of its era as most similar institutions before and since. If bravery was sometimes carried to the point of folly and honour to the point of intransigence, in practice, especially at the operational level, French officers would prove well able to make terms with the changing realities of the Frederician battlefield. Their defeats reflected the quality of their opponent as much as any inherent institutional shortcomings.

The opening rounds of the western campaign seemed to confirm the French army's generally good opinion of itself. On 12 March it

---

40 Kingsley Martin, *French Liberal Thought in the Eighteenth Century*, 2nd edn rev. (London, 1954); and Léonard, *L'Armée et ses problèmes*, pp. 141 *passim*, are good overviews of this subject.

41 Albert, duc de Broglie, *Le Secret du roi (1752–74)*, 2 vols (Paris, 1876), I, p. 342.

began its advance to the Rhine. Not until almost a week later did its principal opponent even have a commander. William Augustus, Duke of Cumberland and third son of the Hanoverian Elector, received the appointment on 17 March. His orders read more like the minutes of a cabinet meeting than an operational document. In essence Cumberland was instructed to protect Hanover, keep his army intact, and defeat the French if possible. He was specifically directed not to prevent the French from marching into Bohemia to reinforce the Austrians – a clause whose publishing would surely have confirmed all existing Continental prejudices regarding 'perfidious Albion'.

Cumberland, though only 36, was an experienced soldier. Best-known for his victory over Charles Stuart at Culloden in 'the Forty-five', he had also seen action at Dettingen and Fontenoy. His name long stood as a symbol of brutality, both for his harshness in pacifying the Highlands after the collapse of the Jacobite rebellion and for his later work in strengthening the punitive clauses of the Mutiny Act. In fact he was well suited for his current post, experienced in leading mixed forces and possessing a significant capacity both to train and to inspire the men under his command. But long odds and ambiguous instructions were the kinds of handicap calling for giftedness, as opposed to mere talent.[42]

Cumberland spent his first days in the theatre of operations trying to decide what to do next, while the French under the Comte d'Estrées pushed forward vigorously into Hanover. Cumberland seems to have hoped that news of the Prussian victories around Prague would inspire negotiations. Instead, the French government ordered d'Estrées to increase his pace. The French main body crossed the Weser River on 16 July. An increasingly alarmed Frederick urged Cumberland to attack. The Duke preferred to stand on the defensive, finally taking up position in the broken ground around the town of Hastenbeck. The French, believing the allies were still retreating, instead stumbled onto their positions at daylight on 25 July. D'Estrées took the rest of the day to concentrate his forces: 50,000 infantry, 16,000 cavalry, sixty-eight guns. Cumberland, with 30,000 infantry, had only 5,000 cavalry and twenty-eight guns – too few, in his opinion, to risk a spoiling attack. Instead he stood in place to have his main positions overrun by a series of dashing French infantry attacks. A successful allied flanking movement lost its significance because of a liaison failure; at 1 p.m. Cumberland gave orders to retreat.

42 For Cumberland's career and capacities, see, most recently, Rex Whitworth, *William Augustus, Duke of Cumberland: A Life* (Hamden, Conn., 1992).

Hastenbeck by itself was not a particular disaster. The French suffered over half again as many casualties as did the allies, 2,300 to 1,400. They also suffered from a change of command when d'Estrées was relieved on 3 August by the Duc de Richelieu – an appointment reflecting the shifting balance of forces at Versailles rather than any particular operational necessity. Cumberland continued his retreat unmolested, to the baffled surprise of his army. By this time, however, politics had begun directly shaping strategy on his side of the battle line as well. England's latest Continental commitment, at best half-hearted, had been badly shaken by news of Frederick's apparent defeat at Kolin. The British minister went so far as to describe Frederick's position as hopeless. In the aftermath of Hastenbeck George II, acting as Elector of Hanover, instructed his son to ask for terms. Instead of obliging, Richelieu pressed forward, driving Cumberland ahead of him. By the end of August the French had taken Hamburg and Bremen, pinning Cumberland's army, now heavily depleted by sickness and desertion, against the North Sea.

Tactically the possibility for a breakout still existed. Operationally and strategically, Cumberland had nowhere to go. Richelieu for his part was primarily concerned with preparing for an invasion of Prussia proper, and willing to let off easily the ragtag force under his guns. On 8 September, Cumberland signed the Convention of Klosterzeven. It provided for the evacuation of Hanover and the disbanding of the Convention army. A week later Richelieu started south-east with the bulk of his forces.[43]

A TIDE STEMMED: THE CAMPAIGN OF ROSSBACH

Frederick had not been exactly idle as his northern strategic front collapsed. Initially, he hoped to draw the Austrians after him into Saxony, obtain reinforcements, and try conclusions in battle. Shortages of food and forage, aggressive Austrian irregulars, and Daun's never failing ability to choose strong defensive positions thwarted the overt intentions of a king perhaps more impressed than he cared to admit publicly by the death-grapples of Prague and Kolin.

Instead, Frederick turned to the council chamber. Specifically, he attempted to choke off the war with France before it had a chance to escalate. In addition to authorizing the offer of a half-million-

---

43 The definitive English-language overview of operations in the western theatre is Reginald Savory, *His Britannic Majesty's Army in Germany during the Seven Years' War* (Oxford, 1966); for this period see pp. 20 ff.

thaler bribe to Madame de Pompadour, Louis XV's current mistress, Frederick sought other back-door entrées to French policy-making circles. He even sent Richelieu a sum of money as a retainer for his good offices in ending the war. All of his efforts proved futile – not least because, as summer turned to autumn, Frederick's fortunes seemed in irreversible decline. British subsidies were uncertain and British aid improbable. French victories in Hanover had inspired an Imperial army that had seemed little more than a token force when it was formed in the spring. To the south, the Austrians were ready to submit another bill for Mollwitz and Chotusitz. To the north, Sweden joined the anti-Prussian coalition in March 1757, and threatened Pomerania with an army of 20,000 men.[44] But the most immediate threat to Prussia was coming from the east.

Russia's mobilization had been episodic, delayed by both diplomatic and administrative factors. The vast distances, by eighteenth-century standards, that lay between the major Russian garrisons and the Prussian frontier exacerbated logistical problems already so clear that pre-war plans assumed the impossibility of maintaining a force of any size in central Europe for longer than a few months. Peculation and corruption were rife at all levels of the supply system. A cumbersome military administration at times seemed to regard civilian contractors as greater enemies than the Prussian army. Keeping paperwork in order was far more important than keeping rats out of the provision wagons. The results, both in the campaign of 1757 and later in the war, were high levels of hunger-related sicknesses that diminished the strength of field armies and debilitated those who kept their ranks. The Russian soldier's physical endurance was already proverbial in the eighteenth century. However, as mentioned earlier in this text, the Russian could not live and fight indefinitely on a few handfuls of flour. One reason for establishing East Prussia as an initial objective was its obvious utility as a forward base.

Despite initial problems of mobilization and concentration, by the end of May 1757 almost 100,000 men were marching towards East Prussia. The province, completely isolated geographically from Brandenburg proper, seemed to be on a serving dish for the invaders. But Elizabeth's troops had no significant experience against a modern western enemy. Their principal commander, Field-Marshal Stepan

44 Klaus-Richard Böhme, 'Schwedens Teilnahme am Siebenjährigen Krieg: Innen- und aussenpolitische Voraussetzungen und Rückwirkungen', in *Europa im Zeitalter Friedrichs des Grossen*, pp. 193–212.

Apraksin, was a court general more impressive in physical appearance than as a strategist or a tactician. The supply system broke down almost completely as the troops lost contact with their magazines in the Baltic provinces. The absence of roads slowed rates of march to a crawl as regiments advanced along forest trails. An unusually hot summer generated insects and humidity in equal measure. Thirsty men ignored water discipline to drink from polluted ponds and streams. Sickness took a correspondingly heavy toll: a fifth of the main army was out of action by the time the Russians reached the Prussian frontier in August.[45]

In the final stages of his advance, however, Apraksin was joined by several detachments that made up most of his losses from disease and straggling. The total strength of his force remained somewhere between 55,000 and 60,000 men. Given his desperate supply situation, Apraksin decided on 23 August to march on the East Prussian capital and major Baltic port of Königsberg. The city's occupation would offer both a political triumph and an opportunity to bring in forage and reinforcements along sea lanes the Russians dominated in the absence of a Prussian naval challenge.

The possible behaviour of East Prussia's defenders, around 30,000 men under the veteran Field-Marshal Hans von Lehwaldt, seems to have influenced Apraksin's thinking only marginally. The Russians moved in a solid block, with no more than a tactical vanguard screening their advance. The large number of Cossacks with the army devoted more attention to plundering than reconnaissance. The well-stocked barns and rich grain fields of East Prussia increasingly tempted foragers, authorized and otherwise, from the best-disciplined of the line regiments. The opportunities for a surprise attack were correspondingly attractive. The Prussian capacity to execute was, however, limited.

Lehwaldt was another one of Frederick's *Haudegen*. He had established a record as a competent subordinate in the Silesian Wars, and as a capable peacetime administrator in his isolated province. He had, however, no experience in independent command, and his infantry included a large number of garrison battalions in whose ranks stood high percentages of the unwilling and the incapable. His cavalry, on the other hand, included some of Prussia's best regiments:

---

45 John L.M. Keep, 'Die Russische Armee im Siebenjährigen Krieg', in *Europa im Zeitalter Friedrichs des Grossen*, pp. 147 ff.; Christopher Duffy, *Russia's Military Way to the West: Origins and Nature of Russian Military Power, 1700–1800* (London, 1981), pp. 73 ff.

East Prussian farmers' sons mounted on well-bred horses. The 6th, 7th, and 8th Dragoons in particular were actually fighting for their homes, and could be expected to give their best. Lehwaldt, moreover, had absorbed enough of his monarch's way of war to regard as folly allowing the Russians to set the terms of battle as they had determined the conditions of the campaign. Early on the morning of 30 August, near the village of Gross-Jägersdorf, he sent his men forward against twice their number.

The Russians were taken completely by surprise, their marching columns collapsing into disorder as officers sought to deploy into battle formation. But Lehwaldt lacked the manpower to break through his enemy's front, and did not possess enough tactical skill to compensate for numerical weakness – particularly against a Russian artillery which on this day began establishing its reputation as the army's backbone. By afternoon it was over, with the Prussians in retreat. Eighteen hundred of their 4,600 casualties were listed as killed in action: grim tokens of the close-quarter fighting that marked the battle's climax. The Russians, however, had lost half again as many men, and Apraksin was sufficiently stunned by the day's experience to order a retreat. His subsequent recall in disgrace was not enough to put new life into the Russian campaign. Frederick's eastern provinces received a welcome respite as their enemy re-evaluated military options by doing nothing in particular.[46]

Apraksin's withdrawal highlighted a major, albeit unexpected, weakness of Kaunitz's coalition. The power the Grand Alliance was potentially able to exert was disproportionate to the perceived threat posed by its enemy. Prussia at its most extreme was generally regarded even in Viennese political circles as a current disturber of Europe's order, not its potential destroyer. Breaking Frederick's power was less a concern in Paris, in St Petersburg, and in the lesser German capitals than benefiting directly from the conflict – or at worst, not emerging as a loser.

That fact was unexpectedly highlighted in the war's western theatre. With the destruction of the Convention army, the burden of continuing the struggle in that sector fell to Prince Ferdinand of Brunswick. Frederick had sent him west in September with six battalions and fourteen squadrons – little more than a token force. Nevertheless, Ferdinand continued to harass the advancing French until, on 3 October, Richelieu proposed an armistice until the next

---

46 Duffy, *Russia's Military Way to the West*, pp. 76 ff., is a detailed account of the fighting.

spring. From a Prussian perspective the decision fell from the heavens. Richelieu's offer reflected less the strategic situation than the logistic one. French administration seemed on the point of collapse. As supplies failed to arrive, the troops turned to self-help in a rich countryside. Discipline suffered proportionally. An energetic commander might have bettered the situation, if only by regularizing the process of living off the land. Richelieu, a notorious womanizer, personally corrupt and fond of the good life, ultimately stole enough from Hanover that he was able to build a palace in Paris with the proceeds. It was scarcely surprising that he preferred to take his men out of the war altogether.

Frederick had spent the late summer testing a broad spectrum of what modern popular psychologists call 'coping mechanisms'. At times he wrote poetry. At times he discussed suicide. At times he proposed to fight to the finish in a hopeless situation. To a degree, his private expressions of despair functioned as a safety valve. Neither the generals nor the diplomats who encountered the King in the daytime had anything but praise – at least in public – for the equanimity with which he confronted his situation.[47] But what exactly could be done to turn the fortunes of war? If Daun and the Archduke seemed too dangerous a foe, Frederick perceived an alternate possibility as early as August.

Since its reorganizing after the Thirty Years War, the Holy Roman Empire had been divided into districts or 'circles'. Each was composed of the sovereign states within its boundaries; each was required to supply specific financial support and military forces in case of war or its threat. Moreover, the contingents of the middle-sized states like Saxony, Electoral Hesse, and Bavaria usually served separately under their own governments or as subsidy forces directly contracted to larger powers or alliances.

Under Austrian auspices, the 'circles' of the Holy Roman Empire were summoned earlier in the year to raise an 'Execution army' to carry out the Imperial sanctions against Frederick. In the aftermath of Kolin as many as 30,000 men had initially concentrated on the upper Rhine. This polyglot and improvised force, under command of the Austrian Prince Joseph von Sachsen-Hildburghausen, offered a promising target of opportunity. Leaving 40,000 men under Bevern, with the still-recovering Winterfeldt as his adviser and orders to keep the main Austrian army in check, Frederick headed west in early

47 Private opinions could be significantly different. See Doran, *Andrew Mitchell and Prussian Diplomatic Relations*, pp. 149, 199–200, for Mitchell's perspective.

September with the remaining 25,000. Initially he hoped to join Cumberland's force, preventing a junction between the main French army in Hanover and the Imperials further south, particularly since the latter were in the process of being reinforced by a further 24,000 men under Marshal Charles de Soubise.

In the first two weeks of September the Prussians marched 170 miles – an unheard-of achievement by eighteenth-century standards. The King had picked the best of his regiments for his task force. Desertion and straggling alike were limited. Morale seemed enhanced by good late-summer weather and the still comfortably remote prospects of a fight. Then on 17 September Frederick learned of Klosterzeven. With Cumberland's army destroyed, a pitched battle seemed the only alternative to disaster. But instead of obliging the King's wish for combat, Soubise and Hildburghausen stayed out of reach. A series of tactical retreats did nothing to draw them on.

Bad news kept coming. Winterfeldt, the keenest mind in Frederick's military entourage, was mortally wounded in a meaningless outpost fight in early October. On the 10th of the same month, Austrian raiders entered a Berlin Frederick had been forced to leave virtually ungarrisoned in order to keep his field forces up to strength. The minor physical and financial costs of an occupation measured in hours were less significant than its clear demonstration of Prussia's current vulnerability, and its corresponding status as still by far the least of the great powers. The notion of Paris or Vienna being similarly harassed by Prussian strike forces was inconceivable no matter how many battles the French or Austrian armies might lose.

Frederick's treasury was empty, his magazines exhausted. He had 90,000 men under arms – three-fourths of the strength with which he had begun the war. The King declared miracles to be necessary. In fact Prussia needed only one 'miracle': a victory in the open field against a major enemy. This would buy time, at least until the next campaigning season: time for Frederick's enemies to fall out among themselves; time for the King to convince Europe of Prussia's continued vitality. And not least, time for him to restore his perspective. Frederick's initial reaction to the Berlin fiasco, a forced march to cut off the Austrians and save his capital, was motivated more by pique than reason. By 20 October it was clear that the operation had been no more than a raid. The perpetrators, moreover, were safely out of range of any effective pursuit. Frederick had outdone the Good Old Duke of York in the nursery rhyme, marching his men first west, then north-east, and sacrificing the better part of a month by the time he turned west again.

On 24 October, at Torgau, the King finally received a piece of good news. Soubise and Hildburghausen were moving forward – in Frederick's mind at least, with Berlin as their probable ultimate objective. By calling in detachments from as far away as Berlin and Magdeburg, he was able to concentrate thirty-one battalions and forty-five squadrons at Leipzig by 28 October. Three days later the Prussians were at the Saale River, primed for a fight.

Their enemies were not so certain. Soubise was ambitious enough for glory and distinction. He owed his appointment, however, to his position at court – specifically, to his intimate, though non-horizontal, relationship with Madame de Pompadour. His troops tended as well to be a cut below the French army's best, most of whom were with Richelieu further north. Nor was Soubise, any more than Richlieu, the man to enforce rigid administrative control and military discipline. If the descriptions of 'lackeys, cooks, friseurs, courtesans . . . and actors . . . dressing gowns, hair nets, sun shades, nightgowns and parrots' have been exaggerated to contrast Prussian virtue with French decadence, Soubise's army did have as many as 12,000 civilian camp followers accompanying its fighting men, who numbered 30,000 after reinforcements joined them from Richlieu.[48]

Perhaps a more serious weakness than this undisciplined *Gefolge-schaft* was the lack of any combat above the level of skirmishing and outpost fights. Soubise's army badly needed tempering. What it had experienced so far in the campaign was more inclined to rot the battalions and squadrons than to season them. Nothing can be more deceiving than the illusion of veteran status – as the French were to learn within a month.

Hildburghausen's German troops were a different story. The Execution army's performance in 1757 has been so universally excoriated that it seems at times as though the army was created with the positive intention of being defeated. In its 'classic' form the *Reichsarmee* developed in the south and west of Germany, where the proliferation of sovereignty since the late Middle Ages had produced an interlocking structure of civil and ecclesiastical authorities patently unable on their own accounts to do more than provide internal security. Most of the small states maintained some combination of rulers' bodyguards, often neither trained nor intended for field service, and a skeletonized battalion and a cavalry squadron or two with a theoretical obligation of Imperial service.

48 The quotation is from J.W. Archenholtz, *Geschichte des Siebenjährigen Krieges in Deutschland*, 5th edn, 2 vols (Berlin, 1840), vol. I, p. 108.

The *Defensionalordnung* of 1681 provided for a force of 12,000 cavalry and 28,000 infantry to be raised and financed by the ten districts of western and southern Germany. In theory, the troops of each district were to form a distinct body, with the command and administrative offices carefully allocated along confessional lines. In practice, the process of levying and organizing these forces was determined by a basic common denominator of confusion. In the Swabian District, for example, no fewer than ninety-three separate sovereign bodies were responsible for raising 4,000 men. In one company the captain was furnished by one town, the first lieutenant by a monastery, the second lieutenant by another town, the quartermaster by a fourth community. This situation was by no means untypical. No general principles for recruitment existed. Every technique, from offering generous bounties to kidnapping unwary travelling journeymen, was used to keep the ranks more or less full. Most of the small states and city-states retained at least theoretical liabilities for service by the peasantry, sometimes by their urban subjects as well. This was normally an undertaking of last resort. Both traditional concepts of paternalism and modern cameralist economic doctrine shrank from deliberately removing productive, settled members of society. Whenever possible, the actual recruiting process was left in the hands of local authorities, who in turn took care to select their conscripts from the community's outsiders – whenever possible, with the lure of bonuses that in any case seldom reached the sums available from the larger states.

In 'home towns' dominated by inward-looking burghers and craftsmen, the local armed forces were seen as employers of last resort for idlers, good-for-nothings, and petty criminals incapable of leading a productive life. Reality could be different: an increasing number of local case studies highlight the number of 'respectable' enlistees unable to find either steady work or a place in the increasingly restrictive guilds. Probably more significant for the nature of the rank and file was the relative absence in the dwarf-state armies of wider motives for volunteering. A young man seeking adventure and advancement was more likely to try his fortune in French, or even Prussian, service than wait to grow old on a soldier's pay in Würzburg or Lübeck. There is some evidence, indeed, that these small forces performed some of the functions later to be assumed by rest camps and soldiers' homes. An individual, that is to say, might desert the Prussian service and spend some months or years in the relative comfort of a circle garrison, then desert again and sign on in France when he felt the urge to do 'real soldiering' once more. Men unfit for the rigours of the campaigning season were similarly likely to find places in small-town contingents willing to overlook even serious physical problems.

Given the nature of the rank and file, the Imperial contingents' efficiency was likely to depend heavily on their officers. Here again, what traditions of military service existed were most likely to be expressed by service in the Habsburg army, which depended heavily on Imperial nobles for its officer corps until well into the nineteenth century. The men who remained in local service were more likely to see their commissions as a form of municipal honour than as a professional obligation. Locked into the routines of garrison service, those retaining any ambition were more likely to seek outlets in the politics of their communities, or by participating in the social, theological, and intellectual controversies of the time.[49]

The final problem afflicting the Imperial army, significant even in an era of improvised organization, involved the total absence of staff systems above the battalion level. Units had no experience in working together, no common drill – not even common words of command. This was not an entirely insurmountable problem. The key to overcoming the weaknesses of the 'circle contingents' was a simple one: time. During the wars of Louis XIV, particularly the War of the Spanish Succession, Imperial troops had performed well as part of larger entities once they learned their trade. In 1757, however, they were being sent against the best fighting army in Europe with less than six months' experience in working together, with supply and administrative services even weaker and more disorganized than those of France, and with no money to support an organized requisition service.[50]

To a significant degree, therefore, Hildburghausen was constrained to keep his army on the move or risk seeing it disintegrate before his eyes into its minuscule component parts. When Soubise refused to cross the Saale, Hildburghausen marched to his ally's camp at Mücheln. Together the allies counted about 34,000 infantry, 7,500 cavalry, and 114 guns. Eleven thousand of these were German, the rest French. Despite the discrepancy between their

49 Roger A. Wines, 'The Imperial Circles: Princely Diplomacy and Imperial Reform 1681–1714', *Journal of Modern History*, XXXIX (1967), 1–29; and Helmut Neuhaus, 'Das Problem der militärischen Exekutive im Spätphase des Alten Reiches', in *Staatsverfassung und Kriegsverfassung in der Europäischen Geschichte der frühen Neuzeit*, ed. J. Kunisch and B. Stollberg-Ringer (Berlin, 1986), pp. 297–346.
50 Karl Brodrück, *Quellenstücke und Studien über den Feldzug der Reichsarmee von 1757* (Leipzig, 1858), remains a useful source for this operation.

forces, Hildburghausen was able to convince Soubise to advance and offer battle. The confident Austrian hoped for an all-out, war-ending fight. The Frenchman advocated a pawn move that could be retracted should Frederick prove uncooperative. On the late morning of 5 November the allies began their advance in three large, ill-coordinated columns.

Frederick for his part had crossed the Saale by 3 November, with 22,000 men and 80 guns. Initially he considered attacking. Then, impressed by the allies' position and by intelligence reports putting their combined strength at 60,000, he decided to give his adversaries the first move. He was eating lunch when a junior officer reported that the Franco-Germans were advancing. Hildburghausen and Soubise planned to march almost directly across Frederick's front to threaten or envelop, depending on one's perspective, the Prussian left flank. They paid little attention to Frederick's possible response in preparing their plan. During the march the regimental officers found quite enough to do in keeping their units in some kind of order and moving towards something resembling the destination given in their orders. No one, in short, was looking beyond his own ranks – always a dangerous proposition against the Prussians!

Once Frederick developed a sense of his enemies' movements, he determined to take advantage of the march capacities of his own men. He ordered the bulk of his army to move first north-east under the cover of a low ridge, then to swing south and west. If the allies deployed into line in the meantime, Frederick intended to reprise the Battle of Prague and roll them up from the right. Should the enemy columns still be on the march, the Prussians would perform a land equivalent of a familiar naval manoeuvre and 'cross their T'.

The key tactical element in either contingency was the cavalry. Frederick had only thirty-eight squadrons, and he placed them all at the head of his line of march. Their commander was a 'new man', one of the few middle-ranking officers to emerge with negotiable credit from the summer's campaign. Friedrich Wilhelm von Seydlitz was 36 – by later standards, an advanced age for a front-line leader of horsemen, but by the Prussian army's standards a mere youth. He had spent over twenty years cultivating his skills in the saddle and indulging his appetite for liquor and women. The latter propensity, and the accompanying venereal infections, had permanently damaged Seydlitz's health while giving him a prodigious reputation among at least the army's junior officers. In addition to his qualities as a rider, Seydlitz was known for his good humour and his willingness to recognize the good work of subordinates – the latter quality of particular significance given the Prussian cavalry's new emphasis on dash and initiative.

Prussia's senior ranks, however, were becoming increasingly strait-laced, and Seydlitz's life style was too reminiscent of an earlier freebooting era to be overlooked – particularly in the context of his propensity for speaking his mind more freely than his rank would support. Despite his experience as hussar, dragoon, and then cuirassier, he was still a colonel in 1756. But his regiment, the 8th Cuirassiers, was one of the best-trained in the service, both in riding and in horsemastership. Its performance at Kolin was one of the few bright spots of that dismal day, and brought Seydlitz to the notice of his king.[51]

Frederick's revamped drill methods had exponentially improved the Prussian cavalry's efficiency. His revised doctrines had provided a solid structure for the army's employment in battle. What remained was to develop a corps of field officers, colonels and brigadiers, able to use the refurbished instrument effectively. Initially Frederick seems to have relied too much on the power of ideas to overcome the effects of age and inertia. Too many regimental commanders were men in their fifties – stout-hearted, reasonably physically fit still, but lacking the dash and *coup d'œil* necessary to employ cavalry effectively as an arm of opportunity. Seydlitz appeared a sufficiently promising exception to be promoted major-general in the aftermath of Kolin, and lieutenant-general a few months later. When Frederick turned against his western enemies he took Seydlitz with him. Now, in the early afternoon of 5 November, Seydlitz had his first, golden opportunity to distinguish himself as a general instead of a battle captain.

Seydlitz lost no time taking charge. Two officers, his seniors in age and rank, politely questioned his new position only to be told, 'Gentlemen, I obey the King and you will obey me.'[52] Around 2.30 p.m. his troopers were on the move, followed by the infantry screened by a few squadrons of hussars and covered by a battery of eighteen heavy guns deployed on the ridge between the opposing armies.

The allied generals were by now aware of the Prussian move; their pickets had seen Frederick's tents struck with a speed and precision unusual in their own ranks. To the French and Austrians

---

51 Seydlitz would well repay a good modern biography. K.A. Varnhagen von Ense, *Leben des Generals Freiherrn von Seydlitz* (Berlin, 1834), remains the best account, presenting its protagonist as he was: chancres and all.

52 Grosser Generalstab, *Der Siebenjährige Kriege, 1756–1763*, vol. V, p. 211.

only one set of circumstances could generate such urgent behaviour. Frederick, conscious of his numerical inferiority, had decided to retreat! Instead of tightening up their formations the allies stretched out in pursuit, with the cavalry of the vanguard pushing forward well ahead of their supporting infantry.

At 3.15 the process of disillusion began when the Prussian heavy guns opened fire. They did some damage, but not enough to halt the advance. Instead, the allied horsemen quickened their forward pace, accepting some disorganization as a fair price for getting out of the artillery's killing zone. Seydlitz had made the opposite decision, deploying into two lines at the first sound of the guns and correspondingly reducing the speed of his advance. The Prussian troopers halted in two lines just behind the ridge that screened their army's advance, and waited. Around 3.30 the allies came within striking distance – about 1,000 paces from the crest of the ridge. Seydlitz ordered the charge.

It spoke volumes for the courage and discipline of the Habsburg cavalry that the two Austrian cuirassier regiments leading the advance were not only able to deploy despite being surprised, but checked the twenty squadrons of Seydlitz's first wave in a combat that dissolved within minutes into a series of furious man-on-man sword duels. Not until Seydlitz ordered forward the eighteen squadrons of his second line did the Austrians, flanked on both sides, give ground. In their retreat they collided with three Imperial regiments that had advanced to support the Austrians, but now broke and scattered. This mass in turn disrupted two dozen French squadrons hastening to join the fray. Attempted countercharges at squadron and regiment level generated neither momentum nor direction. Confusion turned to disaster as the 'furball' of French and German troopers crashed into a sunken road linking two small villages. Those allies who did not surrender drifted south and out of the battle.

Under similar conditions Prussian cavalry had previously tended either to massage its victory laurels or pursue its immediate victims and thereby take itself out of the rest of the fight. Seydlitz instead sounded 'recall', formed his ranks, and led his reorganized force toward the flank and rear of an allied army which in the meantime found itself with all the fighting it ever expected. Frederick's infantry, twenty-four battalions, had marched as rapidly as the King could drive it forwards, initially with the intention of supporting Seydlitz by cutting across the allies' line of advance. Once hearing of Seydlitz's victory Frederick changed his mind. Four battalions continued the original movement. The remaining twenty turned hard left, crossed the ridge in echelon, and swung into battle formation. Instead of the familiar two straight lines of battalions, Frederick used his second line to extend the left flank of the first, forming an obtuse angle. This was done at a certain risk, since the final Prussian formation provided for no significant reserves to plug gaps or cope with surprise tactical threats. Frederick, however, was confident in the quality of his infantry, the ability of Seydlitz to provide timely support – and not least in the capacity of his enemies to make the right kinds of mistakes.

The latter confidence at least was not misplaced. The infantry closest to the Prussian formation were French, confronted first with the rout of their cavalry and then with the unexpected appearance of an enemy line of battle. The decade prior to the Seven Years War had witnessed a heated debate between advocates of linear tactics in more or less traditional form, and a new generation of reformers who favoured the deployment of infantry in columns employed primarily as a shock weapon. Extreme advocates of the latter practice, like the Chevalier de Folard, argued that columns were actually better able to deliver effective fire than linear formations which in practice were impossible to control once battle was joined. Pragmatists suggested that columns were a sensible response to the character of the French infantry. Frenchmen, so the argument ran, could never be disciplined like Prussians or Englishmen, so as to hold their places in a firing line no matter what happened. On the other hand, the French 'genius' expressed itself in the kind of fire-and-movement tactics best employed in a headlong assault by columns.

By the outbreak of war in 1756 extremists on both sides had exhausted themselves. In a way reminiscent on a smaller scale of the events of the Huguenot Wars, an increasing number of military *politiques* advocated combining the systems, seeking the best qualities of shock and fire by alternating columns and lines, one supporting the other. The concept, or at least the principle, made sense to certain colonels.

The latter point was important. Despite the presence, and the increasing influence, of comprehensive manuals of drill regulation, training in the French army still remained essentially a regimental affair – a process enhanced by the lack of permanent tactical units above the regiment, and by the absence of the kind of centralized control provided by Frederick. Confronted with a Prussian line of battle, French officers on the spot rejected immediately the notion of attempting to form their own line in the face of Europe's best infantry. The regiments of Piedmont and Mailly instead formed their eight battalions into columns with fifty-man fronts. Bayonets fixed, they advanced.[53]

Frederick's guns started with solid shot, then switched to canister against the kind of target seldom offered on a European battlefield. As the range closed, the French pushed deeper into the angle created by the Prussian deployment. From the front, then from the left flank, Prussian volleys shredded the enemy advance. The French columns halted, wavered, broke. The fugitives collided with their own supports, confusing efforts to deploy into line and check the Prussian advance with musketry. As the French got in one another's way Frederick's infantry advanced firing, the crashing of its disciplined volleys only increasing the allies' sense of impending débâcle.

Then Seydlitz sent in the cavalry. The weight of his charge struck Imperial troops already demoralized by their allies' discomfiture. The common evaluation of these men as favouring the Prussian cause for reasons of religion or politics was hardly necessary to explain their failure to stand before the long swords and the black horses riding down on them.[54] Three regiments of Franconian *Kreistruppen* threw away their muskets and ran. The French broke along with them, and Seydlitz's troopers sabred the fugitives until early darkness put an end to the pursuit. Over 5,000 French and Germans were killed or wounded. Another 5,000, including eleven generals, were captured that day or surrendered later. Seventy-two guns, twenty-one standards and three sets of kettledrums were among the victory's material tokens. Official Prussian casualties were listed as 169 dead, 379 wounded.

This kind of ten-to-one discrepancy in losses was so unusual in an eighteenth-century battle that it gave Rossbach automatic immediate standing as one of Frederick's greatest victories. It restored a military reputation that the year's events in Bohemia had significantly tarnished. It also showed the Prussian army had by no means lost its cutting edge. Victors and vanquished saw the same reasons for the allied defeat. French and Austrian contemporaries agreed with the Prussians in denouncing the French as poorly trained and worse

53 Brent Nosworthy, *The Anatomy of Victory: Battle Tactics 1689–1763* (New York, 1990), pp. 199 ff., 261 ff. and 329 ff., offers a sound modern overview of French tactics at mid-century.

54 See, for example, Franz Rudolph Mollinger's letter of 11 July 1757 to Georg Wilhelm of Hesse-Darmstadt in Brodrück, *Quellenstücke und Studien*, pp. 78–9.

disciplined, while dismissing the Imperial contingents as no better than a rabble.[55]

Closer analysis of the French performance in particular suggests that a traditional problem of eighteenth-century armies – inadequate tactical reconnaissance – combined with a major and correctable doctrinal shortcoming to produce a disaster as opposed to a defeat. The French infantry formed in columns against a line of battle, then attacked without benefit of skirmishers. The result prefigured experiences from Flanders to Spain in the Revolutionary/Napoleonic Wars. By themselves, unsupported by light troops and artillery, columns had very little chance to overrun a well-disciplined firing line. Unlike their successors in a later era, moreover, the French had no moral mystique to underwrite their tactical *élan*. Frederick's battalions, among the best in his army, were no more intimidated by the French than were Wellington's veterans at Talavera or Vimiero. The French infantry broke when it could stand no more killing; Seydlitz's cavalry was optimally placed to turn retreat into rout.

Politically Rossbach had far-reaching consequences. News of the battle produced throughout Germany a certain *Schadenfreude* at the French catastrophe. Nineteenth-century scholars were prone to emphasize the nationalistic elements of this process, or the triumph of 'Protestant' Prussia over its presumably decadent Catholic rivals. It seems more accurate to stress the pleasure generated by seeing the French having to swallow their own boasting. Rossbach was a sweet revenge for French behaviour in the Rhineland and Palatinate during the reign of Louis XIV. It did not, however, generate a significant bandwagon effect in Frederick's favour among the lesser German states.

Rossbach was also significant for Prussia's relations with England. In the aftermath of Hastenbeck George II had requested that Ferdinand of Brunswick be appointed commander of the Hanoverian army. This was in good part a consequence of the English Parliament's continued reluctance to support a major Continental commitment – a position justified by its advocates in terms of Frederick's failure to provide larger forces for Hanover's defence. Frederick for his part was equally dissatisfied with a British connection that so far had proven disappointingly ephemeral. On the other hand, the accession to power of the Pitt-Newcastle ministry in June 1757

---

55 Dieter Postier, 'Die Schlacht bei Rossbach am 5. November 1757', *Militärgeschichte*, XIX (1980), 685–96, is a brief modern account from an East German perspective.

seemed to promise better times. William Pitt, long one of the sharpest critics of Hanover as a strategic liability, was able to see the specific advantages of tying down French resources in Germany, both directly by sending a new expeditionary force to the north German theatre and indirectly by providing financial assistance to Prussia. From Frederick's viewpoint the circumstances merited at least a pawn move. In the aftermath of Rossbach he urged Ferdinand to accept King George's offer. Despite misgivings, the Prince consented.

In England Ferdinand's appointment combined with the news of Rossbach to modify significantly both public and parliamentary opinion on the value of the Prussian connection. Frederick of Prussia became enough of a folk hero to lend his name to taverns. Lobbyists and propagandists stressed the triumph of Protestant, northern virtues over Latin, Catholic decadence. Not since the early days of William of Orange had a Continental ally been so popular. Both Frederick and Pitt saw the circumstances for a closer relationship between their war efforts as correspondingly promising.[56]

A CORNER TURNED: THE LEUTHEN CAMPAIGN

Negotiations rapidly took second place to fighting. 'The Battle of Rossbach', Frederick later declared, 'merely set me free to seek new dangers in Silesia.'[57] In the King's absence an Austrian army under Prince Charles of Lorraine, with Field-Marshal Leopold Daun as his *fidus Achates*, had overrun in a matter of weeks much of the province of Silesia whose seizure in 1740 had cost Frederick almost twenty years of war, cold and hot. The Duke of Bevern, left to hold in Frederick's absence, had been outfought and outgeneralled at every turn. A man enlightened enough to hire professors to lecture on mathematics to his junior officers and engage foreign enlisted men to teach their native languages, Bevern was out of his depth in independent command against heavy odds. The Austrians took full advantage of superior numbers to hold him in check while overrunning Silesia's fortresses.

These works must not be compared to their massive counterparts in the Low Countries or France. They were simpler, cheaper works, designed more as bases and *points d'appui* than as independent strong points, depending on a supporting field army for their long-term

---

56 Karl W. Schweizer, *Frederick the Great, William Pitt, and Lord Bute: The Anglo-Prussian Alliance, 1756–1763* (New York, 1991), pp. 60–1.

57 Frederick II, *Œuvres de Frédéric le Grand*, ed. J.D.E. Preuss, 30 vols (Berlin, 1846–56), vol. IV, p. 156.

survival.[58] On 13 November Schwednitz surrendered after a three-week siege. On 22 November, more than 80,000 Austrians attacked Bevern's 28,000 men in front of the fortified city of Breslau. The hard-hammered Prussians retreated across the Oder, leaving what amounted to a token garrison of ten battalions in the city. Charles and Daun were more than satisfied with their achievements. Not only had they overrun a good half of the province lost to Prussia in 1740; they had done so in winter – an unusual campaigning season despite unusually mild weather. The Habsburgs looked increasingly like winners, especially to the good citizens of Breslau. Loyalty to the King of Prussia was well enough when that side of the bread was buttered. It did not extend to standing siege and risking bombardment. The fortress commander came under increasing pressure to evacuate the city. Deserters found it significantly easier to disappear among the Breslau's civilian population than was usual under Prussian rule – a circumstance enhanced by Bevern's understandable decision to leave his least reliable troops behind as expendable. On 25 November Breslau surrendered on terms allowing the garrison free evacuation. In fact, only about 600 officers and men rejoined Frederick's army. The rest sold or discarded their equipment and scattered in all directions across the province.

Bevern's field force was in little better shape. Its commander was captured while making a personal reconnaissance – or perhaps looking for a bullet. Frederick had so often ordered the Duke to hold the province or risk his neck that captivity might have been a welcome relief from the all-too-predictable royal wrath. Discipline in the ranks eroded as hungry men looted villages and set fires while officers looked the other way. With disaster looming, Frederick wasted no time turning his attention eastwards. His army began its march on 13 November: eighteen battalions and twenty-three squadrons of cavalry, all that could be spared even after a victory like Rossbach. Ziethen was sent forward to take over Bevern's demoralized regiments. Frederick expected no miracles from the veteran hussar, but Ziethen was popular enough and respected enough to keep Bevern's army in being until the first team arrived. When the two forces joined on 2 December, the King was in command of about 38,000 men. One-third were the heroes of Rossbach. The rest, overmarched, underfed, and badly beaten, would need a deal of work before counting as dependable.

---

58 Duffy, *The Fortress in the Age of Vauban*, pp. 134 *passim*, is the best overview of Frederician Prussia's fortifications.

Frederick had originally intended to use Bevern's army and the Silesian fortresses to hold Charles and Daun in check and set the stage for a major battle under the King's personal command. The Prussians would then pursue the presumably defeated enemy into Bohemia, depths of winter or not. Circumstances had vitiated the grander aspects of this design. Frederick nevertheless was determined to strike the Austrians before they had time to consolidate their Silesian victories. Militarily, he could not afford to begin a new campaigning season with a major enemy army so close to his capital. Politically, the laurels of Rossbach were unlikely to survive a winter of stalemate on what Frederick insisted was Prussian territory. Economically, Silesia's material and human resources were too vital a part of Prussia's war economy to be abandoned, even temporarily.

The King's decision was correspondingly predetermined. The key to its successful implementation involved motivating his army to fight one more time – and win. Frederick's behaviour in the first days of December laid much of the foundation for the subsequent mythology of 'Old Fritz'. Nineteenth-century historians and their successors describe a sick, exhausted monarch moving from bivouac to bivouac, warming himself at the men's fires, listening to their stories and complaints, promising promotion and reward for courage in the field. To the senior officers of Bevern's misfortunate command, who expected at the least massive reproaches, the King instead offered fellowship and preferment. Future performances, Frederick implied, would cleanse past records.

Nor did Frederick rely entirely on his personal resources. Camp discipline was sufficiently relaxed to allow the veterans of Rossbach to tell their stories of victory and plunder to the rest of the army. Extra rations and extra liquor were distributed as far as stocks allowed. The process represented less an emotional appeal to the Prussian warrior spirit than a more or less calculated exercise in reverse psychology. Frederick's normal approach was harsh and demanding. To the officers and men of Bevern's army in particular, their failures in the King's absence had created a sense of anticipatory dread best expressed in the traditional family threat of 'Wait till your father comes home'. Instead the King's unexpected and unconventional behaviour inspired old soldiers and recruits, cynics and idealists, to promise mutual loyalty and support in the hard days to come.

On 3 December Frederick capped his performance by inviting the army's generals and its regimental and battalion commanders to his headquarters. This was in itself unusual. The sense of strangeness compounded itself when Frederick appeared. Instead of a battle captain radiating confidence, the Prussian officers saw their king in a uniform even more worn and snuff-stained than usual. Instead of a master craftsman ready to ply his trade, they saw a tired, ageing man whose voice was too low-pitched to be audible beyond the range of his immediate audience.

The army was marching, Frederick declared, to attack the Austrians at Breslau. The only alternatives were victory or death.

We are fighting for our glory, for our honour, and for our wives and children. The threefold Austrian numerical superiority, the strong Austrian positions, must yield to the bravery of the troops and the execution of my orders. Those who stand with me can rest assured I will look after their families if they are killed. Anyone wishing to retire can go now, but will have no further claim on my benevolence.

As a coda, lest anyone think the King had gone soft, he announced that any cavalry regiment failing in its duty would be dismounted and used as a garrison force. An infantry battalion that flinched faced the loss of its swords and colours, plus the public disgrace of having the ornamental braid cut from its uniforms.

Like all great performances, Frederick's blended sincerity and artifice in a way impossible for anyone to separate. Sir Laurence Olivier could not have recited Henry V's Agincourt speech more convincingly, and the King's words lost nothing in their telling. His 'Parchwitz speech' became the eighteenth-century equivalent of an important contemporary sporting event: even people who were not there could remember every detail of what they saw and heard.[59]

Frederick was conscious enough of what he hoped to achieve by his words that he gave his army a day to simmer before breaking camp on 4 December and marching towards Breslau. That evening the Prussians benefited from what Frederick, at least, regarded as good news. The Austrians had left their positions in front of the city and accepted Frederick's challenge by advancing towards the village of Leuthen. Their decision has often been condemned. Terrain in

---

59 The speech quoted here is taken from that recorded by Prince Ferdinand of Prussia and cited in O. Herrmann, 'Prinz Ferdinand von Preussen über den Feldzug im Jahre 1757', *Forschungen zur brandenburgisch-preussischen Geschichte*, XXXI (1918), 101–2. Duffy, *Frederick the Great*, p. 147, calls this the most authentic account. It certainly lacks the fustian of most other versions.

that area offered no obvious favourable defensive positions. Frederick and his generals, moreover, knew the region well from peacetime manoeuvres.

Charles and Daun, however, had good practical reasons for their decision to seek a battle. Charles was not a distinguished captain by any stretch of the imagination. Neither was he a stereotypical royal nonentity who owed his rank to his position as the Empress of Austria's brother-in-law. He was a seasoned field soldier who had been fighting the Prussians since 1741, and had learned something of his craft by osmosis if in no other way. Daun for his part was a master of the feints and manoeuvres characteristic of eighteenth-century warfare. The winter's events in Silesia reinforced the experience of Kolin: the Prussian army was far from being unbeatable in either siege or battle, even with its king's presence. The Austrian commanders, in short, seemed to agree with Frederick's view of the situation. In their minds, as well, one decisive battle would end the war – only with Prussia's permanent discomfiture rather than Austria's.

A significant factor influencing the Austrians' decision was that Charles and Daun had more chips to bet. Frederick anticipated a fight on equal terms. He had 39,000 men and 170 guns; he believed the Austrian force in front of him was no larger. He faced, in fact, an enemy 66,000 strong, with 210 pieces of artillery, on ground chosen by its commanders.

The Austrians' tactical situation was less favourable than their numerical advantage suggested. Surprised by Frederick's rapid advance, Charles ordered bivouac in battle formation along a $4\frac{1}{2}$ mile front from the hamlets of Nippern in the north to Sagschütz in the south. December's early sunset combined with an overworked road system to keep much of the army awake and unfed until well into the night. It was an ill preparation for the next day. Nor was morale enhanced among the regimental officers when they saw their lines of battle forming on the open, rolling ground around Leuthen. Their troops had performed best against the Prussians with some terrain advantage. What Daun and Charles seemed to have in mind for this day was an eye-to-eye death-grapple, with the Austrians' principal edge being their superior numbers.

The Prussian reveille sounded at 4 a.m. Between 5 and 6 the army was on the march: two columns of infantry in the middle, cavalry on each flank, and a strong advance guard. Frederick himself led the way with a task force of light troops: three irregular battalions, a handful of riflemen, and a half-dozen regiments of hussars. The day dawned clear but cold. When a veteran trooper complained of the temperature

Frederick advised him to have a bit of patience: things would get hot soon enough.

The King's one-line jest was hardly necessary. As they marched, some of the regiments sang Lutheran hymns – behaviour contemporaries and romantics praised as a sign of piety; behaviour also probably facilitated by a general desire to keep from focusing too closely on the coming hours. First contact between the armies came near the village of Borne, where the Prussian vanguard encountered a mixed bag of Saxon light cavalry and Austrian hussars. One quick charge scattered the enemy and Frederick took over 200 prisoners. Frederick ordered the captives paraded past his own men, then rode forward to a small hill. He found himself facing the centre of an Austrian line that, deployed as it was in the open, at first sight appeared even more formidable than its numbers warranted. Two minor terrain features, however, combined to offer Frederick an opportunity. The Austrian left wing was in the air, ending well short of a network of ponds and marshes that offered a potential geographic anchor. In the same sector a series of low hills offered at least some cover for a right wheel across the Austrians' front and a quick turn against the enemy's exposed flank.

The King intended a manoeuvre that was a conventional tactician's nightmare. The flank he proposed to attack was open only in a technical sense. It did not end with a single musketeer or trooper; the Austrians had reinforced it with improvised barricades and battery positions. Reaching the area successfully also involved drawing and fixing the attention of the Austrian commanders away from the threatened sector. This meant dividing an already inferior Prussian force so precisely that the enemy would be deceived as to the decisive point of the attack, while at the same time making the attacking element strong enough to break in and break through instead of hanging itself up against Austrian reserves.

Frederick began his tactical sleight-of-hand by deploying the cavalry of his left wing, eventually supported by infantry, as though he intended to strike the Austrian right. The Prussians took their own time developing the feint. By 11 a.m. the movement was still incomplete. Its effect on the Austrians was nevertheless hypnotic. Previously they had been confident in their ability to finish off the 'Berlin Security Detachment' – a comptemptuous reference to the Prussians' low strength.[60] Now they saw an absurdly small number of their enemies' cavalry preparing for what seemed a suicide attack.

60 Archenholz, *Geschichte des Siebenjährigen Krieges*, vol. I, p. 135.

The commander on the spot called for reinforcements. Charles and Daun not only despatched most of their reserves to the apparently threatened sector; they took position there themselves. Frederick just might have one more trump in his hand; better safe than sorry.

Meanwhile their quarry had turned the bulk of his army south and formed it into two lines of march. Even the detailed Prussian official history fails to clarify the complex pattern of halts and advances, stops, starts, and sidesteps involved in this process. General histories pass over it in corresponding haste. That the manoeuvre succeeded at all, much less in the remarkably short span of one to two hours, is perhaps a greater tribute to the Prussian army's quality than its later performance under fire. Europe's armies at mid-eighteenth century were replete with brave men, well-disciplined men, and officers ready to lead them into the heaviest fire. No army, other than the Prussian, was likely to execute this kind of complicated shuffling in the face of an enemy without tying itself in hopeless knots. Apart from anything else the effect of adrenalin and anxiety on individual judgments was likely to generate enough of what Clausewitz would later call 'friction' to render such a movement an unthinkable risk.

Frederick's men pulled it off – with help from an obliging enemy. Even as the Prussian rightward movement became apparent, Charles took no action. In earlier battles the Austrians had been understandably reluctant to abandon strong positions, natural or artificial, to risk a tactical counterattack against the formidable Prussians. Here nothing stopped them but high-level inertia reinforced by misapplied experience. As the Prussian attack on the left failed to develop, Charles seems to have been pleased at the prospect of bluffing Frederick off the field. 'Our friends are leaving,' he observed *sotto voce* as the Prussians began swinging right. 'Let them go in peace.'

Geography reinforced the Austrian commander's wishful thinking. The high ground Frederick put between himself and the Austrians was not impressive in metres, but the terrain itself was deceptively rolling. The *exact* Prussian line of march remained concealed from the *exact* standpoint of the Austrian commanders – a fact checked after the war in an effort to determine the specific reasons for Charles's inactivity. A horseman carrying a flag along Frederick's route could not be seen from the hill Charles and Daun occupied, even by men looking for him.[61]

Frederick was able to prepare his hammer blow correspondingly undisturbed. Shortly after noon the leading Prussian troops had

61 Duffy, *Army of Maria Theresa*, p. 186.

moved far enough past the Austrian flank for the King to order them to swing to the left. Ziethen, with fifty-three squadrons supported by a half-dozen battalions, deployed on Frederick's right rear. His was to be the exploitation force. The initial breakthrough would be made by three infantry battalions, two of the 26th Infantry and one of the 13th. Their right flank was covered by a four-battalion column: three of grenadiers and one of musketeers from the 18th Infantry plus a battery of *Brummer*, heavy twelve-pounders brought up from the fortress of Glogau. The rest of the main body's infantry deployed in a staggered line by battalions, extending west at intervals of fifty paces.

Frederick made his immediate intentions clear in a brief speech to his first assault wave:

Boys, you see the whitecoats there. You've got to drive them out of the redoubt. All you've got to do is go for them with the bayonet and run them out. I'll support you with five grenadier battalions and the whole army. It's win or die! In front of you you have the enemy and behind you you have the whole army, so you can't find room forward or back except as victors.[62]

The King had not exactly left the composition of this force to chance. The 26th Infantry was one of the army's best. Recruited from Pomerania, its ranks included a large number of Slavic Wends speaking their own dialect and possessing the kind of strong in-group loyalties that, properly utilized, can produce a formidable fighting unit. The 13th was a Berlin outfit, known for its rigid discipline as the 'Thunder and lightning' Regiment, with an NCO corps that was the terror of clumsy and unwilling privates and amateurs and a combat record that had time and again affirmed the worth of hard peacetime training. As for the supports, the royal grenadiers were case-hardened veterans who saw their normal place as at the head of any forlorn hope while the 18th was a crack Brandenburg formation, no more than a cut below its comrades of the 13th and the 26th.

Frederick had learned from his previous experiences that speed was vitally important on a modern battlefield. Getting inside an enemy's loop of initiative was a valuable step towards victory. Haste,

---

62 As recorded by a colour-bearer of the 26th Infantry. C.F. Barsewisch, *Meine Kriegs-Erlebnisse während des Siebenjährigen Krieges 1757–1763*, ed. J. Olmes (Krefeld, 1959), p. 36.

however, often made waste as well. Whatever the Austrians might have been in the Silesian Wars of the 1740s, Prague had indicated and Kolin had proved they could no longer simply be turned out of their positions by a series of limited attacks. This time the Prussian army would hit its enemy with the controlled power of a karate strike, everything focused behind the three battalions that began their advance on the Austrian positions around 1 p.m.

The Austrians in the threatened sector had neither been entirely idle nor remained entirely ignorant. The commander, General Franz Nadasdy, was a veteran hussar who had faced the Prussians too many times to trust entirely in either Fortuna's or Bellona's good will. As the Prussians crossed his front Nadasdy sent repeated requests for support to Charles and Daun. They remained unacknowledged – everyone knew that Hungarians tended to start at ghosts and shadows!

Nadasdy had also been assigned most of the army's *Reichstruppen*. These formations, recruited like their counterparts at Rossbach from the dwarf states of the Holy Roman Empire and middle-sized Austrian allies like Württemberg, were widely and legitimately regarded as unreliable even with a season's victorious campaigning under their belt. Nadasdy's decision to deploy them on the far left of his position was defensible enough as long as the Prussian attack was expected to come from the front and strike further north. The army's weakest links would be correspondingly posted where they were likely to do the least damage. Given Frederick's actual axis of advance the Germans were at exactly the wrong spot, for Nadasty and for the whole Austrian army.

Once they recovered from their initial shock the Imperial colonels on the spot did the best with what they had, refusing their flank and deploying their commands to take advantage of a shallow ditch facing the Prussian line of attack. Most of the men in the first line were Württembergers, Protestants whose willingness to fight the Prussians had been widely questioned in the Austrian camp. They nevertheless held out for a few minutes, blazing away with the valour of limited experience until they saw the Prussian lines continue to push forward through the smoke. *Then* the Württembergers ran, carrying with them the Bavarians of Nadasdy's second line.

Prussian infantry, effectively supported by an artillery spared from any counterbattery fire, drove steadily towards the village of Leuthen as the leading elements of Frederick's main body came into action behind the first wave. These men were under command of Prince Moritz of Dessau, and a colour-bearer of the 26th heard him shout: 'Boys, you've won honour enough! Fall back to the second line.' The answer, at least the one recorded for posterity, was, 'We'd have to be yellow-bellies to fall back now! Cartridges! Cartridges!'[63] Such heroic rhetoric is always suspect. It is, however, a matter of record that the 26th Infantry's officers won no fewer than fourteen *Pour le Mérites* that day, and that Frederick himself donated 1,500 thalers from his own pocket for distribution among the rank and file. 'Your Majesty can trust his crown and sceptre to that regiment', Moritz later remarked, 'When they run from the enemy I don't plan to stay around either!'[64]

The 26th's call for ammunition highlighted another modification of Frederick's pre-war tactics. In the first battles of the Seven Years War, at Prague and Kolin, the Prussian infantry had advanced without firing. The resulting heavy casualties had convinced most of the regimental officers that keeping muskets at the shoulder involved sacrificing one of the Prussian infantry's great material advantages, its fire discipline, in an effort to break enemy morale. At Leuthen the 26th went into battle with the regulation sixty rounds per man. By the time they passed the Austrian first line many of the men had exhausted their supply. But Frederick too had learned from experience. On the day of Leuthen he had ammunition wagons brought up from the artillery park and posted directly behind the advancing infantry. When the 26th despatched an officer in search of replenishment he found the source close at hand. Cartridge boxes filled once more, the 26th closed on Prince Moritz's advance. First the grenadiers' column, then three more infantry battalions, reinforced the drive northward.

Nadasdy had not been idle as his infantry collapsed. Instead of reinforcing defeat by trying to restore the forward line directly with fresh battalions, the old hussar tried to change the battle's dynamic by sending his cavalry against the Prussian musketeers. This was Ziethen's moment – and he almost botched it. His horsemen initially had trouble deploying among the ditches and small woods in their assigned sector. Instead of striking one concentrated blow, the Prussian regiments attacked the Austrians by ones and twos. Ziethen had to commit all fifty-three of his squadrons before the see-saw mounted mêlée was resolved in Prussia's favour. Fortune turned Ziethen's way, however, when the victorious Prussian troopers turned on the retreating German infantry instead of pursuing their mounted foes. Running fugitives offered a more inviting target, especially to

63 Barsewich, *Meine Kriegs-Erlebnisse während*, p. 41.
64 *Ibid.*, p. 38.

the 2nd Hussars, Ziethen's own regiment, which had a major hand in the rounding-up of over 2,000 Württembergers and Bavarians.

With his left flank disintegrating Charles of Lorraine finally realized the real direction of the Prussian *Schwerpunkt*. His projected solution came from the textbook of common sense. While the Prussians dealt with the remnants of Nadasdy's force, Charles proposed to form a new line at right angles to his original main position, one flank resting on the village of Leuthen and the other protected by cavalry from the reserve. The Prince began by redeploying a few infantry battalions from his second line. Then he dispatched his reserves. Finally and belatedly convinced that nothing significant was likely to happen in the northern sector of his original position, Charles ordered his whole army to execute a left turn and meet Frederick's attack face to face.

The proposed Austrian position by now extended on both sides of Leuthen – itself not a bad idea, given the solid construction of the village's buildings and the general tendency for built-up areas to act as magnets for even the best-disciplined attacking troops. Perhaps the Prussians could be enmeshed in a delaying house-to-house fight, buying time to complete the redeployment Charles had ordered. Quick reaction, however, was not one of the Austrian army's strong points. Neither was traffic control. Battalions arrived from everywhere on the field, without specific orders, their men often breathless and sweated from forced marching on a cold day. Too often, instead of shaking out into firing lines the Austrians remained massed together in the killing zone of the heavy Prussian guns now positioned on the high ground overlooking Leuthen.

What was remarkable about this situation was the Austrians' holding their ground when the final Prussian advance began around 3.30 p.m. By this time Leuthen was full of stragglers and fugitives, but the men remaining in ranks fought it out to the muzzle. Let it be said too that a German regiment, supplied by the Franconian Bishopric of Würzburg, held Leuthen's churchyard against Frederick's Guard, and inflicted heavy casualties on that elite regiment and the 10th Infantry before giving way to superior numbers and to the guns brought up to knock down the walls.

As the Prussian advance finally cleared Leuthen, the Austrians mounted a massive cavalry attack. Seventy fresh squadrons were driving on the open Prussian left flank when Lieutenant-General Wilhelm von Driesen earned his footnote in history by launching a counterattack with the forty squadrons of Prussian cavalry which had followed the main army earlier in the day and taken position at right angles to the infantry's left flank instead of forming directly in line with the musketeers. This gave Driesen a tactical advantage that compensated for his inferior numbers. He charged as the Austrians rode across his front.

First to get stuck in were the Bayreuth Dragoons, who found the Austrians altogether tougher to chew than they had been on the regiment's great day at Hohenfriedberg in 1745. The Prussian cavalry's second line took its time engaging – according to one account, because of regimental jealousy. The cuirassiers, who regarded themselves as the elite of the mounted arm, allegedly sat back to appreciate the discomfiture of their social inferiors![65] Once they charged, however, the heavy Prussian horsemen drove the Austrians not back along their original line of advance but eastward, into their own infantry still fighting around Leuthen.

That was enough. The whitecoats panicked and fled by battalions. The few units that stood their ground were mown down by the advancing Prussian infantry. Prussian troopers, again taking advantage of easy prey, sabred the fugitives until night put an end to the slaughter. Frederick, in another departure from custom, attempted to organize a pursuit. He was able to collect no more than a small task force of grenadiers and cavalry which by 7 p.m. reached the bridge across the Wistritz River at Lissa. With snow falling heavily, the King contented himself with ironically begging shelter for the night from a number of wounded Austrian officers who had taken shelter in the local castle: 'Good evening gentlemen; certainly you weren't expecting me here.'[66]

As individual Prussian regiments rallied and reorganized, they followed their king. At first they marched in silence, each man busy with his own thoughts and emotions. Then someone struck up a hymn: 'Now thank we all our God.' The tune and the words were known to everyone, Lutheran or Evangelical, Catholic or unbeliever, in the ranks of Frederick's army. Man after man took up the words of what has ever since been known in Germany as the 'Leuthen Chorale'. For the pious it was an affirmation of God's power over the King's enemies. For the sceptics it was as good a way as any of proving one was still alive.

---

65 According to the memoirs of F.A. von Kalkreuth, a junior officer at the time. Dictated in 1818, their reliability has been called into question. Cf. A. Janson, *Hans Karl von Winterfeldt des Grossen Königs Generalstabchef* (Berlin, 1913), p. 209; and Duffy, *Frederick the Great*, p. 152.

66 Jany, *Preussische Armee*, vol. II, p. 458.

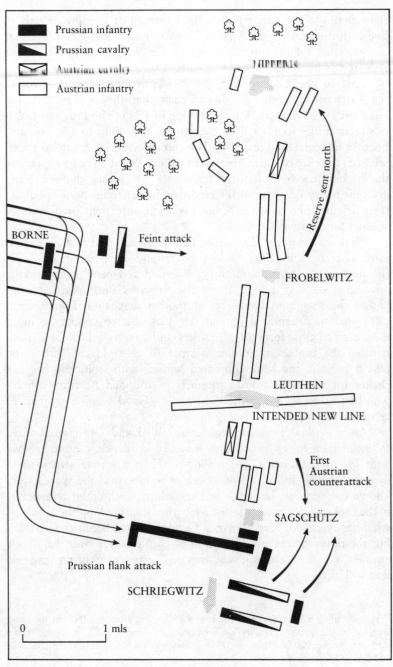

3. Battle of Leuthen, 5 December 1757

Both positions had their justification. The Austrians had come to fight and exacted a high price for their defeat. More than 6,000 Prussians were dead or wounded – a fifth of the men Frederick had taken into battle, and a useful benchmark of the fact that few victories in the Age of Reason were cheaply purchased. The victory, however, was substantial. Fifty-five flags and standards, 130 guns, and more than 12,000 prisoners were among the major physical trophies. Three thousand Austrians were dead and another 7,000 wounded, almost all the latter in Prussian hands. Whole regiments had disappeared from Charles's order of battle, either scattered in the first attack or overrun in the final grapple. A senior Austrian officer reported Charles and Daun 'sunk in the depths of despondency', with the Prince still unable to believe what had happened and Daun attempting to detach himself emotionally and professionally from the disaster.[67] As a footnote to catastrophe, the retreating Austrians abandoned the garrison of Breslau – no fewer than 17,000 men, whose commander surrendered on 20 December.

In addition to its operational virtuosity, Leuthen demonstrated eighteenth-century linear tactics at their best. The Prussian infantry combined fire and movement in textbook fashion; nowhere did the advance bog down in short- or medium-range exchanges of musketry. The cavalry protected the flanks, delivered two tactically significant charges at critical moments, and finally turned the Austrian defeat into a rout. The artillery not only kept pace with the army's movements, no small feat in an eighteenth-century context, but also deployed its guns to take maximum advantage of the ground. The heavy twelve-pounders in particular wreaked havoc on the Austrians bunched around Leuthen, and their distinctive sound did much to heighten Prussian morale at critical moments.

It is also important to note the ways in which Frederick benefited from an obliging enemy. Not only did the Austrian commanders indulge in wishful thinking regarding the thrust of the Prussian attack. They failed as well to use their strong and efficient light cavalry to test realities. Even Frederick remarked that even a single patrol in the right place would have uncovered the truth almost immediately. Arguably even more surprising than this omission at higher levels was Nadasdy's failure to place outposts on his open flank. A light cavalryman with his experience in independent command against the Prussians should have at least considered the possibility of attack from an unexpected direction and taken appropriate precautions.

67 Duffy, *Army of Maria Theresa*, p. 187.

The decisions of Charles and Nadasty to place their least reliable troops in what they regarded as the least threatened sector is more defensible than their condemning themselves to fight a battle while blindfolded. Once Frederick engaged his pile-driver, the south Germans were no more to be blamed for what followed than were the officers and men of the Union XI Corps at Chancellorsville, when struck on their exposed flank. As for the rest of the débâcle, the failure to hold Leuthen and the defeat of the final cavalry attack merely serve to illustrate the truth of the aphorism that, in war, luck is usually a by-product of design.

Leuthen, while the greatest of Frederick's victories, was in no way a crowning mercy. The Austrian army was badly hammered, but still remained an effective fighting force. Ziethen and his hussars were unable to do more than harry the retreating enemy across the Bohemian frontier. To the normal difficulties accompanying operational pursuit under eighteenth-century conditions was added a lethargy similar to that affecting the Union army after Gettysburg. Like that battle, Leuthen had been a moral statement as well as a military victory. Like the Army of the Potomac, the Prussian army had given all it had. Not until the adrenalin had worn off were either the generals or the rank and file likely to be alert in seizing new opportunities. Even Frederick's body reacted to a year's stress: the King was laid low with 'colic' in the aftermath of Leuthen.

Although Leuthen failed to convince Maria Theresa to make peace, the battle was nevertheless decisive in two ways. It kept Prussia in the war. Defeat, or even a draw, might well have compelled Frederick to seek terms while he still retained some negotiating power rather than risk another campaign at a strategic disadvantage. More importantly, Leuthen encouraged Frederick to continue his original grand-strategic design of seeking political victory on the battlefield. For the rest of the Seven Years War, as long as a Prussian army remained in the field under his command, Frederick accepted no military or diplomatic setback as final. In his mind the chance always remained of another, even greater Leuthen: a battle that would turn the tide definitively in Prussia's favour.

5 YEARS OF BALANCE: 1758–59

Rossbach and Leuthen had bought Frederick time. They had not decided the war. Maria Theresa dismissed Charles, replacing him with Daun, and began the slow process of rebuilding an army whose strength at one point sank below 25,000 owing to disease and desertion. Kaunitz in particular remained committed to the war's continued prosecution, insisting that all Austria needed to do was sustain its Grand Alliance and wait for the coalition's superior resources to take effect. In France Foreign Minister Cardinal de Bernis favoured ending a war for which he was never particularly enthusiastic, but his voice was lost in a process of court intrigues that replaced Richelieu with Marshal Louis de Clermont in the field and put the still hawkish Marshal Belle Isle in the war ministry. Elizabeth of Russia, far from considering peace, gave her defeated army a new commander, Count William Fermor, and prepared for a winter campaign against an East Prussia by now almost defenceless.

THE ROAD TO ZORNDORF

Frederick's single ray of hope came from across the North Sea, where Pitt was increasingly ready to negotiate a treaty of alliance, albeit on British terms. Britain and Prussia might have little positive in common. Pitt might have established much of his pre-war parliamentary reputation denouncing the Hanoverian connection in favour of concentration on sea power and colonies. He was, however, shrewd enough to realize that neither the country nor the ministry could contemplate a repeat of Cumberland's disastrous campaign with equanimity. Though the treaty was not concluded until April 1758, Pitt convincingly reassured Frederick that he could count on his British connection – to the ultimate extent of £670,000 sterling annually as long as the Subsidy Convention lasted. At that, Pitt secured a bargain compared with the £1.2 million Parliament voted for the Army of Observation in Hanover.[1]

With continued war a virtual certainty, Frederick considered his options for the next campaigning season. In Prussia's western sector the King benefited from the unexpectedly effective performance of Ferdinand of Brunswick. The Prince had spent the winter reorganizing and reinforcing his army. Frederick sent him fifteen squadrons of regular cavalry. Britain supplied equipment and money. Regularly paid, well-fed, and drilled enough to avert the curse of idleness, Ferdinand's battalions recovered their confidence and assimilated their recruits. After an early phase of shadow-boxing that drew long-distance ire from Potsdam, Ferdinand led his multi-state army in a well-executed winter campaign of manoeuvre that forced the baffled French across the Rhine in six weeks at a cost of not more than 200 battle casualties.[2] With British intervention now assured, Ferdinand seemed in an excellent position to maintain north Germany against a badly demoralized enemy for the coming year. Frederick's attention turned to his other major enemies.

There was no doubt in the King's mind that the greatest immediate threat came from the east. In January, Fermor had led more than 70,000 men back across the East Prussian border. Within six days his forward units had reached Königsberg; the rest of the province was overrun shortly afterwards. The subsequent Russian occupation, mild and humane, succeeded in winning East Prussian hearts and minds far too well for Frederick's comfort.[3] Voices in Paris and Vienna were also raised to protest against trial balloons from St Petersburg suggesting that East Prussia was a legitimate prize of war. Austria hoped to use the Russian colossus for its own ends; establishing Russia as a major central European power was merely to replace one threat with another. As for France, maintenance of a Baltic balance of power had been a significant criterion of its foreign policy since the days of Richelieu. In order to bring Sweden into the

---

1 Karl W. Schweitzer, *Frederick the Great, William Pitt, and Lord Bute: The Anglo-Prussian Alliance, 1756–1763* (New York, 1991), pp. 78 ff.; Patrick F. Doran, *Andrew Mitchell and Prussian Diplomatic Relations during the Seven Years' War* (New York, 1986), pp. 161 ff.; Jeremy Black, *Pitt the Elder* (Cambridge, 1992) *passim*.

2 To this figure must be added around 6,000 sick – a typical cost of winter operations under mid-eighteenth-century conditions. Reginald Savory, *His Britannic Majesty's Army in Germany during the Seven Years' War* (Oxford, 1966), pp. 66–7.

3 Otto von Beren, 'Der Zorn Friedrichs des Grossen über Ostpreussen', *Altpreussische Monatsschrift*, XXII (1885), 145–217.

war, France had concluded a treaty providing for territorial gains in Pomerania and East Prussia – the exact regions coveted by Russia. The French foreign ministry was also concerned that Russia might use the war against Frederick as an excuse to move in force against Poland, with corresponding threats to French influence.[4] Russia, in short, was trading short-term prospects for long-term risks. Should Frederick teach the Muscovites their manners, the reactions of Paris and Vienna were likely to be sighs of relief rather than cries of anguish.

Frederick correspondingly made his initial plans with both eyes on Vienna. He believed that Austria was just on the edge of making peace. Leuthen by itself might not have been quite convincing, but one more victorious campaign should do the trick. The King's design was to mop up the remaining Austrian garrisons in Silesia, then invade the province of Moravia and invest the fortress of Olmütz. Should Daun move to its relief, Frederick proposed to destroy his army in battle, then advance on Vienna. If Maria Theresa were still unwilling to conclude peace at that point, Frederick reasoned, Austria would be too busy repairing damage to provide more than token support to Russian operations whose expected ponderousness presumably offered the Prussians enough time to minimize the direct effect of another campaigning season on the state's still occupied eastern provinces.

Frederick was betting his strategic hand with empty pockets. His peacetime war chest was virtually exhausted. Further scouring of Saxony's already strained economy and systematic forced loans in old Prussian territory together produced results insufficient to finance another campaign. Surplus resources were limited, particularly in terms of the limited range of compulsions available in practice to an eighteenth-century administration. In general, the lands under Frederick's direct control were approaching the stage when the economy was almost as overstressed as the armed forces.[5] The British subsidy enabled Frederick to take the field, but also placed him at significant risk of becoming the client of a state whose lack of vital interests in common with Prussia had been made pitilessly clear by the alliance negotiations themselves.

4 L.J. Oliva, *Misalliance: A Study of French Policy in Russia during the Seven Years' War* (New York, 1964), pp. 73 ff., 95 ff.

5 Lutz Beuten, 'Die Wirkungen des Siebenjährigen Krieges auf die Volkswirtschaft in Preussen', *Vierteljahresschrift für Sozial und Wirtschaftsgeschichte*, XXVI (1933), 209–43.

Once again Frederick was constrained to lead from strength –
in other words, to use his army to escape financial and diplomatic
constraints. But the Prussian army of 1758 was by no means the force
that had crossed the Saxon border two years earlier. Casualties and
disease had taken heavy tolls of the best regiments, whose exhausted
men were correspondingly easy prey for even minor campaign illnesses like diarrhoea. The canton depots had been almost emptied of
trained men in the summer and autumn of 1757. Drastic changes in
the conscription system would threaten a social system already shaken
by economic pressures. Instead, Frederick sought replacements outside Prussia. Prisoners of war were coerced to change sides. Those
who remained intransigent were exchanged – a process that brought
more than 12,000 veterans back under Prussian colours. Saxony,
Pomerania, Mecklenburg and western Germany were scoured for
recruits. By late spring Frederick's ranks included between 160,000
and 170,000 men. At least 50,000 of these, however, were counted
as garrison and regional security forces rather than field troops.[6]

An increasing number of the field army's battalions were *ad hoc*,
irregular organizations, the 'free battalions'. Prussia initially counted
four of these units in its order of battle. Raised by foreign officers in
the autumn of 1756 from a pool of adventurers and hard cases, they
were effective enough when suitably employed, though no more than
marginally useful for the kind of pitched battles Frederick sought to
fight. The half-dozen or so raised in late 1757 and early 1758 were,
however, another story, especially in terms of their poorly qualified
officers. They were as much a problem to Frederick's generals as
Frederick's enemies, and their unreliability and indiscipline were
harbingers of a steady decline in the Prussian army's cutting edge.[7]

Willy-nilly, Frederick crossed the Austrian frontier on 29 April.
On 3 May he blockaded Olmütz, but his siege train did not begin
arriving until 20 May. Not until 31 May were the battery positions
ready to open fire, and then Olmütz proved an unexpectedly tough
nut to crack. The fortress had been recently modernized and was well
garrisoned, without the large civilian populations that had influenced
the sieges of Prague and Breslau. Daun, moreover, refused to play
the role assigned him in Frederick's plans. Instead of immediately

6 Curt Jany, *Geschichte der Preussische Armee*, 2nd edn rev., 4 vols (Osnabrück,
1967), vol. II, pp. 472 *passim*.

7 K. Schmidt, *Die Tätigkeit des preussischen Freibataillone in den beiden ersten
Feldzügen des Siebenjährigen Krieges (1757–8)* (Leipzig, 1911).

marching to Olmütz's relief, he continued to build up his army in the fortified camp of Skalitz, well out of Frederick's reach. His light troops constantly harassed the Prussian positions, a process culminating on 30 June when a vital convoy of over 3,000 wagons coming from Silesia was ambushed and almost destroyed. Two days later Frederick cut his losses and raised the siege. It was better, he said, to make an unpleasant decision than to decide nothing or to wait until the situation became untenable. Though it took a month, the Prussian army regained its own territory without further significant losses. Frederick had, however, suffered a strategic defeat by playing his enemy's game. The Olmütz campaign was a routine eighteenth-century operation, whose very ordinariness highlighted the limitations of Frederick's tactical and operational innovations. The King could neither conclude a siege nor force a battle without the cooperation of his adversary – which on this occasion was not forthcoming.[8]

Nor had the virtuosity of Frederick's withdrawal been anything more than a temporary distraction from events in the east. The Russian advance, initially at least, was conducted in the style Frederick expected and hoped: ponderous columns accompanied by swarms of Cossacks and other irregulars more concerned with plunder than reconnaissance. In mid-August the army halted before the small fortress of Küstrin on the Oder River and began a half-hearted siege. Fermor was unwilling to push further on his own, given what he regarded as the continued passivity of Russia's Swedish and Austrian allies. On the other hand he did nothing strategically or operationally to prepare for Frederick's arrival in the theatre.

The Prussian situation ranged from serious to desperate, depending on the day and one's perspective. In September a Swedish army of 17,000 invaded Prussian Pomerania, then halted in place. This relative lack of enterprise was a welcome relief for Prussian generals and administrators constrained to rely heavily on recruits and locally raised militia for much of their order of battle in the province. In the aftermath of Gross-Jägersdorf, Frederick's commanders in the east were able to do little more than keep their forces in being, even in the face of Russian depredations that generated increasing civilian protests. The largest of these, twenty battalions, thirty-six squadrons and eighty-two guns, Lehwaldt's old army, had been placed under the

---

8 Heinrich Köhler, 'Friedrichs mährische Feldzug 1758', PhD dissertation, Marburg, 1916.

command of General von Dohna in March and reinforced by nine battalions, two solid regiments of cuirassiers, and thirty-six guns. But for all Frederick's good advice from a long distance about the best way to defeat the Russians, Dohna took no chances with his still outnumbered force. He contented himself with a watching brief through the high summer.

Once again Frederick was the catalyst. On 10 August, he started 15,000 picked men and forty guns from Silesia for the Oder. The Prussians moved by forced march – 15 miles a day. On 21 August they reached the river. Two days later they crossed it in the face of inconsequential Russian opposition. Fermor in turn abandoned the siege of Küstrin and marched north-east to the village of Zorndorf. The terrain, a mixture of low hills and marshy bottom lands, offered solid opportunities for neutralizing the Prussian army's skill in tactical manoeuvre. Fermor, however, instead of deploying on the heights, merely left his wagons leaguered there. He advanced the bulk of his force into a hollow surrounded by swamps and commanded by higher ground to the east and south.

Fermor's original force of 34,000 men was reinforced by a further 9,000 just before the battle, giving him about 6,000 more men than Frederick could command even after his task force was joined by Dohna's provincial garrison. No one on either side expected the Russians to do much more than fight where they were placed – but exactly *where* were they placed? The terrain was heavily wooded. Frederick's hussars were intimidated by the Cossacks. The King's intelligence was correspondingly vague. He proposed to mount a flank attack against the less obvious Russian flank: the one farthest from the Prussian line of advance. To find that flank, the King planned to march his army across the entire Russian position – albeit at a greater distance than he had employed at Kolin and Leuthen. The overwhelming Prussian superiority in heavy cavalry – 10,500 troopers against 3,300 – would guarantee the security of the march even should the Russians show some unexpected initiative. The chances of a successful countermove seemed so limited that Frederick slept well the night before the battle.

Some of the King's apparent peace of mind may have reflected his sense of an ace in the hole. Like everything else in Prussia the woods were regulated, and Frederick had been able to obtain two local foresters as guides. One would accompany the cavalry at the head of the advance, keeping Seydlitz's troopers from losing their way in the underbrush. The other would guide Frederick and his main army around the Russian left flank. Small wonder that the

King slept soundly and on leaving his quarters in the early hours of 25 August, informed his entourage the battle was already won.[9]

The advance began at 3 a.m. By daylight the vanguard was through the woods and well into open country south of Zorndorf. The Prussians' first sight of their enemy was not the Russian army proper, but its supply wagons, isolated on high ground to the south-east. Then and now Frederick's critics have questioned his failure to divert enough troops to seize the lightly defended baggage train and thereby put Fermor in the position of having to attack, surrender, or starve.[10] The idea does not seem to have crossed the King's mind. He was committed to fighting the Russians, not playing tag with them. Perhaps he remembered what had happened at Olmütz; certainly he had no intention of resigning the tactical initiative to a second foe. The Russian wagons would still be there after the victory Frederick expected to win.

Initially the Russians were taken by surprise – not least because the smoke from Zorndorf village, fired by Cossack looters, blew back across their main camp. The Prussian columns passed the hamlet of Batzlov, then swung sharply right towards Walkersdorf. Given the expected Russian inactivity, this move would have brought the Prussians directly opposite the right flank of a Russian army facing eastward and set the stage for a second Leuthen. Paradoxically, however, the Russians' initial slow reactions worked to their advantage. Since Frederick had not planned to replicate his December triumph, a key aspect of the Leuthen manoeuvre was omitted: a feint credible enough to convince the enemy to look in the wrong direction. Instead, Fermor kept his army in place long enough to calculate the Prussians' probable route of advance closely enough to decide that the main attack would come from the south. He deployed accordingly – and with significant attention to Prussian tactical doctrine and practice. The Russians' flanks were reinforced. Their reserve forces were strong enough that some Prussian observers thought they faced a square instead of a line. The Russian dispositions did have a major drawback: the ground to the rear varied from soft to swampy. Any kind of orderly retreat would be correspondingly difficult. Fermor, however, expected that all retreating would be done by the Prussians.

Frederick made his final inspection of the Russian positions with

9 Heinrich de Catt, *Unterhaltungen mit Friedrich dem Grossen*, ed. R. Koser (Leipzig, 1884), p. 158; C.G. Kalisch, *Erinnerungen an die Schlacht bei Zorndorf* (Berlin, 1828), p. 50.

10 Christopher Duffy, *Frederick the Great: A Military Life* (London, 1985), pp. 164–5.

a certain perturbation. All of his army's well-executed operational manoeuvring had done nothing more than create the preliminaries for another frontal attack. His new intention was to use the oblique order tested at Leuthen against the Russian right, which stood somewhat at an angle to the rest of the army and where marshy ground would help screen the left flank of the Prussian attack.

The honour of striking the first blow was given to Manteuffel – a significant hint that Frederick's earlier criticism of the general's performance at Kolin was self-serving. Six of his eight battalions were grenadiers, the best assault troops in the Prussian army. There are two ways of handling an elite force. One involves holding it as a reserve, to complete a victory or screen a defeat in the pattern of Napoleon's Guard. The other depends on using one's best troops first, to confound or demoralize an enemy in the pattern of the Panzer divisions of 1940, or contemporary air assault formations. At Prague and Kolin, even Rossbach, the infantry formations selected to begin the day had been selected more or less randomly. At Zorndorf, Frederick led trump. The grenadiers were the cutting edge of an axe blade. The weight would be provided by a further fifteen battalions under Lieutenant-General H.W. von Kanitz. Twenty squadrons of cavalry were in sector reserve. Thirty-six more, under the personal command of Seydlitz, would cross the low ground and advance on its far, or west, side, moving parallel to the main attack. The rest of the army under Dohna formed a 'refused' wing, with the mission of securing the Prussian right flank against any Russian initiatives in that sector.

Without the advantage of tactical surprise he had enjoyed at Leuthen, Frederick turned to his artillery to make up the difference. Sixty guns, an unheard-of number for this era, opened fire on the Russian right flank around 9 a.m. When too many rounds fell short, the gunners redeployed to their front and blasted the Russian lines with a mixture of solid shot and canister that decimated the solid Muscovite formations. A single cannon ball was described by an eyewitness as inflicting forty-eight casualties.[11] Dust and smoke added to the Russians' discomfiture and rendered their attempts at counter-battery ineffective. Yet the Russians stood their ground, replacing gaps in the ranks from the second lines, then from the reserves. After two hours the Russian human wall remained unbroken. At 11 a.m. Frederick sent his infantry forward.

---

11 Christopher Duffy, *Russia's Military Way to the West: Origins and Nature of Russian Military Power, 1700–1800* (London, 1981), pp. 88–9.

The grenadiers and musketeers advanced in silence. First the thumping of the drums beating the advance carried to the Russian positions. Then one of the regimental bands began playing a hymn: 'Now, Lord, I am in Thy keeping'. A German pastor with the Russian army noted the melody. Frederick too, ever the secularist, asked one of his generals what the band was playing and repeated the words to himself as the sound faded.[12] Lest the romance of battle be carried too far, it must be noted that the musicians dropped out of the advance well before coming in range of the Russian muskets!

The bandsmen were more fortunate than the rest of the rank and file. Things started to go wrong with the attack from the beginning. The weather at Leuthen had been clear and cold. The day of Zorndorf was hot, with just enough wind to dry tongues and keep the air full of dust and smoke. The Russian position, with its long lines of silent men, so riveted everyone's attention from colonels to privates that the Prussian task forces began losing contact. Manteuffel's men stepped out briskly, not least from a general desire among all ranks to end the suspense. They moved so quickly, however, that they lost contact with Kanitz's supporting battalions. Kanitz in turn understood *his* primary mission not as directly supporting Manteuffel with every musket he could bring to bear, but as keeping touch with Dohna's wing. Instead of following in Manteuffel's tracks, therefore, Kanitz shifted his axis of advance to the right and made his own way towards the Russian position only to have his lines of march disordered by broken ground to his new front.

About 11.15, Manteuffel's leading files broke through a literal fog of war and found themselves no more than forty paces away from the Russian line. The Prussians opened fire at once, and for a few minutes shot their way forward into the enemy ranks. But the Russians responded with an even heavier counterfire. Musketry and canister cut the Prussian strength by a third within minutes. More seriously from a tactical point of view, Manteuffel's veterans compensated for their losses in approved textbook fashion, by closing on the centre. This meant that the left-flank unit, the 2nd Infantry, lost touch with the boggy ground protecting them from a cavalry attack. Had Kanitz's battalions come up in support, the gap might have been filled and the situation relegated to the might-have-beens that kept nineteenth-century general staff historians busy. Instead, with a clear field in front of him, the brigadier commanding the Russian cavalry on Fermor's right threw fourteen squadrons at the

---

12 Duffy, *Russia's Military Way*, p. 88; Duffy, *Frederick the Great*, p. 166.

dangling target offered by the 2nd Infantry's open flank. Manteuffel's survivors broke ranks and ran, Russian troopers cutting them down at every step.

Things were going no better in Kanitz's sector. His battalions, under heavy fire from the Russian centre, overextended themselves and fell into confusion as the second line mixed with the first to carry the charge forward. The Prussians broke into the Russian lines and captured a few guns, but they were too disorganized to break through before the fugitives of Manteuffel's task force rushed into their ranks from the left, seeking shelter from the Russian sabres. The musketry of Kanitz's disorganized battalions, already disrupted by the normal patterns of a Frederician fire-fight, became random. A junior officer in the 7th Infantry described its fire as doing more damage to its own troops than to the Russians, whose infantry took advantage of the unexpected confusion to mount a local counterattack of their own.[13] Kanitz's battalions followed Manteuffel's in a retreat at best disorganized and at worst panic-stricken, depending on where one was standing.

Once again Frederick was saved by his enemies. The Russian counterattack not only remained unsupported; it came to a staggering halt when its own support troops opened fire into its ranks, in the dust and smoke mistaking the Russians for the enemy. With the issue of the day hanging in the balance, Seydlitz turned the tide. His squadrons had moved uneventfully into position on Manteuffel's left flank and thus far had remained unengaged despite, according to some accounts, repeated orders from an increasingly desperate king to do something – anything at all. 'Tell the King', he allegedly replied, 'that after the battle my head is at his disposal, but meantime I hope he will permit me to exercise it in his service.'[14]

Seydlitz's delay was not entirely the product of his cavalryman's eye for a situation. It took time to move his squadrons of big men on heavy horses across the marsh separating them from the main army. Nor was Seydlitz blind to the risks of being caught on the move on unfavourable terrain. Nevertheless, his troopers struck the Russian cavalry's flank at better than two-to-one odds sometime around 1.30, scattered them, then rode into the Russian infantry. A few minutes later they were joined by twenty more squadrons initially held in reserve behind Kanitz's wing.

13 C.W. von Prittwitz und Gaffron, *Unter der Fahne des Herzogs von Bevern* (Berlin, 1935), p. 253.
14 Quoted in Duffy, *Frederick the Great*, p. 167.

The fighting in this sector was as desperate as any during the entire Seven Years War. The Russians, caught in the open and with no time to form squares, might reasonably have been expected to break under the sheer physical shock of the Prussian charge. Instead, enough of them stood their ground, whether as formed units or as clumps of survivors, to force the dragoons and cuirassiers to repeat their attacks instead of flowing over the Russian right wing in a single coherent movement. By the time the last resistance was broken the Russians had been able to bring up fresh units, rally shaken ones, and form a new front despite the disappearance of thousands of their men into the woods and swamps, or under the hooves of the Prussian horsemen.

Thus far the battle had been fought by only half the Prussian army. Its right wing had not moved, and about 1.30 a badly shaken Frederick rode over to galvanize Dohna into battle. Moritz of Dessau, seeing his monarch's discouragement and himself aware that all was not well at the designated *Schwerpunkt*, brought one regiment into action by shouting that the battle was won, that the confused masses of troops barely visible to the west were Russian prisoners![15] This Platonic 'noble lie' helped start the advance, but it came to a halt within minutes when thirty-six Russian squadrons, again on the initiative of their immediate commander, attacked Dohna's flank, capturing a full infantry battalion and a battery of heavy guns. Another battalion was shaken when civilian artillery drivers and their teams fleeing the lost position broke through its ranks to escape the Russian sabres. A battalion of the 18th Infantry stood its ground and kept up its fire, but the Russian troopers simply rode around the musketeers in search of more vulnerable targets.

Once again Prussian cavalry intervened decisively to stabilize the battle. Dohna's wing had included five mounted regiments; three of cuirassiers, one each of dragoons and hussars. These, reinforced by another two regiments of dragoons, charged the Russians with the courage of desperation. They received unexpected but decisive support from Seydlitz, who had replicated his performance at Rossbach by rallying his excited squadrons north of Zorndorf. He now sent some and led others right across the Prussian rear into the new fight. The Russian cavalry retreated, leaving behind not only the guns but also the battalion, whose captivity proved as brief as its embarrassment was enduring.

Dohna's infantry colonels took full advantage of the breathing

15 Catt, *Unterhaltungen mit Friedrich dem Grossen*, pp. 159–60.

space to rally their ranks. About 4 p.m. the Prussian right wing strode forward for a final try at deciding the battle. Many of these men were Brandenburgers, counted by Frederick among his best troops. They had seen enough of Russian deprodations to know that their homes would be next if they failed today. Supported brilliantly by the artillery, they forced the Russians back in hand-to-hand fighting so brutal that musket butts and bayonets gave way to teeth on at least one occasion, when a dying Russian was found savaging a mortally wounded Prussian.[16]

However, such close-gripped fighting was by no means every man's taste. As twilight set in an increasing number of Prussians and Russians alike dropped out of the ranks, some to breathe, others to drink. It seemed that almost every vehicle accompanying the Russian army carried a supply of high-proof alcohol, vodka, schnapps, or brandy. Other opportunities beckoned as well. The 5th Hussars was an East Prussian regiment with a reputation of mustering some of the toughest troopers in Frederick's army. When they stumbled across Russian paymasters' chests, temptation proved too great. The hussars reverted to their origins and began dividing the spoils.

By 8.30 the battle was over, halted by exhaustion and confusion as much as by the intentions of generals. The armies drew off to nurse their hurts. These had been considerable. More than 18,000 Russians and almost 13,000 Prussians were dead, wounded, or missing. The combatants had engaged everywhere on the field with a ferocity that shocked even the most case-hardened of Frederick's veterans. 'Even a shot to the body', noted one participant, 'was often not enough to bring [the Russians] down.'[17] Another officer, who had fought with Manteuffel's task force and had a correspondingly detailed perspective on Zorndorf at the sharp end, noted 'the ferocity still written on the faces' of the cavalrymen slain in Seydlitz's first charge.[18]

Though at day's end the Russian position was significantly vulnerable, neither Frederick nor his army possessed the will to continue the fighting on 26 August. Fermor re-established contact with his supply train, which had been left undisturbed despite its vulnerability – another indication of Zorndorf's impact on the Prussians. In the early morning of 27 August what remained of the Russian army slipped past indifferent Prussian outposts and withdrew to the east.

16 J.W. Archenholtz, *Geschichte des Siebenjährigen Krieges in Deutschland*, 5th edn, 2 vols (Berlin, 1840), vol. I, p. 169.

17 *Ibid.*, p. 167.

18 Prittwitz, *Unter der Fahne des Herzogs von Bevern*, p. 235.

More than any other battle of the eighteenth century, Zorndorf established the paradigm for western evaluations of Russia's military performance. When Frederick asked Seydlitz on the day after the battle whether or not he thought the Russians were useless, the general responded more or less curtly that such an appellation hardly fitted men who had repulsed Prussian troops so decisively.[19] The King's apparent dismissal of the Russians was the equivalent of a child whistling to keep up his courage while walking past a cemetery. Before 1756 Frederick had been consistent in describing Russian troops as worthless, insisting a disciplined army would make short work of any number of them. After Zorndorf he could ignore neither the stolid courage of the Russian gunners and musketeers nor the numerical resources available to Russian commanders. An additional point overlooked in many general accounts of the battle, but clearly noted by contemporaries, was the relatively high degree of tactical initiative shown by the Russians. The cavalry charges on the flanks and the infantry counterattack against Kanitz demonstrated all too clearly the significant vulnerability of the oblique order to even small-scale disruptions. What would be its fate against an enemy able to coordinate its response?[20]

Zorndorf was arguably far more significant for the Seven Years War than either Leuthen or Rossbach. Unlike its predecessors, the battle created a new paradigm. The Russians had become permanent, direct participants in the struggle for power over central Europe. They had shown they were an enemy not to be despised in battle. They had fought the best army in Europe to a bloody draw. Frederick may have held the field; his army was in no shape to challenge Fermor's withdrawal. Even Russian occupation policies posed a double threat. East Prussia was the carrot, the positive example of Russia as a magnet. The Zorndorf campaign, with its indiscriminate pillaging, was the stick. Frederick could neglect the security of Prussia's eastern provinces only at the risk of breaking the state's social contract beyond easy restoration.

Given the increasing importance of the Prussian army's tactical

19 Carl von Warnerey, *Campagnes de Frédéric II Roi de Prusse, de 1756 à 1762* (Amsterdam, 1788), p. 275.

20 For general accounts of Zorndorf, cf. O. Herrmann, 'Zur Schlacht von Zorndorf', *Forschungen zur brandenburgischen und preussischen Geschichte*, XXIV (1911), 547–66; and Kurt von Unger, 'Die Schlacht bei Zorndorf am 25. August 1758', *Militär-Wochenblatt*, 1901, *Beiheft* IV, 221–58; and Stefan Hartmann, 'Eine Unbekannte Quelle zur Schlacht bei Zorndorf', *Zeitschrift für Ostforschung*, XXXV (1985), 176–210.

efficiency as the key to the state's strategy, Zorndorf was suggestive in other ways as well. The cavalry had performed superlatively. From Seydlitz through the regimental and squadron commanders to the rank-and-file troopers, the Prussian horsemen had demonstrated that Mollwitz was long in their past. But even at its apogee the mounted arm showed its essential weakness. It could not, with its own resources, ride down unshaken infantry under normal battlefield conditions.

The Prussian artillery for its part showed an increasing capacity to prepare and support attacks. Dohna's final advance in particular would have gone nowhere without the guns. Gunner officers regarded their craft as a science, and tended correspondingly to dislike upsetting their careful calculations of ranges and trajectories by changing positions constantly. They had a point in their argument that the temporary masking, or even the temporary loss, of a battery meant little if the original site were well chosen. The guns could not easily be removed. The guns could not be easily disabled. Sooner or later the guns would have their say. Nevertheless, Prussia's 'long arm' had neither the mobility nor the *mentalité* to participate in a flexible battle. It took so much time to move even field pieces from place to place that their role in a fast-moving fight was likely to be no more than marginal.

That left Prussia's infantry as the pivotal force on the battlefield. Frederick never forgave some of the regiments that broke under the Russian guns and sabres at Zorndorf. Not until the royal review of 1773 were the East Prussian regiments of Kanitz's command restored to something like favour. A year later Frederick reminded the Pomeranian 7th Infantry that it too had fled the field of Zorndorf, and such behaviour could neither be corrected nor forgotten.

Reality was more complex than questions of provincial courage or regimental honour. That regiments whose depots and families were under Russian control may have felt the effects of poor replacements and low morale is hardly debatable. The East Prussian battalions were worn thin from a summer's fruitless campaigning. They were sent into battle under less than favourable weather conditions. Zorndorf clearly demonstrated, however, the crucial gap between Frederick's tactical doctrine and the Prussian infantry's organizational articulation. The absence of any permanent structure above the regimental level meant a corresponding absence of intimacy, of *Tuchfühlung*, among units which stood next to each other in the line of battle as virtual strangers. Nor were senior officers familiar, except by accident, with either their assignments or the formations under them.

As a result command decisions like Kanitz's change of direction or Dohna's delay in advancing tended to compound themselves, particularly in the context of even minor, local enemy initiatives. The oblique order demanded an obliging enemy, one that not only made all the right mistakes, but allowed itself either to be deceived by Prussian feints or intimidated by the final advance. A foe willing to stand its ground and able to throw even a little grit in the Prussian machinery had a correspondingly good chance of seeing the oblique order self-destruct because of its inflexibility.

Zorndorf also highlighted the limitations of a command system depending on one man. Frederick could oversee a single major attack in the style of Leuthen. When events began to unravel, as at Zorndorf, he could not be everywhere at once. Any negative effects of haste and emergency, however minor, on the King's demeanour tended to become all too obvious to the officers and men he needed to inspire to renewed efforts. When all the positives and negatives were collated, the Battle of Zorndorf clearly indicated that the short, decisive campaigns basic to Frederick's strategy would be increasingly difficult to achieve.

HOCHKIRCH: THE UNEXPECTED BLOODY NOSE

Frederick took no time for such reflections in the final days of August 1758. The aftermath of Zorndorf indeed showed one of the major practical reasons for the Prussian army's maintaining a task-force structure, as opposed to more permanent groupings. What remained of Frederick's army was split up. Twenty-one battalions and thirty-five squadrons were left under Dohna to keep an eye on the Russians. Frederick took fifteen battalions and thirty-eight squadrons westwards, again at the double, to counter the Austrians.

Frederick's enemies validated the King's decision. Fermor had been so stunned by the carnage of Zorndorf that he withdrew completely from the theatre of operations, spending the rest of the campaigning season blaming his soldiers for the battle's outcome and desultorily pursuing a siege of the Baltic port of Kolberg. The Austrians, however, had developed and implemented plans for a major strategic counteroffensive into Prussia's heartland. Their principal commander has gone down in military history as an archetypical eighteenth-century general, a master of magazines and manoeuvres, disinclined to risky offensive actions. But Marshal Leopold Daun was also a man who knew himself and his army. Hot strategic pursuits and brilliant tactical combinations only played to his great opponent's

221

principal strengths.[21] While Frederick was beating his army to pieces at Zorndorf, Daun shifted his base of operations to Saxony, where he joined a reorganized Imperial army now under Prince Frederick of Zweibrücken. Initial plans to overrun the relatively weak covering force Frederick had left behind under the command of Prince Henry foundered on the always vexed issue of allied cooperation, then were abandoned completely with the news of Frederick's imminent arrival in the theatre.

Once again the speed of the King's strategic movements were impressive. His men, despite their Herculean efforts at Zorndorf, marched as many as 20 miles a day, and on 11 September the King joined his brother's forces in Saxony. Daun responded by moving his army to the broken country east of Dresden. Fire-eaters among his subordinates were disappointed. Nevertheless, this was Daun's kind of ground: ideal for the defensive operations in which he specialized, while offering favourable opportunities for tactical initiatives should the Prussians make a mistake. To encourage the latter process Daun detached flying columns and raiding parties to harass Frederick's outposts and communications.

The King for his part had no intention of obliging Daun by launching another head-on attack. Zorndorf had been quite enough for one year. Instead, Frederick proposed to manoeuvre *Daun* out of position by threatening *his* logistics. For over a month the armies jockeyed back and forth in a stately gavotte that achieved nothing significant. Then on 9 October Frederick marched the bulk of his troops, about 36,000 men, into camp around the village of Hochkirch.

It was an administrative move. Frederick planned to remain only until he could be resupplied, and he took correspondingly limited pains with the layout of his positions. The Prussian camp straggled in a more or less north–south direction, facing eastwards towards Daun's last reported location. Its left, nine battalions supported by a battery of heavy guns, was essentially an outpost force intended to secure communications with a detached force observing another part of Daun's army. The centre, north of Hochkirch, was more or less well dug in. The right was another story. It included eleven battalions and twenty-eight squadrons based in and around Hochkirch itself, a community dominated by a large walled church. Strengthened by batteries and redoubts, garrisoned by some of Frederick's best troops, the position was strong in itself. It was dominated, however, by high

---

21 F.L. Thadden, *Feldmarschall Daun* (Vienna, 1967), is a sympathetic but balanced analysis of its subject's character and capacities.

ground to the east – high ground increasingly occupied by Austrian light troops, appearing where they had no right to be according to Prussian intelligence. Any anxiety at battalion levels failed to communicate itself to the King. Frederick had once more fallen prey to the sin of judging his enemy's intentions by his own requirements. Daun had done nothing all summer. The Prussians badly needed fresh supplies. A day or two of theoretical risk in a less than favourable position seemed perfectly acceptable.

The Austrians had other ideas. Daun by this time had 80,000 men at his disposal – almost a three-to-one superiority over Frederick. The Austrian commander was cautious, but he was no poltroon and he knew how to compensate for his negative tendencies by choosing his subordinates. Specifically, his chief of staff, Franz Moritz Lacy, was an aggressive, hard-driving officer. He had been mentored earlier in his career by Marshal Browne, and he was a sufficiently solid administrator that his support for vigorous action could not be easily confused with the head-down enthusiasms of the older *Haudegen* who had learned their craft in easier schools than that kept by Frederick of Prussia.[22]

Urged on by Lacy, Daun spent several days personally scouting the Prussian camp, on one occasion himself coming under fire. The most remarkable thing about these missions, from an Austrian perspective, was the Prussian failure to respond in any significant fashion, either by altering their deployments or by increasing their security. The circumstances seemed ideal for an attack. Daun's decision was also influenced by the spirit of his own army. The regimental officers were spoiling for a fight and they reported their men in a similar mood. The latter point may be open to question. The summer campaign had nevertheless been successful enough and bloodless enough to dim the memories of Leuthen. Daun had every reason to believe a major victory would erase them completely, and a long list of other reasons to believe himself in a position to win just such a battle.

The Austrian commander's intention was simpler than his plan. Daun proposed to take the Prussian right flank by surprise with the best troops in his army. Forty-two battalions of infantry and grenadiers and eleven regiments of cavalry would converge on Hochkirch in five columns. This was Lacy's idea: columns for shock power but

22 E. Kotasek, *Feldmarschall Graf Lacy. Ein Leben für Österreichs Heer* (Horn, 1956), is the definitive biography.

small columns for control, since the advance to the objective would be made under cover of night. The timing of the attack – a nice touch – was to come from the Prussian position. When the Hochkirch church clock struck 5 a.m., the Austrians would charge.

Simultaneously the rest of Daun's army, twenty-one battalions of infantry and seven cavalry regiments, would engage the Prussian left and centre, holding it in place as a hand positions a nail for the hammer. If all went reasonably well the results would be a Leuthen in reverse, with Frederick's army rolled up from its broken right flank. The Prussian position around Hochkirch might be naturally strong and improved by artifice. The Austrian advance, however, could take advantage both of the high ground referred to earlier and of numerous small woods that masked fields of vision and fire. The killing zones to be crossed by the final assault would be narrow ones. Once Hochkirch was taken, moreover, there were no terrain features in the area on which the Prussians could rally for a stand. Perhaps Daun's projected Leuthen might be followed by a counterpart to Rossbach, with Frederick's army shattered beyond easy repair.

Weather as well as terrain favoured the Austrians. The night of 13/14 October was starless, the early morning foggy. The Austrians left their tents standing and their campfires burning. Working parties, taking care to make as much noise as possible, cut trees for field entrenchments, as though Daun feared a Prussian attack. The Austrian columns successfully maintained individual cohesion despite the broken terrain. At 5 a.m. the clock struck and the Austrians went forward, screened by their irregulars.

Frederick still had not changed his camp routines, despite reports from Austrian deserters that their army was on the move. Two free battalions, surprised and unsupported, were the first to collapse. Next came the turn of the right wing's three grenadier battalions. Some had time to seize their muskets and form ranks before the Austrians burst out of the fog. Others were bayoneted in their tents, or as they struggled to free themselves from the canvas that enveloped them as ropes were cut and poles broken. The Prussian guns fired as fast as their desperate crews could sponge out and reload, but most of the salvoes were wasted firing blindly into the fog. The Austrian artillery, on the other hand, found clear targets in the Prussian camp. Their shell-firing howitzers in particular inflicted heavy and horrifying casualties on sleep-stupid infantrymen who grouped together less from any instinctual rallying to the colours than because there seemed nowhere to go. As weight of numbers forced the struggling mass away from the main camp site and towards the outskirts of Hochkirch the shouts of the Austrians, echoing in a half-dozen languages, were matched by the Prussian officers and NCOs: 'Fall in! To arms!'[23]

Initially Frederick dismissed the sounds of battle as just another outpost skirmish. When he saw a regiment forming line he said, 'Boys, go back to camp. They're only Pandours.' Only when cannon-balls from Prussian twelve-pounders captured in the redoubt began whistling over his head did Frederick shout for his horse and order a general alert.[24]

By that time day had broken. The fog had cleared enough to enable the adversaries to distinguish friend from enemy at other than eyeball ranges. Prussian cavalry mounted a series of regimental-scale counterattacks that stung the Austrians but failed to stop them. A battalion of the 23rd Infantry charged, then fell back as Austrians closed in on its flank and rear. By this time Hochkirch was starting to burn as roof after straw-thatched roof caught fire. The battery south of the village, with its twenty twelve–pounders, was lost at bayonet-point, the surviving defenders streaming back into Hochkirch. But the fight was far from over. A battalion of the 19th Infantry manned the churchyard: stone walls acting as a magnet for both Prussian stragglers tired of running and Austrian battalions whose commanders would have been better advised to bypass this kind of strong point. Elements of a half-dozen Habsburg regiments ultimately became involved in trying to capture a position that could only be approached on narrow fronts, and Major Simon von Langen's musketeers of the 19th held their ground with bullets, bayonets, and clubbed muskets against everything the desperate Austrians could bring to bear.

The time bought in the Hochkirch churchyard was not wasted. Marshal Keith, with an old soldier's sense of danger, had mistrusted Frederick's casual attitude from the first. If the Austrians do not attack us here, he had said, they deserve to be hanged.[25] Now Keith rode to the sound of the guns, and along with Moritz of Dessau, began reasserting tactical control in the battle zone. The situation was too desperate to allow time for massing reserves; regiments were

23 C.D. Küster, *Bruchstück seines Campagnelebens im Siebenjährigen Krieg* (Berlin, 1791), pp. 36 *passim.*, is a vivid account by an army chaplain of the first phase of the fight for Hochkirch. Cf. C.F. Barsewisch, *Meine Kriegs-Erlebnisse Während des Siebenjährigen Krieges 1757–1763*, ed. J. Olmes (Krefeld, 1959), p. 72.

24 *Ibid.*, pp. 73–4.

25 Jany, *Preussische Armee*, vol. II, p. 500.

fed into the fight as they arrived. A slashing local counterattack, led by Keith in person, retook the battery south of Hochkirch, but could not maintain its position in the face of Austrian musketry from the village. Around 6 a.m., three more Prussian regiments rushed Hochkirch itself, with Prince Moritz rallying stragglers and detachments to support the charge.

The Prussians swept through the village, out the far side, and fell on the battery at bayonet-point. The advance by that time had become a mass of shouting men, most order lost and with no impetus beyond initial shock. It was seen off by the disciplined volleys of the Austrian reserves, ably supported by guns there had been no time to spike that were now turned against their former owners. Moritz, badly wounded, was carried from the field. Keith was smashed out of the saddle by a cannon-ball, dead when he hit the ground. The Prussians fell back, rallied briefly under cover of Hochkirch's walls and gardens, then flowed out of the village in full retreat.

Langen's battalion, unlike most of the Prussians in Hochkirch, had held its position instead of joining the counterattack. Now its muskets crashed again, checking the Austrian pursuit and acting as a beacon for the rest of the army. By this time Frederick was on the scene. Whatever his earlier shortcomings in an emergency, on this morning the King kept his head. No more men, he declared, were to be wasted in house-to-house fighting. Instead, three regiments, including the Guard, would envelop Hochkirch from the west, with Ziethen's cavalry covering their right flank. But the troopers were drawn into a duel with the horsemen of Daun's left-flank column, winning honour rather than participating in the battle. As the counterattacking Prussian infantry ran into increasingly heavy Austrian fire, they behaved in a manner prefiguring the Union army's Philadelphia Brigade at the stone wall of Gettysburg, at the height of Pechett's charge on July 3. They did not break to the rear and run, but neither did they drive forward and win. Instead, they engaged in a fire-fight at medium range until their ammunition ran out and small-scale cavalry charges began tearing holes in their formations.

Frederick's brother-in-law was beheaded by a cannon-ball, and the King himself helped rally the shaken regiment that observed the incident. Langen and his forlorn hope held out in Hochkirch churchyard, beating off attack after attack until their cartridge boxes were emptied. The major rallied all the survivors still on their feet, then charged in a desperate attempt to regain his own lines. In minutes he went down mortally wounded. The attack collapsed, and with it any real hope of a Prussian victory in this sector.

On the other end of the battle line Frederick's left wing had been under heavy attack since 7 a.m. It finally retreated with the loss of no fewer than thirty heavy guns, and an entire grenadier battalion surrounded and captured by Austrian cuirassiers. Meanwhile, the King had formed a new fighting line north of Hochkirch, but it was little more than a rallying point for stragglers and survivors of the morning's débâcle. Frederick, no gambler, knew when it was time to cut his losses. Around 10 a.m. the Prussians began falling back to the north-west.

'Just look at how many brave men I have lost!' Frederick mourned to one of his attendants.[26] Hochkirch cost him over 9,000 men. Austrian casualties were 2,000 fewer, and the bulk of Frederick's losses were men he could ill spare, from regiments whose memories were of Leuthen and Rossbach rather than the slaughterhouse of Zorndorf. The 13th Infantry had more than 800 dead, wounded, or missing. Other proud regiments, the 19th and the 26th, had suffered in proportion. A hundred guns were gone. So were too many of the bravest regimental officers. Among the army's higher ranks Keith was dead, and it was left to the Austrians to honour his stripped and plundered body. Moritz of Dessau was captured, then paroled, but would never again lead troops in battle. He developed cancer unrelated to his wound and died in 1760.

Tactically the Austrian army was too disorganized to pursue immediately. Some of the senior officers seem to have been so surprised by their victory that they had difficulty believing it was real – time enough to shake hands with friends, and to sort out battalions and squadrons still hunting stragglers in the ruins of Hochkirch or dispersing to plunder the dead and wounded of both sides.[27]

Hochkirch's direct strategic consequences were limited by the rapidity and efficiency of Frederick's withdrawal, and by Daun's reluctance to pursue an enemy so quickly able to get out of effective range. The remainder of the 1758 campaigning season in the war's central sector only emphasized the limited value of the Austrian victory. Frederick briefly considered trying another round with Daun, but was instead compelled to advance into Silesia to relieve the blockaded fortress of Neisse. In the meantime Daun moved in the opposite direction and placed Dresden under a desultory siege. With Neisse

26 Catt, *Unterhaltungen mit Friedrich dem Grossen*, p. 190.

27 Norbert Robitscheck, *Hochkirch* (Vienna, 1905); and Curt Jany, 'Hochkirch', *Militär-Wochenblatt*, 1905, *Beiheft* III, 99–114, summarize this often overlooked battle from the viewpoints of the respective participants.

safe for the winter, Frederick returned to Saxony in early November. Daun promptly withdrew to winter quarters in Bohemia.

If the Prussians did little fighting in the final weeks of 1758, they showed that they still knew how to march. Straggling and desertion seem to have been limited in the aftermath of Hochkirch, if for no better reason than the cumulative effect of a year of long marches and hard fighting. By this time the weaker bodies and the frailer spirits were gone. Faith in God or belief in the King, pride of caste or craft, simple stubbornness – the motives varied widely, but transcended the bonds of formal discipline. If the army's ranks were thinner than they had been since the war's beginning, they were by now filled with men who had in common a will to be there and the experience to make that will an effective military factor.

In evaluating his situation at the turn of the year Frederick had reasons for short-range optimism. Silesia and Saxony were safe until spring. The Russians had been driven away from Prussia's eastern frontiers. The Swedes had demonstrated clearly that they possessed neither the will nor the capacity to threaten Prussian Pomerania seriously. In the west Ferdinand of Brunswick had approached, if not quite crossed, the line separating a 'good ordinary general' from a *Feldherr*. Reinforced during the summer by a British contingent of first-rate infantry and cavalry, he had conducted a campaign of feint and manoeuvre that kept his French enemies consistently off-balance, and finally compelled them to evacuate Hanover entirely. Small wonder that a grateful King George bestowed on Ferdinand a life annuity of £2,000, or that Frederick made him a field marshal – without, however, any accompanying gratuity![28]

From a broader perspective, however, Frederick's position had deteriorated significantly. Tactically, battlefields had changed utterly from the days of the First Silesian War. Frederick was particularly impressed by the Austrians. In the winter of 1758, he composed a set of 'reflections' praising the contemporary Austrian skill in choosing and improving their camps and positions. Not only did they show great energy in constructing redoubts and abatis; their defences were organized in depth, featuring snares and traps to disorganize an enemy force after its initial breakthrough. Frederick also noted the Austrians' sophisticated use of combined-arms tactics, with cavalry deployed to invite an attack, infantry concentrated to ambush the attackers, and artillery in position to complete the discomfiture. Frederick emphatically denied any implication that the Austrians

---

[28] Savory, *His Britannic Majesty's Army*, p. 115.

had suddenly become invincible. But his text acknowledged somewhat ruefully that frontal attacks in the style of Kolin offered little
prospect against an Austrian army that had the choice of position.
The Prussian infantry, usually advancing uphill, could do almost no
damage with its musketry. Their Austrian opponents were extremely
unlikely to be intimidated by a silent advance with fixed bayonets,
as prescribed in pre-war doctrine. The King now urged the exploitation of Austrian errors in deployment while simultaneously taking
advantage of any opportunities provided by unoccupied terrain in the
battle zone. Above all, Frederick urged the seizing of high ground
for artillery positions, the bringing of as many guns as possible into
battery as quickly as possible and using them to prepare the attacks
of the other arms.

The King's dismissal of Austrian willingness to stand under artillery fire may itself be dismissed; the Austrians in 1758 had shown
themselves no worse and no better in that respect than any other
reasonably well-trained and disciplined force. What was important
was Frederick's insistence that attacking without first having fire
superiority, or at least equality, was the same as facing muskets with
sticks – an impossibility.

This was a far cry from the tactical doctrine with which Prussia
had gone to war in 1756. Frederick expressed further caution in
advising against all-out attacks in the style of Prague or Kolin. They
were too dangerous, he declared. Keeping one wing refused, engaging
only part of the army, ensured the presence of a force to cover retreat
in case of defeat. Select a point in the enemy's line, Frederick urged.
Concentrate artillery on that point. Then send forward the infantry.
If the enemy's line was broken in one place he could be destroyed just
as effectively as if he were overwhelmed in every sector. But it was
vital to secure the flanks of the assault, and at least as vital to keep
the infantry battalions well in hand once they secured their objectives.
The Austrian cavalry were a particularly dangerous enemy in local
counterattacks against disorganized troops.

Some of Frederick's points uncannily prefigure conclusions drawn
by British and US commanders about the best ways of attacking
German troops from 1943 to 1945. Defence organized in depth,
skilful use of combined arms tactics, prompt counterattacks against a
disorganized enemy – these patterns call to mind Hitler's Wehrmacht
more readily than the Austrian army of Maria Theresa. The similarity
in argument nevertheless highlights the deep respect Frederick had
developed for the Austrians. He argued, indeed, that the only way to
secure decisive victories over the Habsburgs was to lure their generals

away from the forests, the mountains, and the broken ground of Bohemia, Moravia, and Upper Saxony. On the other hand, the plains of Lower Silesia offered, in Frederick's opinion, an ideal killing ground. He fully expected Austrian greed – or more accurately, Maria Theresa's determination to recover her lost province – to lure the Habsburg army to its destruction eventually![29]

FREDERICK TAKES STOCK

The final word was the rub. Manoeuvring the Austrians into the open would at best take time, and time was something Prussia was not likely to have available in the coming year. Heinrich de la Motte Fouqué had known Frederick since he was a junior officer in the Crown Prince's shadow court. A man who combined the skills of a field soldier with the tastes of an intellectual, Fouqué was one of the King's favourites and among the few who risked, in the German phrase, 'pouring him uncut wine'. He questioned whether the Austrians would ever be obliging enough to give their enemy the chance to fight a second Leuthen. Daun, declared Fouqué, was too old a fox to be tempted from his den by anything but a favourable opportunity in the style of Hochkirch.[30]

Fouqué's pessimism matched Frederick's concern in the new year of 1759. The Austrians might be the most obvious enemy, but the Russians had received no more than a few pinpricks compared to their massive resources. In his own mind at least, moreover, Frederick had serious reasons to question the endurance of his eastern provinces in the face of another full-scale invasion. In the war's western sector, Ferdinand's victories had pulled Britain's Hanoverian chestnuts from the French fire. This was important, if only for the sake of the subsidy Frederick considered necessary if he were to field an army in 1759. It did not, however, contribute directly to resolving Prussia's strategic crisis. Ferdinand, moreover, was a general of his times, better at manoeuvring than at fighting the kind of pitched battle that had by now become the centrepiece of Frederick's way of war. The Prince's cape-and-sword techniques might baffle the French for

29 Frederick II, 'Réflections sur la tactique et sur quelques parties de la guerre, ou, Réflexions sur quelques changements dans la façon de faire la guerre', Œuvres de Frédéric le Grand, ed. J.D.E. Preuss, 30 vols (Berlin, 1846–56), vol. XXVIII, pp. 154 ff.

30 G.A. Büttner, Denkwürdigkeiten aus dem Leben des Konigl. Preuss. Generals von der Infanterie Frieherrn de la Motte Fouqué, 2 vols (Berlin, 1788), vol. I, pp. 77 ff.

another summer or two. They could also serve as a school of war for an army that had proved a formidable enemy from Rocroi to Fontenoy, and scarcely seemed afflicted by irreversible decay. What might be Prussia's fate, Frederick pondered, should he in the next winter face composing an equivalent memorandum on the fighting style of the French, or even the Russians?

Frederick's own forces, moreover, had been badly weakened, especially the infantry, rank, file, and regimental officers. Frederick sought to fill his depleted ranks by every means possible. The cantons were combed pitilessly for young men and recovered convalescents. The occupied territories of Swedish Pomerania and Saxony were laid under ruthless contributions. The Estates of Saxony were bluntly informed that either they provided the requisite number of recruits or the army would procure them by any means necessary. Neutral Mecklenburg was subjected to a razzia in the style of the Thirty Years War. Frederick also sought men in the Empire, paying a bounty of 15 thalers per 'volunteer' to the colonel in charge of the operation. By this time almost any German honestly interested in a soldier's life had long since donned a uniform. It required all the tricks of the crimp's trade to provide a few thousand recruits from southern Germany and the Rhineland. Some younger sons of middle-class families were even promised officers' commissions in Frederick's army, only to find themselves unceremoniously disposed of as enlisted replacements. Small wonder that these *muss-Preussen* had to be regularly escorted by armed guards.[31]

Far more reliable as replacements were the prisoners of war whose exchange Frederick secured during the winter. More than 18,000 officers and men returned to Prussian service by this process. Most of them had been captured at Hochkirch. They had had correspondingly little time to lose their health and discipline, and were welcome additions either to their former regiments or to other formations badly in need of experienced personnel. Because the balance of exchange in the past year had favoured Prussia, enough enemy soldiers remained in Frederick's hands to make worthwhile a systematic combing of prison camps for prospective coat-changers. Prussian recruiters worked correspondingly at encouraging 'volunteers'.

The overall results were decidedly mixed. Official accounts describe an army that spent the winter integrating its recruits and replacements, and that by the beginning of the 1759 campaigning season was as ready for the field as it had ever been. The cavalry

31 Jany, *Preussische Armee*, vol. II, pp. 511–12.

was by all accounts in good order. The artillery was stronger than ever. As early as November 1758, Frederick proposed to take almost 300 heavy guns into the field in the coming year. Fifty of these were heavy twelve-pounders taken from Prussian fortresses — the famous 'Brummer' of the war's later years. Seventy more were Prussian copies of the light Austrian twelve-pounders that had been so effective on so many battlefields. In addition, Frederick proposed to create a strategic artillery reserve totalling eighty pieces, six- and twelve-pounders. To provide the manpower for these guns, and to supervise the civilian drivers and the large teams necessary in particular for the heavy pieces, the strength of the artillery corps was doubled to almost 4,000 officers and men.

Frederick added another major innovation to his artillery in the spring of 1759. Russian tables of organization provided for every cavalry regiment a three-pounder cannon and a light mortar or two as direct fire support. Frederick took this idea a step further by organizing 'flying artillery' that could be sent rapidly to any part of a battlefield, either to check an enemy attack or to assist the heavy, semi-mobile pieces in securing the fire superiority the King now regarded as necessary for successful infantry attacks. The first battery consisted of a half-dozen light six-pounders, each drawn by a six-horse team. The seven-man crews were individually mounted as well, and all the horses were chosen with the same kind of attention paid to cavalry remounts. Frederick personally observed this unit at drill before the campaign began, and was impressed with both its performance and its potential.[32]

A look below the surface generated more alarm than reassurance. Except for a few free battalions, increasingly composed of men no one else wanted, the army's order of battle remained unchanged from 1758. Its strength was almost the same — 163,000 as opposed to 166,000 a year earlier. Numbers, however, told only part of the story. The infantry, the heart of the army, was fragile by comparison to the men of Kolin, Leuthen, and Rossbach. They would need careful handling and a victory or two under their crossbelts before they could be fully trusted in an emergency. The shortcomings of the replacements have been described earlier. Too many of the veterans, moreover, had crossed too many start lines since the war began.

32 Cf. R. von Bonin, 'Über die Errichtung, Formation, und Ausrüstung der preussischen reitenden Artillerie', *Archiv für die Offiziere der Königlich Preussische Artillerie- und Ingenieur-Korps*, IX (1839), 202–37; von Strotha, *Die Königlich Preussische Reitende Artillerie vom Jahre 1759 bis 1816* (Berlin, 1868).

Depression, fatigue, and a sense of declining odds characterized the mood even in some of the army's best regiments.

These problems were less significant under eighteenth-century conditions than in the individualized warfare of later eras. If Kipling's 'Sergeant Whatsisname' had a charm for making riflemen from mud, Prussia's drillmasters could produce musketeers from manure. The army's cadres, however, were not what they had been in earlier years. At the beginning of his reign Frederick had forbidden the worst excesses of discipline and hazing in the Cadet Corps, and ordered greater emphasis on academic instructions. Practical results of the measures were limited. Not until General J.J. von Buddenbrock became governor in 1759 did living standards, academic standards, and standards of behaviour begin to improve. In the intervening two decades the Royal Prussian Cadet Corps continued to produce generations of junior officers whose knowledge of higher mathematics and minor tactics was alike rudimentary, but who would die before they would run.[33]

And die they did in the fierce battles of Frederick's great war. By 1759 almost half of the officer corps had been lost. Those who returned to their regiments after recovering from wounds or sickness not infrequently bore physical or psychological scars that diminished their effectiveness. Frederick sought to fill the gaps by commissioning experienced NCOs and scions of the middle class, and by hiring foreigners. Cadets as young as 13 were sent to the field, where, instead of being introduced gradually to their responsibilities, they were assigned line commands immediately.

Boy officers might inspire certain levels of sympathy among the mixed bags of war-weary veterans and King's hard bargains that by now filled the ranks of most of the infantry regiments. They were not likely to command the kind of respect that generated prompt obedience in a pitched battle – nor could they inspire a compensating fear in the men they were supposed to command.

The army's higher command structure had also suffered major damage. Schwerin and Keith were dead; Moritz of Dessau was dying. Seydlitz's fragile health rendered him a dubious quantity. Winterfeldt was dead, and the army's staff work would never be the same. The King's younger brother, Prince Henry of Prussia, had emerged as a reliable theatre commander. Ziethen remained as durable and as

---

33 J.K. Zobel, *Das preussische Kadettenkorps. Militärische Jugenderziehung als Herrschaftsmittel im preussischen Militärsystem* (Frankfurt, 1978), is a sharply critical survey of this institution.

irrepressible as ever. But the list of failed commanders and uninspired brigadiers had grown with each campaign – Dohna, Bevern, Manteuffel, Kanitz. Too many promising colonels had fallen at the head of their regiments. Captured officers were no longer exchanged as a matter of course. A few new faces had begun emerging from the scrum. Whether they would continue to develop – if they survived – no one could be certain, not least because of the extremely polarized demands Frederick's way of war made upon his generals. On the one hand they were expected to be interchangeable cogs in the King's machine, fulfilling his intentions as well as his orders to the last detail. On the other, they were expected to manifest initiative in crucial operational situations, responding to events created by enemy action in the confusion of a Zorndorf or a Hochkirch. Confederate General Stonewall Jackson would create a similar paradox a century later. The high-spirited individualists of the Army of Northern Virginia responded to Jackson's command in ways that provoked arrests and quarrels from the Valley Campaign to Chancellorsville. Frederick's generals were a good deal more passive, but no more able to resolve the double binds imposed by egocentric genius.

The Prussian army's internal quality was particularly significant in the context of Prussia's strategic situation. Frederick had spent 1758 putting out fires, rushing from theatre emergency to theatre emergency. The coming year offered little prospect of relief. Prussia's enemies were strong enough to deter the King from taking the risk of concentrating his army. Twenty-eight thousand men under Dohna, still the best command alternative, remained in the east to watch the Russians. Another 5,000, based in Stralsund, kept an eye on the Swedes. Prince Henry was given about 30,000 men, and the mission of securing Saxony against invasion by either the Austrians or the *Reichsarmee*. Thirteen thousand men under Fouqué held down Upper Silesia. After making a few other, smaller detachments for the sake of local security Frederick was left with a main army of only 50,000 men – and that force was constrained to keep watch on both Saxony and Silesia, since neither Henry nor Fouqué could be expected to do more than screen and delay a major attack in their respective theatres.

Frederick's situation resembled that of the proverbial chameleon on a plaid shirt, with a similar risk of self-destruction trying to meet the challenge. Diplomacy in such a context was useless. Remaining passive seemed a certain recipe for disaster. But where and how could Prussia take the initiative? In the western theatre Ferdinand of Brunswick had proved he could win battles. Perhaps as much to the point, that sector was the focal point for a Britain whose enthusiasm for Continental wars could never be entirely relied upon. In December the Commons had expressed support for Prussia: support to be manifested in both financial and military terms. Might it be time, in gamblers' parlance, to ride a hot hand?

In the winter of 1758/59, Ferdinand's army was significantly strengthened and improved along lines indicated by Frederick's battles against the Russians and Austrians. The artillery was reinforced. The light troops were increased – not by a marauding rabble like the free battalions, but by disciplined regular soldiers given special training as skirmishers and marksmen. The base structure was overhauled. Transport was streamlined and reorganized. Shortly into the new year Ferdinand commanded a solid force of sixty battalions and seventy-seven squadrons. He was anxious to take the offensive, even against superior French numbers.[34]

Frederick was willing enough to support the wager. Prussia's enemies were finding it more difficult to coordinate plans than intentions. They had gone to war with the general agreement that Prussia needed curbing. But each power had its own ideas of what that meant. France was primarily concerned with the war on the high seas and in North America. In that context the principal enemy was Ferdinand's army and the principal objective was Hanover. Austria wanted to regain Silesia and 'liberate' Saxony, the latter in a way that would solidify Habsburg primacy in the Holy Roman Empire. Russia hoped for extensive territorial gains in the east – perhaps the entire province of East Prussia – along with recognition of its primacy/hegemony in that region. Even Sweden expected Prussian Pomerania as a suitable recompense for its presence in the game.

The problem lay in achieving these objectives. During the American Civil War Abraham Lincoln would offer the homely metaphor of each Union field army taking hold of a leg and beginning the skinning process *somewhere*! The French proposed to help their allies buy knives. Despite the country's growing financial weakness the government of Louis XV provided subsidies to Austria and Sweden, cash sweeteners that helped justify France's determination to concentrate the bulk of its own forces against Ferdinand. The subsidies were far from regularly paid, and in the winter of 1758–59 those to Austria were significantly reduced. They were nevertheless better than nothing at all.[35]

34 Savory, *His Britannic Majesty's Army*, pp. 117 ff.
35 James C. Riley, *The Seven Years' War and the Old Regime in France: The Economic and Financial Toll* (Princeton, NJ, 1986), pp. 83 ff. and 132 ff., offers the best treatment in English of the limits French finances placed on French ambitions.

KUNERSDORF: RUSSIA TAKES CENTRE STAGE

This left the Russians and Austrians to deal directly with Frederick and his army. In theory at least, that task seemed less formidable in 1759 than it had proved in earlier years. The Russians informed the Austrians that Frederick became discouraged when his headlong offensives did not produce expected results. The Austrians declared with equal sagacity that Frederick owed his victories to a strategic central position allowing him to turn against his enemies one by one. The solution seemed obvious: develop a plan for concerted action against Frederick's now-divided forces. Daun, with more than 100,000 men, among the largest armies Austria had ever put into the field, would concentrate against Saxony and Silesia. Thirty-five thousand Imperial and Austrian troops, largely paid for with French money, would concentrate west of Daun and threaten Leipzig. Forty thousand Russians, plus whatever Swedes could be induced to move, would invade Brandenburg and Pomerania. Another 70,000 Russians would march from central Poland, cross the Oder River, and meet Daun somewhere in Silesia.[36]

These kinds of large-scale troop movements were impossible to conceal, and almost equally impossible to execute quickly. As suggested earlier, the first opportunities to check Prussia's enemies came in the west. In March Ferdinand, after making a few feints against the French in the Rhineland, declared his intention of turning against the Imperial army, concentrated by now around Bamberg. Frederick urged Prince Henry to support the operation. When his brother proved reluctant, encouragement became orders. In the end nothing came of the operation. Instead on 13 April Ferdinand was defeated at Bingen by the French whom his own movements had galvanized into action.

Henry, a younger son and a cautious general, was reluctant to attack the Imperials with his own resources, but on 6 May finally launched his advance. The *Reichsarmee* fell back before him, losing more men to desertion and straggling than in the few skirmishes their commanders actually risked. Neither Frederick nor Henry, however, had intended a pursuit *à outrance*. If the enemy stood and fought, well and good, but the Prince's offensive was basically a raid to

---

36 Dietrich Bangert, *Die russisch-österreichische militärische Zusammenarbeit im Siebenjährigen Kriege in den Jahren 1758–1759* (Boppard, 1971), remains the best analysis of this complex political and strategic relationship. For details of the 1758 plan, see pp. 52 ff.

destroy bases and disrupt supply systems. By 1 June Henry's men were back in their original area of deployment.[37] The operation had, however, been something more than an eighteenth-century military gavotte. It had demonstrated beyond doubt just how little was to be expected from the Imperials in the coming summer. It had also enhanced Prussia's reputation in the western German area of operations. The well-disciplined battalions of Ferdinand and Henry were an institutional argument for Frederick's ways of war when compared to the disorderly Imperials and the scarcely less controlled French.

Increasingly, however, Henry's achievements resembled the successful curing of a cancer patient's facial warts. In June, the French moved against Ferdinand in what seemed overwhelming force. They captured the city of Münster, then the crucial supply depot of Minden, without a serious fight, using the techniques of masking and manoeuvre that Ferdinand had employed so successfully a year earlier. Frederick bombarded his subordinate with long-distance good advice to remember Rossbach and accept the gage of battle even at the risk of defeat.[38] Unfortunately for Ferdinand, the advice was unaccompanied by troops and guns. Frederick had none of either to spare. His main army was effectively held in place by Daun. Even if the Austrian commander was reluctant to move, even though he continually frittered away his strength in detachments, Frederick was able to do no more than spar a few rounds with Habsburg outposts and light forces as the summer progressed.

The immediate situation was not entirely disadvantageous, as Frederick was able to season his unusually mixed bag of troops under field conditions. Waiting, however, told heavily on the royal nerves. Ferdinand of Brunswick was not the only subordinate harassed by constant advice, warnings, recriminations, and orders, the last sometimes mutually exclusive. In late June, Daun finally moved – but no further than the broken ground of Upper Silesia. The initiative in this case came less from Daun himself than from the Russians, who began their advance to the Oder on 25 June. By virtue of previous agreements they expected the Austrians to follow suit, but, instead

---

37 The best analysis in English of Henry's campaign is Chester Easum, *Prince Henry of Prussia: Brother of Frederick the Great* (Madison, Wis., 1942), pp. 95 ff. This is also the best biography, but can usefully be supplemented by Werner Gembruch 'Prinz Heinrich von Preussen, Bruder Friedrichs des Grossen', in *Persönlichkeiten im Umkreis Friedrichs des Grossen*, ed. J. Kunisch (Cologne, 1988), pp. 89–120.

38 Frederick to Ferdinand, 1 July 1759, PC, XVIII, 370–1.

of moving his entire force towards the river, Daun despatched only 24,000 men under Marshal Gideon Laudon. The decision, though made from Daun's continued fear of Frederick, was not an objectively bad one. Laudon was one of the best of the Austrian army's younger generation of commanders, a Baltic-born free-lancer initially rejected by Frederick. He had found a place in the more open ranks of the Habsburg officer corps, but his saturnine temperament and his habit of speaking his mind won him few friends as he climbed the rank ladder. In particular he did not get on well with Lacy, and in the aftermath of Hochkirch Lacy had Daun's ear as much as anyone in the army's headquarters. Laudon, moreover, was a field soldier who had made much of his reputation commanding moderately sized independent forces. Detaching him solved at least two problems at once for Daun – by decreasing friction among his subordinates, and by removing a man whose criticism of his superiors' style of command was obvious even when Laudon never said a word.[39]

Nor was Daun ungenerous in drawing up the orders of battle. Laudon received some of the army's best fighting regiments: the Birkenfeld Cuirassiers, the Württemberg Dragoons, the Light Horse Regiment Jung-Löwenstern. Laudon's infantry included the south Germans of the 35th, the Low Countrymen of the 9th, the Hungarians of the 19th – a cross-section of the Habsburg Empire and its army. They would fight if well-led, and Laudon was just the man to secure maximum results from his multicultural task force.

Daun's strategy depended on keeping Frederick and Henry pinned in south Germany while Laudon and the Russians chopped into Prussia's exposed rear. Even Maria Theresa saw the connection – and the weak link. Daun was unlikely to fix the King of Prussia by the basilisk effect of his dynamic personality. The Habsburg Empress ordered her principal commander to advance and fight Frederick at the first favourable opportunity, absolving him in advance for any consequences of defeat.[40] Daun moved slowly, no more than a

---

39 Franz Pesendorfer, *Feldmarschall Loudon. Der Sieg und seine Preis* (Vienna, 1989), is the best modern study. Cf. also Johannes Kunisch, 'Feldmarschall Loudon oder das Soldatenglück', *Historische Zeitschrift*, 236 (1983), 49–72.

40 Maria Theresa to Daun, 24 July 1759, in Johannes Kunisch, *Das Mirakel des Hauses Brandenburg. Studien zum Verhältnes von Kabinettspolitik und Kriegführung im Zeitalter des Siebenjährigen Krieges* (Munich, 1978), pp. 95–100. Cf. the general analysis in Bangert, *Die russische-österreichische militärische Zusammenarbeit*, pp. 204 *passim*.

few miles a day, digging himself in at every opportunity. Frederick referred scathingly to 'the fat excellency with a lead butt'. Nevertheless, Daun gave the King no openings for the battle Frederick hoped to fight and expected to win. And meantime the situation on Prussia's eastern frontier approached critical mass and imminent meltdown.

Frederick had left Dohna in command of that theatre for no better reason than *faute de mieux*. He had assigned General Moritz von Wobersnow as Dohna's 'adviser' in the same spirit. Wobersnow's personal life was dissolute even by the standards of a Prussian hussar, and he seemed to save most of his intellectual and physical energy for liquor and women. In June he proposed a raid towards Thorn to threaten the long and disorganized Russian supply lines. Frederick responded with more enthusiasm than the project deserved, describing it as a potential campaign-winner. The actual results were limited, partly by Wobersnow's lack of enterprise and more by Russian refusal to oblige the would-be raiders by uncovering their communications. The King's exasperated comment that Wobersnow had made every mistake possible and his campaign deserved immortality as a negative example was perhaps excessively harsh. It did accurately reflect Frederick's growing concern for the threat from the east.

By mid-July approximately 70,000 Russians had assembled around Posen, ready for the march westward. They were under a new commander. General Peter Saltykov had relieved Fermor, discredited in court circles for his clumsy handling of the previous year's campaign. At 61 Saltykov was elderly for a major field command, and had more experience as an administrator than a battle captain. He possessed something resembling a common touch and manifested an unusual concern for the day-to-day well-being of his men. Whether these regimental virtues could be translated into victory against the Prussians was, however, by no means certain.

Nor were Russian policy-makers speaking with a single voice. Elizabeth's health was fragile. She was overweight, colicky, and constipated – conditions exacerbated by an unhealthy life style swinging from indulgence to asceticism and back again. In June 1756, she had suffered a stroke her doctors believed life-threatening. She continued thereafter to have periodic seizures – perhaps other, smaller strokes, perhaps *petit mal* epilepsy.[41] Although her hatred for Frederick remained unabated, her nephew and heir was an extreme Prussophile. How committed a particular general might be to a particular cam-

41 Tamara Talbot Rice, *Elizabeth Empress of Russia* (London, 1970), pp. 194 ff.

paign plan at a particular date depended significantly on the degree of his future orientation.

Saltykov was the Empress's man. Once the campaigning season of 1759 opened, the unprepossessing Russian commander surprised everyone by making his basic moves correctly – a process enhanced by Dohna's passivity. Outnumbered by more than two to one, the Prussian commander seemed virtually hypnotized by Saltykov's feints until a disgusted Frederick replaced him by Lieutenant General Johann von Wedell. Frederick charged his new commander with being to his army what a dictator was in the Roman Republic – not an ignoble comparison for a general able to execute the intention. Wedell unfortunately was a typical product of the Frederician system. Brave and aggressive in battle, he had no experience of independent command and could conceive of no better way to execute his monarch's orders than to go looking for a fight at the first opportunity.

American readers may well perceive similarities between the situation in East Prussia in 1759 and the relief of Joseph Johnston by John Bell Hood before Atlanta in 1864. Then too a cautious general was replaced by a thruster. Saltykov, even more than William T. Sherman, was perfectly willing to let his enemy run his head into a noose. He deftly manoeuvred his main body across Wedell's lines of communication, then set out to give the Prussians a lesson in defensive fighting. The Russian main army deployed in two lines around the village of Paltzig. A shallow, swampy river covered the front, and Saltykov extended his left to take advantage of the river's relative unfordability outside of the main battle zone. His right was deployed on and around a number of small hills south of Paltzig. With his guns well dug in, the batteries' fields of fire overlapping, Saltykov was content to wait. The July weather was hot. Prussian canteens would be as empty as Prussian haversacks by the time the musketeers reached Saltykov's killing ground.

Wedell obliged his adversary nicely. Apart from his head-down temperament, he had no real alternative but attack. His force was too small to make manoeuvring the Russians out of their position a favourable option. Nor was Wedell's army, heavily East Prussian in original composition, with a high proportion of the winter's polyglot replacements filling out its ranks, likely to endure deprivation willingly. On 23 July scouts discovered the Russian position. Desertion and straggling had reduced Wedell's strength by now from 28,000 to around 23,000 men. Nevertheless, he prepared to attack off the line of march.

Critics later argued he would have been better advised to keep his force as an army in being, to threaten and harass the Russians as they continued their march to the Oder. Wedell's troops had at least ten days' basic rations in their supply wagons, and could in an emergency have drawn on the magazines at Glogau in Silesia. Wedell's answer was that the King expected him to fight at any cost. He led the first infantry wave in person, through the village of Kay against the Russian right. A second task force was ordered to find a way across the river further south and envelop the flank Wedell attacked in front. The rest of his little army Wedell retained in reserve, to be committed as the situation developed.

Wedell at least led from strength. His advance guard, consisting of two of his best regiments, the 3rd and the 7th, reached the Russian gun positions despite heavy losses from artillery fire, but then lost touch with the rest of the army and was driven back in disorder. A second frontal attack, this one six battalions strong, met no more success. An attempted flanking move collapsed under heavy artillery fire. Wedell unleashed his cavalry, but the troopers achieved nothing against unshaken Russian batteries supported by a series of deftly timed counterattacks. Wedell brought up reinforcements, rallied his first waves, and sent them in once more over their own dead and wounded in the waning light of the summer day. Once again Russian guns brought the infantry to a halt, then to retreat. The misfortunate Wobersnow ended the day by leading eight battalions against a sector of the Russian line that had been neither prepared by artillery fire nor shaken by earlier attacks. His death at the head of his men might indeed have seemed a preferable alternative to facing his King.

By 7 p.m. it was all over. Wedell, himself wounded, drew his survivors away from the battlefield and across the Oder. Eight thousand of his men were killed, wounded, or missing – including a disconcertingly high proportion of deserters even by Prussian standards. Saltykov had not won his victory without loss. Forty-eight hundred Russians, over 10 per cent of the troops on the field, were killed or wounded – a good reason for doing no more than keeping the field. Saltykov's reluctance to pursue his beaten foe only enhanced his reputation with the army's rank and file, who had a chance to savour their triumph in full before the army took up its march to the Oder in the wake of Wedell's remnants.[42]

The consequences of this battle, Paltzig to the Russians and Kay to the Prussians, did not depend on its tactical results. Even before

---

42 Duffy, *Army of Frederick the Great*, p. 187; and *Russia's Military Way to the West*, pp. 105 ff., combine for the best modern summary in English.

Zorndorf, only optimists had assumed the possibility of successfully attacking Russians possessing 100 per cent superiority in numbers in a position they had chosen and reinforced. In that sense Frederick's relatively sympathetic reaction to Wedell's dispatch informing him of the defeat was logical. The King may have been influenced as well by a certain sense that despite Wedell's shortcomings, he was the best man available – the man, indeed, whom Frederick had picked for the mission. Instead the outcome of Kay/Paltzig only reinforced Frederick's belief that one successful battle would restore 'order' on his eastern frontier. Wedell's men had done well against odds. Suitably reinforced, they would do better. On the evening of 29 July, Frederick turned command of the main army, 40,000 men, to Prince Henry. Supported by Fouqué's 18,000 men, by now concentrated around Landeshut, this seemed a force strong enough to keep Daun in play. Frederick himself struck out for the Oder with twenty-one battalions, thirty-five squadrons, and over seventy heavy guns, plus the new horse artillery: the remaining cream of a hard-tried army.

Daun, instead of slipping away from Henry and driving his whole force towards the Oder in Laudon's tracks, despatched only 22,000 men under General Andreas Hadik, who proved at least as unenterprising as his superior. A few skirmishes with Frederick's flank guards convinced the Austrian that his men were too fatigued to risk venturing further into the blue. Laudon for his part kept moving. He reached the Oder on 2 August. The Russians had arrived on the opposite bank a day earlier. A disappointed Saltykov, who had expected the presence of Daun's whole army, was reluctant to chance a crossing with Frederick somewhere in the neighbourhood. Laudon for his part wanted to fight, and saw no reason to strain the alliance by arguing the point. On 5 August he moved his force to the Oder's east bank and joined the Russians in their fortified camp at Kunersdorf.

By most reckonings the allies were on the wrong side of the river. Should they defeat Frederick, the theoretical possibility of pinning the King against the Oder and destroying his army did exist. In practical terms Saltykov was not the man for such an operation, while Laudon was more a battle captain than a master of operational art. The generals, moreover, did not get along. Saltykov suspected foreigners on general principle, and seems to have regarded Laudon as more show than substance. Laudon described Saltykov as untrustworthy, though 'inscrutable' might have been a more accurate characterization. The generals, their staffs and interpreters, continued to debate the next move until Saltykov grumblingly conceded to crossing the Oder after all and marching towards Silesia to meet Daun.[43] Frederick's speed drew a line through his enemies' intentions. Reinforced by Wedell's troops and another smaller detached force, on 10 August he crossed the Oder on improvised bridges with a force of 50,000 men. He intended 'to advance on the enemy in order to attack him early the day after tomorrow'.[44] Tents and haversacks were left on the west bank of the river; the crossing site was secured by three regiments that had suffered such heavy losses at Kay, they were no longer considered fit for front-line service. That left Frederick with about 48,000 men – fifty-three battalions, ninety-five squadrons, and over 140 heavy guns, not counting battalion pieces.

The King would need everything he could put into the field against the combined forces of Saltykov and Laudon: 52,000 infantry, 12,000 cavalry, and over 250 guns. As so often during the Seven Years War, Frederick's enemies also had the advantage of position. Saltykov's men had dug themselves into the sandy soil of a ridge extending south-west from the village of Kunersdorf, about 5 miles east of Frankfurt an der Oder. The Russians were deployed in two lines, their front strengthened at intervals by fortified batteries of heavy guns. Laudon's corps was concentrated in the right rear of the position, partly as a reserve and partly as a striking force. The left flank, facing low, boggy ground, seemed well enough secured by entrenchments on the high ground overlooking Kunersdorf itself – the Mühl-Berge, the locals called this network of hills. They would play a key role in the coming battle.

Frederick made his customary personal reconnaissance on the evening of 11 August, accompanied, as at Zorndorf, by local guides: a forest ranger and an officer who had been stationed in Frankfurt before the war. All accounts agree that the King badly overestimated the suitability of the terrain for complex tactical manoeuvres. Even to an optimist, most of the allied line seemed to offer distinctly unpromising possibilities for an attack. Frederick concluded that his best prospects lay in marching against the allied left. Through his telescope, that sector seemed relatively unprotected – a bit of wishful royal thinking perhaps enhanced by the presence of wooded hills, outside the Russian entrenchments, that Frederick believed could be used to screen a Prussian advance. Replicating his dispositions at

43 Bangert, *Die russische-österreichische militärische Zusammenarbeit*, pp. 224 ff.

44 Frederick to Finckenstein, 10 Aug. 1759, *PC*, XVIII, 481.

Leuthen the King detailed a diversionary force of eight battalions and a dozen squadrons of cavalry to attract the enemy's attention. The main Prussian body would envelop the allied position, smash its flank, and drive any survivors towards the Oder River. Frederick, however, had made one major blunder. He mistook the direction in which the enemy positions were facing! The attack which he projected to strike a relatively open flank, perhaps even a vulnerable rear, was instead aimed at a fully entrenched front!

The Prussians broke camp between 2 and 3 on the morning of 12 August. The badly broken terrain both hindered the Prussian infantry and delayed the deployment of the heavy artillery upon which Frederick relied to prepare his attack. As the day dawned clear and hot, heavy clouds of dust thrown up by boots, hooves, and wheels gave Saltykov and Laudon ample warning of the Prussian axis of advance. Frederick was further discomfited when he caught sight of the low, marshy ground across which he had proposed to deliver his main attack – to say nothing of his reaction to the bristling network of fortifications that daylight revealed to his troops.

More than any period to date in Frederick's military career, the morning of Kunersdorf confronted the King with the tactical consequences of conceptual and institutional failures at the operational level. There existed no objective reason why the King could not have supplemented his personal observations with the detailed reports of scouts and patrols – none, that is, except Frederick's belief that anything he did not execute personally was *ipso facto* unreliable. The continuing evolution of the hussars into battle cavalry meant that the Prussian army no longer had any troops with reconnaissance as even a major secondary mission. Nor did it have any systematic means of combing its ranks for reliable men with some knowledge of the terrain on which its commander proposed to fight. The result at Kunersdorf was an elaborate series of marches and manoeuvres that ended by bringing Frederick to one of the strongest points in the enemy line, facing terrain that could only retard an attack whose success depended heavily on speed and shock – particularly given the blistering heat of the day.

In battle at least, the King of Prussia was no longer a man who took counsel of his fear. He reoriented the tactical axis of attack on the spot to avoid the worst of the soft ground. He ordered his guns into position. Around 11.30 a.m., over sixty pieces, twelve- and six-pounders, opened fire against the Russian positions on the Mühl-Berge. The Prussians had the advantage of numbers and position. After an hour's shelling, most of the Russian guns were silenced, their crews dead or driven to cover. The infantry holding the redoubts, packed elbow to elbow, suffered as much from thirst and heat as from Prussian fire. At 12.30 Frederick reckoned the enemy position to be *Sturmreif*, and sent his infantry forward in two waves. The first included four elite grenadier battalions. The second, following at a short interval, consisted of two more battalions of grenadiers and a line regiment, the 43rd Fusiliers.

The latter was a relatively new creation, a Silesian formation whose men Frederick regarded as neither as loyal nor as hardy as his 'old Prussian' veterans. That it was entrusted with such a key assignment suggests clearly the effect of two-and-a-half years of war on Prussia's infantry. Today, however, the Silesians held pace and won honour with the men of the grenadiers. Taking full advantage of small irregularities in the ground, the Prussians closed to volley range through heavy musket and canister fire, then charged. Some of the Russians ran. Others, too exhausted or too shell-shocked to move, simply threw themselves on the ground, or stood dumbly in ranks to be spitted by the Prussian bayonets. Prussian troops were not normally especially atrocity-prone even in the midst of battle. But here the Russians were not surrendering, and they were so crowded as to constitute a genuine obstacle to the advance. Bayoneting an unresisting man grew easier with repetition.[45] Within minutes the Mühl-Berge were in Prussian hands, the defenders scattered, eighty or ninety guns lost.

It was a neat first-stage victory, executed with relatively little loss to the front-line units. It was also a greater success than Frederick's preparation deserved. Some of the King's entourage urged him to rest content. The allies, they argued, could not maintain their present position and were unlikely to mount a successful counterattack so relatively late in the day. Let the Russians and Austrians for a change throw themselves against a Prussian defence. Or let the allies disengage, abandon the field, and perhaps create opportunity for just that kind of encounter battle in the open that Frederick himself had recommended earlier in the year as so suited to Prussian methods.

Instead, the King decided to continue the fight. He ordered some of his twelve-pounders to leave their original positions and move up to the Mühl-Berge. He ordered his feint against the allied right to press forward, perhaps becoming a real attack in its own right. And he sent his victorious advance guard straight ahead – into the teeth of a revitalized defence.

45 Warnerey, *Campagnes*, p. 312.

A little valley called the Kuh-Grunde separated the Mühl-Berge from the main allied position. Well before the Russian defences collapsed Laudon had started a dozen companies of grenadiers to their support, and the whitecoats reached the right place at the right time. Instead of crossing the Kuh-Grunde and being caught in the Russians' defeat, the Austrian grenadiers formed a firing line on the far side of the valley. Reinforced by further Austrian and Russian troops, they shot it out at point-blank range with their equally determined adversaries and stopped the Prussians in their tracks.

According to one account at least, Saltykov substituted prayer for tactics during this phase of the battle.[46] His behaviour reflected conditions in the front lines at least as clearly as a more orthodox style of command might have done. Frederick had originally intended to commit his infantry in echelon, the better to probe for flanks and weak spots. But by now the field was shrouded by a thick blanket of powder smoke. Confused officers tended to lead men half-paralysed by thirst and heat to the sound of the heaviest fighting. Battalions piled up one behind the other, so disorganized that it proved impossible even to relieve the sorely tried units in the front lines. Major Ewald von Kleist, one of Prussia's best-known poets and bravest fighting men, was mortally wounded here. Cavalry from both armies attacked and counterattacked with no result – not least because the infantry on both sides were too densely packed to make flight a readily available option.

Frederick's initial efforts to get his stalled attack moving met with frustration as his reserve battalions and squadrons were absorbed relentlessly into the fire-storm around the Kuh-Grunde. Then the King called for Seydlitz. At such close quarters the Prussian heavy cavalry was unlikely either to find the opening or to develop the impetus for one of the battering charges that had become its speciality. The army's *beau sabreur* successfully charged a small force of allied cavalry, but his men flinched when faced with the musketry of three fresh Russian infantry regiments. Then Seydlitz himself was wounded – not badly, but painfully enough to force him to retire. His successors in command possessed neither Seydlitz's energy nor his *coup d'œil*. Fresh Russian and Austrian horsemen closed in on Prussian troopers already disorganized by close-range artillery fire. The 6th Dragoons, whose nickname of the 'Porcelain Regiment' embodied the army legend that the regiment had been originally acquired from Saxony in exchange for tableware, rode into range of a Russian battery and

---

46 Quoted in Duffy, *Russia's Military Way to the West*, p. 110.

was put out of action in a matter of minutes. Other regiments seeking to disengage and rally found themselves penned against lakes and ponds, or driven into boggy ground where their heavy mounts were no match for the steppe ponies of Saltykov's Cossacks and Tartars.

Some of the Prussian troopers were forced back into the ranks of their own infantry. For men who had marched and fought for sixteen hours, much of the time with empty canteens, for men who had seen their ranks decimated – not least by Prussian cannoneers who seemed to pay no attention to the colour of their targets' uniforms – this was the final discomfiture. Frederick subsequently dismissed what began around the Kuh-Grunde about 5.30 as 'the absurd fear of being transported to Siberia'.[47] Perhaps there may have been some feeling, conscious or subconscious, that if the Russians were by no means immortal as individuals, they were close to unconquerable *en masse*. Laudon's men too had fought with a fury unfamiliar on the battlefields of Saxony and Bohemia. With battalions reduced to the strength of companies and companies melted to platoons, they held their ground at bayonet point when their cartridges ran out. And over it all lay the sickening smells of blood and excrement, the clouds of powder smoke that blinded eyes and thickened tongues, the growing miasma of confusion.

It was the Prussians who flinched first. Lack of ammunition furnished the overt excuse for seeking safety in the rear. In contrast to Leuthen, the infantry's ammunition wagons had no chance at all to overcome the obstacles of soft ground and Russian artillery fire that seemed deliberately to seek out any target larger than a single man. It took only minutes for unsteadiness in the ranks to flare into full-fledged panic. No one, officer or man, wanted to be the last one left to hold on a stricken field. Frederick, whose decisions had contributed so heavily to the catastrophe, plunged in to stem the tide. Two horses were shot from under him. His coat was pierced by musket balls as he seized a regimental flag and shouted for a rally. His words were lost in the roar of gunfire. His example went for naught when some of the allied cavalry, instead of pursuing its defeated Prussian counterparts, turned instead on the infantry.

Battalions that by now consisted of no more than a few files around the colours broke and ran for the shelter of the small woods and copses dotting the field. Frederick rallied a few hundred men in an effort to form a new line, only to see them melt away under Russian canister fire. A few beacons guttered through the fog of

47 Frederick to Finckenstein, 16 Aug. 1759, *PC*, XVIII, 487.

defeat. The Prussian artillerymen, from whom traditionally no sense of warriors' honour had been expected, fought their guns to the muzzle. A Silesian fusilier regiment, converted from labour troops only the previous year, advanced from its inglorious assignment of guarding the artillery park. Surrounded in minutes, the rear echelon soldiers made a heroic stand in square until, all of hope of relief gone, the survivors grounded their arms in surrender. Frederick himself had a musket ball stopped by a snuff box he carried in his pocket, and was saved from falling into the hands of the Cossacks only by the desperate charge of a detachment of the Ziethen Hussars.

The Prussian army had not been defeated. It had been routed. No more than 3,000 or 4,000 men remained under Frederick's command as he left the field, and many of those were stragglers who could think of nowhere else to go. A thunder-and-lightning storm, albeit unaccompanied by rain, added to the terror of defeat on a pitch-black night illuminated only by occasional lightning flashes. The disorganized mass that had at daybreak been an elite fighting force sought to regain the Oder bridgeheads ahead of the Croats

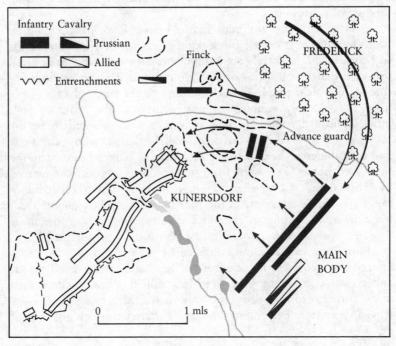

4. Battle of Kunersdorf, 12 August 1759

and Cossacks everyone was sure were on the fugitives' heels. It was small comfort that instead of pursuing a beaten enemy these irregulars devoted their attention to plundering corpses and cutting the throats of the wounded.[48] Frederick was in despair. He turned command of Kunersdorf's survivors over to a subordinate – a sign of belief that nothing mattered any longer. He informed his foreign minister that he would not survive this cruel turn of fortune and did not propose to outlive the ruin of his country.[49] In truth, the King had much over which to grieve. Of the 50,000 men he had taken into battle, more than 19,000 had become casualties. One hundred and seventy-two guns, including no fewer than eighty-five of the nearly irreplaceable twelve-pounders, had been left on the field. Even the artillery's new pride, its horse artillery battery, was lost to the Russians. No fewer than twenty-eight flags and standards had been captured, and some of these were scavenged from where they had been abandoned by their terrified bearers. Eight regimental colonels were dead – no small loss to a field-officer corps whose quality was an increasing subject of concern.

Serious as these material losses were, Frederick also confronted the inescapable fact that, however inadvertently, he had fought his enemies' kind of battle. Instead of finding and developing a weak spot in the allied lines, the King had directed his oblique order against a strong point. Instead of utilizing his infantry's capacity for tactical manoeuvre, he had committed it to a killing ground where the only real question involved which side would break first. Instead of the cavalry and artillery serving as force multipliers to change the nature of battle, they had merely been part of an effort to use a heavier hammer against the Kuh-Grunde. Even had the Prussians held the field of Kunersdorf, a 40 per-cent casualty rate was more than the army and the state could afford unless the battle in question was likely to decide the war. And even at his most wildly optimistic Frederick could scarcely have hoped that the defeat on Prussian territory of an Austrian task force and a Russian expeditionary corps would somehow impel the enemy empresses to suspend hostilities.

Paradoxically, the Prussian position brightened when viewed from the enemy's perspective. Kunersdorf had been a triumph of

---

48 Turn-of-the-century accounts of Kunersdorf include Albert Naudé, 'Zur Schlacht bei Kunersdorf', *Forschungen zur brandenburgischen und preussischen Geschichte*, VI (1893), 251–64; and von Eberhardt, 'Die Schlacht bei Kunersdorf', *Militär-Wochenblatt* (1903) *Beiheft* IX, 389–420.

49 Frederick to Finckenstein, 12 Aug. 1759, *PC*, XVIII, 481.

regimental determination and allied cooperation. The Russians and Austrians had outfought Frederick's best in an eyeball-to-eyeball confrontation that tested nerve and courage at least as much as military skills. Elizabeth promoted Saltykov to Field-Marshal and issued a medal to every participant. She even sent Laudon a sword of honour – fitting recognition of the Austrians' contribution to the victory. But as Saltykov informed his monarch, the King of Prussia sold his defeat at a high price. Nineteen thousand Russians and Austrians had been killed or wounded; the victors were almost as badly shaken and disorganized as the vanquished. Laudon rhetorically urged an immediate tactical pursuit. When Saltykov demurred, the usually hard-driving Austrian was content enough to cooperate in a gentlemanly advance to the Oder. On 17 August, the Russians finally crossed the river in the context of Daun's agreement to guarantee his allies' supplies.

MAXEN: SYMBOL OF DECLINE

That was all. For the next month, both Russian and Austrian armies remained inactive. Maria Theresa regarded the next logical step as a joint advance on Berlin, a city less than a week's marching distance even by easy stages. The Austrian Council of War urged Daun not to let Frederick's beaten army out of his sight, but instead to pursue and destroy it. Elizabeth was less sanguine. She urged Saltykov to avoid further general action, which she described as too expensive and too risky to be worth taking. Saltykov regarded his army as having done all of the campaign's serious fighting, and had no intention of taking further decisive action without ironclad guarantees of cooperation. In the event, Daun was more concerned with possible Prussian threats to his supply lines from Bohemia than with striking at either the political or the military vitals of his enemy.[50]

The result was what Frederick later described as the first miracle of the house of Hohenzollern.[51] The Russians and the Austrians neither combined their forces nor acted individually, either to seize the Prussian capital or to destroy what remained of the army so badly beaten at Kunersdorf. Left undisturbed, that force rapidly increased in strength. Stragglers reported to Frederick's camp singly and in detachments, by hundreds, then by thousands. For all of the horror stories about service in the Prussian army, surprisingly few

50 Bangert, *Die russische-österreichische militärische Zusammenarbeit*, pp. 242 ff.; Thadden, *Feldmarschall Daun*, pp. 395 ff.
51 Frederick II to Prince Henry, 1 Sept. 1759, *PC*, XVIII, 510.

men took advantage of the situation to surrender to the Russians or Austrians, or simply to disappear. Some had nowhere to go. Some were hungry enough to welcome army rations once more. Others, however, cantonists and mercenaries alike, chose not to abandon their service. By 15 August, 24,000 men stood under the colours salvaged from Kunersdorf. They were tired; they were demoralized; but they were present.

The next day Frederick resumed personal command. He replaced part of his lost heavy artillery by stripping Berlin of its available twelve–pounders. He sent cavalry patrols to scour the countryside for men still missing. By the month's end, however, the King could still count no more than 33,000 men under arms, and he consistently denigrated both their quality and their willingness to fight.

Prussia's cause may well have been saved by Frederick's brother. On learning of the news of Kunersdorf, Prince Henry abandoned his habitual caution and marched eastwards into Saxony. By 12 September he turned Daun's fears to reality by reaching Görlitz, astride the main Austrian supply line – which now, by agreement, must support the Russians as well. On 22 August, when Daun and Saltykov met to discuss possible next moves, Daun insisted on the importance of securing the allies' logistics in the face of this new threat westwards, towards Bautzen. Saltykov saw the move as a political one, designed to secure Austria's interests in Saxony at the expense of any meaningful cooperation against Frederick. Russia's main field army would not be a Habsburg cat's-paw. Instead, it moved in the opposite direction from Daun, to the Oder River.

Saltykov was by no means abandoning Daun or the alliance. His initial intention was to lay siege to the fortress of Glogau in the stated hope of drawing Frederick into Silesia and bringing Frederick to action; and with the underlying expectation of at least occupying a useful *point d'appui* for next year's campaign. When the Austrians failed to provide supplies and siege materials, Saltykov expressed willingness to keep Frederick's revitalized army in play while Daun finished off Prince Henry.[52]

That, however, proved to be a difficult option. Initially the situation seemed promising for the Austrians. A *Reichsarmee* that had shed the worst of its troops and the least efficient of its commanders had been gobbling up undermanned Prussian fortresses and strong

---

52 Saltykov's report of his meeting with Daun is reprinted in Bangert, *Die russische-österreichische militärische Zusammenarbeit*, pp. 399–401; the allies' moves are analysed in *ibid.*, pp. 252 *passim*.

points for most of the summer. On 4 September, Dresden itself surrendered to the hitherto despised Imperials. Frederick sent Henry what reinforcements he could spare, but the Prince had no intention of facing Daun in a pitched battle. By mid-October he had retreated to a strong position near Torgau. The Prussian prince and the Austrian marshal exchanged feints for a month, despite Frederick's repeated insistence on the Habsburg army's vulnerability to just one more big battle. Then, on 24 October, Saltykov made Frederick's course of action easier by ordering his Russians back to Thorn on the Vistula River. There the army would go into winter quarters and prepare for the next year. Laudon, downcast and angry, led the survivors of his corps back into Bohemia to join Daun. Frederick promptly betook himself to Henry's camp, arriving on 13 November. Arguably even more welcome were the 16,000-odd troops he had sent ahead, bringing Henry's strength up to around 60,000 men.

It was a numerically strong army whose morale on the whole had not been directly affected by the blood-letting of Kay and Kunersdorf. Frederick, however, was not at his physical or emotional best in the last months of 1759. Some good news had arrived from the west. On 1 August, Ferdinand of Brunswick had won a neat tactical triumph over the French at Minden. He followed up his victory by manoeuvring his enemy out of Westphalia and back to the start lines of the spring campaign.

The Prince of Brunswick's performance was significant both negatively and positively. Minden was the last major Anglo/Prussian base in western Germany. Its loss would have left Prussia's heartland open to a French invasion, as well as to the Russian/Austrian thrust that never quite came off. Instead, by the third week of August Ferdinand was seriously considering a march to the Rhine, perhaps even a move into France itself. His German troops, however mixed their origins, were by now tested veterans, confident in themselves and their general. The British contingent might have been regarded as a potential weak spot in the weeks before Minden. After the brilliant feat of arms of its infantry, routing French cavalry on open ground by musketry alone, no one doubted the redcoats' fighting qualities. All that was needed was a free hand from Frederick – perhaps as well a few more troops, and something more than the meagre trickle of supplies which the King had heretofore allowed the war's western theatre.[53]

---

53 Piers Mackesy, *The Coward of Minden: The Affair of Lord George Sackville* (New York, 1979), incorporates a solid analysis of the campaign and the battle.

Instead, Ferdinand received a letter asking for help in Kunersdorf's aftermath. Frederick wanted an advance south-east, towards Halle and Leipzig, to attract the *Reichsarmee*'s and Daun's attention.[54] Ferdinand decided that the best support he could offer would involve pushing the French backwards towards Frankfurt and eventually out of Germany. For the next month Ferdinand advanced slowly, outrunning his supplies as the French drew strength from their own magazines. Frederick, disconcerted by the stately pace of his cousin's advance, repeatedly wrote urging haste while imploring Ferdinand to send him reinforcements. Ferdinand continued to temporize as October gave way to November. Meanwhile, the French prepared a counter-stroke designed to teach the Prince of Brunswick his military manners.

The French were not the only army planning a riposte. Frederick was as convinced of his moral ascendancy over Daun as he was of his superiority as a strategist over anyone in Europe. The King anticipated little difficulty forcing the Austrians to evacuate Dresden by threatening their supply lines in time-honoured fashion. To this end he organized a task force under Friedrich August von Finck and sent it on an end run around Daun's army to the plateau of Maxen, where it could 'command' the main road from Bohemia while avoiding contact with large or belligerent opponents.[55] Finck, a veteran officer who began his career in Russia, stood about as well with his monarch as anyone at this time. He had performed reasonably well commanding the screening force at Kunersdorf, and better in the everyday work of restoring order to a thoroughly beaten army while Frederick was recovering his psychic equilibrium. He also had some experience commanding detached forces, and Frederick gave him some of the army's best troops. Finck's order of battle included four grenadier battalions, a half-dozen reliable infantry regiments from the 'old Prussian' provinces, and the crack 6th and 7th Cuirassiers, recently distinguished respectively at Hochkirch and Rossbach. Admittedly not all of the task force was of the same quality.[56] The King's orders also left Finck cut off from any reasonable possibility of support from the main army. Nevertheless, 15,000 men, eighteen battalions and thirty-five squadrons supported by seventy guns, posed a formidable threat to Daun's logistics, and could be reasonably expected to give

54 Frederick to Ferdinand, 15 Aug. 1759, *PC*, XVIII, 484.

55 Frederick to Finck, 15 Nov. 1759, *PC*, XVIII, 639.

56 Max Immich, 'Die Stärke des Finkschen Armeekorps bei Maxen', *Forschungen zur brandenburgischen und preussischen Geschichte*, VII (1894), 548–56.

a good account of themselves if brought to battle. Moreover, Daun's apparent commitment to making war by detachments left Frederick reasonably sanguine about this move to the Maxen plateau.

Finck was at least as optimistic as his master. Despite his exposed position, he made little use either of his single hussar regiment to provide operational security, or of his 3rd Free Battalion – one of the better formations of its type – as a tactical outpost and picket force. Meanwhile, General Lacy was urging Daun to move in force against this tempting target. Prince Charles Joseph de Ligne describes in his memoirs the reluctance not only of Daun, but also of most of the army's senior commanders, to take the risk of attacking across broken, wooded terrain that seemed an ideal natural defence.[57] Lacy was convinced that he could do against Finck what he had done against Frederick at Hochkirch: plan a march table that would bring the Austrians into the Prussian positions before the enemy knew what was happening. Finally he overcame Daun's resistance. The Prussian rook would be threatened by a knight fork.

Finck received warning of the Austrian advance from Frederick himself on 19 November, well before the Habsburg task force was in any position to threaten his camp and in ample time to withdraw his men from their exposed position. The King, however, did not describe the situation in urgent terms nor did he authorize a retreat.[58] Finck refused to risk Frederick's wrath without direct orders. He also seems to have been confident that if he held his position Frederick somehow would come to his aid. Critics of Finck's apparent lack of 'civil courage' tend to overlook both Frederick's repeated ability to perform similar operations and his propensity for keeping his grand designs to himself. Finck can hardly be blamed for remembering his master's propensity for boldness, or for believing that he was only one of the King's chess pieces. In his own mind his task was to hold out, and he believed he could perform that mission until relieved.[59]

The Austrians disabused him. Daun had allocated 32,000 men for the attack on Finck's camp. Nine thousand men, *Reichstruppen* stiffened by a few Austrian units, advanced from the south-east. Six thousand more closed in from the north. The main force of 17,000, accompanied by Daun himself, deployed to the south-west. All three columns took advantage of broken ground to approach

57 Quoted in Duffy, *Army of Maria Theresa*, pp. 195–6.
58 Frederick to Finck, 18 Nov. 1759, *PC*, XVIII, 651.
59 Jany, *Preussische Armee*, vol. II, p. 546, summarizes Finck's reasoning without defending it.

Finck's position unobserved, and then to deploy their heavy guns so as to bring the Prussians under a withering cross-fire. Not until 3.30 p.m. did the Austrian infantry go forward. As at Hochkirch the main force was formed in columns of battalions, sacrificing fire effect for speed and mass. Even more than at Hochkirch, the effect was devastating. The Prussian line gave way at several points. Desperate cavalry counterattacks were seen off by Austrian horsemen superior in numbers and morale. Maxen itself was successfully defended for a time, but then Finck's infantry began to collapse. Saxon conscripts, Russian and Austrian prisoners who had changed their coats rather than endure captivity, saw no reason now to engage in a hopeless last stand. More and more of them threw down their muskets and called for quarter. With daylight almost gone Finck tried to retreat, but found his chosen route blocked – blocked, furthermore, by the hitherto despised *Reichstruppen*.

Most of Finck's artillery had been captured. Over half his infantry had vanished from the ranks. Frederick had dispatched a relief force in Finck's direction, but snow-drifts delayed its march. Finck spent an anxious night waiting for orders and listening for gunfire. On the morning of the 21st the Austrians offered terms and threatened to renew their attack. Finck responded by surrendering his entire corps – 13,000 officers and men, including stragglers. Total Austrian casualties were fewer than 1,000. And the impact of the disaster was multiplied when Daun refused to exchange prisoners. The rank and file might be considered expendable. The 500 officers surrendered by Finck were now virtually irreplaceable.

Frederick lapsed into a depressive rage, asking melodramatically why bad fortune should pursue him to Saxony and descend on his unfortunate and unhappy life. Despite his declared intention not to judge the events without the facts, the King put the 'Maxen regiments' at the very bottom of his preferment list. Finck, who remained in Austrian custody until the end of the war, was court-martialled and sentenced to a year's confinement on his return.

Blame for the first large-scale surrender in Prussia's history has been tossed back and forth ever since. Prince Henry seems to have regarded Frederick as responsible for an operational approach that was 'contradictory and uncertain'.[60] Certainly Frederick exaggerated the capacity of his mere presence in the theatre to frighten an Austrian army that had shown an amoeba-like resilience in the face of the Prussians. Finck's task force, moreover, was an awkward size. Too

60 Easum, *Prince Henry of Prussia*, pp. 121–2.

small for a pitched battle, it was far too large for a raiding party, and correspondingly likely to attract hostile attention. On the other hand, Daun did not have a name for risk-taking. Frederick was not merely indulging in an all-or-nothing gamble by reasoning that Hochkirch had been an isolated event. Some of Finck's subordinates were also close to the mark in arguing the battle had been fought clumsily.

These criticisms ignore, however, the skilful Austrian planning and execution. Lacy for the second time in a year was able to achieve operational surprise. The Austrian column commanders proved themselves tactically proficient. The rank and file, infantrymen and gunners, overcame snow and cold to achieve surprise and the moral superiority that went with it. Finck's men were no worse, and arguably a bit better, than a cross-section of the Prussian army at the end of 1759. But their approach to military service was by now contractual rather than patriotic even among the native Prussians. Surrounded in the middle of winter, with no significant indication that their superiors had more than a vague idea of what was happening, it was scarcely remarkable that the 'Maxen men' decided fairly quickly that they had done enough to earn their pay from the King of Prussia.

Maxen was not, moreover, an isolated event. Two weeks later at Hussen, three more battalions on detached duty capitulated to the Austrians, albeit after a harder fight. By this time Frederick could do no more than hang on and hope the Austrians would retire. As winter deepened, the question became which army would first dissolve from cold and privation. Under conditions prefiguring those of George Washington's army at Valley Forge, Prussian troops on starvation rations crowded together not in cabins as usual, but in tents, seeking some protection from the snow and wind of the high country. Proximity-transmitted diseases, dysentery and respiratory infections spread like wildfire. Morale sagged accordingly. It suggests a good deal about Frederick's charisma, as well as his discipline, that his main army did not erupt in mutiny or erode in mass desertion. Perhaps the men were too miserable, and any reasonable destination too far away, to make anything beyond brute endurance an impossible option.

Circumstances elsewhere were no more promising. The Russians had withdrawn to winter quarters, but there was no doubt of their return in the spring. In any case Frederick had already reduced his forces in the eastern theatre to a minimum, able to do little more than screen those provinces still unoccupied. To the west the French, now under the duc de Broglie, a competent field soldier, took advantage of Ferdinand's overextension and reinforcements of fresh French and

Imperial troops to mount a counterattack that pushed the Prince's forces, now diminished significantly by detachments sent to Frederick, back almost into Hanover. Frederick's strategic position could hardly be worse. In the context of the inconsequential autumn operations of Daun and Saltykov, voices had been raised in Vienna and St Petersburg questioning the wisdom of continuing a war whose original objectives now seemed attainable only for disproportionate outlays of men and treasure. Maxen offered a seemingly irrefutable answer. In December, Kaunitz proclaimed that the King of Prussia was as good as destroyed. Russia's war hawks, including the Empress, agreed. The French were not quite so sure. The continental war in their sector was at best a stalemate. Nor had Broglie engaged the Prussian first team. Frederick's overtures to Paris for a separate peace were not rejected out of hand – but neither were Louis and his ministers anxious to take any drastic unilateral action. Perhaps instead the Anglo-Prussian alliance might self-destruct on grounds of mutual incompatibility if given enough time.[61]

That this was by no means a pipe dream was suggested by the negative reply Pitt gave to Frederick's request for a British squadron to operate in the Baltic. The Prime Minister's continued protests that the Royal Navy was stretched too thin for such a risk were at best imperfect camouflage for Britain's continued reluctance to risk its Baltic trade by provoking the Baltic maritime powers: Denmark, Sweden, and Russia. This defence of British self-interest was in part a response to a French strategy that hoped to provoke Britain into sending a fleet into the Baltic – a measure likely in turn to cause a Russian declaration of war.[62]

British reluctance to extend European commitments also in good part reflected a major shift in French national strategy. In December 1758, the duc de Choiseul became foreign minister and in effect first minister of France. He brought to his offices fresh energy and a fresh perspective. Britain, Choiseul argued, was France's principal enemy, against whom the country's limited resources must be concentrated. In March 1759, the Third Treaty of Versailles substantially reduced French military and financial commitments to the Continental war.

61 Bangert, *Die russische-österreichische militärische Zusammenarbeit*, pp. 291 ff.; Oliva, *Misalliance*, pp. 92 passim.

62 Richard Middleton, *The Bells of Victory: The Pitt-Newcastle Ministry and the Conduct of the Seven Years' War, 1757–1762* (Cambridge, 1985), pp. 58–9, 149–50; Oliva, *Misalliance*, pp. 138 ff.

Choiseul proposed instead to apply Continental principles to the British Isles. Rather than treat the French navy as a supply and transport force for colonial operations, Choiseul proposed to mount an invasion of England itself, with support from a Jacobite movement whose collapse after the abortive rising of 1745 was as yet plain neither in Paris nor in London. In the final version of his plan a squadron from Toulon and one from Brest would combine to escort a task force of 20,000 men to the mouth of the Clyde, then sail to meet another 20,000 at Ostend and shepherd them across the Channel to the Essex coastline. The prospects for Britain's collapse under this replication of the Spanish Armada were limited. Choiseul, however, was confident that the landing force could maintain itself as a kind of 'army in being', compelling Pitt – or his successor – to conclude peace on terms more favourable than those justified by French performance in the war to date.

The latter point was highlighted by the growing weaknesses of France's North American position. The massive imbalance between the military resources of French Canada and those of the British colonies began to take effect after two years of arm's-length sparring. Even before the loss of Québec in 1759, it was plain that the operational situation could not be restored without massive reinforcements from the mother country. Rather than accept the risks inherent in transporting and convoying large forces across the Atlantic, it seemed the better part of strategic wisdom to use these naval and military resources to strike at Britain itself.[63]

Choiseul initially hoped for the cooperation of the Dutch and the major Baltic powers, the Swedes and the Russians, whose war with Frederick did not yet extend to his island ally. Britain's conciliatory behaviour in the matter of a Baltic commitment combined with the implied threat of the Royal Navy's power to keep these states, already suffering from overextension, out of the French camp. Ultimately, therefore, the success of Choiseul's proposed operation depended on the French navy's direct capacity to elude British blockading forces and to establish control of the English Channel. The squadron from Toulon made it through the Strait of Gibraltar only to meet defeat off

---

63 Choiseul's grand design is outlined in G. Lacour-Gayet, *La Marine militaire de la France sous le régime de Louis XV* (Paris, 1902), pp. 318 ff. The practical obstacles to its implementation are highlighted in James Pritchard, *Louis XV's Navy 1748–1762: A Study of Organization and Administration* (Kingston, Ont., 1987). Cf., as well, C.F.G. Stanley, *New France, the Last Phase, 1744–1760* (London, 1968).

the Portuguese coast on 19 August. Any still lingering hopes for the next year vanished at the Battle of Quiberon Bay on 29 November, when the Brest fleet was almost destroyed by Admiral Hawke in one of the century's most decisive naval victories. Hawke's goal was less the checking of a specific French initiative than the destruction of the French fleet as such.[64] When the numbers were tallied, seven French sail of the line had been sunk or taken. Three more were eventually lost to storms. With them went any reasonable chance that France could shift the balance of the colonial and maritime war.

Might it not be time for the Bourbon monarchy to cut its losses? Pitt had boasted in Parliament of raising Ferdinand's army to a strength of 100,000 for 1760, and hinted that might be only a beginning. While bodies in uniform did not automatically equal effective soldiers, France's depleted treasury had at best a limited capacity to keep pace with such an effort. The British government was willing to talk. It issued through the Netherlands on 25 November an invitation to a peace conference. Tentative efforts to initiate systematic negotiations, however, bore no fruit. The French proposed to separate Continental and Imperial issues. When the British refused, Choiseul, handicapped by growing Austrian concern at his behaviour, abandoned the effort.[65] The war continued, by now with no one able to win it or willing to end it.

64 Ruddock F. Mackay, *Admiral Hawke* (Oxford, 1965), pp. 200 ff.
65 Middleton, *The Bells of Victory*, pp. 134–55.

6 PRUSSIA CONTRA EUROPE, 1760–63

From Frederick's perspective the new year offered nothing except grim prospects. The King suffered through the winter from a variety of nagging ailments, most of them stress-related. He complained constantly of his inability to change the diplomatic circumstances that threatened not merely Prussia's future, but even its existence. 'We have nothing left', he wrote on 1 January 1760. Nor, in an environment where everything ultimately depended on the man at the top, was Frederick able to draw emotional support from his subordinates. Even his brother blamed him for the war and its continuing.

FEINTS AND INITIATIVES: THE SUMMER CAMPAIGN OF 1760

Yet Frederick never quite yielded to despair. Samuel Johnson's famous aphorism that a man under sentence of hanging develops remarkably improved powers of concentration might well have been composed with the King of Prussia in mind. Since diplomacy had failed, one tool remained in Frederick's hands: the army. And the increasingly obvious defects in that institution offered a welcome outlet for energy that otherwise consumed itself in fretting. Among Frederick's first concerns was the reorganization of the units captured at Maxen and elsewhere. Some regiments, particularly those recruited in areas previously spared battle or invasion, were still able to call up enough cantonists to set the tone of their rank and file. Others depended on a volatile mixture of enemy deserters – the *Reichsarmee* seems to have contributed many men disgusted with incompetent commanders and haphazard administration – Saxons impressed into Prussian service, and recruits from western and southern Germany and the Low Countries. The latter were often obtained by the most dubious methods, and had a corresponding reputation of involving almost their own number of more reliable men to prevent mass desertion.

These were not the only sources of manpower. Neither the Russians nor the Austrians were any longer willing to exchange prisoners. On the other hand, many of the best Prussian formations had fought at Zorndorf, Kay, or Kunersdorf, and had corresponding numbers of recovering wounded in hospitals or convalescent units. Not a few veterans succeeded in escaping from an Austrian captivity that was neither particularly restrictive nor particularly oppressive. Prussia's depots also furnished their share of dug-outs and comb-outs – many of them rear echelon heroes of the purest strain, but at least possessed of technical skills that could be turned to account in the field.

The replacement of officer losses posed far greater problems. As in 1759 Frederick found himself constrained to draw many company officers from teenagers assigned from the cadet corps or sponsored by regimental colonels, from NCOs commissioned in the field, and from foreigners with swords for hire. Garrisons and depots provided other men who at least wore epaulettes. Some were full of spirit, but too old for field duty, or too debilitated by wounds and sickness. Others, perfectly willing to spend their war in relative comfort while enlisting and training prospective heroes, suddenly found themselves with field commands.

When all the rosters were prepared and cross-checked, Frederick's order of battle had undergone significant changes. A half-dozen of the weakest and hardest-hammered regiments were assigned to fortress duty. Some of these had once counted among the army's best: the 11th from Königsberg, or the Pomeranian 29th. They were replaced at least on paper by nine garrison battalions, more or less the best in their category, shorn of their least fit personnel and given enough supply wagons to keep pace with the rest of the army. Another nine regiments were reduced to a single battalion each. Six grenadier battalions were combined into three, their parent regiments now able to provide only a single company of these purportedly elite troops.

The mounted arm was less drastically affected. A half-dozen regiments were reduced to one, two, or three squadrons and temporarily amalgamated. In order to compensate, Frederick withdrew the 9th and 10th Dragoons from Ferdinand's army, where they had performed sterling service since the start of the war. The artillery posed a more serious problem. Frederick had drastically depleted his reserves of guns to make up the losses of Kunersdorf. Now he ordered the casting of 140 twelve- and six-pounders. The former were of a new type, copied from the Austrian design that had wreaked such havoc in Prussian ranks ever since Lobositz. It was lighter and more mobile than the 'Brummer', the fortress guns on field carriages which Frederick had previously relied upon for heavy fire support. The artillery also received an improved organization, with the heavy guns and howitzers grouped into 'brigades' of ten pieces under the command of a captain or senior lieutenant. In the spring these new formations also benefited from a manual describing the techniques of employing heavy pieces in battle.

One final organizational point merits attention. Prussia's original brigade of horse artillery had been left at Kunersdorf. A second, organized by Prince Henry, was captured at Maxen. Frederick did not consider the mobile guns worth replacing. The Prince, however, organized another battery in July 1760 and initially attached it to the Bayreuth Dragoons. When that regiment joined Frederick's army a month later, the guns accompanied it. Frederick, whose affection for the *Bayreuther* was as remarkable as it was unusual, adopted the horse battery as well. For the rest of the war he kept it near his headquarters, frequently assigning its guns to reconnaissance parties and advance guards.[1]

Sustaining Prussia's army for another year's fighting posed at least as complex a challenge as reorganizing it. Frederick had originally proposed to finance the war's costs by a combination of the state's war chest, contributions levied on occupied territory, and the British subsidy. The notion of paying the state's bills by increasing the ongoing tax levies was unacceptable for two reasons. It challenged what might be described as Prussia's *mentalité*. Precisely because Frederick ruled over subjects rather than governing citizens, an emerging social contract implied the state's responsibility to protect its productive elements from unusual burdens.

More specifically, Prussia's tax structure was heavily based on indirect levies whose continued collection implied a strong and stable economy. By 1760 circumstances had changed. Prussia's geographic 'heartland' remained intact, but revenues from the border provinces either were not forthcoming at all, as was the case in East Prussia, or fell off sharply, as in Pomerania where the Swedes remained a constant threat and a viable excuse. Even before the war, moreover, Prussia's trade had been affected adversely by a general economic downturn in central Europe. A poor harvest in 1756 – made worse

---

1 Curt Jany, *Geschichte der preussische Armee*, 2nd edn, rev., 4 vols (Osnabrück, 1967), vol. II, pp. 550 ff.; and Christopher Duffy, *The Army of Frederick the Great*, (New York, 1974), pp. 189 ff., summarize the reconstruction of the Prussian army for the campaign of 1760.

by the absence of cantonists who, recalled to active service, had been and unable to plant or harvest – had generated a steep initial rise in the price of food and agricultural products. The transformation of the prosperous regions of Saxony and Silesia into theatres of war disrupted industrial production and commercial distribution. Inflation reduced the value both of fixed salaries and of government contracts negotiated on long-term bases.[2]

Frederick met the challenge by biting the bullet and debasing Prussia's currency. As early as November 1757, the royal plate was converted into coin at the rate of 21 thalers per mark of silver, instead of the usual 14. By December 1759, the official ratio was almost twenty to one. Saxon currency was debased to an ever greater extent. Frederick's officials took advantage of Poland's long-standing contract with the Saxon mint to issue Polish coins of slightly more than one-third their official silver content. The English subsidy for 1759 had been coined into 5.3 million thalers. The subsidy for 1760 produced another million thalers from the same amount of bullion – a piece of fiscal sleight of hand that not even the King's most ardent supporters could ignore.

Frederick was all too conscious of the long-term consequences of his inflationary monetary policy. The Prussian thaler lacked the historic credibility of the pound sterling, but nevertheless had been one of the stronger currencies of central Europe. Diminishing confidence in its acceptability was an expenditure of public resources at least as debilitating as more obvious outlays of blood and treasure.[3]

Combined with strict and comprehensive instructions that the new coins be accepted as full-value payment for government purchases, while at the same time forbidding their acceptance by government agencies, the monetary 'reform' enabled Frederick to put approximately 100,000 men in uniform into the field for the campaign of 1760. The choice of words reflects the fact that many of the

---

2 Cf. *inter alia* Lutz Beutin, 'Die Wirkungen des Siebenjährigen Krieges auf die Volkswirtschaft in Preussen', *Vierteljahresschrift für Sozial- und Wirtschaftsgeschichte*, XXVI (1933), 209–43; Hubert C. Johnson, *Frederick the Great and His Officials* (New Haven, Conn., 1973), pp. 156 *passim*; and Karl Born, *Wirtschaft und Gesellschaft im Denken Friedrichs des Grossen* (Wiesbaden, 1979).

3 Cf. Jörg K. Hoensch, 'Friedrichs II. Währungsmanipulationen im Siebenjährigen Krieg und ihre Auswirkung auf die polnische Münzreform von 1765/1766', *Jahrbuch für die Geschichte Mittel- und Ostdeutschlands*, XXII (1973), 110–75; and Reinhold Koser, 'Die preussische Finanzen im siebenjährigen Krieg', *Forschungen zur brandenburgisch-preussischen Geschichte*, XIII (1900), 340–51.

men were hardly soldiers in the sense in which Prussia had understood the term in 1756 – or even in 1759.

The shortcomings of this approach were becoming apparent even on its home ground. Frederick was well aware of his army's shortcomings – deficits likely to be most clearly manifested at the tactical level, where he had hoped to decide the war. In 1760 Johann Jakob Friedrich Bielfeld, a leading Prussian theoretician of cameralist economics, published a two-volume analysis of political institutions. In it he argued for a distinction between the 'real' and the 'relative' power of a state. Real power depended on a combination of size and riches, its 'opulence'. These meant nothing if not translated into political and military effect by a combination of 'power and system'. Only systematic mobilization and systematic employment of resources made 'real power' politically effective. The sting of Bielfeld's argument lay in its tail: a conclusion that a state's 'relative power', the relationship of its particular product of resources multiplied by systems to those of its neighbours, depended to a significant degree on the 'real power' that was the multiplicand.[4]

Bielfeld's point was not lost on European observers. A year after his work appeared, an Austrian official, Egidius von Borié, conceded that Prussia, through long and painful economies and the concentration of its total resources on preparation for war, had so increased its power that no one of Europe's great Continental powers was its direct match. Nevertheless, Borié argued, France, Russia, and Austria in combination had essentially nothing to fear from the Prussian army. On the contrary, they were in an excellent position to overwhelm the interloper – providing that they held together and held out until Prussia collapsed from stress.[5]

In the context of two centuries' hindsight, the advice seems obvious enough to appear banal. In an eighteenth-century environment, with its pattern of abandoning allies and ending wars for relatively marginal advantages, Borié's position paper was an innovative demand for long-term commitments with an essentially economic basis. Wars of attrition were common enough, but the attrition had previously been on a tactical level: killing an enemy's soldiers and ravaging his territory. Borié was describing strategic

4 Jacob Friedrich Bielfeld, *Institutions Politiques*, 2 vols (The Hague, 1760).

5 E.V. Baron Bové 'Staatsbetrachtungen über gegenwärtigen preussischen Krieg in Teutschland . . .', in Johannes Kunisch, *Das Mirakel des Hauses Brandenburg. Studiem zum Veriältnes von Kabhnettspolitik und Kriegführung im Zeitalter des Siebenjährigen Krieges* (Munich, 1978), pp. 101–41.

attrition: wearing down Prussia without giving its king a chance to redress the situation in the area where he remained an acknowledged master, the battlefield. Kaunitz had relatively little use for this cautious, almost negative, approach. Perhaps more clearly than his subordinate, the Chancellor saw that a protracted war would run down Austria's resources as well as Prussia's. The states were diametric opposites. If Prussia resembled a finely tuned, high-performance engine, Austria was like an old, often repaired one, replete with ersatz parts and improvised connections. Both, however, were significantly vulnerable to long-term stress: one by seizing up, the other by collapsing.[6]

Kaunitz's perceptions were influenced by another factor as well. From the beginning his diplomacy and his grand strategic designs had alike been shaped by a desire to bring Russia onto the European scene as a regular player. France's reduced role on the Continent after 1759 led to a growing reliance on Russia to make up the loss of men, if not money. Nevertheless, the risks of the Tsarist Empire becoming an even greater threat than Frederician Prussia to the continent's political balance were never forgotten in Vienna. Events in the autumn and winter of 1760 seemed to confirm Kaunitz's concerns. The Empress Elizabeth was adamantly opposed to concluding peace with Frederick on any terms conceivable to the latter. But exactly how determined was Russia to follow her own perceived interests in the context of the alliance? St Petersburg had opened negotiations with Poland regarding the possible exchange of territory for Prussian lands Russia expected to acquire at the end of the war. The occupation of East Prussia had taken on an increasingly permanent appearance. From the governor downwards, Russian officials overtly and assiduously courted the provincial notables. They took pains to employ German-speaking staffs, and to be generous with invitations to official social functions. In Königsberg, army officers ostentatiously attended the lectures of Immanuel Kant. Russia's frontiers had expanded on far smaller bases of good will.[7]

---

6 A point highlighted in Bernhard R. Kroener, 'Die materiellen Grundlagen österreichischen und preussischen Kriegsanstrengungen 1756–1763', in *Europa im Zeitalter Friedrichs des Grossen. Wirtschaft, Gesellschaft, Kriege*, ed. B. Kroener (Munich, 1989), pp. 47–78.

7 William C. Fuller, *Strategy and Power in Russia, 1600–1914* (New York, 1992), p. 134 *passim*, is a solid general discussion of Russia's strategic problems at mid-century. E.C. Thaden, *Russia's Western Borderlands, 1710–1870* (Princeton, NJ, 1984), pp. 5 *passim*, stresses the role of positives in expanding Russia's influence at this period.

Elizabeth's government correspondingly requested an Austrian guarantee not to oppose a permanent change in East Prussia's status. The Austrian ambassador to St Petersburg regarded the demand as reasonable – not least because possession was at least seven or eight points of international law as generally understood. Elizabeth's health, moreover, continued to be a wild card. In September 1759, she collapsed and could not be revived for several hours. Peter was coming closer to the throne with each of his aunt's erratic heartbeats and no one could comfortably predict exactly what he was likely to do – or to whom he would listen.

Opinions in Vienna were less favourable, particularly in the context of France's insistence that giving East Prussia to Russia was directly contrary to French interests in the Baltic. Choiseul, however, was unwilling to take the risk of refusing Russian claims directly. On 1 February 1760, a French note declared that the Russian war aims were so extensive that they required a new treaty, to be negotiated between Russia and Austria. France, the document stated, would offer its comments once the preliminary work was done.[8]

This put the ball squarely in Austria's court. Kaunitz had no real choice. Austria needed Russia too badly to risk its alienation, and the Russians refused to discuss future military cooperation until Austria accepted their territorial claims. After months of negotiations in the spring of 1761, Austria finally and unwillingly concluded a secret agreement by which Russia would secure East Prussia – on the condition that Austria recovered Silesia and Glatz.

Even more than in the previous year, the Russian government sent a broad spectrum of signals that its army's behaviour would depend heavily upon the performance of the Austrians. No more Russian blood would be spilled to pull Habsburg chestnuts from the Frederician fire. Elizabeth and her advisers were bluffing. Saltykov initially found strong political support when he proposed an independent campaign against the Baltic coast. He might have achieved even more success had he not defined the operation primarily in terms of sieges. Instead, the Empress and her immediate advisers decided for an offensive directed against Breslau. This operation would test Austrian good will while providing a basis for independent operations should these prove necessary. Elizabeth might be dying

8 L.J. Oliva, *Misalliance: A Study of French Policy in Russia during the Seven Years' War* (New York, 1964), p. 150. Cf. also Grégoire Wolkonsky, 'La France et la menace d'expansion russe pendant la guerre de Sept-Ans (1756–1763). Pendule Est–Ouest', *Revue d'Histoire Diplomatique*, LXX (1956), 193–9.

on her feet, but she was all the more determined to take her enemy down with her.[9]

Austria's response was influenced to a degree during the first months of 1760 by a desperate Prussian effort to bring Turkey into the war. The armies of the Sublime Porte were by now in such a state of decline that no one seriously assumed they could defeat the forces of Russia and Austria singly, much less combined. Frederick, however, was desperate enough to authorize over three-quarters of a million thalers as bribe money. Perhaps an even clearer sign of his desperation was his enduring hope that the Sultan and his officials would do more than smile, promise, and extend their hands for further payment.

From Kaunitz's perspective Turkey was more a nuisance than a threat – but a nuisance that could not be summarily dismissed. Even under favourable military circumstances, Turkish raiding parties backed by regular troops could make the summer very unpleasant along Austria's south-eastern border. Nor was Kaunitz so entirely certain of Hungary's loyalty, particularly in the context of the Empire's new demands for men and money. The blandishments of Constantinople had proved all too effective all too often in the Transleithania. If open, large-scale revolt was less likely than in the days of Gabor Bethlen, disaffection and foot-dragging were at least likely consequences of Turkish intervention.[10]

Not until late spring was it reasonably clear that the Ottoman Empire was too conscious of its own weaknesses to risk involvement in a European war. This left Kaunitz free to advocate a strategic plan developed, in outline at least, by Laudon. Albeit for different reasons, the general shared the diplomat's concern with the probable consequences of another year spent sparring with Frederick like the proverbial cat circling a plate of hot soup. Laudon's attitude was also shaped by a deepening personal and professional rivalry with Lacy, whom he by now dismissed as the true author of Austria's embarrassingly dilatory policies in what was still the principal theatre of war.

Instead, Laudon proposed and Kaunitz accepted a policy of

9 Christopher Duffy, *Russia's Military Way to the West: Origins and Nature of Russian Military Power, 1700–1800* (London, 1981), p. 113; Tamara Talbot Rice, *Elizabeth Empress of Russia* (London, 1970), p. 206.

10 Cf. Rudolf Porsch, 'Die Beziehungen Friedrichs des Grossen zur Türkei vor Beginn und während des siebenjährigen Krieges', PhD dissertation, Marburg, 1897; and Karl A. Roider, *Austria's Eastern Question 1700–1790* (Princeton, NJ, 1982), pp. 104 ff.

bolder strokes. The main Austrian army would remain in Saxony, acting aggressively enough to keep its Prussian counterpart fixed in place. Laudon would repeat his performance of 1759 on a larger scale by taking 40,000 men into Silesia, joining the Russians, and mopping up whatever resistance Prussia's eastern provinces could muster. This plan was strongest at its extremes, on the tactical/operational and the political levels. It reflected Laudon's conviction that neither the Prussian army nor the Prussian King were what they once had been. The allied armies should be able to win a free hand in the Silesian theatre even if Kunersdorf were refought as a preliminary. From Kaunitz's perspective the proposed operations offered prospects of restoring on the battlefield a situation that had become seriously unbalanced in the council chamber. Should Austria take a leading role in the war against Frederick, should Silesia be rewon by the force of Austrian arms, should Laudon add to the laurels won at Kunersdorf, then perhaps the recent concessions to Russia might be renegotiated. At worst, military success during what remained of the summer would provide a counterweight to the growing Austrian nightmare of Russia's emergence as the primary power of east-central Europe. Prussia might be dangerous enough, but Kaunitz had no desire to exchange King Log for Tsaritsa Stork.[11]

Frederick was able to do no more during the first weeks of the new campaigning season than match Daun feint for feint along the Saxon border. There was no possibility of aid from the west. Despite substantial reinforcements during the winter, Ferdinand of Brunswick was significantly outnumbered by the French to his front. Ninety-two battalions and 112 squadrons faced 163 battalions and 187 squadrons – and Ferdinand, for all his capacities, was not the kind of *Feldherr* who could work miracles at long odds.

Brunswick's limitations were highlighted in May when two strong French forces began advancing into central Germany. The French commander in chief, the duc de Broglie, was a sound operational planner who had also vastly improved the training, discipline, and administration of his troops. Through the summer he consistently outmanoeuvred Ferdinand. The latter successfully avoided being forced into a major battle until, on 31 July, he gave part of Broglie's force a bloody nose at Warburg. This tactical victory, however, could not save Kassel, which the French occupied on the same day. The city's possession provided both a potential springboard into Hanover

---

11 F. Jihn, *Der Feldzug 1760 in Sachsen und Schlesien mit besonderer Berücksichtigung der Schlacht bei Torgau* (Vienna, 1882).

and a *point d'appui* against allied operations in Hesse. It also finalized the absence of any help, direct or indirect, for Frederick. Ferdinand faced all he could manage in cleaning his own operational plate.[12] Laudon's Silesian offensive began in the last week of May. His first objective was the small detached force of 12,000 men which was all Frederick had been able to spare as a field force for the province. Its commander, Lieutenant-General Heinrich Fouqué, was a welcome sight on a stricken field but possessed neither the operational insight nor the capacity for rapid movement of his Austrian rival. For a month the two generals feinted back and forth, each seeking an opening. It was Fouqué whose guard slipped first. Under royal orders he reoccupied the road junction of Landeshut on 17 June. Attempting to screen the kind of broken ground which the Austrians had used to such effect at Hochkirch and Maxen, Fouqué and his subordinates spread their seventeen battalions and fifteen squadrons far too thinly. As usual, Prussian tactical security was virtually non-existent. On 23 June, Laudon took advantage of indifferent pickets and a stormy night to cut Fouqué's line of retreat and strike his exposed eastern flank with 35,000 men.

The Prussian infantry fought with the courage of desperation, yielding the high ground on which they were deployed a foot at a time while inflicting heavy losses on Laudon's equally desperate musketeers. At the end, Fouqué gathered the survivors and tried to cut his way out at bayonet-point. Austrian cavalry broke the Prussian formation. Fouqué, his horse shot under him, bleeding from three sabre cuts, was taken prisoner. His captors praised his courage. Even Frederick compared Landeshut to Thermopylae. But no fine words could disguise the loss of almost 2,000 dead, plus no fewer than 8,000 wounded and prisoners. Nine hundred troopers managed to escape Laudon's net, collect a few hundred more stragglers, and retreat to Breslau. But they were survivors, not a field force.[13]

Meanwhile Frederick, with 55,000 men at the Saxon city of Meissen, confronted Daun's 80,000 concentrated around Dresden. His efforts to surprise isolated elements of the Austrian force came to so little that the King once declared he would be best advised

---

12 Reginald Savory, *His Britannic Majesty's Army in Germany during the Seven Years' War* (Oxford, 1966), pp. 201 ff.

13 A. von Sodenstern, *Der Feldzug des Königlich preussischen Generals der Infanterie Heinrich August de la Motte Fouqué in Schlesien 1760*, 2nd edn. rev. (Kassel, 1817), is a detailed narrative sympathetic to Fouqué's position and problems.

to hang himself.[14] The sentiment reflected frustration rather than depression, but news of Fouqué's annihilation gave point to the King's despair. For one of the few times since 1756, he had lost the initiative. With Laudon on the loose in Silesia and the Russians looming on the province's horizon, there seemed no alternative to breaking away from Daun and securing what was still not only Prussia's only permanent prize of war but a source of manpower and resources more important even than Saxony.

The Prussian main army started eastward by forced marches on 3 July. Bad roads and burning heat compounded the tribulations of a force whose rank and file included too many unfit men and convalescents. More than 100 men died of exhaustion on a single day, to no strategic purpose. Daun not only reacted to Frederick's move; for once he outpaced his rival. The Austrians were actually ahead of Frederick on the high roads to Silesia! Accepting the axiom that a stern chase is a long chase, the King decided on 7 July to return his army to Saxony. Frederick had more than aimless raiding in mind. The city of Dresden, in Austrian hands since the previous autumn, seemed ripe for plucking. Not only was it weakly garrisoned; neither the 20,000 men Daun had left in Saxony as a rearguard nor the 20,000 warm bodies of the *Reichsarmee* were within easy supporting distance. On 13 August, Frederick reached the city and set the stage for one of the most controversial actions of the Seven Years War.

For Frederick, Dresden was a means to an operational and strategic end. He hoped to draw Daun back from Silesia and into a major battle on Frederick's terms – a replication of the Battle of Prague in 1756, only this time presumably with more positive results. For the lure to work, the threat to Dresden had to be something more immediate and more spectacular than a formal siege, for which in any case Frederick lacked the resources. Instead, he brought up a dozen heavy guns and opened a general bombardment of the city on 19 July. In sharp contrast to normal eighteenth-century practice, civilian buildings, especially the centrally located Kreuz-Kirche, were specifically designated as targets.[15] The resulting fires burned down much of the city without affecting the 14,000-strong Austrian garrison.

The moral impact was correspondingly negative. Even in his own

14 Heinrich Catt, *Unterhaltungen mit Friedrich dem Grossen*, ed. J. Koser (Leipzig, 1884), p. 426.

15 J.W. Archenholtz, *Geschichte des Siebenjährigen Krieges in Deutschland, 1757–1763*, 5th edn, 2 vols (Berlin, 1840), vol. I, pp. 327–8.

camp Frederick's actions were interpreted as the product of malice or frustration. The King's principal modern military biographer charitably suggests that Frederick did not expect Dresden to be so inflammable after his experience at Prague.[16] In fact, when Frederick ended the blockade it was because of Daun's continued reluctance to meet the King's expectations. Daun had followed Frederick back to Saxony and taken position close enough to Dresden that the wind carried debris from the burning city into his camp. Yet despite growing open criticism from his subordinates, the Austrian commander had no intention of obliging his old enemy by fighting him. Dresden was a bone in Frederick's throat. A little bit of patience, a little bit of pressure, and the King of Prussia would dance once more to Austria's strategic piping.

Was this inertia or wisdom? Certainly it was a decision that tightened the operational screws on Frederick. On 21 July he raised the siege, bitterly blaming the officers of his technical arms, the engineers and artillery, for its failure. An even clearer indication of the King's frustration came when a night-time sortie by the Dresden garrison scattered two battalions of the 3rd Infantry to the four winds. This had once been the Old Dessauer's proprietary regiment, winning fame as such in the Silesian Wars. Many of its recent replacements, however, came from Saxony and had correspondingly little lust for serving the King of Prussia. The 3rd had suffered heavy losses in prisoners at Kay. Seven of its companies had been involved in the capitulation of Maxen. This was the third strike. The officers and men of the unfortunate regiment had to remove the distinctive braid and ornament from their uniforms. The rank and file were also deprived of their swords.[17]

The loss of several pounds of wrought iron, seldom by now used for anything more martial than carving meat rations, might seem inconsequential to contemporary soldiers concerned with lightening wherever possible the loads carried on the march and into battle. The general reaction to Frederick's punishment was, however, one of shock. Prussia's infantry might have been a sadly mixed bag compared to their predecessors of 1756. They nevertheless had sustained a pride of status and of craft that was deeply wounded

16 Christopher Duffy, *Frederick the Great: A Military Life* (London, 1985), p. 199.

17 Jany, *Preussische Armee*, vol. II, p. 560; *Geschichte des Infanterie-Regiments von Anhalt-Bernburg*, reprinted with introduction by H. Bleckwenn (Osnabrück, 1974), pp. 81–2.

by what seemed a gratuitous insult to a regiment whose failure could be explained as the product of ill fortune and poor generalship rather than lack of courage. It was not, after all, the sergeants and privates who had sent the 3rd in broken ground and on a dark night to cover the withdrawal of a few siege guns whose loss would hardly be missed in any case. In the ranks of the main Prussian army, men began to talk darkly of 'next time', and a drowning of shame in Austrian blood.

That time would not come in Saxony. While Frederick watched Dresden burn, Laudon's corps had taken free rein in Silesia. On 29 July, the Austrians carried the fortress of Glatz by a *coup de main* against a weak garrison composed largely of deserters and recruits from Prussian prison camps. Liegnitz and Parchwitz fell without a fight, opening the way for a junction with the Russians. The Austrians reached the gates of Breslau itself, and only Laudon's lack of a siege train saved the city from investment and bombardment. Substituting bravado for round shot Laudon summoned the garrison to surrender, melodramatically threatening to tear the unborn children from their mothers' wombs. The city's commander, a hard case named Bogislaw von Tauentzien, dryly replied that neither he nor his soldiers were pregnant and invited Laudon to 'come and get us'.[18]

Tauentzien's defiance nevertheless conveyed a distinct sense of spitting against the wind in the final days of July. On the 26th the Russians began their march westward from Posen, 60,000 strong with an advance guard of 25,000 specifically assigned to join Laudon in Silesia. Once again Frederick determined to 'try our luck in combat', even if it meant only 'dying four weeks sooner or four weeks later'.[19] He began the process of translating melodrama into strategy on the night of 29 August, when he set out for Silesia from Dresden with 30,000 men.

Frederick was less alone than his rhetoric implied. The ever-reliable Prince Henry had been sent east in the spring, to stand off Swedes and Russians as best he might with whatever he could scrape together. By midsummer that amounted to about 37,000 men, most of them facing eastwards to keep an eye on the Russians. Once the latter began to move, Henry responded by bringing his own force into Silesia by forced marches. The Prince was well aware that Silesia had once again become the war's focal point. Should Laudon and the Russians be able to join forces unopposed, the operational results

18 Jany, *Preussische Armee*, vol. I, p. 334.
19 Frederick to Finckenstein, 27 July 1760, *PC*, XIX, 524–5.

could spell disaster for Prussia. By 5 August he had reached Breslau, seen off Laudon at least temporarily, and positioned his troops to block a direct Russian advance on the city. But Henry had good reason to complain to his brother that he faced an almost impossible task, one showing few signs of becoming easier.[20] His mixed bag of cantonists, convalescents, and convicts could hope by itself to do no more than delay the allies, even as a force in being.

Frederick responded by driving his army mercilessly on its second set of forced marches in a month. In five days the Prussians covered over 90 miles despite high losses from straggling, desertion, and heat exhaustion. Frederick's subsequent denunciation of the propensity of his men to desert on the march ignored the fact that the pace he ordered as a response to what he perceived as a desperate situation exceeded the physical capacities of men who had spent the past six months in camp. A significant number of men marked absent at the end of a day seem as well to have rejoined their regiments within a relatively brief time. Certainly, the force under Frederick's command was hardly decimated when it stopped for a day's rest on 8 August.

Another useful indication that eighteenth-century fighting men were not the unwilling warriors of today's mythology is the continued ability of Daun's army not merely to keep pace with the Prussians, but to outmarch them – and across rougher country with fewer roads. Frederick initially hoped to prevent Daun from making contact with Laudon. When that effort proved vain, the King sought to sidestep the combined Austrian force, now approximately 90,000 strong, in order to join his brother and eventually get between the Austrians and the Russians with the expectation of defeating – or at least intimidating – his enemies separately.

By this time Daun was under more fire from his own camp than from the Prussians. Daun's primary concern, at least as understood by his officers, was to stick closely enough to Frederick to prevent the King's gaining the shelter of the fortresses of Breslau and Schweidnitz. This was as far as it is possible to imagine from Frederick's actual intentions, which were to fight rather than hide. At the same time Laudon repeatedly insisted on the folly and the risk – based on his own recent experiences in Silesia – of attempting siege operations with two undefeated Prussian armies still in the field. Kaunitz warned that it was now or never for Austria. Finally in desperation, Maria

---

20 Prince Henry to Frederick II, 5 Aug. 1760; and Frederick's reply of 9 Aug., *PC*, XIX, 540–1.

Theresa not only sent Daun specific orders to fight; she also absolved him beforehand of responsibility for the battle's consequences![21]

General, minister, and monarch alike underestimated the man on the spot. No revisionist can transform Leopold von Daun into a great captain, even relative to his times. He was, however, neither a poltroon nor an incompetent. His own self-image as the summer campaign progressed seems rather to have been that of an experienced knife fighter, circling patiently, waiting for his opponent to give him an opportunity for one quick and fatal thrust. By mid-August his army was so close to Frederick that one observer said the Austrians looked like a fourth Prussian column.[22] No matter how the King dodged and twisted, whitecoats blocked his way. The seizure on 10 August of Lacy's personal baggage, including some very useful maps, offered Frederick the chance to make a grand gesture and return the Austrian general's belongings, but only confirmed the desperate situation in which the Prussians found themselves.

When all the heads were counted Daun had a three-to-one superiority in numbers. Attempting to create a tactical opportunity by further marching and countermarching generated a corresponding risk of exhausting men and horses to the point that neither would be able to fight at all. Most discussions of the campaign's hardships focused on the infantry. The cavalry's horses, however, were accustomed far more even than their nineteenth-century descendants to regular fodder and regular rest. Under the regimen of the past month, the mounts were losing both flesh and spirit faster than regimental colonels liked, especially in the heavy regiments that provided so much of the army's shock power. Camp rumours had the Austrians boasting that they had Frederick in the bag, and at least some of the King's subordinates were talking in private about a replay of the Maxen débâcle on a larger scale.[23]

Daun proposed to translate rumour to reality on the evening of 14 August by sending his main army against the Prussians in four columns. At the same time Laudon was ordered to take his 24,000 men north across the Katzbach River, near the town of Liegnitz. The Austrian general expected, if not to defeat Frederick himself, at least

21 Alfred Ritter von Arneth, *Geschichte Maria Theresias*, 10 vols (Vienna, 1863–79), vol. VI, p. 139. Cf. von Webern, 'Die Operationen welcher der Schlacht von Liegnitz am 15. August 1760 vorangingen, *Militär-Wochenblatt*, 1897, *Beiheft* IV, 205–20.

22 Mitchell to Holdernesse, Aug. 16, 1760, note for Aug. 10, Andrew Mitchell, *Memoirs and Papers of Sir Andrew Mitchell, KB*, 2 vols, ed. A. Bisset (London, 1850), vol II, p. 192.

23 Note for Aug. 12, *ibid.*, 194.

to force him back against Laudon – who was just the sort of battle captain to hold the Prussians in place until Daun could arrive and complete the victory.

Only one thing was necessary for success: that Frederick stand still for the hammer. Instead, the King implemented his own plan. Unaware of Daun's intentions, he ordered a night march north in one last effort to shake the stubborn Austrians loose. The Prussian movement was well under way when a junior officer dismissed from the Austrian army, an Irishman, took his revenge by reporting Daun's intentions to the King. Since the man was dead drunk, his information did not receive immediate credence. Forcibly sobered up, the wild goose volubly insisted on his veracity.[24] Frederick was convinced. For one of the few times in his military career, he stood to benefit from a stroke of pure luck. The Prussian movement had incorporated the usual security measure of leaving detachments behind to keep bivouac fires burning and provide similar evidence of an occupied camp. Barring both an unusual degree of enterprise and a high level of flexibility at all levels of command, Daun would attack into empty air and throw his whole army off balance.

Instead of continuing his originally planned march, Frederick took position north-east of Liegnitz on a low plateau, itself commanding the even lower open ground to the south and west. He was sufficiently aware of the risk of being caught between Daun and Laudon that he deployed in two wings facing in opposite directions, ready to react to whichever Austrian force first reached battle range.

It was a detachment of the by now ubiquitous Ziethen Hussars, the Red Second, who tripped the battle's trigger by – almost literally – running into Laudon's force marching down 'Frederick's' bank of the Katzbach. The hard-driving Austrian general had brought his men across the river with little delay and less confusion, but for the sake of haste had paid less attention to screening his advance than was his usual practice. The hussars drew rein and rode back to Frederick's camp to give the alarm. It speaks significantly, both positively and negatively for the structure of the Prussian army after four years of war, that the hussar commander did not bother with chains of command, but made his report directly to his commander-in-chief.

Frederick responded by deploying three brigades of infantry against Laudon. In the dim light of an early morning, after a complicated night march, the manoeuvre took more time than the Prussians possessed. Laudon's cavalry vanguard rode forward, driving back two hastily deployed regiments, then being checked itself by a charge of the 2nd Cuirassiers, Prince Henry's regiment. The heavy troopers gave their infantry just enough time to form a line of battle when the Austrian grenadiers made the first in a series of ferocious attacks, designed to take advantage of early-morning ground fog and tactical surprise to sweep the Prussians from the field.

Much of the surprise, however, was on Laudon's side of the battle line. He had not expected to find the Prussians so far north, much less deployed for battle. Tactically as well, it was the Austrians who faced an unexpected challenge. In organizing his army for the march to Silesia, Frederick had assigned a ten-gun battery of twelve-pounders, preferably the lighter 'Austrian' versions, to each of his infantry brigades. The reason most usually cited for this dispersion highlights the King's alleged belief that his infantry had so declined in quality that it required the direct support of heavier metal than the regimental guns.[25] Events at Kunersdorf suggest another possibility. On a stricken field the Prussian heavy artillery was 'nobody's child'. To perform its assigned mission of preparing the decisive infantry attack, it had to deploy almost in the enemy's face. Should the day go badly, the clumsy guns with their civilian drivers were easy meat left to their own devices. Infantry presumably demoralized by defeat was unlikely to risk life and limb to see the guns safely away. Brigading the two arms offered at least the possibility of generating a sense of common identity and a spirit of mutual cooperation.

Thus far in the campaign the results had been the exact reverse. The twelve-pounders obstructed lines of march. They threw up clouds of dust. They got stuck or bogged, and the infantry had to get them on their lumbering way once more. The previous night's march had been a particular mess, with the twelve-pounders seemingly ubiquitous in causing inconvenience. Now, as the fog cleared and the early-morning sun lit the plateau, the heavy guns proved their worth as a brigade-level weapon. Canister at short range tore huge gaps in the attacking formations as the Prussian gunners fought their pieces almost to the muzzle. On the Prussian right flank, when a local counterattack was checked by Austrian artillery, Saldern offered 10 thalers to anyone who could silence the battery. A few minutes later a howitzer shell landed on an Austrian powder wagon.[26] The shot

---

25 As in Duffy, *Army of Frederick the Great*, p. 120.
26 C.F. Barsewisch, *Meine Kriegs-Erlebnisse während des Siebenjährigen Krieges 1757–1763*, ed. J. Olmes (Krefeld, 1959), p. 115.

may have been a lucky one, but it meant that the Prussian advance continued.

Laudon responded by pressing his own attack against the Prussian left wing. For a few minutes the lines of battle resembled a revolving door, and the day's outcome appeared to depend on which army would first reach the other's rear. The Austrian infantry, led by its grenadiers, made one more desperate effort. Then Prussian reserves moved up behind their front – a brigade including the 3rd Infantry, the byword of the army since its disgrace at Dresden. No one gave the order to charge, but enough officers, NCOs, and high privates sought to clear their names that the 3rd surged forward on its own initiative, with the less willing heroes of the regiment carried along in the crush. The general commanding the sector shouted at the 3rd's brigadier to keep his men together. His injunction was lost in the shout of 'honour or death' that rose from the 3rd's ranks. They hit the Austrians like 'furies and devils', breaking through in a hand-to-hand brawl of musket butts and bayonets.[27] Another regiment of infantry and the 2nd Cuirassiers followed the 3rd into the breach, and when the Austrians broke, the cuirassiers reaped them like grain.

The charge of the 3rd Infantry, the Regiment of Anhalt-Bernburg, entered Prussian/German military history as an example of fighting spirit at its highest. The immediate aftermath, however, bore a certain resemblance to the fate of the Light Brigade at Balaclava. As the Prussian musketeers pressed forward, they were disorganized both by the momentum of their charge and by the broken terrain over which it passed. An Austrian cavalry counterattack scattered a grenadier battalion, inflicted heavy losses on an infantry regiment, and captured ten standards before being halted by the musketry of less-shaken battalions and seen off by two Prussian cavalry regiments hastily ordered to the scene.

For Laudon it was enough. His men had suffered heavy and unexpected losses. As much to the point, there was still neither sight nor sound of Daun's army. Laudon was the kind of aggressive general willing enough to fight at long odds on his own responsibility. But he disliked Lacy, mistrusted Daun, and was just frustrated enough by the situation to withdraw his badly shaken troops around 6 a.m. Austrian losses amounted to 1,400 dead, more than 2,200 wounded, and 4,800 prisoners, many of the latter victims of their own courage in charging up to the muzzles of Prussian guns. Eighty guns, twenty-three flags and standards were the visible trophies of victory in this hard-fought

27 Jany, *Preussische Armee*, vol. II, p. 566; *Der Siebenjährige Krieg*, vol. XII, 210.

sector. Frederick who, as was increasingly his custom, had been in the thick of the fighting, did not order pursuit. Instead legend has it that he rode to the 3rd Regiment, where some of the surviving old soldiers begged him to reinstate the regiment in his favour. 'Yes, boys', the King is supposed to have answered, 'everything will be returned to you. All is forgotten.'[28] It was an event that should have happened even if it did not. Certainly the army believed the story; certainly Frederick took no pains to deny it. Certainly too, the King took more documented pains than usual to congratulate his infantry for their discipline and their fighting spirit. That very evening he paraded the army to announce an unusually long list of promotions and rewards – concluding with a statement that not only had the 3rd Infantry restored its honour, but that the King himself would pay for new hat tresses for the enlisted men!

That Frederick was able to indulge this unusual generosity owed much to a negative event: the failure of Daun's troops to come anywhere near the fighting. When Frederick turned to face Laudon he gave Ziethen about half the army, with orders to slow Daun by every means possible. In one sense the old hussar was the best choice for a delaying action. An infantryman accustomed to pitched battles might have been correspondingly tempted to a stand-up fight. Since Ziethen had no more than 15,000 men to oppose the 60,000 Daun could deploy, the likely outcome of such a course of action was plain. Not the matador's sword, but his cape, would be needed.

In the event, the Austrians did most of Ziethen's work for him. In contrast to their efforts at Hochkirch, their staff work was deplorable – a probable reflection of Lacy's promotion and assignment to a field command. Daun's subordinates were slow to begin their marches and had difficulty keeping their troops in order. The abandonment of Frederick's original camp was discovered and reported far too late to make any adjustments in the axes of advance. Austrian vanguards were initially unable to find fords over the Katzbach and its small tributary the Schwarzwasser – a process rendered even more difficult by Ziethen's artillery, which kept up harassing fire on likely crossing spots. The few squadrons of cavalry that managed a timely passage were easily checked by their Prussian counterparts. It was 5 a.m. before most of Daun's army was in something like a position to advance, and then Daun hesitated, awaiting developments in Laudon's sector. By 7.30 it was clear that Frederick held the advantage. Rather than seek to reverse the day's fortunes, Daun took

28 J.W. Archenholtz, *Geschichte des Siebenjährigen Krieges*, vol. II, p. 68.

his own troops – who still outnumbered Frederick's by better than two to one and were fresh, to boot – back to his original camp.[29] Liegnitz stands as a classic example of a battle that was lost as well as won. It is an even clearer illustration of the ultimate dependance of strategy and operations on tactics. Daun's plan was not merely sound; it was excellent. Nor did its implementation challenge beyond capacity the Austrian army and its commander. They had executed at least as demanding an operation at Hochkirch. Instead, the Austrians fell victim to self-generated fog and friction. Liegnitz was by any calculation the single worst performance of Daun's career. On this day all of his virtues became defects through exaggeration. The initial over-cautious, bumbling advance of the main army was compounded in its consequences by Daun's refusal to take even minor risks once the fighting started. The Prussian King's moral ascendancy over his principal opponent never bore richer fruit than on the morning of 15 August.

Laudon was correspondingly bitter. Frederick later quoted deserters' accounts of Laudon thrashing about on the ground, bewailing the loss of his cannon and cursing Daun in the most lurid terms.[30] These stories may be presumed to have been significantly improved in the telling, but there is no doubt that Laudon initially at least believed he had been deliberately left in the lurch by a commander jealous of his growing fame.

In reality, Laudon bore a fair share of responsibility for the day's outcome. Apart from his failure to scout effectively in front of his line of advance, Laudon committed his troops to a series of frontal attacks against an enemy whose strength was unknown, but whose dangerousness had long been established. Laudon was ambitious. He was also contemptuous of Daun. His assigned mission as commander of a blocking force offered little more than a chance to play valet to Daun's virtues. Breaking the Prussians in a heroic encounter battle opened an entirely different spectrum of possibilities. Had Laudon remained in place, perhaps even fallen back and established defensive positions on ground of his choosing, Frederick would have had nowhere to go. The Prussian army would have been constrained to fight not only in two directions, but almost in reality back to back. At Liegnitz, in short, Laudon as well as Daun played the role of an obliging enemy – albeit for different reasons.

---

29 Baerecke, 'Die Schlacht von Liegnitz am 15. August 1760', *Militär-Wochenblatt*, 1906, *Beiheft* IV, 187–204.
30 Frederick to Prince Henry, 21 Aug. 1760, *PC* XIX, 554–5.

Liegnitz was also the moral tonic the Prussian army needed. Frederick's actual role in directing the battle remains difficult to reconstruct. The King himself credited fortune: his initial decision to make the night march and the subsequent timing of his arrival on the battlefield.[31] His contemporaries – and many subsequent analyses – dismissed this as a modest disclaimer, manifesting exemplary diffidence or false humility, depending on the writer. In fact, Frederick's evaluation seems reasonably accurate. Liegnitz was a soldier's battle – or at most a brigadier's, despite Ziethen's promotion to full general for his success in keeping Daun from doing what Daun was reluctant to do in the first place. The restoration of the army's self-confidence was a collective act, projected onto Frederick because at that desperate stage of the war a heroic figure in full command of events was a major requirement of public morale. Had he been defeated at Liegnitz, Frederick remarked to Mitchell, there would have been an end of all.[32] This time the King did not exaggerate. It is one of the dialectical ironies in Prussian history that the monarch who more than any of the state's rulers governed from the top down in response to his own internal dynamic, increasingly became the stuff of legends created from the bottom up.

With his enemies now safely divided morally, if not physically, Frederick marched towards Breslau. He also ordered Prince Henry to leave 14,000 men to keep an eye on the Russians and join him with the rest of his army. On 29 August the Prince reached the city at the head of twenty-six battalions and forty squadrons. After a few exchanges of units that had suffered heavily at Liegnitz, Frederick had about 50,000 men under his direct command. The price he paid was his brother's withdrawal from the campaign. Henry was tired and ill, frustrated by the loss of his independent command, and not a little jealous of Frederick's seemingly uncanny ability to restore his fortunes and his image at the edge of disaster. He remained in Breslau when the King resumed his search for a decisive battle with the Austrians.[33]

With the most favourable numerical balance he had possessed all year, Frederick proposed to bring Daun low before the year ended. Daun, however, was easier to track than to fix. The Austrian marshal had a remarkable capacity for shrugging off the consequences

---

31 Mitchell to Newcastle, 17 Aug. 1760, Mitchell, *Memoirs and Papers*, vol. II, 201 ff.

32 Mitchell to Holdernesse, 17 Aug. 1760, *ibid.*, 203–4.

33 Chester Easum, *Prince Henry of Prussia: Brother of Frederick the Great* (Madison, Wis., 1942), pp. 147 ff.

of his own mistakes. Liegnitz seemed forgotten as once again he shifted ground cleverly in response to the King's repeated flanking movements. As Daun stayed just out of reach, Frederick developed his by now usual spectrum of stress-related illnesses: cramps, fever, and haemorrhoids. Nor was the Austrian general a purely passive opponent. Periodically his manoeuvres impelled Frederick to change position involuntarily. On 17 September, his artillery even bombarded Frederick's columns of march – an unusual circumstance for the eighteenth century. In contrast, the King's planned blows landed on thin air. His forced marches did no more than draw the Prussian army further into the kind of wooded, broken country that was ideal for Daun's approach of bob-and-weave, but correspondingly unsuited for the kind of stand-up battle that had become Frederick's trademark.

TORGAU: THE FINAL KILLING GROUND

With Frederick playing tag in the Silesian uplands and Henry nursing his health and his grievances in Breslau, the allies considered their options anew. Saltykov's infirmities had finally caught up with him. In September he resigned, replaced by none other than Fermor, the best-qualified man immediately available. Fermor had no illusions about his prospects for being permanently confirmed in the appointment of which he had been deprived two years earlier. But a spectacular coup, something to make them sit up in Vienna and St Petersburg, might change his circumstances significantly. He was ready to listen when the French observer with his army proposed a joint Russian-Austrian thrust at Berlin. The Prussian capital was almost bare of troops. A fast-moving task force had every chance of seizing the city. Operationally, such a success might draw Frederick back north and expose him to a full-scale allied attack. Politically, the loss of his capital might be enough of a blow to dispel the *mana* that still surrounded Prussia's King. At the least a thrust against Berlin, even if barren of wider results, would be something worthwhile to end a year that from the allies' perspective had been entirely wasted.

Daun, already under pressure from Kaunitz and the Empress to do more than spar with Frederick, responded by sending Lacy north on 28 September, with about 15,000 men. Fermor assigned another 18,000 Russians under Chernyshev to the mission. A vanguard of 5,600 picked light cavalry, Cossacks, and grenadiers reached Berlin's outskirts on 2 October and appeared before the city itself the next day – an unusually fast pace.

Berlin's garrison, a mixed bag of recruits, convalescents, and militiamen, had little chance of making a long defence even after being reinforced by detached forces operating in the neighbourhood. The city's commander, Lieutenant-General von Rochow, was able to turn back initial Russian probing attacks, but the arrival of Chernyshev's main body and Lacy's corps between 5 and 7 October sealed the city's fate. A council of war decided that Prussia could not afford the loss of another army in a hopeless defence. On the night of the 8th, 16,000 Prussians slipped past the Russian outposts and marched in the direction of Spandau. Rochow stayed behind, to surrender the city to an allied force champing at the bit for the pleasing prospects of a storm and a sack.

The terms of capitulation have been described as generous to the point of folly. At least the Russian occupation is correspondingly dismissed as benign to the point of indifference. From a Russian perspective, however, the approach made sense. A light hand had been remarkably successful in East Prussia. If, moreover, the occupation was the short-term consequence of a strategic raid, a certain level of cooperation from the city's more prosperous elements was likelier to produce quick results than was a policy of unrestrained exploitation, to say nothing of the wastage such a policy entailed.

This at least was the position of the Berlin merchant Johann Gotzkowsky. Perhaps with an eye to the future, he had done much to improve the living conditions of Russian officers detained as prisoners in the city after Zorndorf. Now he argued that the original demand for 4 million thalers was impossible to fulfil under any reasonably likely conditions. The prompt reduction of the contribution by over half, to 1.5 million thalers, may suggest a certain economic illiteracy on the part of the Russian commander – or a lack of sales resistance. The decision can also can be taken as proof of common sense. As Berlin's business community busied itself with raising the ransom lest worse befall, the allies turned to sorting out material assets. Austrian hussars and Saxon cavalry plundered Frederick's palace at Charlottenburg. Russian light troops scourged the countryside around the city.

Within Berlin itself things went better – at least from a Prussian perspective. Facilities crucial to the war effort, like Splitgerber and Daun's foundry, were spared as private property. Even public buildings, the arsenal and the *Gold-und-Silber-Manufaktur*, escaped destruction. An effort to destroy the powder supplies held in Berlin miscarried when a premature explosion cost a dozen or so Russian lives. Some military equipment was buried. Some muskets were thrown into the Spree. A large number of horses, not all of them government property, changed owners. But the musket factory at Potsdam was only slightly damaged. A battalion of convalescents defied the Russians and kept the gates of Spandau. A fair number of the Berlin garrison managed to escape a custody more nominal than strict. Perhaps the greatest human tragedy of the occupation was the fate of around 100 11– and 12–year-old boys from the Cadet Corps. These children were marched to Königsberg under conditions of extreme hardship; not until 1762 were they released as part of a general peace treaty.[34]

The relatively minor nature of the damage in Berlin cannot be ascribed entirely to allied fecklessness. Devastation is easier than destruction. Demolishing machinery, destroying solidly built factories and public buildings, takes certain levels of skill not widespread in the Russian army. Nor did the allies have unlimited time to render Berlin useless to Frederick's war effort. Living off the land, even in the aftermath of the harvest season, had its limitations.

Frederick, moreover, had not remained idle. In Saxony a revitalized Imperial army, 30,000 strong and heavily reinforced by Austrian regulars, was waging a successful campaign of manoeuvre against an inferior Prussian screening force. Then the King's scouts and agents informed him of the detaching of Lacy's corps. Whether it would march on Saxony or Berlin was initially uncertain. Frederick had no real choice but to abandon his position confronting Daun, withdraw into the Silesian plain, and await developments. But Russian security in 1760 was as bad as it would prove in 1914, with junior officers boasting to all and sundry about what they were going to do in Brandenburg. Further reports of his enemies' movements convinced the King his capital faced the greatest threat.

The Prussians moved rapidly without forcing the pace. Frederick was still a good five days' march away when the allies left the city on 11 October. Their evacuation highlights the eccentric nature of the mission. It was a true raid as opposed to an operational manoeuvre. Had anything like a coordinated plan existed, Berlin could well have been held for a few days as a ploy to draw Frederick further north

---

34 By far the best summary of the Berlin raid is in Duffy, *Russia's Military Way to the West*, pp. 114 ff. Cf., as well, Herman Granier, 'Die Russen und Österreicher in Berlin im Oktober 1760', *Hohenzollern-Jahrbuch*, II (1898), 113–45. J.C. Gotzkowsky's *Geschichte eines patriotischen Kaufmann*, 2 vols (Augsburg, 1768–69), vol. I, *passim*, is good for details and more self-serving than might be expected. A.F. Crousaz, *Geschichte des Königlich-Preussischen Kadetten-Corps* (Berlin, 1857), pp. 123 ff., tells the story of the boy soldiers.

and open Saxony and Silesia to the Austrians. As matters stood, the King was well able to halt on receiving news that the city was free – and relatively undamaged.

The Russian strike force rejoined the main army unmolested. Fermor spent the rest of the campaigning season negotiating with Gotzkowsky over a reduction of the agreed financial 'contribution' from Berlin – much of which still remained to be paid![35] It says much for the climate of eighteenth-century warfare that neither of the principal parties to this discussion considered it in the least unusual that such an obligation remained anything but moot, absent the presence of an occupying force. Apart from financial gains, the Russians could congratulate themselves on having humiliated their principal enemy at least for a few days, and for having conducted the campaign so prudently that their field army was well up to strength at the year's end. The latter fact also uncomfortably highlighted a significant general improvement in Russian logistics and administration. The animals had indeed learned something.

Critics might observe that the entire summer had been an exercise in smoke and mirrors, making a show of activity while achieving nothing of substance. Russia's ultimate aims, however, were regional, not local; and a cat can be killed by choking it with cream. Their moderate, conciliatory behaviour in Berlin convincingly replicated their ongoing policy in East Prussia. To the extent that the Russians could generate a sense in Brandenburg's businessmen and officials that the war was no longer worth fighting in terms of its costs, they might strike an ultimately mortal blow at a Prussian state already suffering seriously from over-stretch. Overt challenges to Frederick's authority were neither necessary nor desirable. A sense that Russia was a good neighbour, and at least thinkable as an alternate master, would suffice.

Prussia, moreover, was in certain respects becoming a secondary objective for the Empress and her advisers. The real prospects for making long-term territorial and political gains lay to the south-east, in Poland. Much of the original tension between France and Russia had reflected the former state's concern with maintaining its influence with the Polish monarchy. An unwelcome side effect of the series of defeats and checks suffered at British hands had been to diminish significantly the diplomatic and financial resources available to sustain French interests along the Vistula. As early as 1758, Choiseul

35 Gotzkowsky, *Geschichte eines patriotischen Kaufmanns*, vol. I, pp. 63 ff.

had declared privately that Poland could no longer be regarded as under French protection – at least, not at the price of risking the Russian alliance. Russian troops had used Poland as a transit route since the war's beginning. With more and more of the great magnates of the land testing the winds blowing from St Petersburg, a policy of *suavitur in modo* towards Berlin was a relatively cheap price to pay for a case study suggesting that Russian hegemony over Poland, or even direct Russian rule, would be an acceptable fate, if not one lightly borne.[36]

While Russia looked to grand strategy, Austria fought its war on the operational level. As Frederick marched beyond immediate striking range, Daun's army, more or less recovered from its high-summer exertions, took the field again, this time into Saxony. The Austrian commander-in-chief proposed to unite first with the *Reichsarmee*, then with Lacy's task force coming south from Berlin. Despite leaving 30,000 men under Laudon to keep an eye on the 10,000 or so 'odds and sods' Frederick had left behind in Silesia, Daun could count on assembling between 85,000 and 90,000 men under his immediate command before the end of October. That force, Daun reasoned, would be strong enough to create a choice. He could neutralize and occupy much of Saxony before winter put an end to field operations, or Frederick could fight another battle against long odds. And surely the King's tactical luck could not last for ever.[37]

Part of Daun's mosaic fell into place on 23 October, when Lacy's men joined their comrades complete with tales of wild nights in Berlin and enough loot to make the stories credible. Some of the advantages of that morale boost were lost, however, when the *Reichsarmee* withdrew beyond Leipzig in the face of a Prussian feint. Its commanding general, the Prince of Zweibrücken, had too clear a sense of the limitations of his motley force to risk thrusting it into what he regarded as the lion's very jaws.

A case might be made that Daun was better off without the Germans, even though the 11,000 Austrians in the *Reichsarmee's* ranks would have been a useful reinforcement. Daun, however, was not at his best on a level playing field. Frederick, by 28 October, had collected enough troops from around Berlin to bring his force to a strength of something like 50,000 with 250 guns. Daun had a few

36 L.J. Oliva, *Misalliance: A Study of French Policy in Russia during the Seven Years' War* (New York, 1964), pp. 156 ff.; Cf. H.H. Kaplan, *The First Partition of Poland* (New York, 1962).
37 F.L. Thadden, *Feldmarschall Daun* (Vienna, 1967), pp. 424 ff.

thousand men more, but by no means enough to give him an obvious edge going into battle. Yet a battle was exactly what he was under pressure to fight. On 23 October Maria Theresa had ordered him to defend Saxony even if that meant fighting under doubtful conditions, or achieve something else decisive.[38] Daun responded by occupying an old Prussian position near the town of Torgau on the Elbe River.

Daun had not chosen this site at random. Operationally, Torgau was the most important crossing point on the middle Elbe, and correspondingly useful as a choke point. Tactically the terrain was well suited for defence – so well suited, indeed, that Prince Henry had bluffed the Austrians under Daun off the same ground earlier in the year. The main Austrian position was established facing south, along a low ridge to the west of Torgau. Its left was anchored by Torgau's fortifications and its right by a series of wooded hills. The front slope of the ridge was dominated by vineyards, while the bottom of the slope featured marshes, ponds, and other assorted forms of wet ground to retard an enemy advance.

Torgau's defences were not exactly state of the art, but with an army supporting them they effectively denied access to that flank of the Austrian army. The right as well seemed secure enough, but Daun respected Frederick's mastery of tactical flanking movements through rough country sufficiently to deploy a good part of his cavalry to cover that area. With a network of redoubts and batteries covering his front, Daun was reasonably confident even though the position was uncomfortably small relative to the forces deployed. The ridge was so narrow that the Austrian lines were almost on top of one another; nor was there much room to shift troops. This disadvantage was arguably balanced by the fact that the broken terrain and sandy soil was not conducive to rapid manoeuvring by the defenders. To a certain degree Daun had learned from experience – his own and that of the Russians. Recent battles, from Leuthen to Kunersdorf, had demonstrated the difficulty of defeating Frederick in a tacticians' game of scissors-paper-stone. On the other hand Zorndorf, and especially Kunersdorf, suggested the Prussians were relatively vulnerable to a close-gripped fight. Daun's men might not have the stolid endurance traditionally associated with the Russians. But most of them had not been seriously engaged all year. Given his strong position it was not unreasonable for Daun to expect to take the Prussians' first shock, then bleed them to death along the ridge line. Moreover, Daun's sovereign and his enemies in court and camp

38 Arneth, *Geschichte Maria Theresias*, vol. VI, p. 174.

would have no immediate grounds for disparaging his own attitude towards battle.

Frederick too was looking for a fight, declaring that he regarded the prospect of death in battle from a stoic's perspective and never would conclude a disadvantageous peace. Instead, he announced himself ready to take any risk, even the most desperate, to end the campaign with a victory or a glorious death.[39] In terms of policy his rhetoric made sense. If after four years the King of Prussia could not protect his own capital, if the business community whose good will was so vitally important felt it necessary to enter long-term negotiations with the King's enemies, then it was time and high time to bring the fighting to an end. At the tactical level, however, matters seemed different. Prince Henry could not understand why his brother proposed to risk another fight with an enemy who had such obvious advantages of numbers and position. In Frederick's ranks senior and junior officers doubted the wisdom of a battle so late in the year when weather could set at naught the best of tactical plans. The deciding factor was Saxony. As long as Daun maintained his position at Torgau, Frederick was effectively cut off from what remained of that state's resources. Without Saxon conscripts, Saxon provisions, and Saxon money, Prussia's prospects of enduring another year of war without suffering permanent damage to its own infrastructure were grim indeed.

By 2 November, the Prussian army was within striking distance of Daun's position. Frederick had about 49,000 troops in ranks against Daun's 53,000, and 250 guns against 275. His principal material advantage was in his 180 twelve-pounders and heavy howitzers – a threefold superiority over the Austrians' heavy metal. The King was correspondingly free of any worries about being outshot, or of having his infantry massacred by mutually supporting enemy batteries.

As in several other major battles of the Seven Years War, Frederick had the further advantage of detailed knowledge of the terrain. Prince Henry's earlier manoeuvres in the region meant that some regiments had occupied the positions they were supposed to attack, and there seemed no shortage of reliable guides. The Prussian army's final marches had brought it to about 6 miles south of the Austrians, but Frederick had no intention of taking the most obvious route of attack and going against an enemy left flank that had all the advantages of terrain. Instead, as he reconnoitred the position in the late afternoon of 2 November, Frederick developed

---

39. Frederick to Prince Henry, 7 Oct. 1760, *PC*, XX, 141.

the idea of a flank march across the Austrian position. This time he proposed to take advantage of the woods that lay from 2 to 5 miles away from the enemy's lines. These, he reasoned, could screen a large-scale movement not merely to the Austrian right flank, as at Leuthen, but *around* it, to strike their positions from the rear. The tight deployment of the enemy's forces along the ridge made such a manoeuvre doubly inviting. Should they advance to disrupt it, the Austrians risked throwing their forces into irretrievable confusion.

One major problem stood in the plan's way. By this time Frederick's penchant for tactical flanking manoeuvres was familiar throughout Europe. At Prague and Kolin he had been able to ignore the Austrians, secure in the knowledge that his march was unlikely to be challenged. At Leuthen he had been able to attract and distract their attention with an exercise in military sleight of hand. Now at Torgau, a mere feint was unlikely to prove sufficient. To hold Daun's army in place called for a major secondary attack, commanded by someone who knew how to bite and hold on.

Frederick had the right personality ready to hand in Ziethen. The old hussar, general's dignity still fresh on his shoulders, was not a sophisticated tactician. His assignment, however, demanded no great finesse. Frederick gave him 18,000 men and ordered him to attack the Austrian left. His detailed instructions were verbal, and it remains a matter of debate whether the attack was intended merely as a holding operation or as an eventual component of a pincer movement designed to pin Daun against the Elbe River. Evidence favours the former – not least because of the King's unconcern for establishing any kind of systematic liaison with a man whose limitations were familiar and whose competence in conducting this kind of a battle was unknown. The distribution of force is also suggestive. Ziethen had 11,000 infantry and 7,000 cavalry – a task force structured both to draw on itself the enemy's horse and to complete a tactical victory. Frederick took 24,000 infantry, but only 6,500 cavalry, on his flank march. This at least suggests he expected to decide the battle in his sector, with Ziethen standing ready to exploit the decision as far as might be feasible.

The Prussians broke camp as early as the winter light permitted on 3 November; by 6.30 a.m. they were on the march. Frederick's operational goals may remain opaque, but his tactical intentions were clear. His main body marched in four columns. The first, under his personal command, was to strike the principal blow against the Austrian right. Its twenty-five battalions included ten of grenadiers, and some of the best of the army's line infantry. It was accompanied by no fewer than fifty twelve-pounders. Two dozen more, and ten howitzers, marched with the second column. Its infantry strength was less than half the first, but it counted five grenadier battalions to only seven of musketeers. The Prince of Holstein's third column had thirty-eight squadrons, but only four infantry battalions. Column four, the artillery train and some of the baggage wagons, had the extra responsibility of covering the army's rear against any surprise attacks by Austrian light forces. Ziethen's task force moved out at the same time, following Frederick's route for a short while, then turning right on the high road to Torgau, led by a mixed bag of hussars and *Freitruppen*.

It was a raw, wet morning, and the Prussian main body had 12 solid miles of ground to cover before reaching its position. That meant six hours' marching if everything went reasonably well, eight or more should the weather, the terrain, or the Austrians intervene. All three factors took a negative hand. Physical discomfort exacerbated pre-battle tension enough to diminish alertness at all levels. Frederick's guide, a local forester, misdirected the King's column, thereby forcing the second column to alter its line of march. The third cavalry column got a late start, then had its movements disrupted time and again by soft ground and narrow paths. Nor had the Austrians trusted entirely to natural forces for their protection. Daun's front was strongly outposted, and a bit before noon Frederick ran into one of his detachments. The resulting brief exchange of fire sounded the alarm even before the first general reports of Prussian movements arrived at Daun's headquarters.

The Austrian commander was less surprised than Frederick had hoped. He was already aware of Ziethen's presence on his left; the latter's advance guards had stumbled upon a small force of *Grenzer* and hussars just a bit earlier. The Croats, though quickly driven out of their improvised field works by a bayonet charge, nevertheless performed admirably as a trip-wire. Lacy commanded this sector of the Austrian line and behaved with his usual cool efficiency, keeping Ziethen well in play with a minimum of effort.

That left Daun free to cope with Frederick. He responded by changing his front slightly, so that a dozen battalions faced north while six more formed front to the west. When the manoeuvre was completed the main Austrian line formed a three-sided rectangle, one long line facing north and another south, with the short end on the west. On a map the Austrians seem deployed virtually back to back. On the ground the position was so crowded that some regiments had to do little more than execute one about-face to fulfil their movement orders. Retreat would be extremely difficult. Daun saw no reason to expect a negative outcome from the day's work. Just in case, however, he sent the army's baggage trains to safety across the Elbe. Should anything go wrong the fighting units would not be impeded by carts, wagons, and their civilian drivers.

Frederick's advance had progressed more slowly than the King wished or intended. Not until around 1 p.m. was he close enough to the Austrian positions to make a detailed reconnaissance. The King was anything but pleased with his observations. His projected axis of attack was now confronted by Austrian infantry deployed in line of battle. There was some open ground between the left wing of Daun's main position and the outskirts of Torgau, but an attack in that sector would put Frederick between Daun's and Lacy's forces – with no guarantee that Ziethen could hold the latter foe in place. The terrain itself, moreover, lay under the gun muzzles of several Austrian batteries: too much a potential killing ground for Frederick's liking.

The King's decision was to shift his weight further west and attack the far end of Daun's new line. This meant those of his battalions that had already deployed into their fighting lines now had to re-form into march columns. More seriously, the second column and the cavalry still had not caught up to Frederick's main body. The new battle plan meant therefore that the Prussian army would be split not merely into two but three parts at least, for what might be a crucial period of time.

Despite the risks, Frederick felt unable to wait. No more than four hours of daylight remained to him by the most generous reckoning. The weather threatened to break at any moment. And the sounds of Ziethen's grapple with Lacy were by now clearly borne on a strong wind. At about 2 p.m., Frederick ordered his infantry forward: ten battalions of grenadiers, the best in the army. They would need all of their fighting power. Heavy underbrush and a sudden storm combined to retard movements and disrupt order. The grenadiers could form line only when they reached open ground – and that placed them squarely in front of Daun's cannon.

The Austrian artillerymen were able to work their guns virtually undisturbed by Prussian counter-battery fire. The heavy guns on which Frederick had originally set such hopes remained far behind the front lines. Only a few battalion pieces were in position to support the advance. The small size of Daun's position meant that the Prussians came under fire from what seemed like every direction at once. One combatant spoke of 'a fire more intense than any known in land warfare since the invention of gunpowder'.[40] Nevertheless the grenadiers advanced, winning praise from the enemy both for their disciplined courage and their by now 'usual ceaseless musketry'.[41] The latter was a far cry from the shouldered firelocks of Prague or Kolin, but a futile gesture against the storm of cannon shot. Even Frederick, who was well up with the forward troops, noticed the 'frightful cannonade' and asked whether anyone had heard anything like it.[42] Over half the grenadiers fell in a few minutes; the survivors took shelter in the woods.

Any thoughts Frederick might have entertained of breaking off the action were deterred by a local Austrian counterattack. Itself easily repulsed, the charge suggested that Daun or at least his subordinates, were unlikely to remain passive in the face of a Prussian withdrawal. Instead, the King sent forward a second attack, the reserves of his own column reinforced by a half-dozen battalions from the second one, which had just reached the field. These men almost carried the day by sheer courage. They crossed the killing zone, still carpeted with dead and wounded grenadiers, stormed the heights, and began spiking Austrian guns whose fire was masked by their own retreating infantry. Daun responded by personally leading a counterattack. Initially the Prussians held their ground, trading volleys with the Austrians at point-blank range. Then enemy cavalry struck the line of musketeers in front and flank. The Prussians fell back – whether in good order or by running for their lives depends on the man telling the story.

The King meanwhile had sent messenger after messenger urging his cavalry forward. The troopers finally reached the scene around 3.30, coming up at a brisk trot and led by five regiments of cuirassiers. A royal adjutant begged one of the colonels to support the hard-pressed infantry who had been rallied for a third try. The rest of the Prussian horse followed, charging into and riding down Austrian infantry already disorganized by their efforts against the earlier attacks. With no local reserves to stop them, the leading Prussian squadrons broke through onto the high ground, only to be checked by the musketry of three grenadier battalions deployed in line.

Instead of promptly attacking this new enemy, the Prussian horse-

---

40 Archenholtz, *Geschichte des Siebenjährigen Krieges*, vol. II, pp. 106–7.

41 The comment of a Swedish officer with the Austrian army, quoted in Jany, *Preussische Armee*, vol. II, p. 587.

42 Archenholtz, *Geschichte des Siebenjährigen Krieges*, vol. II, p. 107.

men allowed themselves to be distracted, rounding up prisoners and dragging away guns. They paid for their error when four regiments of Austrian cuirassiers charged into their ranks and forced them off the plateau. By 4.30, Frederick's battle seemed over. His grenadiers were dead, his musketeers disorganized, and his cavalry mounted on exhausted horses. Frederick himself was stunned by an almost spent musket ball, and carried from the field by his anxious entourage.

In his absence the Prussian army turned the battle of Torgau around. Most of the credit goes to Ziethen – or perhaps better said, to the officers and men under his command. The process of recovery began around 4 p.m. Ziethen had been reluctant to push Lacy too hard. The broken, wooded terrain was uncongenial to the kinds of open-field battles on horseback he was experienced in fighting. Instead, Ziethen chose to wait until Frederick's portion of the battle developed – a polite euphemism for what seems to have been his hope that the King would settle matters decisively and take his loyal subordinate off the hook. But time passed; nothing happened; and Ziethen grew more nervous. For the old hussar tension was best dispelled by action. With twilight already beginning, he decided to march north and join Frederick.

Although many troops and guns had been withdrawn from the original Austrian position, enough of both remained to give Ziethen substantial concern for his flank. He left two of his four cavalry brigades in front of Lacy, moved two more in succession around his rear, then started the original brigades north as well. It was a manoeuvre more easily described than executed. Nevertheless the Prussians succeeded in breaking away. Then the lieutenant-colonel commanding the 15th Infantry, the Royal Guard, learned from an orderly officer that the Austrians had left unguarded a causeway leading to the western flank of Daun's position on the ridge. He reported the opportunity to his brigadier – perhaps the one man in Frederick's army best qualified to seize such an opportunity. On his own initiative Friedrich von Saldern took five battalions across the causeway. When his men were stopped by heavy Austrian fire, Ziethen moved up reserves in support. The Austrians were able to reinforce their position only by drawing battalions, many of them already heavily engaged, from in front of Frederick. Any numerical advantage gained thereby, moreover, was balanced by the growing number of stragglers, lightly wounded, and men who simply had done enough for the day, who crowded through the already congested rear areas of the Austrian position on their way to Torgau and the Elbe.

By this time the Austrian high command had lost control of the fighting. Daun, wounded during the counterattack, was convinced the day was his. 'Doesn't he know it will do him no good?' was his reaction to Frederick's apparent determination to throw away the best of his army in frontal attacks.[43] Around 6.30, his wound stiffening in the cold, Daun instructed Lacy to support the main army's left, turned command over to his next-ranking subordinate, and himself left the field – or was carried off.

Lacy remained inactive, held in place by Ziethen's cavalry and his own lethargy. It was Frederick, or more likely one of his staff officers, who determined to make a final effort to turn the day in Prussia's favour. Two regiments of infantry which had originally marched with the cavalry column still remained unengaged. The sounds of the fighting in Ziethen's front grew louder as in the growing darkness, flames from the village of Suplitz showed Austrians forming front to the south against Ziethen instead of the north against Frederick. Drummers beat the rally. Majors and captains shouted orders and regimental names. Fugitives and stragglers returned to their colours. The battalions may have been hollow shells of their morning selves, but the men remaining in their ranks would fight, and circumstances furnished a leader.

Johann von Hülsen, no stranger to these pages, was the kind of general whose style had been obsolescent since the turn of the century. Uneducated and unpolished, he had spent fifteen years in the rank of ensign. He owed his current rank of lieutenant-general to bravery and biddability rather than any more subtle talents. His command of Frederick's second column on the day of Torgau was more a reflection of the army's increasing lack of senior officers than to any gifts for task force command. But Hülsen possessed the kind of unquestioning courage that simply took no conscious notice of enemy fire. His rough manners and spectacular profanity reminded the native Prussians in his regiments of their *Gutsherren* and fathers back home, while the mercenaries responded to his coolness under fire. Now Hülsen massed the survivors for one more try. His horses had all been killed or wounded earlier. He was far from the days when he could lead a charge afoot, even without the painful foot wound he had suffered earlier. Instead he mounted a cannon and shouted 'Pull!' to the men around him.[44] With every drummer who retained two sticks and a whole skin beating the charge, the Prussians

---

43 Quoted in Duffy, *Frederick the Great*, pp. 213–14.
44 Archenholtz, *Geschichte des Siebenjährigen Krieges*, vol. II, p. 110.

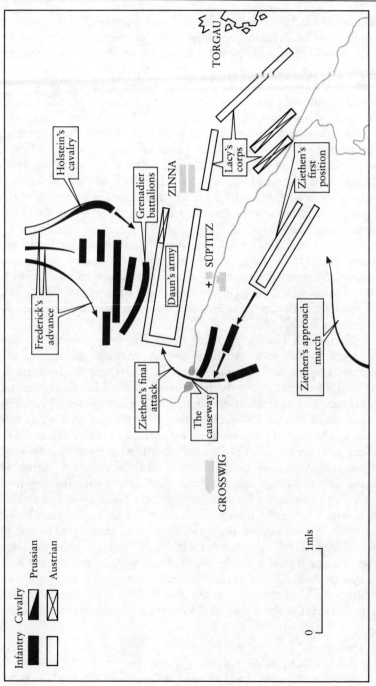

TORGAU

Holstein's cavalry

Grenadier battalions

ZINNA

Lacy's corps

Ziethen's first position

Daun's army

Frederick's advance

+ SÜPTITZ

Ziethen's final attack

Ziethen's approach march

The causeway

GROSSWIG

Infantry Cavalry

Prussian

Austrian

1mls

0

5. Battle of Torgau, 3 November 1760

followed Hülsen up the slope at about the same time Ziethen's exhausted men mounted an attack in their sector.

It was just enough. The Austrians left the field under cover of darkness – less in panic than in exhausted confusion. The Prussians were little less bewildered. A mixed bag of infantry and artillery formed something like a firing line and managed to beat off the half-hearted local counterattacks that were all the Austrians could manage. Lacy's corps had scarcely been engaged the whole day, but the hour was too late and the situation too confused for a general of Lacy's careful habits to risk trying to turn the day on his own initiative. Instead, he used his force to cover the army's retreat across the Elbe.

Austrian stragglers were left to roam the field, mixed with Prussians who had lost their regiments. A Prussian lieutenant-colonel became the prize of four bemused Austrians, while an Austrian general found himself a prisoner after giving orders to a Prussian battalion. Even Frederick came close to falling into the hands of a wandering troop of Habsburg cavalry. The night was cold; canteens and haversacks were empty. Deserters, camp followers, and local villagers with small cause to favour either side plundered wounded and dying with fine impartiality.

Frederick's mood was a microcosm of the battle. The King carried the shame of once again having been effectively distant while the battle was being decided. At least this time he had a reason. Stories of his dissolving in tears before Hülsen's attack are consistent with the kind of wound he had received.[45] A spent ball hurts; and thoughts of what *might* have happened could scarcely have remained entirely subject even to Frederick's vaunted self-control. After his recovery Frederick remained downcast. He ignored the captured flags and standards presented to him the next day. Instead he devoted an unusual amount of attention to determining his casualties, then concealing them.

They exceeded his worst fears. Almost 17,000 Prussians were dead, wounded, and missing – over 40 per cent of the army, and 1,000 more than the Austrians, whose losses included 7,000 prisoners who could be exchanged to fight once more. Again, moreover, the casualties had fallen disproportionately on the army's best forma-tions: the grenadiers and the low-numbered regiments from the 'old Prussian' provinces. The fifteen grenadier battalions that went into

---

45 Carl von Warnerey, *Campagnes de Frédéric II Roi de Prusse, de 1756 à 1762* (Amsterdam, 1788), p. 439.

the fight were consolidated into six afterwards. Most of the infantry regiments could muster only enough men to field a single battalion. Two of them suffered such ruinous losses that they were temporarily combined into one battalion instead of the regulation four. The Prussians could show fifty guns and thirty colours as trophies – but Daun's men had taken no fewer than forty-five flags, most of them from Frederick's main body. And even in retreat the Austrians brought off eight guns and 3,000 Prussian prisoners.[46]

Arguably more than Leuthen, Torgau stands as the archetypical 'Frederician' battle of the Seven Years War. The King's determination to destroy Daun's army has been exaggerated by nineteenth-century general staff historians committed to demonstrating Frederick as a proponent of *Vernichtungsstrategie*. There nevertheless seems no doubt that Frederick hoped and expected to redress an unfavourable political and strategic situation by a tactical victory sufficiently one-sided to impress Austria's allies and encourage Maria Theresa to reconsider her policies. Instead, he had occupied a patch of ground with little or no inherent value, and hammered his army to a pulp in the process. The Russians still held East Prussia and much of Pomerania. The Austrians still threatened Saxony and Silesia. Frederick was unable to consider even the limited option of reinforcing Ferdinand of Brunswick, whose polyglot army continued to keep the French and Imperials in play, with more than a token detachment.

1761: YEAR OF EXHAUSTION

On the other side of the line, the strategic situation seemed no more promising. By itself Torgau was marginally significant. The Habsburg army had lost battles before, and would lose them again. If Lacy had been supine in battle, he proved himself once more a master of administrative manoeuvre as a temporary replacement for Daun. The survivors of Torgau were brought very neatly around Frederick's shocked army, back to Dresden and safety.

Austria's problems lay deeper. It was no closer to defeating

---

46 Torgau has been the subject of several unusually solid secondary treatments: Emil Daniels, *Zur Schlacht von Torgau am 3. November 1760* (Berlin, 1886); Eberhard Kessel, 'Friedrich der Grosse am Abend der Schlacht bei Torgau', *Forschungen zur brandenburgischen und preussischen Geschichte*, XLVI (1934), 179–88; *Quellen und Untersuchungen zur Geschichte der Schlacht bei Torgau* (Berlin, 1937); and Helmuth Schnitter, 'Die Schlacht bei Torgau 1760', *Militärgeschichte*, XVIII (1979), 216–24.

Prussia than it had been when the war began, four-and-a-half years earlier. With Dresden firmly in Austrian hands, both armies went into winter quarters. But what prospects existed for the Habsburgs in the spring? Militarily, no new faces had emerged from the ruck. Laudon had too many enemies, and had shown nothing of a *Feldherr*'s talents in his independent commands. Torgau had highlighted pitilessly Lacy's limitations in any situation that did not go exactly to plan – which meant any situation involving King Frederick. Daun, who accepted responsibility for the defeat and refused to use his wound as an excuse to transfer blame, remained in command by default. No one expected him, however, to perform in drastically different fashion at his next opportunity.

Liegnitz and Torgau also ended for practical purposes any hope that France would reinvigorate its commitment to the Continental war. The Russian army might still mount a decisive campaign, but thus far had shown no more than a capacity to win battles. Austria's own financial situation ranged from serious to desperate, with little required to cross the line into catastrophe. Its administrative system had been strained to its limits and beyond by the demands of a war that had lasted longer and made more demands than anyone had foreseen in the halcyon days of 1755/56.

The logic of Austria's situation dictated a policy of peace, retrenchment, and reform. The latter two were forthcoming. In 1761 Maria Theresa inaugurated what has been appropriately called an administrative revolution aimed at completing Austria's transformation to a modern bureaucratic state with a coherent financial system. Preparing and inaugurating the new rules diminished even the human energy available for continuing the war. After a quarter-century Silesia's loss had become familiar, if not necessarily comfortable. Kaunitz began to consider the possibility of negotiating terms with his old enemy. Maria Theresa pondered the continued wisdom of risking everything in order to salvage something. Despite arguments to the contrary, however, Austria's initiatives for peace in the winter of 1760–61 were few and feeble. Whatever Austria's problems, Maria Theresa, Kaunitz, and their advisers were convinced that Frederick's resources and artifice were even closer to the point of exhaustion, unlikely to survive another year's operational stalemate. This perspective was reinforced wherever the Austrians looked.[47] In the German theatre of war, Ferdinand took the unusual step of

[47] Reginald Savory, *His Britannic Majesty's Army in Germany during the Seven Years' War* (Oxford, 1966), pp. 283 ff.

mounting a winter campaign against a French army that had gone into virtual hibernation. The Prince justified his decision by the quality of his own force, by now battle-seasoned and fully confident in its leader. But an early thaw and an unexpectedly swift French counteroffensive brought Ferdinand back to his start lines by the end of March, and gave a dispirited French army a significant infusion of confidence that bade fair to shape the summer's operations in a way not to Prussia's liking or advantage.

The year 1760 had also marked the final running-down of the Franco-British colonial war. The Royal Navy checked every French effort to reinforce Canada during the spring and summer. In September, Montreal fell to a British task force. The western outposts of Detroit and Michillimackinac surrendered by the turn of the year. On the other side of the globe British troops and their Indian allies and auxiliaries conquered one French strong point after another. The investment of Pondicherry and its surrender in January 1761 signalled the final end of French political pretensions on the sub-continent.

Paradoxically, this very run of British victories encouraged Austrian policy-makers to stand firm. All of Pitt's rhetoric could not sustain parliamentary support for a Continental commitment always expensive and now apparently increasingly irrelevant. Britain also had a new chief executive. George II, who sometimes seemed in practice more Elector of Hanover than King of Great Britain and Ireland, died in 1760. His grandson and successor, George III, was determined to establish the British character of his house. He was supported in this position by the Earl of Bute, one of Pitt's more determined political foes.[48]

It required no great flashes of insight in Vienna to conclude that Britain's commitment to Frederick was likely to depend heavily on Pitt's continuance in office – or to perceive that the scale of that commitment was likely to be diminished whether Ferdinand lost or won his battles in 1761. The temptation to hold on, to draw just one more card in a game with such high stakes on the table, was overwhelming. Kaunitz had not, after all, come to power as a domestic reformer. His emphasis had been on an assertive, indeed a revolutionary, foreign policy. To suggest now that it was time for Austria to fold its hand and accept the *status quo ante bellum* was to abandon all hope for a place in history – except at the losers' table.

---

48 Richard Middleton, *The Bells of Victory: The Pitt-Newcastle Ministry and the Conduct of the Seven Years' War, 1757–1762* (Cambridge, 1985), pp. 171 ff.; Karl W. Schweizer, *Frederick the Great, William Pitt and Lord Bute: The Anglo-Prussian Alliance, 1756–1763* (New York, 1991), pp. 99 *passim*.

Russia too was uninterested in peace with Frederick. Its main army had withdrawn into winter quarters in unusually good shape. Saltykov had been relieved in the aftermath of the Berlin raid. His successor, Alexander Buturlin, was a favourite of the Empress and a first-rate administrator. He took full advantage of his position to overhaul the logistics arrangements of his new command. In part this involved modifying, when not abandoning, conciliating East Prussia. Requisitions increasingly supplemented purchases – a policy Buturlin described as by the end of the year having saved 400,000 roubles, whatever its longer-term political consequences. Buturlin's 85,000 men could reasonably be expected to take the field in top condition once the winter broke and the 1761 campaigning season could begin.

The crucial question was what was this well-found army was to do? Elizabeth and her council by this time had developed a respect amounting to awe for the recuperative powers of Frederick's Prussia. All the more reason, then, to finish the King while his strength was at its nadir. The Russians proposed essentially to repeat the strategy of the previous two years: advance towards the Oder, link up with the Austrians, and bring Frederick to battle. At the same time a task force would advance through Pomerania and capture the Baltic port and fortress of Kolberg, consolidating the Russian operational and political position in that crucial northern sector.

The Austrians, for all their abstract determination to continue the war, were significantly passive in terms of operational planning. Daun retained command, but no one in Vienna regarded him as more than a figurehead – at best, a buffer among increasingly factionalized senior officers. He urged that Austria concentrate its forces and resources in Saxony for a decisive spring campaign. Instead, Kaunitz and the Empress once again put their trust in Laudon. He was given more than 70,000 men, and ordered to advance through Silesia to cooperate with Buturlin in securing the province and defeating the Prussians. Daun's 'main army', in contrast, had a strength of only 55,000, and a mission of doing no more than attracting Frederick's attention – an assignment that Vienna regarded as incorporating more hope than expectation, given Daun's record.[49]

Frederick had also spent an anxious winter. His glass, depending on one's perspective, was half-full or half-empty. On the positive

49 Eberhard Kessel, 'Der russisch-österreichische Feldzugsplan 1761', *Forschungen zur brandenburgischen und preussischen Geschichte*, XLIX (1937), 142–60; and F. Jihn, *Der Feldzug 1761 in Schlesien und Sachsen* (Vienna, 1884).

side, Torgau and its aftermath had won the King four to six months of badly needed time to secure men, horses, supplies, and money. Not only the familiar hunting grounds of Saxony and Mecklenburg but the ostensibly independent petty states of Thuringia as well, experienced the attentions of Prussian recruiters and foraging parties. Sometimes it came to armed clashes between Frederick's men and French troops engaged on similar errands.

Manpower was so short that at least on one occasion prisoners of war were incorporated directly from their point of capture into the Prussian army. By March, nevertheless, the Prussian main army was only 1,600 men short of its authorized paper strength. Three-fifths of the replacements came from the regimental depots – though whether all of them were cantonists in the strict sense of the term is at least debatable. The remaining 40 per cent were foreigners, mostly north and central Germans. Whether a regiment's home district was in enemy hands continued to make a significant difference. By this time the Pomeranian and East Prussian formations were taking anyone they could get, keeping them in ranks with ever more draconian punishments, formal and informal, administered by ever-shrinking cadres. Even Frederick was reluctant to dilute his veteran units too heavily with the kind of replacements brought in by his press gangs during the winter of 1760/61. Instead, he more than doubled the number of free battalions.

Almost two dozen of these improvised formations, infantry and cavalry, stood on the army's rolls in 1761. Their quality ranged from adequate to miserable. Their commanders were a collection of adventurers. Some of them would have been perfectly at home in the American Civil War, riding with bushwhackers like William Quantrill or James Jennison. Others, like Charles Guichard, had intellectual as well as military pretensions. He had written a book on the art of war in antiquity, and Frederick nicknamed him 'Quintus Icilius'. Nothing in the King's character suggests that the christening was anything but sarcasm. Guichardt, however, adopted it as his *nom de guerre*, and proudly called his collection of gallows-bait the 'Roman Free Legion'.

Whatever their shortcomings, the free battalions could no longer be relegated to secondary missions or used as fillers for the order of battle. A half-dozen regular regiments were so badly hammered that they were assigned to garrison duties. Another half-dozen took the field with heavily reduced establishments. The grenadiers, Frederick's shock troops, were mere shadows of the proud formations that strode out of their garrison towns in 1756. The cavalry was in better state. Its losses had been lighter. The number of cantonists among its replacements was much larger than in the infantry. And the irregular mounted units seem to have attracted a higher quality of volunteers, including teenagers who still believed in glamour and sought adventure. No one, however, was confusing this force with the men of Leuthen, Zorndorf, or even Torgau.

Frederick's training programmes during the winter were both more rigorous and more practical than in the war's earlier years. It remains easy to exaggerate the brutality of Prussian discipline at the cutting edge. Whatever the King's increasingly misanthropic rhetoric, his captains and majors were well aware of the numerous ways their men could evade duty and avoid fighting if driven to extremes. Prussia's field officers were by now well aware that fear alone could not bring men forward on days like those of Kunersdorf or Torgau. At the same time, the new men in the ranks were not exclusively victims forcibly dragged from the plough and the cart's tail, or cozened by a recruiter's promises. They too were survivors in their ways. Some were hard-cased veterans of a half-dozen campaigns in as many uniforms. Others were Prussians, Saxons, or Mecklenburgers still with ties to their home villages, but who had seen enough service to know what they were expected to do. A reasonable parallel might be drawn to the militias of the American colonies in the last years of the Revolutionary War: men who in a perfect world might not have chosen to fight for the King of Prussia or anyone else, but who had lost their innocence long before and who knew what they were about when the guns went off. They might no longer go into action singing hymns – but fight they could and march they could, given the right conditions.[50]

Their supreme commander proposed to match his strategy to his army. Rebuilding his forces was easier than paying for them. Britain was no longer the cash cow of the war's earlier years. Pitt managed to steer the Prussian subsidy treaty through Parliament, but only after lengthy, vehement, and hostile debate on the question. His private assertions that should England conclude peace with France Prussia would still receive enough funds to maintain 40,000 men may have been sincere. They were correspondingly hollow. For Frederick as for Kaunitz, it did not require great experience of parliamentary systems to realize that Pitt's term in office was unlikely to survive a separate peace, and that the subsidy would vanish with him.[51]

Frederick responded by debasing his coinage, this time to the

50 Jany, *Preussische Armee*, vol. II, pp. 598 *passim.*
51 Schweizer, *Frederick the Great, William Pitt and Lord Bute*, pp. 106 ff.

tune of 6 million talers. He increased the pressure on Saxony, draining that unhappy country of almost 20 million talers. He levied a contribution on the city of Leipzig that was so heavy that fifty leading merchants accepted imprisonment rather than pay their shares. Occupied Mecklenburg was scoured for grain and livestock. Even private property was no longer safe. The palatial estate of the Saxon prime minister-in-exile was looted, on Frederick's orders, by Quintus Icilius. What did not vanish into the pockets and knapsacks of the freebooters was sold or sequestered, at a neat profit for Frederick.

The King's policy generated widespread criticism both on the Continent and in England, where the Protestant paladin of 1756 bade fair to become the Prussian reiver of 1761.[52] It must be noted, however, that Frederick was still at some pains to keep his exactions within bearable limits. The extent of his Saxon extortions was exceeded – if only slightly – by Saxony's ability to produce the goods and specie without collapsing. In Prussia proper, there remained money to be made through army contracts on scales never before heard of in central Europe. Splitgerber and Daun prefigured modern conglomerates by taking advantage of their base in arms production to diversify into trading, banking, and other industrial enterprises. The firm of Ephraim and Sons, lessees of the royal mints, grew rich by squeezing even more Saxon thalers out of a pound of bullion than the King required. Those who stayed on top of the current profited. As for the others, there remained the motto 'Pray and obey' – and the hope of peace.

The latter was not mere wishful thinking. Frederick was so heavily outnumbered in so many sectors that his initial strategy could be no more than one of pure reaction: wait and see what his enemies proposed to do, then outmarch and, when necessary, outfight them. He kept, however, a particularly sharp eye on the build-up of Laudon's force in Silesia, if for no better reason than the necessity for holding that province if Prussia were to survive. In late March the King himself set out for Silesia with 30,000 men to join the Prussian forces already on the ground. Prince Henry, who had rejoined his brother for this campaign, was left in Saxony to 'observe' Daun with the 30,000 men Frederick trusted least, including most of the free battalions.

---

52 Even Mitchell, one of the King's great admirers, was shocked by the turn the war was taking. See his letters of 7 and 16 January in Mitchell, *Memoirs and Papers*, vol. II, pp. 214, 217–18.

The King's earlier tactical aggressiveness, as well as his strategic energy, had been significantly curbed. Kunersdorf and Torgau had taught him the risks of attacking even fortified field positions.[53] He kept his army as a force in being while Laudon was reinforced and Buturlin's Russians advanced slowly and carefully towards the Oder. Frederick did benefit during this period from a well-executed piece of intelligence work. The Russian force sent against Kolberg was commanded by General G.K. Todleben who had proceeded with kid gloves against Berlin. A Prussian merchant, Isaac Sabatky, acted as go-between, offering money and eventual asylum in exchange for information on Russian war plans and a policy of sparing occupied territories. Not until the end of June was the contact uncovered. It took another two months for the Russians to get their Baltic campaign under way once more.[54]

Operations in the western theatre were significantly less fortunate. A well-executed French counterattack took Ferdinand off balance and showed the weaknesses inherent in a polyglot army held together by money and its commander's charisma. Supply arrangements had deteriorated to the point where the rank and file had begun drawing their own rations directly from the countryside – a major danger signal in the eighteenth century. Morale continued to go downhill even after Ferdinand successfully withdrew beyond immediate striking range. Subordinates quarrelled with one another and criticized their chief while the French assembled two armies, 160,000 strong, for the purpose of forcing a decisive battle somewhere in central Germany.

Despite France's growing economic weakness, the employment of such apparently disproportionate force made solid grand strategic sense. With Ferdinand's army destroyed or scattered, Britain might be rendered considerably more amenable to negotiating an end to a war that had long since ceased to offer France even remote possibilities of economic or diplomatic profit. France's aggressive military strategy in the summer of 1761 was also closely linked to its Spanish policies. The latter state's relations with Britain had been increasingly strained by economic and naval policies that, at least from Madrid's perspective, appeared inappropriately heavy-handed. France, on the other hand, saw Spain as a highly desirable makeweight in a negotiated

---

53 Frederick II to Prince Henry, 24 May 1761, *PC*, XX, 412.

54 Eberhard Kessel, 'Totlebens Verrat', *Forschungen zur brandenburgischen und preussischen Geschichte*, LXIX (1937), 371–8.

peace. The Spanish navy, even combined with what remained of its French counterpart, was hardly likely to threaten Britain's maritime position. Spain's colonies, indeed, offered renewed possibilities of rich pickings to an island empire that had exhausted most of its obvious targets. But the possibility of continuing the war at sea indefinitely might well inspire a peace-minded British Parliament to reconsider its commitments – particularly if the Continental sword currently wielded by Ferdinand of Brunswick could be dulled or broken.[55]

Not until August was Choiseul able to overcome Madrid's reluctance and conclude a formal Franco-Spanish alliance. Meanwhile, on 19 July Laudon broke out of the frontier zone and into the Silesian plain. Frederick countered by interposing his main body between Laudon and the Russians. Despite a significant numerical superiority, Laudon refused to try conclusions with Frederick on ground of the King's choosing. He fell back westwards. Frederick retired east, his army *en vedette* like a boxer balancing on the balls of his feet. But it was the allies who finally won the manoeuvring game. Frederick had kept his focus on Laudon, regarding the Austrian as his most dangerous enemy. On 12 August, however, Buturlin's Russians crossed the Oder without opposition. On the 15th they linked up with a strong force of Laudon's cavalry. Frederick, well aware of the risks in the new situation, turned against the Russians only to find them entrenched so strongly that any serious thoughts of attacking were buried under memories of Zorndorf. Instead, Frederick stood in place and allowed himself to be feinted out of position once more, as Buturlin led his men from under the King's nose to a successful union with Laudon's main body.

This proof of the Russian army's quality left Frederick facing an allied force of more than 70,000 Austrians and almost 50,000 Russians. Against them he had 55,000 men – too few to risk in open battle even had they possessed the quality of the regiments destroyed at Prague, Kunersdorf, or Torgau. The King responded to his circumstances with a conventional eighteenth-century manoeuvre worthy of Daun himself. He moved his army into camp at Bunzelwitz, north-west of the small fortress of Schweidnitz, and began fortifying his positions in expectation of an allied attack.

Field engineering was a major, and often overlooked, strength of

---

55 Cf. Alfred Bourguet, 'Le duc de Choiseul et l'Angleterre, mission de Bussy à Londres. Le duc de Choiseul et l'alliance espagnole', *Revue Historique*, LXXI (1899), 3–32; and Allan Christelow, 'Economic Background of the Anglo-Spanish War of 1762', *Journal of Modern History*, XVIII (1946), 22–36.

the Prussian army. Frederick's engineer officers were more competent than the King deserved given his tendency to treat his technicians shabbily, and Frederick himself had a good eye for ground. Not least of the Prussian advantages was the willingness of the rank and file to do the donkey work of trench-digging and timber-cutting – an attitude not shared in the French and Austrian armies, whose private soldiers tended to view manual labour as a reminder of the servile estate they ostensibly left behind on joining the colours. The Prussians worked around the clock in two shifts, and within three days had a defensible position that took full advantage of the broken, swampy terrain.

Bunzelwitz was not an entrenchment. Its perimeter was not continuous. Frederick instead established a series of battery positions, redoubts, and fortified villages with gaps between them, both to permit counterattacks, and to lure attackers into killing grounds covered by the cross-fire of over 450 guns including heavy pieces taken from Schweidnitz. The camp's extensive size meant that most of the infantry was deployed along the perimeter. Counterattacks would be the responsibility of the cavalry – another good reason for the position's relatively open layout. Since Schweidnitz was also a major supply depot the Prussians were in no danger of starving, or of becoming too weak to continue work on a system that for decades remained a model of field fortification. Instead of following normal camp routine, the entire army struck its tents and stood to just before dawn, ready every day to meet a second Hochkirch. The King himself slept in one or another of the main batteries every night. In sharp contrast to earlier, more or less cavalier attitudes about tactical security, the Prussians constantly kept their field works manned strongly enough to resist even the first stages of an assault that Frederick expected would cost his enemies at least 30,000 men by the time their discomfiture was completed.

Frederick's preparations did not deter Laudon. Initially at least, the fiery Austrian was determined to attack. Buturlin was less sanguine. His army was far from home. Its casualties could not be easily replaced. The weather, moreover, was as hot as it had been in any summer since the war began. The Russians in their heavy uniforms suffered badly from heat exhaustion. The army was also plagued with camp diseases caused by thirsty men drinking any water available, no matter how polluted. Laudon, however, was persistent. He finally convinced his Russian opposite number to cooperate in an attack on 1 September. Most of the fighting was to be done by the Austrians, and Laudon's plans promised initial success: a break-in, at least. But they came to nothing, in practice, when Buturlin refused at the last minute to participate. Perhaps he knew enough about bear-hunting to recognize that the real risk came not on entering the den, but when seeking to leave!

The next ten days were anticlimactic. Laudon made one more attempt to force Buturlin's hand by declaring that a growing shortage of supplies would soon force the allies to separate. Buturlin agreed so heartily that on 9 September he broke camp and marched towards the Oder! As a token of good will, the allies exchanged troops. Twenty thousand Russians, most of them infantry, remained with Laudon. Forty Habsburg squadrons rode north-east with Buturlin. Whether these would be allies or hostages remained to be seen.[56]

The pseudo-siege of Bunzelwitz was arguably a tactical victory to rank with Leuthen or Liegnitz. Frederick had absorbed the attention of his enemies' two major field armies for most of the campaigning season at virtually no loss to his own forces. A year's breathing space and a summer's seasoning had, moreover, done much to improve the quality of the main Prussian army. Instead of fostering what a later generation would call 'bunker psychosis', the entrenchments of Bunzelwitz had given the infantry back its confidence. If it was still far from the levels of 1756 and 1757, most of its battalions were far more stable in September than they had been in May. In the war's major secondary theatres, Daun and Prince Henry had fenced to a predictable stand-off in Saxony. And Ferdinand of Brunswick had again proven to have more military lives than the proverbial cat. On 15–16 July he won a significant tactical victory at Vellinghausen against two French armies whose divided command more than compensated for their combined strength. The defeated generals quarrelled, agreed to conduct operations separately henceforth, and left themselves correspondingly vulnerable to Brunswick's gifts as a counter-puncher – implemented by his veteran army, which by this time had fully recovered both its fighting spirit and its confidence in the commanding general.

The fragility, as opposed to the brittleness, of eighteenth-century armies is easily exaggerated. The contingents that marched with Ferdinand were the usual mixture of conscripts and professionals, but whatever their origins the men were by now a case-hardened lot who took an approach to war that is best described as short-term contractual. Breach of agreement, whether because of inadequate

---

56 Eberhard Kessel, 'Friedrich der Grosse im Lager von Bunzelwitz', *Die Welt als Geschichte*, III (1937), 38–57; Duffy, *Frederick the Great*, pp. 221 ff.

supplies or too many one-sided defeats, generated what amount to a military strike. But let the provision trains and the paymasters arrive once more, let the 'old man' convey a sense that he knew a hawk from a handsaw at least on most days; and the marauders and grumblers of one month could become transformed in the next into men able to defeat twice their numbers and march their feet bloody for the opportunity. So it proved in central Germany. By October Ferdinand himself was exhausted to the point of illness. His men's tongues were hanging out. But their tails were so well up that Ferdinand was planning another major winter campaign against opponents by now almost paralysed by the Prince's feints and thrusts.[57]

Thus far, so good – so good, indeed, that Frederick felt able to take a risk. His position at Bunzelwitz was in the long term untenable. With more than 50,000 men in what was a relatively confined space, camp diseases, diarrhoea and respiratory problems, were taking increasingly heavy tolls. As yet few were dying, but many were debilitated. Schweidnitz's magazines, moreover, were not an inexhaustible source. They held basic supplies for no more than a month, and allied light troops and raiders were rapidly increasing the risks and costs of foraging in a depleted countryside. Frederick decided, logically enough, to shift his base of operations to the other major Prussian base in south Silesia. Dismantling its Bunzelwitz defences, the Prussian army marched towards Neisse on 26 September as a first step to moving into winter quarters in Saxony. 'The campaign is over', Frederick informed Henry, 'for neither the Austrians nor ourselves are capable of any initiatives.'[58]

Frederick's opinion provided exactly the opportunity Laudon had sought all summer. Schweidnitz had grown slack under the protection of the King's army. Its commandant was unenterprising. Its garrison was built around four battalions of Silesians whose operational records to date were at best uneven. Laudon was at heart less a battle captain than a raider, a man in the mould of Confederate General Nathan Bedford Forrest.[59] With Frederick at a safe distance,

57 Savory, *His Britannic Majesty's Army*, pp. 312 ff. H. Little, 'The British Army Commissaries in Germany during the Seven Years' War', PhD dissertation, London University, 1981, further develops the relationship between administration and morale.

58 Frederick to Prince Henry, 27 Sept. 1761, *PC*, XX, 630.

59 Johannes Kunisch, 'Feldmarschall Loudon und der Kleine Krieg', in *Formen des Krieges. Vom Mittelalter zum 'Low-Intensity Conflict'*, ed. M. Rauchensteiner and E.A. Schmedl (Graz, 1991), pp. 45–70, makes this point while demonstrating that Loudon himself regarded his skills in this area as a professional liability.

Laudon moved against Schweidnitz. At dawn on 1 October, he stormed the fortress with a mixed bag of Russian grenadiers and Austrian infantry. Despite some stout local resistance, by full daylight Schweidnitz was under the double eagle. Over 200 cannon, almost 4,000 men, and hundreds of tons of supplies were victory's tangible rewards. No less significant was the shock to Frederick's army. The King himself initially could hardly credit the news. From generals to privates morale sagged. Desertion rates soared. And Frederick's troubles were just beginning.

In September the Baltic port of Kolberg came under siege once more, this time by a Russian commander who meant business. Lieutenant-General Peter Alexandrovich Rumyantsev was one of the army's rising stars. The son of one of Peter the Great's most trusted advisers, he was as well read as he was brave and ambitious. He had served briefly in the Prussian army – more a gesture of youthful independence than a serious career move – and admired the Prussian way of war inordinately enough to be aware of its shortcomings as well as its strengths. He had fought at Gross-Jägersdorf and Kunersdorf; this was his first independent command and his first chance at real glory.

Initially Frederick was not inordinately alarmed. In the aftermath of the Todleben affair he had reinforced the garrison and strengthened the fortress. In September he had also detached 10,000 cavalry and light troops from his main army on a raid against the Russian depots in Posen, with the secondary mission of swinging north to support Kolberg's defence by harassing the besiegers. These moves seemed more than enough, particularly given the previous desultory nature of the war along the Baltic coast, where neither Swedes nor Russians had shown much enterprise.

Rumyantsev was a different prospect entirely. His cavalry and light infantry, the latter a new institution in the Russian army, kept Frederick's raiders well in check while the main army, supported while the weather permitted by Swedish and Russian warships, took Kolberg by the throat and squeezed. Initially the fortress commander proposed to seek battle but was dissuaded by the King, who doubted the garrison's capacity to defeat the Russians in the open field.[60] Despite the Russians' failure to isolate Kolberg entirely, its supply situation grew steadily worse. In mid-November most of the garrison broke out along the coast to Mecklenburg. Four battalions remained behind, keeping the colours flying until the Russian artillery finally

60 Jany, *Preussische Armee*, vol. II, p. 609.

established practicable breaches a month later. On 16 December Kolberg finally surrendered, giving the Russians full mastery of Eastern Pomerania.

1762: THE END-GAME

Diplomatically as well as militarily, the final weeks of 1761 brought only misfortune to Prussia and its King. Despite the failure of the French campaign in Germany, Spain in August concluded a treaty with France that amounted to an alliance against England. Pitt responded by arguing for a declaration of war. Denied by a Parliament weary to death of war without end, he resigned. His successor was the Earl of Bute, no pacifist but a peace-minded statesman. He began his term in office by rethinking England's relationship with Prussia.

Bute's revisionism accelerated in January, when despite his best efforts war broke out with Spain. This not only revived a maritime/colonial struggle that had appeared ended with the fall of French Canada. It also created possibilities for direct British intervention in the Iberian peninsula. 'Descents', small-scale landings in the neighbourhood of naval bases or in regions presumed to be disaffected, had been a feature of British strategy since the days of William III.[61] Spain offered a broad spectrum of apparently fruitful prospects for similar operations.

In December Bute had informed Frederick that instead of asking Parliament to renew the subsidy treaty, he would request a specific grant at an 'opportune' time – preferably between the twelfth of never and the thirty-first of June. Bute's next step was to urge Frederick to seek terms with Austria, cutting his strategic coat to his military cloth even if that involved significant territorial concessions. Neither Britain's pockets nor its patience, Bute declared in effect, were bottomless.[62]

For Frederick this represented a final catastrophe. With the port of Kolberg in Russian hands, the logistics of their next year's

---

61 Cf. W. K. Hackman, 'English Military Expeditions to the Coast of France, 1757–1761', PhD dissertation, University of Michigan, 1969; and Robert McJimsey, 'England's Descent on France and the Origins of the Blue Water Strategy, 1690–1693', unpublished manuscript.

62 Schweizer, *Frederick the Great, William Pitt and Lord Bute*, pp. 142 ff. According to the King some officers helped make ends meet by selling muskets to the free battalions, who presumably had greater opportunities to 'acquire' negotiable assets. Letter of 15 May 1762, PC, XXI, 439–40.

campaign would be simpler than ever before. Forces already strong could be enlarged almost at will, with supplies and reinforcements transported by sea across a Baltic that from Prussia's perspective was now a Russian lake. The administrative and economic integration of Prussia's occupied eastern territories into the Tsarist Empire was also likely to be significantly facilitated by the opening of the coast to Russian and Swedish merchantmen and traders.

Prussia's situation seemed no more promising in the south. With Schweidnitz in Austrian hands, the Habsburg army was able to establish most of its winter camps on the Prussian side of the Silesian border, with corresponding impact on Frederick's ability to tap that province's resources for the coming campaign. Russian troops cantoned almost on the border of Brandenburg rendered chances of compensating by purchasing grain and remounts in Poland significantly limited.

Perhaps the most devastating aspect of Prussia's strategic dilemma was that the allies had achieved their advantage by expending no more than military pocket change. For the past four years, Frederick had compensated for his state's geo-strategic disadvantages by his own tactical skill and the fighting power of his army. Each in its way, Kolberg and Schweidnitz demonstrated that even the battlefield balance was beginning to shift away from Prussia. Whether by a brilliant *coup de main* or in conducting a complex combined arms siege, the Russians and Austrians had shown levels of improvement that were threatening both in themselves and in the context of the Prussian army's changing structure.

At the start of the war Frederick had been able to maintain several subsidiary forces in addition to a main army that alternately served as a striking force and a fire brigade. These 'theatre armies', including large numbers of second-line troops, were never intended to win victories by themselves. Their task was rather to keep the ring until Frederick arrived to tip the balance. By 1761, however, the quality of troops available for the secondary theatres had sunk so low that ordinarily competent commanders, the only kind Frederick possessed, were best advised to avoid taking significant risks. The disasters of Kolberg and Schweidnitz suggested that Frederick could no longer afford to assign military leftovers to these regions. But to reduce or dilute the main army to underwrite sideshows was an even more certain way to disaster.

It was scarcely remarkable that Frederick's personal and professional behaviour showed renewed signs of stress as the year ended. Whether dreaming of a Turkish attack on Hungary in the coming spring or proposing to unite the whole Prussian army and attack one of his enemies as soon as possible, Frederick confronted the problem Bute had put in such brutally simple terms. Prussia could no longer keep the field in the style it had maintained since the war began. Its civil and military administrations were disorganized – so disorganized that the economic core of the army, the system of company administration, was by now in danger of collapsing. Captains were not receiving the money necessary to purchase clothing and equipment for the next year. And Frederick's army by this time was no different than Ferdinand's in being unlikely to endure long-term everyday continued privation with equanimity.

From a more general perspective Frederick could not escape the fact that the core of his state, the provinces of Brandenburg and Pomerania, now lay wide open to raid and invasion on a regular basis. As has been previously suggested in these pages, the 'social contract' between Frederick and his people involved the exchange of service for protection. Even if the enemy should be unable to overrun what remained of the Prussian kingdom, razzias and sorties could do much to make the state ungovernable.

Prussia's situation was restored by an event no reviewer of historical fiction would credit as a novel's plot. Empress Elizabeth's health had long been uncertain. In early December she suffered what was probably a final series of small strokes. Their effect proved cumulative; the Empress died on 6 January 1762. Frederick learned of her death two weeks later, but initially did not hope for much from it.[63] In fact, Elizabeth's last illness proved the turning point of Prussia's fortunes. Her successor, Peter III, was a prince of Schleswig-Holstein with an inordinate admiration for everything Prussian, including above all its King.

Russian nationalist historians have made much – perhaps too much – of Peter's shortcomings as a man and an emperor. He was certainly susceptible to Frederick's flattery. When awarded the Order of the Black Eagle and made an honorary general in the Prussian army, Peter's sycophantic responses disgusted even the Prussians in his entourage who benefited from the Tsar's obsession. Peter, however, was at least something more than a weak-minded man jealous of his spouse. His Prussophilia and his status as the heir-apparent had made him the symbol, if not quite the leader, of the faction at court

---

63 Frederick to Benoît, Prussian secretary at Warsaw, and to Prince Henry, 19 Jan. 1762, *PC*, XXI, 189, 190–1.

that had from the beginning criticized war with Prussia as ultimately inimical to Russia's interests.

Prussia, these men argued, represented nothing like a serious long-term threat to Russian security. Had Russia kept the peace in 1756, Frederick might at worst have been in a position to challenge directly Russian influence in Kurland – hardly a major problem. As for Poland, any Prussian gains on the western borders of that ramshackle state could easily be balanced by Russian annexations in the Polish east and Russian influence in Warsaw, the latter an advantage beyond the annexation of East Prussia. Reality, in the latter case, was certain to be a nightmare, generating a permanent anti-Russian coalition of German states under Prussian or Austrian leadership, perhaps even encouraging these enemies to make common cause against a new, greater threat from the east.

Territorial speculations aside, critics argued, the war had brought Russia recognition as a first-rank military power, at a cost of tens of thousands of lives and 30 million roubles. The latter was a loss more serious than the former to an undeveloped economy. Both were good reasons to reconsider a war that, from the perspective of St Petersburg, seemed no closer to ending now than five years earlier. Even before Elizabeth's death the French alliance had for all practical purposes been abrogated. As for Austria, nothing in the behaviour of its field commanders suggested even remotely that the Habsburgs regarded Russia as anything beyond an instrument for achieving Kaunitz's grand designs for Europe. Certainly even Laudon, the alliance's most vociferous defender, had from Kunersdorf to Bunzelwitz shown a distressing eagerness to fight to the last Russian.[64]

To speak, in short, of Peter's search for peace with Frederick as a 'great betrayal' is defensible only in the context of equating eighteenth-century Prussia with Wilhelmine or Hitlerian Germany as a permanent, objective threat to the rest of Europe.[65] By 1762 it was arguable, if not quite self-evident, that Prussia's only real challenge was to Austria. Whatever might have been strategically defensible, moreover, in Elizabeth's original intention to reduce Prussia to the

---

[64] Carol S. Leonard, *Reform and Regicide: The Reign of Peter III of Russia* (Bloomington, Ind., 1993), pp. 122 *passim*, incorporates a solid revisionist analysis of the roots of foreign policy in the Tsar's short reign. Cf. also Georg Küntzel, 'Friedrich den Grossen am Ausgang des Siebenjährigen Krieges und sein Bündnis mit Russland', *Forschungen zur brandenburgischen und preussischen Geschichte*, XIII (1900), 75–122.

[65] The phrase and the concept are Duffy's, in *Russia's Military Way to the West*, p. 122.

status of a middle-ranking German power, events since 1756 strongly suggested that such a policy was no longer feasible. Prussia might and could be broken. But a peace concluded on that basis was likely in turn to aggrandize Austria's German position to a degree making it a more than uncomfortable neighbour for Russia. Such a peace indeed might well require underwriting by a permanent Russian military presence on Prussia's eastern frontier, with all the unpredictable diplomatic consequences certain to accompany such a situation.

If Peter's Prussian policy deserves more serious consideration than it usually receives, its implementation can only be described as feckless. He opened negotiations by sending a private envoy to the King, who responded by despatching Baron Bernhard von der Goltz to St Petersburg. Goltz's primary mission was to restore peace with Russia and detach her from France and Austria. For all of Frederick's public intransigence on the subject of frontiers, the King was willing to consider ceding East Prussia should that be necessary to end the war. The only condition was that Prussia be compensated elsewhere – presumably in Poland.[66] And even that concession might have been negotiable had not the Tsar fallen over himself in his desire to give away the diplomatic store. Peter received Goltz with enthusiasm, housed and entertained him lavishly, spoke of Frederick as his master. The King, who regarded words as tools to be used as needed, lavishly praised Peter's wisdom and insight. Peter responded by calling Frederick one of history's greatest heroes.

The love feast was briefly interrupted by a report from the Russian ambassador to London. This described Bute as hoping Russia would remain in the war long enough to impel Frederick to end the fighting. It must be understood, the document continued, that Britain had no wish to see Prussia destroyed. At the same time it was unwilling to continue a war to support Frederick's Continental pretensions to the final jot and tittle. Reasonable sacrifices on the King's part, Bute allegedly concluded, could be expected. When sounded on the precise meaning of that term, East Prussia was brought into the conversation – at least according to the ambassador's report.[67]

Peter responded in a fashion completely unexpected. He sent a summary of the document to Frederick and declared his willingness to receive concrete peace proposals immediately.[68] The effect on a

66 Frederick to Goltz, 7 Feb. 1762, *PC*, XXI, 234 ff.

67 Karl Schweizer and Carol Leonard, 'Britain, Prussia and the Galitzin Letter: A Reassessment', *Historical Journal*, XXVI (1974), 531–56, is the most accessible of several versions of the latest analysis of this issue.

68 Goltz to Frederick II, 13 March 1762, *PC*, XXI, 311–12.

man already close to the edge of nervous exhaustion was predictable. Frederick described the British minister as deserving to be broken on the wheel, and descanted on his grievances in public to a degree unheard of even among his immediate entourage.[69] Frederick had more than a second-hand ambassador's report to fuel his rage. Bute had informed him that Prussia would receive no more English money for the prolongation of the war. If, however, the subsidy should be devoted to securing peace, the King (meaning Bute) would 'immediately' request it of Parliament.

From Bute's perspective the proposal reflected both the altered diplomatic circumstances of 1762 and the fact that the Anglo-Prussian alliance had never been more than instrumental, reflecting the respective needs of the partners at a specific time. With a Spanish war on his hands, Bute wished at the very least to reallocate funds from a German war increasingly irrelevant to Britain's security. He had no particular intention of throwing Frederick to the wolves. Indeed, he was to take substantial pains to safeguard Prussia's Rhineland territories, long under occupation, during the eventual peace negotiations with France. Bute, however, was equally determined that the Prussian tail should not wag the British dog. His approach may have been forceful – but nothing in Frederick's previous career suggested that Prussia's King was particularly susceptible to more subtle means of persuasion.[70]

Bute's pressure was by itself not a necessary cause of an Anglo-Prussian rupture. At least as serious were the implications of a piece of secret diplomacy simultaneously undertaken by Newcastle. The Duke, surviving the fall of Pitt, still believed in the potential of an Austrian connection. With the tacit support of Bute, he sent Kaunitz a carefully couched note suggesting the possibility of British good offices in negotiating a settlement of the Silesian question 'satisfactory' to the court of Vienna. Kaunitz, whose distrust of Britain was by this time hardly less than his distaste for Prussia, rejected the proposal as likely to jeopardize a French alliance whose importance to Austria was increasing with every day Peter III remained on Russia's throne. But the Prussian minister in London learned of the *démarche* and informed Frederick. The letter, by ironic coincidence, was dated 23

69 Frederick II to Knyphausen, 9 April 1762, PC, XXI, 355.
70 Karl Schweizer, 'The Termination of the Prussian Subsidy', and 'Britain, Prussia, and the Prussian Territories on the Rhine 1762–1763', in *England, Prussia, and the Seven Years' War* (Lewiston, NY, 1989), pp. 240–60, 261–78; Patrick Doran, *Andrew Mitchell and Prussian Diplomatic Relations during the Seven Years' War* (New York, 1986), pp. 318 *passim*.

March – the date Frederick learned of the Galitzin despatch. One lent credibility to the other. Particularly given his own past behaviour in similar circumstances, Frederick was not exactly unjustified in thinking that he was about to be sold by his ostensible ally. Even if the confusion surrounding Britain's intentions could have been resolved to Frederick's immediate satisfaction, the King would scarcely have been willing to accept the conditions of Bute's original proposal if he had *any* feasible alternative, to say nothing of the prospects opened by Peter's generous proposal.[71]

Frederick authorized his ambassador to sign anything Peter drew up. In the event, this *noblesse oblige* proved unnecessary. Peter agreed first to an armistice, then to a peace restoring all territory lost by Prussia, and finally to a defensive alliance that put 20,000 Russians at Frederick's disposal in Silesia! In return, Peter received Frederick's promise of diplomatic and military support in obtaining the duchy of Schleswig from Denmark – a legacy of his origins as Prince of Holstein. Potentially far more important was the King's pledge of a common policy in Poland, and his accompanying expressed readiness to urge both the Turks and the Crimean Tartars to concentrate their efforts against Austria rather than Russia. These shifts in focus came to nothing militarily. They did, however, clear Russia's southern frontier at a time when the Empire was suffering a significant case of strategic over-extension.[72]

Sometimes overlooked, but deserving more than a footnote, was Sweden's departure from the war by treaty in June. The terms were essentially *status quo ante bellum*. The Swedish threat to Pomerania had always been more potential than real; Frederick periodically regaled himself with jests of the 'Is Sweden still in the war?' variety. Nevertheless, the removal of another active combatant was welcome – and by this time the second-line troops who had spent the war keeping the Swedes under observation looked like Julius Caesar's legions in the context of the rest of the Prussian army.

That point, at least, soon became obvious. With Russia seemingly in his pocket, Frederick prepared for what he hoped once again would be the final campaign against Austria. Once again Prince Henry was assigned the secondary theatre, this time Saxony, with

---

71 Karl Schweizer, 'Lord Bute, Newcastle, Prussia, and the Hague Overtures: A Re-Examination', in *England, Prussia, and the Seven Years' War*, pp. 129–74, convincingly revises standard accounts emphasizing that Newcastle acted on his own responsibility and Kaunitz leaked the information to Prussia.

72 Frederick II to Peter III, 23 March 1762, *PC*, XXI, 314.

about 30,000 men. Frederick's main army in Silesia consisted of somewhere around 70,000 men: the exact number depending by now on captains' honesty and privates' fleetness of foot. The cavalry were still solid, still able to draw recruits and replacements from farmers' sons. The infantry, by contrast, were the dross of once-famous regiments: grenadier battalions reinforced from a bewildering variety of sources; provincial formations with little more than their flags to recall their original identities; a jumble of 'free battalions', the King would once have scorned as good for no more than cannon-fodder in a pitched battle.

Frederick reinforced this mixed bag with some of the better troops from Pomerania. He also acted with great – and arguably unseemly – haste to reintroduce military service in the recovered territories. As early as 6 March the King had ordered regiments whose recruiting districts lay in East Prussia to select officers to return to the cantons. On 10 April he instructed the levying of 5,800 men as soon as peace should become final. These recruits, he declared, should be substituted for the least reliable men in the East Prussian regiments, with the provision that the latter not simply be turned loose, but instead assigned to garrison duty. Recruiting officers assumed their duties at the end of May. The first contingents were not available until mid-October – not least because of high levels of passive resistance at all levels of East Prussian society. From the salons of Königsberg to the churchyards and taverns of the remotest villages, complaints of arbitrariness and harshness joined with unfavourable comparisons to a Russian regime that had combined policies of benevolence with good-humoured inefficiency in practice.[73]

Apart from the general political consequences, the dismantling of the province's military administration during the occupation meant that most of the recruits levied were despatched to the field armies without receiving any significant training. In such contexts Frederick initially placed great hopes in his new Russian allies. But their com-mander, Zakhar Chernyshev, and most of his senior officers, were far less eager than their Tsar to take arms for Frederick against Austria. The Russians moved neither quickly nor consequently to support the King's initial moves.

By comparison with the practice of earlier years, those manoeu-vres had a limited objective. Frederick's stated goal was to retake

73 Jany, *Preussische Armee*, vol. II, p. 617; Stefan Hartmann, 'Die Rückgabe Ostpreussens durch die Russen, 1762', *Zeitschrift für Ostforschung*, XXXVI (1987), 405–33.

Schweidnitz and reoccupy southern Silesia. Daun's intentions mirrored the King's. Control of Schweidnitz made Austria mistress of half the province. By this time, moreover, the Habsburg government was reaching the outer limits of its mobilizable financial resources under wartime conditions. Since 1756 Maria Theresa and her financial advisers had eschewed Frederician combinations of force and fraud for both moral and pragmatic reasons. Austria did not as yet possess the kind of powerful, centralized bureaucracy that could enforce such draconian policies effectively over any period of time. In 1748 a compromise had been struck with the provincial estates. In return for exemption from the direct responsibility of feeding and housing troops, these bodies provided cash raised primarily through a complex structure of property taxes. These were supplemented by direct state fees and taxes, and by the income from public monopolies. Although the system was essentially designed to maintain a stable peacetime establishment, it worked well enough in the war's earlier years. From Kaunitz downward, however, no one in the Austrian government had expected such a drawn-out, close-gripped conflict. The Empress made appeal after appeal to the patriotism and the self-interest of the estates. The administration sharpened its wits and its pens to develop and collect fresh taxes. The government borrowed – and borrowed – and borrowed again. In 1762 the state bank issued central Europe's first fiat money: notes backed by the credit of the Habsburg lands. While these were not exactly shin plasters at first, they did represent straws – or paper – in the wind. Unless expenses were curbed significantly, another year or eighteen months might bring the entire system to the edge of collapse, or beyond.

In the winter of 1761/62, the Habsburg government embarked on a broad programme of economies. Those most directly relevant to the war effort involved paying every officer above the rank of captain in paper, redeemable only after the war, and cutting the strength of most regiments by two companies. The latter move involved no significant reductions in strength: the rank and file were redistributed to the regiment's other companies, which were usually undermanned in any case. The reorganization did, however, reduce by 15 per cent the number of 'company administrations' with their opportunities for peculation and inefficiency.[74]

74 P.G.M. Dickson, *Finance and Government under Maria Theresia 1740–1780*, 2 vols (Oxford, 1987), vol. II, pp. 8 ff.; Christopher Duffy, *The Army of Maria Theresa*, (Newton Abbot, 1977), pp. 123 *passim*.

It is difficult to support the frequently expressed position that the Austrian army of 1762 was directly and immediately weakened in any significant, immediate way by the state's developing financial crisis. What did happen was that the cuts provided a clear signal to the commanders in the field that the war was about played out. Daun responded in predictable terms. If Frederick was determined to reconquer Schweidnitz, Daun was just as determined to hold it. In mid-May he moved his main army forward to cover the fortress, itself garrisoned by 12,000 of his best troops. Given the weaknesses of Frederick's army, a more aggressive strategy might have achieved greater operational results. There seems no doubt that at regimental levels the Austrian infantry was by now significantly superior to that of the Prussians. Their artillery was at least marginally better. If Frederick retained any advantage it was in the mounted arm, and by now the limitations of cavalry against good infantry had become obvious.

Nor was the Russian contingent, when it arrived, much of an improvement. It consisted of 18,000 men, give or take 2,000 or so on any given day – statistics reflecting its high proportion of Cossacks and other irregulars. Frederick took special pains to win the good will of their commanders. He also did his best to use his lemons to make lemonade. If the Russo-Prussian army was not an ideal tool for pitched battles, its large number of light troops and irregulars harassed Daun's outposts, foraging parties, and supply lines with notable success.

Frederick sought in the meantime to manoeuvre Daun away from Schweidnitz. Six weeks of feints and starts left marginal honours with the Prussians: Daun had taken up a position in the Waldenburg hills that was just on the edge of being out of communication with Schweidnitz, but too strong to be attacked by any force Frederick was able to muster. As the King probed the defences of the 'Burkersdorf Camp', he received another shock. On 18 July he was informed that Tsar Peter III had been deposed by his Prussophobic wife Catherine, and his Russian allies were correspondingly unavailable for future operations.

In what was perhaps the greatest diplomatic achievement of his career Frederick convinced Chernyshev not only to stay with him for three more days, but also to deploy his corps for battle albeit without engaging. That in turn drove Frederick to the kind of operational improvisation that had never been his strong point. He had less than seventy-two hours to plan and execute an attack on Burkersdorf. The results, while virtually lost to history, were tactically suggestive and diplomatically significant. With Russian help the King arranged a series of feints to attract Daun's attention. The real attack was delivered not by the Prussian army as a single entity controlled from above, but by three separate strike forces assigned schedules of movement and timing that might well have daunted the victors of Leuthen and Rossbach. In the event Frederick's subordinates passed their final exam with credit, coordinating their advances, using the broken ground to maximum advantage, and forcing the Austrians to withdraw from part of their fortified lines. Daun was sufficiently intimidated to abandon the rest of his position – and his communications with Schweidnitz.[75]

In terms of casualties Burkersdorf was little more than a skirmish: 1,600 Prussian casualties to 2,100 Austrian. Whether it might have proved a portent had the war continued, whether Frederick would have continued to experiment with coordinating multiple attack forces, must remain a subject for speculation. Daun's new position was in country too broken to invite further Frederician initiatives. The King may well have felt, in his heart of hearts, that he had already used a year's worth of luck. The siege – better described as a blockade – of Schweidnitz continued until 9 October, when the fortress finally surrendered.

Three weeks later, that 'good ordinary general' Prince Henry sank another *banderilla* into Austria's hide at Freiberg in Saxony. As usual the Prince had been given the troops Frederick did not want. A summer's campaigning had hardened the men, but cost heavily in horseflesh and supplies. When superior Austrian-Imperial forces moved into Saxony in September, Henry fell back and dug in around Freiberg. A series of indecisive battles in mid-October left Henry convinced that he could mount a successful offensive against an enemy whose measure the prince now believed he had taken.

His decision to attack was probably fostered by the familiar hectoring criticism and advice from his royal brother. Like Frederick at Burkersdorf Henry planned a coordinated attack by four independent columns – a complex operation perhaps excessively risky against better troops, but the Austrians were war-weary and the Imperials still the Imperials. On 29 October the Prussians went forward at daybreak. Well before noon they were in full control of the allies' positions, beginning the process of tallying almost 4,500 prisoners.

75 Achim Kloppert, *Der Schlesische Feldzug von 1762* (Bonn, 1988), is a definitive operational analysis. Cf. also Curt Jany, 'Das Treffen bei Burkersdorf am 21. Juli 1762', *Militär-Wochenblatt*, 1907, *Beiheft* IV, 77–91.

Another 2,800 Austrians and Imperials were dead or wounded. Prussian losses were fewer than 1,500.[76]

Prince Henry's pride in his victory might well have been greater had he known of its impact in Vienna. With Schweidnitz lost, with the situation in Saxony at best a stalemate, the Austrian government confronted uncomfortable prospects. Russia remained a wild card. Prospects of drawing Catherine into the war against Frederick were reasonably good. But who would dominate such an alliance? France and Britain had been negotiating for peace since March, and no sane diplomat could expect the government of Louis XV to devote any of its remaining resources to a major campaign in central Europe. Austria stood on the edge of exhaustion. The original prize, Silesia's recovery, had absorbed so much of the Empire's resources that the war bade fair to acquire a life of its own, with the amount of money in the game so large that the original bet was forgotten. As Prussian raiders scoured the city-states of Franconia, as the Imperial Diet demanded action from Vienna, Maria Theresa decided to cut her losses. After some preliminary sparring, peace negotiations began on 30 December.

It was appropriate that the delegates met at the royal Saxon hunting lodge of Hubertusburg – a once pleasant estate devastated by marauders. Even the terms were simple. Austria still held the fortress of Glatz, a sally-port into Silesia. In return for its abandonment Frederick offered to restore Saxon independence. The gesture was less generous than might first appear, given the improbability that Prussia could hold the electorate or any part of it without continuing the war. When talk emerged of indemnity for Saxon losses and suffering, Frederick alluded to the impossibility of unscrambling an egg. Let peace lead to reconstruction, his envoys argued. On 18 February, 1763, Austria, Prussia, and Saxony agreed to restore the frontiers of 1756, *status quo ante bellum*.[77] By 30 March, the King was back in Berlin. He sought no parades, no fanfares. Legend has it Frederick was at work the next day – his father's true son at last.

---

76 Easum, *Prince Henry of Prussia*, pp. 210 ff., is an excellent description of this overlooked action.

77 Carl Freiherr von Beaulieu-Marconnay, *Der Hubertusberger Friede. Nach archivalischen Quellen* (Leipzig, 1871), is still the most detailed account of the negotiations.

7 CODA: 1763–86

Frederick's prompt return to normalcy was more than either a grand gesture or a personal quirk. He recognized, more clearly than either his foes or his steadily increasing number of admirers, just how near-run a thing had been Prussia's experience. The Peace of Hubertusberg established Prussia as a great power beyond question – but not beyond challenge. Frederick's contemporaries were generally united in agreeing that any state able to hold its own for seven years against three major enemies itself belonged in the first rank. But given Prussia's exposed geography and limited resources, the feat itself was difficult to explain. If not exactly the product of accident, it nevertheless might be susceptible to reversal at some later date – particularly since the King himself had become an old man. Contemporaries were appalled at his physical deterioration since 1756. Exhaustion exacerbated his sense of vulnerability and his fears for his life's work.

PRUSSIA'S RECOVERY

Prussia's King recognized, as he had not recognized in his younger years, the importance of chance to his survival. The death of Empress Elizabeth seemed in particular an actual act of God. Frederick conceded as well the importance of his enemies' errors: the failure of the allied cabinets to develop and implement a common strategy, and the shortcomings of the allied field commanders. But if the former had been stubborn and the latter prone to what Frederick called amateurs' mistakes, those facts offered no guarantees for the future. Prussia could do nothing about its former enemies working to improve themselves. In particular, Frederick feared Russia: 'a power which will become the most dangerous in Europe' once it mobilized its immense resources.[1] This represented a direct reversal of his pre-war

---

1 'Politisches Testament Friedrichs des Grossen (1768)', in *Politisches Testamente des Hohenzollern*, ed. R. Dietrich, (Munich, 1981), p. 353.

dismissal of the Russian state and army as a barbarian mob, and led to an assiduous search for a Russian alliance. But in order to negotiate on equal terms, Prussia needed to recover its strength as quickly as possible.

The Seven Years War might not have been a total war in the twentieth-century sense. Prussia nevertheless had survived by evolving towards the modern model of a warfare state, with army, economy, and society combined in a symbiosis devoted to establishing and maintaining Prussia as a great power. In this model the army's requirements took first place even in peacetime. To meet them required a comprehensive tax system. That system in turn needed not only a sound economy, but also compliant taxpayers.

Neither could be taken for granted in 1763. Frederick returned to a state shaken to its physical and moral foundations. Between 160,000 and 180,000 of his subjects had been killed in action or died of wounds or disease. One noble family had lost twenty of its twenty-three males of military age, while throughout the kingdom peasant households had suffered in proportion.[2] Eighteenth-century armies on the whole were less destructive than either their seventeenth-century predecessors or their nineteenth- and twentieth-century successors. On the one hand they were better disciplined; on the other they were smaller and possessed less physical capacity to damage their environments. The normal patterns of devastation involved strips rather than swaths. But campaigns conducted in the same theatres year after year left marks like those of repeated floggings.[3]

Brandenburg and Silesia, East Prussia and Pomerania, had paid top prices for their sovereign's ambitions. Russian armies in particular, operating at the end of long and tenuous supply lines and including large numbers of Cossacks and similar irregulars, left their marks everywhere they went. Not a little of the no-quarter mentality that affected the Prussians at Zorndorf and Kunersdorf was a reaction to the destruction they had witnessed – or smelled, as the smoke of burning villages and farmsteads drifted across the countryside. The Austrian army's borderers were no whit behind their Russian

---

2 Christopher Duffy, *The Army of Frederick the Great* (New York, 1974), p. 199.

3 Horst Carl, *Okkupation und Regionalismus. Die preussischen Westprovinzen im Siebenjährigen Krieg* (Mainz, 1993), is a brilliant and exhaustive analysis of this process in an often neglected area of Prussia.

counterparts in their search for loot and their love of destruction for its own sake. As the war progressed, even regular armies took the gloves off. The Austrians bombarded open towns as well as fortified ones in their former province of Silesia. As early as 1758, for example, little remained of Schweidnitz but its fortifications. On their way to Zorndorf the Russians virtually demolished the town of Küstrin, burning most of the houses in their effort to smoke out the Prussian garrison.

Some results can be expressed in numbers. By war's end Prussia had lost 60,000 horses and 13,000 houses. One-fifth of the population of Pomerania, 70,000 people, died of disease and privation between 1756 and 1763. In Neumark-Brandenburg, a quarter of the civilian population, almost 60,000, died or disappeared. East Prussia, despite the officially benevolent Russian occupation policies, had been harrowed alike by invaders and defenders. In particular, many of the agricultural colonies established prior to 1756 had disappeared, as immigrants without generations of roots in the land sought better lives elsewhere. Ninety thousand people were listed as dead or deported.[4]

As significant as the physical devastation was the damage done to Prussia's moral framework. By the standards of Russia, Austria, even France, Frederick's had remained a model government. Far from being indifferent to the fate of his subjects, in the depths of the war Frederick provided relief to a Pomerania that had exhausted its own resources maintaining a local defence force against the Swedes. The government never established new taxes or raised old ones without consulting prominent taxpayers, merchants as well as aristocrats – who frequently made the case for lower assessments or complete remission. As for the bureaucrats, they initially accepted with loyalty, if not enthusiasm, the suspension of salaries and pensions in 1757 and again in 1762.[5]

These specifics reflected the widespread acceptance in Prussia of an implied social contract referred to earlier in this text, offering

4 Walther Hubatsch, *Frederick the Great*, trans. P. Doran (London, 1973), p. 148.

5 Hubert C. Johnson, *Frederick the Great and his Officials* (New Haven, Conn., 1975), pp. 177 ff., surveys the nature of wartime administration in Prussia's core provinces.

protection and stability in return for service and loyalty.[6] Enemy invasions arguably damaged that agreement less than did debased currency, inefficient administration, and the general lack of grip that characterized Frederick's government, particularly in the war's final years, when the King and his councillors were preoccupied with the state's survival. Peasants burned out of their farms, merchants without stock or capital, officials taking promissory notes in lieu of pay, were not promising human material for a great power.

Austria's experiences during the Seven Years War, France's repeated financial crises in the 1760s and 1770s, only highlighted for Frederick the impossibility of systematically raising funds in the face even of passive resistance to the process. The Prussian army existed to fight Prussia's foes, not to levy contributions from Prussia's people. The first step in restoring and stabilizing Prussia's military strength, therefore, involved re-establishing the social contract so badly shaken by a quarter-century of war and preparation for war.

This process in good part involved developing Frederick's image as statesman and patriarch. The King's professed indifference to public opinion – an indifference manifested in the last quarter-century of his reign by behaviour ranging from erratic to eccentric – had the paradoxical result of enhancing his appeal to what a later scholar has called 'political pilgrims', who came to Berlin prepared to admire its master for their own reasons. The earlier generation of intellectuals, whom Frederick had disillusioned by his apparent indifference to the ideals of the Age of Reason, was giving way to new men with new visions.

Frederick's very inaccessibility made him an object of interest to proto-Romantics, while the men of the *Aufklärung* saw the King as a potential focal point for intellectual perspectives consciously challenging those emanating from Paris. That Frederick continued to prefer French as a language of discourse, that he was consistently indifferent to the works of German scholars like Johann Wincklemann and German men of letters like Gotthold Lessing, was outweighed by

---

6 T.C.W. Blanning, 'Frederick the Great and Enlightened Absolutism', in *Enlightened Absolutism, Reform and Reformers in Later Eighteenth-century Europe*, ed. H.M. Scott (Ann Arbor, Mich., 1990), pp. 265–88, establishes as convincingly as can be done both the psychological and actual reality of Prussia as an Enlightened state by contemporary standards. Cf. Theodor Schieder, *Friederich der Grosse. Ein Königtum der Widersprüche* (Frankfurt, 1983) pp. 264 ff.; and H.B. Nisbet, "Was ist Aufklärung?" The Concept of Enlightenment in Eighteenth-Century Germany', *Journal of European Studies*, XII (1982), 77–95.

his tolerance of intellectual freedom and open discussion – at least in the realm of abstract ideas.[7] In the 1760s Berlin began developing as an intellectual centre in its own right, where bureaucrats and army officers exchanged ideas with members of the Berlin Academy and sons and daughters of a rising Jewish bourgeoisie. The restrictions, official and unofficial, limiting comment on public affairs, were not a significant burden to men and women nurtured in the traditions of duty to the state and society.

In such contexts Frederick's actual behaviour and attitudes were far outweighed by his function as a symbol. The process manifested itself even among his comrades in arms. Post-war adulation of Frederick as a military genius was by no means common among officers who remembered their monarch's behaviour at Mollwitz and Lobositz; the blindfolded slaughterhouses of Kolin and Kunersdorf; the arbitrary outbursts of vengeful ill-temper against men whose only fault was being in the wrong place at the wrong time. Stories were exchanged over pipes and brandy when the veterans came together. Memoirs were written and circulated confidentially in manuscript form – an early version of Soviet Russia's *samizdat*.[8] Yet while the King lived, his officers kept silent.

Fear of consequences may have influenced their behaviour. Significant as well was a growing retrospective sense of having been part of a world-historical event. At the time Frederick's wars had been part of the day's work – at most, a matter of survival until the next battle. After 1763 a process seems to have taken place among Prussian officers similar to that described for Civil War veterans in Gerald Linderman's *Embattled Courage*. The Seven Years War became the defining point of their lives, and as such an event not lightly to be trivialized. Perhaps it had really been the famous victory memorialized in song, story, and statuary. Perhaps things had not been as bad as they still might seem in the late watches of the night, when the dreams came.[9]

With his moral leadership increasingly secure, Frederick turned to the task of physical reconstruction. He began with a personal tour

---

7 G.B. Volz, *Friedrich der Grosse im Spiegel seiner Zeit*, vol. II, *Der Siebenjährige Krieg und die Folgezeit bis 1778* (Berlin, 1926), includes a broad spectrum of contemporary opinion on Prussia's monarch.

8 Christopher Duffy, *Frederick the Great: A Military Life*, (London, 1985), pp. 257–8.

9 Gerald Linderman, *Embattled Courage: The Experience of Combat in the American Civil War* (New York, 1987).

of inspection through his ravaged provinces – an event that, like the Parchwitz speech, was remembered long afterward at first hand by thousands who were miles away from the royal coach. He opened the magazines and the stables. Grain no longer needed for the next campaign and horses now superfluous to the army's requirements were made available free of charge to civilians in need. In the first year after the war 6 million thaler flowed into the cash-starved Prussian economy – and these were good coins. In contrast to many a victorious government before and since, Frederick was at pains to curb inflation by withdrawing and reminting the debased wartime currency. By 1764 the Prussian thaler once again passed current throughout central Europe.[10]

Direct financial reform was only part of the King's grand, post-war plan to concentrate banking and manufacturing under state regulation, when not state control. This remained incomplete, in good part because of the hostility of bureaucrats and businessmen unwilling to accept state monopolies as a necessary element of international competitiveness. Specifically, however, Frederick enjoyed a series of triumphs. His encouragement of emigration brought as many as a quarter-million new subjects to Prussia after 1763. Nor were these indigent refugees. Many had skills and resources, and were actively courted by Prussian agents. Others were attracted by guarantees of jobs or land – guarantees the Prussian administration was usually able to fulfil. Royal estates were subdivided into peasant holdings. Weavers, tailors, day labourers, found work and housing in the remotest corners of Prussia and Silesia. And most thanked the king who made their new lives possible.[11]

When immigrant labour fell short, Frederick turned to the army. As billets gave way to barracks in the larger garrison towns, soldiers and their families were put to work in state enterprises. They were joined by drafts from orphanages, poorhouses, and prisons – an early form of 'workfare' perhaps less shocking to late-twentieth-century sensibilities than to those of earlier, more expansive eras. The Prussian army's contribution to the state's workforce in the final years of Frederick's reign has been estimated as high as three-quarters of a

10 Reinhold Koser, 'Die preussischen Finanzen von 1763–1786', *Forschungen zur brandenburgischen und preussischen Geschichte*, XVI (1903), 445–76.

11 Cf. Heinrich Beeger, *Friedrich der Grosse als Kolonisator* (Giessen, 1896); and August Skalweit, 'Wieviel Kolonisten hat Friedrich der Grosse angesiedelt?' *Forschungen zur brandenburgischen und preussischen Geschichte*, XXIV (1911), 243–8.

million when soldiers' families are included. Nor were the jobs entirely dead-end grunt labour. Frederick encouraged the development of a class of skilled workers that incorporated not a few soldiers' sons. By 1786 Prussia counted as many as 165,000 such men, and industry directly supported as high as 9 per cent of the state's population.[12]

Much of that industry was government-owned: everything from iron mines and small steel factories in Eberswald to clock manufacturers in Berlin. Tobacco, timber, and coffee were state monopolies. The direct revenues accruing to the state from these and other monopolies were supplemented by a comprehensive system of indirect taxes. Frederick regarded such taxes as the least painful way of raising revenue, involving as they did relatively small amounts easy to overlook in the pleasure of acquisition.[13] Like their modern successors, VATs and sales taxes, they were regressive, exacting relatively higher costs from the poorer classes of the population. On the other hand, pre-industrial Prussia was still largely a subsistence economy. Even in towns, established households could be self-sustaining to a degree unknown a century later, partly by direct production and partly by the widespread practice of informally exchanging goods and services. As increasing amounts of their business never appear on formal records, the developed Atlantic economies of the late twentieth century are doing no more than taking leaves from the book of Frederician Prussia.

Frederick's economic policies came under heavy and increasing fire from physiocrats in France and German cameralists, who advocated systems of direct taxation as being more predictable and more profitable than the Prussian approach of collecting small change. But as a slightly bowdlerized German proverb states, 'little cows also give milk'. Frederick's scorn for academic intellectuals, moreover, was by this time Olympian. From his perspective, arguably developed in his years at the head of an army at war, most human beings were most comfortable with familiar patterns. Change even for purposes of reform not only fostered unhappiness; it also increased suspicion, with individuals and classes sourly eyeing one another to see who was favoured by the changes. The balance of grievances referred to in Chapter 1 had served Prussia well in the eighteenth century. The

---

12 C.B.A. Behrens, *Society, Government, and the Enlightenment: The Experiences of Eighteenth-Century France and Prussia* (New York, 1985), p. 177.

13 'Politisches Testament Friedrichs des Grossen (1768)', Dietrich, p. 263.

King saw no reason to risk overhauling it, particularly in financial contexts.[14]

REMODELLING THE ARMY

And the system worked. By 1786, the year of Frederick's death, Prussia's public income was three times what it had been in 1740. Most of it was spent for a by now traditional purpose: maintaining Prussia's army. Frederick's military policies after 1763 were shaped by his confirmed sense of the army's importance as a strategic deterrent. The King had perhaps been slow to learn, but the last half of the Seven Years War seems to have convinced him beyond doubt that the capacity and the readiness to make war were far more important to Prussia's security than the waging of war itself. Frederick correspondingly welcomed the mythology that increasingly surrounded not only his victories, but also his defeats. Anything fostering Prussia's image as a formidable opponent, a Kunersdorf as well as a Leuthen, could only enhance the reluctance of Prussia's neighbours to risk further trials in arms against Old Fritz and his faithful grenadiers.

Myths cannot be sustained for long without some basis in reality. If after 1763 most of the European powers demobilized, Prussia reorganized. Wartime formations like the free battalions were disbanded. Regiments returned to their home districts. When the post-war shakedown was completed Frederick's army counted more than 150,000 field and garrison troops, and that number steadily increased while the King lived. Fewer than half of them were immediately available outside of the drill and manoeuvre season in late autumn, but by now no one doubted the quality of Prussia's cantonists. Certainly no one confused them with peasants in uniform.

The large size of the Prussian army had to be matched, in Frederick's mind, by its high quality. Here too, after 1763 the King did no more than follow patterns he had developed during and after the Silesian Wars: insisting on the importance of creating a front-loaded military system able in the first instance to frighten off potential enemies, and in the second to win the kind of decisive

---

14 Ingrid Mittenzwei, *Preussen nach dem Siebenjährigen Krieg. Auseinandersetzungen zwischen Bürgertum und Staat um die Wirtschaftspolitik* (East Berlin, 1979); and Stephan Skalweit, *Die Berliner Wirtschaftskrise von 1763 und ihre Hintergründe* (Berlin, 1937).

victories the old Prussian army, for all its good qualities, had failed to achieve.[15]

Two possible paths to Frederick's goal lay open. One involved capitalizing on the developments in the craft of war that had begun to suggest themselves by 1763. In France an initial, uncritical tendency to copy Prussian methods directly began giving way to consideration of combined-arms divisions as a counter to the operational and tactical arteriosclerosis characteristic of Frederick's army. Tacticians debated the use of small, manoeuvrable columns, depending on speed and shock, as counterparts to the three-deep Frederician line. Logisticians evaluated the prospects of living off the land, reducing dependance on magazines and supply trains. Kunersdorf and Torgau suggested the importance of such mundane items as accurate field maps. And were light troops really as useless as Frederick seemed to believe?[16]

These and similar ideas spread across the Elbe in the 1770s. They were accompanied, at least among Prussia's junior officers, by a growing concern with what later generations would call 'personnel policies'. A key role in this development was played by Count Friedrich Wilhelm zur Schaumburg-Lippe-Bückeburg. His career had been that of a military cosmopolitan: service with the English-Hanoverians at Dettingen in 1743 and under Austrian colours in Italy in 1745, commander of Ferdinand of Brunswick's artillery in the Seven Years War, and finally organising Portugal's successful resistance to Spanish invasion in 1762–63. Returning to his home state, he introduced universal military service as part of a comprehensive structure of reforms designed to make his subjects into citizens and his citizens into soldiers. He also founded a military academy that accepted students from everywhere in Germany.[17]

The Count was by no means a pure idealist. He believed firmly in the rights – and the value – of small states like his in the interna-

---

15 Frederick II, 'Das Militärische Testament von 1768', in *Die Werke, Friedrichs des Grossen*, ed. G.B. Volz, 10 vols (Berlin, 1912–14), VII, pp. 246 ff. W. Lotz, *Kriegsgerichtsprozesse des Siebenjährigen Krieges in Preussen* (Frankfurt, 1981), offers a valuable perspective on Frederick's expectations of his officers.

16 Cf. Robert Quimby, *The Background of Napoleonic Warfare* (New York, 1957), pp. 106 *passim*; and Jean Colin, *L'Infanterie au XVIII siècle. La tactique* (Paris, 1907), pp. 86 *passim*.

17 The Count's writings can be found in C. Ochwadt (ed.), *Wilhelm Graf zu Schaumburg-Lippe: Schriften und Briefe*, 3 vols (Frankfurt, 1977–83). The best treatment of his career, despite its limited focus, is Christa Banaschik-Ehl, *Scharnhorsts Lehrer, Graf Wilhelm von Schaumburg-Lippe, in Portugal, Die Heeresreform 1761–1777* (Osnabrück, 1974).

tional system. His advocacy of mobilizing moral as well as physical resources was shaped by his belief that states organized for war on such lines could operate to deter their greedier, more ambitious neighbours. One might call Lippe's approach 'Prussia written small', and it had not a few antecedents in Prussia's experience. The Old Dessauer's appeals to the good will of the rank and file, the relative humanity of pre-war recruit training, were foundations on which genuine camaraderie had been built during the Seven Years War. Some Prussian company and field officers in university towns like Berlin and Königsberg were touched by the humanitarian tendencies of the *Aufklärung*. Others read Rousseau on their own time. Perhaps, these men suggested, common soldiers did perform better when treated as men with at least the potential to reason and feel.

Frederick took an exactly opposite tack. Military effectiveness, he had declared in 1752, depended on strict discipline, unconditional obedience, prompt execution of orders.[18] Nothing in the intervening years had changed his mind. Frederick still regarded it as vital for Prussia to win quick, decisive victories. This outcome the King perceived as depending on a military system rigorously controlled in every possible detail from the top down.[19]

It is possible to compare Frederick's reforms after 1763 with the evolution of the Schlieffen Plan between 1894 and 1914. In both cases military planners faced with potentially overwhelming odds sought to develop what Arden Bucholz calls a 'Great Symphony', synthesizing state-of-the-art technical procedures and high levels of will power in systems designed to achieve their ends through an endless capacity for taking pains.[20] In Frederick's case the technical procedures involved human beings. No other option was open in a pre-industrial era: the only real force multipliers were the men in any army's ranks.

After 1763 the Prussian common soldier's transformation into a military cyborg was facilitated by every means possible. Frederick's dictum that the soldier must fear his officer more than the enemy has usually been described as reflecting his experiences in the Seven Years

18 Cf. 'Über die Aufklärung des Militärs', *Militärische Monatsschrift*, I (1785), 590–601; Col. J. von Scholten, *Was muss ein Offizier wissen?* (Dessau and Leipzig, 1782); and the summary in Max Jähns, *Geschichte der Kriegswissenschaft, vornehmlich in Deutschland*, 3 vols (Munich and Leipzig, 1889–91), vol. III, pp. 2439 ff.

19 'Politische Testament Friedrichs des Grossen (1752)', Dietrich, p. 229; and 'Politische Testament Friedrichs des Grossen (1768)', Dietrich, pp. 287 *passim*.

20 Arden Bucholz, *Moltke, Schlieffen and Prussian War Planning* (New York, 1991).

War, processed through his growing misanthropy. An alternative interpretation is that Frederick sought to achieve with his rank and file what the Great General Staff sought in a later century to achieve with mobilization plans. The King was looking forwards, not backwards, seeing Prussia's salvation and Prussia's glory in an army so comprehensively drilled and so well-integrated that what Clausewitz calls 'fog and friction' would find no room to enter.

The sacrifice of flexibility engendered by this approach seems to invite its dismissal as a dead end, particularly when other armies were discussing and experimenting with techniques of going with the flow of events as opposed to imposing predetermined patterns on unpredictable processes. Frederick, however, recognized the disadvantages of the latter mind-set. Command and control systems had not significantly improved since the beginning of his reign. Organizing permanent peacetime units above the regimental level risked weakening the direct royal influence Frederick regarded as vital in sustaining morale and ambition.[21] Prussia, moreover, had relatively few areas that could support large permanent garrisons without significant social and economic disruption. Berlin, Königsberg, Magdeburg – outside these urban centres a regiment or two was the practical upper limit.

Another factor encouraging Frederick's post-war approach to his army was the existence of a clearly defined Prussian military culture. Armed forces, particularly armies, are not infinitely malleable institutions to be transformed at the will of kings, presidents, or generals. In victory and defeat armies develop patterns, doing some things well, others indifferently, and still others not at all. The weaknesses the Prussian army had demonstrated in the Seven Years War were not the kind of structural problems that broke the French army in 1940 and frustrated the United States in Vietnam. They appeared instead to involve specific flaws of doctrine, such as the initial de-emphasizing of fire-power. Or they reflected the consequences of heavy casualties in battles like Kolin, Zorndorf, and Torgau – battles which arguably need not have been fought if the army and its commander-in-chief had been up to their initial responsibilities and settled the war from a standing start.

Frederick was all too conscious of his own mistakes as war leader and battle captain – conscious enough of them to do everything in his power to avoid their repetition. Standards of discipline were tightened

---

21 'Politische Testament Friedrichs des Grossen (1768)', Dietrich, p. 299.

and made more comprehensive. Punishments that earlier had been applied selectively to the unwilling and the incapable became general practice in regiments whose colonels increasingly vied for the King's attention at reviews and manoeuvres. Drill movements, always precise and demanding, became exacting to the point of impossibility even for experienced men. Frederick's principal concern was to perfect the quickest possible deployment from columns of march to the complex attacking lines required by the oblique order. Here in particular Friedrich von Saldern played a significant role. His own experiences in the Seven Years War had convinced him of the importance of precision. After 1763 his example supplanted that of the Old Dessauer in the Prussian infantry. Clockwork regularity was the order of the day, and woe to any critic of the principle or the practice.[22]

It is important to reiterate Frederick's belief that discipline and drill were not ends in themselves, but facilitators of war-fighting. The King's ultimate vision was best expressed in an artefact: the redesigned musket issued to the infantry in 1782. Gerhard von Scharnhorst and Carl von Clausewitz alike dismissed it as the worst firearm in Europe. A junior officer with more direct experience of the weapon described it as neither firearm, pike, nor club.[23] Tolerances for the *Infanteriegewehr* M1782 were wide enough for standardization to be almost non-existent. The calibre of individual muskets ranged between 20.4 and 18 mm. Weapons varied as much as 3 inches in length. Windage, the clearance between ball and barrel, was so great that a musketeer who pointed his loaded weapon toward the ground ran some risk of having the ball roll out by itself. Apart from its ballistic deficiencies, the M1782 was so constructed as to make aiming nearly impossible. It was badly balanced. It weighed over 10 pounds. The butt was in an almost straight line with the stock. Viewed in context, however, the *Infanteriegewehr* M1782 was the culmination of a century's effort. The smoothbore flintlock musket was never regarded by its most enthusiastic advocates as a precision weapon suitable for individual feats of marksmanship. Instead it was refined and developed along the lines of the modern assault rifle.

22 Curt Jany, *Geschichte der Preussische Armee*, 2nd edn rev., 4 vols (Osnabrück, 1967), vol. III, pp. 81 ff.; R. von Priesdorff, *Saldern. Der Exerziermeister des Königs* (Hamburg, 1943).
23 F Meinecke (ed.), 'Aus den Akten der Militärreorganisationskommission von 1808', *Forschungen zur brandenburgischen und preussischen Geschichte*, V (1892), 139.

Instead of improving its ballistic qualities, gun designers and practical soldiers alike sought to enhance its rate of fire. Its ramrod was made of iron – more durable than the wooden versions favoured elsewhere in Europe, less likely to swell and stick in a barrel heated by rapid fire. The ramrod was also cylindrical, eliminating the necessity of reversing it in order to ram down a charge. Unlike any other military musket of its era, the M1782 had a cone-shaped touch-hole which carried the spark directly to the charge. The great windage contributed to easier loading.

In its final form the Frederician musket was designed not to minimize its limitations of accuracy but to maximize its advantages as a quick-firing weapon. Aiming was not only discouraged, but forbidden. The musketeer was simply ordered to point his weapon in the general direction of the enemy's crossbelts, fire on command, and reload as quickly as possible. And the musket's very imbalance, specifically a muzzle-heaviness caused by the iron ramrod and the heavy bayonet, enhanced the effectiveness of this process by limiting the normal tendency of excited men in combat to shoot too high.[24]

Yet the friction Frederick worked so assiduously to eliminate in his army persisted in entering by the back door and through the windows. Some of the King's own decisions had significantly adverse effects on the army's performance. The quality of uniforms issued to the rank and file steadily decreased – an important morale factor, and a not insignificant financial burden on men required to make up loss and damage from their pay. Grain allowances for the cavalry were cut to the point where in spring and summer the horses depended on grazing for much of their nourishment. Frederick continued to stockpile resources in the royal arsenals and magazines. By 1776 Breslau and Berlin held between them 72,000 bushels of grain – enough to feed 60,000 men for two years. Reserve stocks of weapons, uniforms, and equipment were also maintained at high levels. It was only on an everyday basis that the King behaved like the proverbial farmer who sought to save money by reducing his ox's feed by a half-cup of oats per day. Just when the animal had been put of a diet of nothing at all, it inconveniently died.[25]

This cheese-paring had a particularly unfortunate impact on a

---

24 W. Eckardt Morawietz and O. Morawietz, *Die Handwaffen des branden-burgisch-preussisch-deutschen Heeres, 1640–1945* (Hamburg, 1957), pp. 43 ff. is technically accurate but typically critical in evaluating the M1782.

25 Duffy, *Army of Frederick the Great*, pp. 199 ff., highlights the nature and consequences of these false economies.

particularly vital element of the army. Frederick had always preferred high numbers of professionals, whether foreigners or Prussian subjects without roots in their society. His extensive reliance on cantonists during the Seven Years War had been a move of desperation. The 'Political Testament' of 1768 asserted that even in wartime recruits should be raised in one's own country 'only when sternest necessity compels'.[26] The military usefulness of these regulars had been long established: few colonels were happy at having to rely entirely on native conscripts. It was small wonder, then, that Prussian recruiters began scouring central Europe almost as soon as the guns fell silent.

Results were to say the least disappointing. The number of foreigners steadily increased. By 1786, 110,000 of the 190,000 men under Prussian arms were outlanders. These numbers alone would suggest a relative decline in quality; prior to 1756 only 50,000 aliens had served Prussia's King. Frederick's often expressed contempt for these men as no more than cannon-fodder, a contempt shared by nineteenth-century nationalist historians and twentieth-century writers of military history, has obscured the continuing importance of the mercenaries in establishing the peacetime tone of regiments whose cantonists spent large amounts of time on leave, or out of uniform except for parades. All authorities are agreed that between 1763 and 1786 the foreigners in Prussian service were a far cry from what they had once been. Most explanations stress an increasingly brutal discipline that discouraged enlistment under any circumstances. Others focus on such details as the replacement of regimental recruiting by a pool system that destroyed the incentive of captains and colonels to seek the best men possible.

Personal economics played a role as well. The rampant inflation of the Seven Years War might have been curbed, but prices of staples never went back to what they had been in 1756, to say nothing of 1740. Instead, as Prussia's economy developed, prices rose steadily. Foreign soldiers were among the first to feel the pinch as a growing gap between their pay and their expenses forced more and more of them to seek employment in the civilian economy. Here they found themselves at a significant disadvantage compared to cantonists with claim to local loyalties and identities, and handicapped as well in competition with civilian workers who could devote full time to a job and who lacked the legal and social protection a uniform conferred even on a private.

26 'Politisches Testament Friedrichs des Grossen (1768)', Dietrich, p. 289.

The obvious results were consistently empty pockets and a never-ending search for whatever casual labour might be available. Desertion was a logical consequence, facilitated by the growing reluctance of foreigners to establish even informal long-term relationships. A woman one could not support, children one could not feed were burdens no sensible man assumed. Lacking such ties, desertion seemed an ever more favourable option. It is no accident that most of the worst horror stories of Prussia's preventive and punitive measures against 'French leave' date from the period after 1756.[27] Prussian recruiters faced as well the consequences of a changing *mentalité*. On one level the Enlightenment, with its rejection of war as violent and unnatural, had begun penetrating to village pulpits. Pastors and schoolmasters may not have turned pacifist, as so many of their French counterparts did after 1918. They were, however, more likely than their predecessors to stress the morality of peacefully cultivating one's garden. In practical terms the direct experience of the Seven Years War had burned away much of the popular belief that change and adventure could be found in uniform. Not until the 1780s would a new generation of young men begin to listen to recruiters' blandishments. The general economic upturn in central Europe after 1763 attracted some potential volunteers. Others joined, or were conscripted into, the expanding forces of their native states: Hesse-Cassel, Saxony, or Bavaria. And for the real tearaways, service in one of the German regiments maintained by the French government offered better pay and better maintenance than that provided by a Prussian army on the path to implosion.[28]

Another of the King's significant contributions to the Prussian army's confusion of ends with means involved the growing capriciousness of his critiques at reviews and manoeuvres. The post-war Prussian army was too large, the King by now too remote, to sustain the network of informal contacts that had served in earlier years to diminish, if never to eliminate, the consequences of Frederick's whims. Now regiments would be commended one year and con-

27 Cf. Jany, *Preussische Armee*, vol. III, pp. 447–8; and Kurt Schützle, 'Über das Rekrutierungssystem in Preussen vor und nach 1806/07 und seine Auswirkung auf die geistig-moralische Haltung der Soldaten', *Militärgeschichte*, XVII (1977), 28–35.

28 Cf. Henri Brunschwig, *Enlightenment and Romanticism in Eighteenth-century Prussia*, trans. F. Jellinek (Chicago, 1974); Geoffrey Best, *Humanity in Warfare* (New York, 1980), pp. 31 ff.; and as case studies, Charles Ingrao, *The Hessian Mercenary State: Ideas, Institutions and Reform under Frederick II, 1760–1785* (Cambridge, 1987); and James A. Vann, *The Making of a State: Württemberg, 1593–1793* (Ithaca, NY, 1984), pp. 270 *passim*.

demned the next. The careers of field and general officers, their places in the army's pecking order, followed no predictable pattern. Nor could they easily be readjusted by improving next year's performance, since no one could ever be sure what Frederick wanted. Under these circumstances it was only logical to concentrate on doing everything *in* the book *by* the book as well as it could be done. If one nevertheless met professional disaster, at least there remained the satisfaction of having met official standards.[29]

This was hardly an environment calculated to foster independent thinking in the rising generation of officers. Frederick's ruthless purging of commissioned bourgeoisie after 1763 had less significance in this respect than is commonly asserted. Just because a man was born without 'von' before his name did not automatically bless him with insight and wisdom genetically denied to an aristocrat. The reverse indeed was often true. Consciousness of their marginal position, few non-nobles were anxious to risk already shaky careers by injudicious boat-rocking. Bourgeois officers, coming from a milieu without a significant military heritage, usually learned their craft by direct experience, and often tended to guard jealously their limited stock of knowledge won at such high prices. A reasonable parallel might be drawn to the post-Civil War army of the United States, whose officer corps was for two decades lumbered with men commissioned and brevetted for gallantry in the field against the Confederacy but who too often lacked any of the qualities appropriate to their rank except courage.

Milieu was more important than birth in stifling the intellectual development of Frederick's officer corps. In the years after 1763, the King insisted that cadets and subalterns be rigorously separated from the enlisted men in order to discourage what he regarded as an inappropriate pattern of familiarity that had developed during the late war. He did little to encourage the systematic study of military affairs in a broad context. As the generals of the Seven Years' War died or retired, they were replaced by men who had been colonels or majors, had learned all about commanding a regiment, and continued to ignore everything else. A taste for *belles-lettres* on the part of a subaltern or a captain was an acceptable private

---

29 Jany, *Preussische Armee*, vol. III, pp. 99 ff., describes the process from a more or less sympathetic perspective. Cf. Hyppolite J.R. de Toulengeon, *Une Mission militaire en Prusse in 1786*, ed. J. Finot and R. Galmiche-Bourer (Paris, 1881), and J.A. Guibert, *Journal d'un Voyage en Allemagne, fait en 1773*, 2 vols (Paris, 1803), vol, I, pp. 170 ff.

eccentricity. Concentrating on one's profession tended to be regarded as an attempt to show up one's elders and betters – a risk few were willing to take in an army where promotion was slow and depended heavily on personal connections and personal impressions.[30]

For all its shortcomings, the later Frederician army nevertheless performed almost to perfection the role intended by its creator. It was a successful deterrent. To a significant degree that success was a product of its reviews and manoeuvres. After the Seven Years' War these became public spectacles open to foreign observers. Military or civilian, few failed to be impressed by the disciplined precision and rapid fire of the infantry, the speed and control shown by the cavalry. Critics there were – but mostly of the 'we could do that better if only we wished' variety. Everything from drill regulations to uniform styles found their imitators in France, in Britain, in Russia. The revitalization of the American Continental army under Friedrich von Steuben owed much to the Baron's introduction not only of Prussian drill suitably modified, but of the original Prussian approach to recruit training, with its emphasis on patience and repetition.[31] Certainly no one with any influence in Europe's decision-making circles seems to have left a Prussian manoeuvre ground without the sense that the Prussian army was an opponent best avoided – particularly in a war's initial stages.

TESTING THE DETERRENT

One risk of an effective military deterrent is the exaggeration of its threat potential to a point generating a reverse effect. States with powerful armed forces that use those forces as an instrument of blackmail run a steadily increasing risk of convincing their negotiating partners that war, even at long odds, is preferable to conceding issue after issue. That point was particularly significant because Frederick, unlike Otto von Bismarck a century later, retained some territorial ambitions. Poland's increasingly rapid decline offered a particular temptation in the form of West Prussia.

30 Gottlieb Friedländer, *Die Königliche Allgemeine Kriegs-Schule und das höhere Militär-Bildungswesen 1765–1813* (Berlin, 1854); F.K. Tharau, *Die geistige Kultur des preussischen Offiziers von 1640 bis 1806* (Mainz, 1968). Cf. also U. Waltzoldt, *Preussischen Offiziere im geistigen Leben des 18. Jahrhunderts* (Halle, 1937).

31 Charles Royster, *A Revolutionary People at War: The Continental Army and American Character, 1775–1783* (Chapel Hill, NC, 1979), pp. 213 ff., is the best modern discussion.

Nor was Prussia in a position to drop out of the diplomatic game
for a few rounds even had its King been so inclined. Under Empress
Catherine, Russia was intensifying pressure on a Poland whose throne
fell vacant in 1763 with the death of Augustus III. In the perpetually
divided Sejm, a significant number of delegates, whether from conviction or through material encouragement, favoured electing a monarch
who would cultivate closer ties with Russia. Other factions disagreed,
and their feuding provided common ground for a Russo-Prussian
agreement.[32]

Catherine's post-war hostility to Frederick reflected antagonism
to her late husband's Prussophilic position rather than any positive conviction that Prussia offered a meaningful threat to Russia.
Frederick stood alone in Europe. He had just completed a seven-year
course in the importance of allies even if they were no more than allies
of convenience. In positive terms, Russia and Prussia had a common
interest in keeping the Polish crown out of the hands of France,
Austria, or Saxony, which had furnished the previous incumbent.
On 11 April 1764, Frederick and Catherine concluded a treaty.[33] The
Russian connection was for Frederick as much a security blanket as a
stepping stone. When in 1768 Catherine went to war with the Ottoman Empire, Frederick initially urged mediation – not least because
the terms of the treaty required Prussia to pay subsidies to Russia!
This seemed, given Prussia's history and Frederick's parsimony, a
violation of the laws of nature. Prussia *received* money; it did not
expend it![34]

Austria too desired peace in east-central Europe. Maria Theresa
explicitly denied any intention of changing existing power relationships in that region, or challenging the current occupant of the Polish
throne. Kaunitz was equally cautious; Frederick was even more so.
He had long entertained the goal of acquiring western Prussia –

32 Cf. Tadeusz Cegielski, 'Preussische "Deutschland- und Polenpolitik" in dem
Zeitraum 1740–1792', *Jahrbuch für die Geschichte Mittel- und Ostdeutschlands*,
XXX (1981), 21–7; and G.T. Lukowski, 'The *Szlachta* and the Conference
of Radom, 1764–1767/68: A Study of the Polish Nobility', PhD dissertation,
Cambridge, 1976.
33 Cf. Georg Küntzel, 'Friedrich der Grosse am Ausgang des siebenjährigen
Krieges und sein Bündnis mit Russland', *Forschungen zur brandenburgischen und
preussischen Geschichte*, XIII (1900), 75–122; and H.M. Scott, 'Frederick II, the
Ottoman Empire, and the Origins of the Russo-Prussian Alliance of 1764', *European
Studies Review*, VII (1977), 153–75.
34 W. Stribrny, *Die Russlandpolitik Friedrichs des Grossen 1764–1786* (Würzburg,
1966), is a solid history of the alliance.

'Polish Prussia', as it was described in contemporary correspondence – in order to link East Prussia with Brandenburg and to create a glacis between his kingdom and Russia. The King did not propose, however, to risk his state that was still being rebuilt directly for a stake less valuable than Silesia had been. Instead, Frederick sought to act as a broker between Russian and Austrian governments increasingly suspicious of each others' intentions.[35]

For Frederick, the longer the Russo-Ottoman war continued, the greater the risk of Prussia's being drawn in by accident. A series of Russian victories culminating in the occupation of the duchies of Moldavia and Wallachia only alarmed the King further – particularly as anti-Catherine forces in Poland brought that unfortunate country to the edge of civil war and beyond by the summer of 1770. In October, Prince Henry travelled to St Petersburg, bearing his brother's urging for a policy of moderation based on allowing Austro-Prussian assistance in ending the Ottoman war and restoring order to Poland. Catherine gave the Prince an easy answer – neither yes nor no. Frederick responded by outrageously praising the Empress, mediator; and eventually grumbling that he would not become the slave of Russia's ambitions.[36]

Meantime, the Austrian government took concrete action. The Habsburg Empire had established a security zone on its eastern frontier, both to fend off raiders and stragglers from the opposing armies and to keep out the plague, endemic to southeastern Europe and likely to flare up during a war. That 'cordon' had been unofficial but increasingly extended into south-western Poland. In December 1770, the County of Zips was formally annexed to the Kingdom of Hungary, while the Habsburgs advanced further claims in Polish territory bordering what remained of Austrian Silesia.[37]

Frederick initially showed little concern at this nibbling. Russian reaction was far more extreme. Austria, Catherine's advisers reasoned, had begun a process ultimately impossible to stop: dismembering a Poland no longer able to maintain its borders. Better to ride

---

35 E. Reimann, 'Friedrich der Grosse und Kaunitz im Jahre 1768', *Historische Zeitschrift*, XLII (1879), 193–212.

36 Frederick to Henry, 30 Oct. and 2 Nov. 1770; and 11 Jan. 1771, *PC*, XXX, 239, 234–5, and 384–5. Chester Easum, *Prince Henry of Prussia: Brother of Frederick the Great* (Madison, Wis., 1942), pp. 259 ff., is the best overview of the Prince's mission.

37 Derek Beales, *Joseph I*, vol. I, *In the Shadow of Maria Theresa 1741–1780* (Cambridge, 1987), summarizes a complex process.

the waves than be submerged. In January Frederick's ambassador to St Petersburg reported a Russian proposal that the allies compensate themselves for Austria's gains by slices of Polish territory along their respective frontiers. Frederick was both dubious and interested. 'Polish Prussia', he declared, 'would be worth the trouble,' even if Danzig were not included.[38] When Prince Henry returned home in February, he completed the process of convincing his brother to change his policies. While his diplomats spun the cobwebs of legal justification, the King acted to move Vienna and St Petersburg to decisive action. After eighteen months of complex negotiations, Prussian troops took possession of 20,000 square miles of land and over a half-million new subjects.

Ruling Poles was not altogether a new problem. The eastern region of East Prussia contained enough Poles that part of the province's administration was conducted in that language. Some of Frederick's generals might compare Poles to apes, but the King ordered his successor to learn Polish and encouraged bilingualism among the bureaucrats assigned to the new territories. Aristocrats and peasants in general responded positively to a system that was at least predictable, subject to laws other than the whims of the most powerful local magnate. And they paid their taxes. Frederick benefited by annual revenues of 1¾ million thaler – over two-thirds of which were devoted to paying for the five infantry regiments and their supporting troops raised in the new territories.[39]

The eastward shift represented by West Prussia's acquisition had significant consequences for Prussia's future development. Most of them, however, became apparent only after Frederick's death. More relevant for present purposes is the role Prussia's army played in Prussia's aggrandizement. While Frederick carefully eschewed overt sabre-rattling, Russian and Austrian diplomatic correspondence during the partition crisis was informed, when not shaped, by the conviction that Prussia was an undesirable enemy, and Prussia's king

---

38 Solms to Frederick, 8 Jan. 1771; Frederick to Henry, 31 Jan. 1771, *PC*, XXX, 405, 417–18.

39 Iselin Gundermann, 'Westpreussen im Staatshaushalt Friedrichs des Grossen: Ein Finanztaschenbuch für die Jahre 1775/76 bis 1777/78', *Zeitschrift für Ostforschung*, XXXIV (1985), 421–48, surveys the King's initial plans for the new province. Helmuth Fechner, 'Westpreussen unter friderizianischen Verwaltung', in *Deutschland und Polen 1772–1945*, ed. H. Fechner (Würzburg, 1964), pp. 30–46; and Walther Hubatsch, 'Friedrich der Grosse und Westpreussen', *Westpreussen-Jahrbuch*, XXII (1972), 5–14, are positive general evaluations of the new order.

a monarch worth conciliating even at a high price – particularly when he took the field at the head of Prussia's army. The next test of the Prussian deterrent came six years later. On 30 December 1777, Maximilian Joseph, Elector of Bavaria, died, leaving a vacant throne and no direct heirs. The situation was no surprise. For years the lawyers and diplomats of the Holy Roman Empire had debated Bavaria's fate. For almost as many years the Austrian foreign ministry had been considering how to acquire the major part of the Bavarian inheritance without provoking either a German or a European war. Max Joseph's closest – albeit distant – relative, the Elector of the Palatinate, had his own ideas. As early as 1776 he had suggested to Vienna that the Empire guarantee his Bavarian claims against Prussia and Saxony as a preliminary for one of the biggest land exchanges in modern history. Austria would receive Bavaria; the Austrian Netherlands would go to the Elector. Kaunitz too was intent on annexation.

Maria Theresa and her son and co-ruler, Emperor Joseph were of two minds on the subject. Maria Theresa was reluctant to sacrifice a province that had for decades been part of the Habsburg legacy. Joseph sought to rationalize the frontiers of an empire altogether too ramshackle for the programme of centralized reform he favoured. He viewed the Austrian Netherlands as an obvious and increasing strategic liability: vulnerable on all sides and too far away from Austria's centre of power to be relieved or secured in any serious crisis. The heir and the minister carried the day. A few days after the Bavarian ruler's death the bargain was struck. Austrian troops entered lower Bavaria.[40]

Karl Marx's aphorism that history repeats itself first as tragedy, then as farce, might well have been composed in honour of this situation. Austria's claims to Bavaria were almost as shadowy as Prussia's had been to Silesia forty years earlier. Nor was Joseph's action exactly ignored elsewhere in Europe. Frederick in particular realized that major Austrian aggrandizement in Bavaria would do much to restore the status quo he had spent his reign struggling to revise. Austria plus Bavaria made Prussia once again a clear second runner in the German pecking order.

At the same time the King was not anxious to go to war. Instead, he played a wide variety of diplomatic cards – this time assisted by

40 Paul Bernard, *Joseph II and Bavaria* (The Hague, 1965), is the most detailed English-language analysis. Beales, *Joseph I*, pp. 386 ff., is more recent and incorporates trenchant criticisms of earlier studies.

Maria Theresa's increasing hostility to the entire project. Austria, the Empress declared in March, was outnumbered by up to 40,000 men. To meet Frederick on equal terms meant exposing large parts of the Empire to attack from other quarters. Even if the Austrian army should win initial victories, the possibility of destroying or crippling Frederick's army was so remote as to be ephemeral. Instead, the result was likely to be a general European war with Austria playing the role assigned to Prussia in 1756. Isolated, without support from any quarter, she could expect nothing but disaster.[41]

In spite of, or perhaps because of, his mother's support for a policy of conciliation Joseph pursued the Bavarian succession with an energy worthy of a more practical goal. In this he was encouraged by Kaunitz, still the grey eminence of Austria's foreign policy, still hoping to reverse the results of 1740, and still contemptuous of Frederick as a statesman.

Prussia's King and his diplomats meanwhile had not been idle. The great powers and the German states alike were disturbed by what seemed a major alteration in a balance that had remained stable for twenty years. Austria's role in the partition of Poland might be explained as a one-time event, actually facilitating the preservation of Europe's order by diminishing Poland's potential as an apple of discord. Bavaria was another matter, lying as it did in the heart of Europe. In Paris, London, and St Petersburg, Frederick insisted on his commitment to do no more than restore the *status quo* by acting as the executor of what Rousseau might have called the powers' general will. In Germany the King emphasized his role as defender of the rights and integrity of a Holy Roman Empire threatened by the ambitions of a heedless youth and a malicious chancellor.

The King had not become an altruist in his old age. Prussia had long-standing, and this time defensible, claim to the small principalities of Bayreuth and Ansbach – claims that Frederick reasserted in this new context. Nevertheless on both diplomatic fronts Prussia was an easy winner in the first stage of the war: the struggle for moral and political high ground. Even Saxony, Frederick's victim two decades previously, now sided with its erstwhile despoiler, promising troops should *démarches* give way to cannon-balls.

Frederick's preparation for the second, military stage of the confrontation were anything but *ad hoc*. As early as 1775 he had

---

41 Maria Theresa to Joseph, 14 March 1778, in *Maria Theresia und Joseph II: Ihre Correspondenz sammt Briefen Josephs an seinen Bruder Leopold*, ed. A. Ritter von Arneth, 3 vols (Vienna, 1867–1868), vol. II, pp. 186 ff.

outlined a plan for war against Austria based on a mutually supporting, two-pronged offensive against the Czech crown lands. Only the
exact force structures needed to be established. Sixty-five thousand
Prussians, more or less reinforced by 20,000 Saxons, would open
the ball by advancing from Dresden into Bohemia. Their commander
was Prince Henry, who by now inspired almost as much respect in
Austrian military circles as Frederick himself. Once the Austrians'
attention was engaged in that sector, Frederick himself would strike
from Silesia into Moravia at the head of 87,000 of his best troops.
The King's intended result was the overrunning of Bohemia, either
after a major battle or as a consequence of Austrian withdrawal in
the face of Frederick's pincers.

The war's next step would be political. Bohemia would become
a hostage for negotiations or, that failing, serve as a springboard
for a campaign against Austria's heartland. Whatever the King's
private dreams might have been, no significant evidence suggests
that Frederick had any concrete plans for incorporating Bohemia
into his kingdom. Such behaviour would only invite a reversal of the
situation he had been at such pains to create, this time with Prussia
left isolated as the threat to Europe's diplomatic balance.[42]

The King was confident of his army's capacity either to win the
war's initial battles or so to over-awe the Austrians that they would
concede the field after a few skirmishes fought for the sake of honour.
Events began suggesting different results even before the outbreak of
hostilities. Frederick had been so impressed by the Austrian artillery's
performance in the Seven Years War that he assembled over 800 guns
to support his operation. The effect of this huge artillery train on
largely unpaved roads, even in the dry season, was to enmesh the
Prussian army in its own fire support. Supply arrangements strained
and broke under the pressure of feeding larger numbers of men and
horses than Prussia had ever concentrated for a single campaign.
Under-fed and over-protected cavalry mounts collapsed, went lame,
or contracted disease by hundreds and thousands. Unseasoned, poorly
uniformed infantrymen, unused to sleeping rough and living hard,

---

42 Cf. generally from a Prussian perspective, Gustav Berthold Volz, 'Friedrich der
Grosse und der bayerische Erbfolgekrieg', *Forschungen zur brandenburgischen und
preussischen Geschichte*, XLIV (1932), 264–302; and more recently and generally,
Karl von Aretin, *Heiliges Römisches Reich 1776–1806: Reichsverfassung und
Souveranität*, 2 vols (Wiesbaden, 1967), vol. I, pp. 110 ff. The King's basic
operational plan is sketched in the 'Projet de campagne' in *PC*, XXX, 270 ff.

dropped out of ranks in clusters with everything from blisters to pneumonia.[43]

Not until 4 July 1778 did Frederick's main body cross the frontier. Henry's men entered Bohemia about the same time. The Prince was not particularly optimistic, believing the contending armies would be too large to do anything but glare at each other.[44] The Austrian high command agreed. Both sides had begun mobilizing early in the year, and about 160,000 whitecoats had been concentrated in Bohemia by the time the shooting started. Their role was purely defensive. Politically, the Empire could not risk appearing the aggressor. Militarily, against Frederick the best offence was a good defence. About 80,000 troops under Lacy were sent to confront the King. Laudon, with about 65,000, was assigned to cross swords with Henry.

The Prince did well enough initially, driving well into Bohemia without firing a shot. But even Henry's often-demonstrated skills at manoeuvre warfare could not compensate for his supply problems. His army could not carry enough food and forage to support its movements without depending on supply trains that proved less and less able to maintain the shuttle between magazines and haversacks, to say nothing of nose bags. It could not live off the countryside unless it kept moving. To keep moving invited confronting Laudon in the kind of head-on fight Henry believed would cost a third of his men to no purpose. And the Prussian Prince was too much a man of the eighteenth century to test his enemy's morale in a pitched battle.[45]

Frederick fared no better. His relative indifference to logistics was part of the calculated risk involved in maintaining a front-loaded military deterrent. Frederick had not projected the kind of campaign where supply problems would be a long-term issue. He expected to draw the Austrians into a quick fight on ground of his choosing. Instead, Lacy drew back to the Elbe River and entrenched. Frederick followed suit. For over a month he reconnoitred Lacy's position seeking a weak link. He found none. The Austrian, by this time commanding almost 100,000 men, kept them massed. Facing a force too large to bypass and too formidable to attack, Frederick reacted by sending to the shop for a bigger hammer: reinforcing his own army from Prussia's depots and garrisons. As supply trains failed to keep pace with troop concentrations, hungry soldiers sought a new

43 Jany, *Preussische Armee*, vol. III, p. 114; Duffy, *Army of Frederick the Great*, p. 204.

44 Prince Henry to Frederick, 10 March 1778, *PC*, XL, 231.

45 Easum, *Prince Henry of Prussia*, pp. 304 ff.

source of calories. The potato had been known in Europe since the seventeenth century, but was widely regarded with suspicion, blamed for causing a broad spectrum of diseases. As late as 1774 the citizens of Kolberg refused to eat them even in the midst of a famine.[46] But in a countryside stripped of more conventional foodstuffs, potatoes offered an alternative to privation. Foraging parties traded sickles for pitchforks, and the war went down in history as the 'Potato War'. The rank and file on both sides found the new vegetable tasty as well as nourishing: the potato's emergence as a diet staple in central Europe arguably owes a good bit to the problem of the Bavarian succession.

The operational stalemate in good part reflected the King's loss of physical vigour and intellectual flexibility as a general. As a statesman, however, Frederick was also responding to a series of Austrian overtures modifying Habsburg claims on Bavaria while at the same time acknowledging Frederick's long-asserted claims to the principalities of Ansbach and Bayreuth. Frederick wanted to win the war, not escalate it. Bringing up more troops was a diplomatic gesture as well as a military one: matching Austria's raise without calling the hand. Yet Maria Theresa was old and her son and successor ambitious. Their councils were correspondingly divided.[47] As weeks passed with no progress, Frederick declared it necessary 'to beat these buggers in order to inspire in them more reasonable sentiments'.[48]

With the King stymied at gun-barrel length, the task of beating the buggers devolved on Henry. The Prince solidified his reputation as Frederick's best general by going against his established patterns. Still critical of his brother for starting the war, in late July and early August the Prince feinted Laudon out of position by taking advantage of secondary roads and mountain passes deemed unusable by any sizeable force. Laudon fell back to the Iser River, and was ready to retreat further when Henry halted and began demanding reinforcements. The Prince was worn out, and so badly stressed that his health collapsed. He spent more time worrying about his own lines of retreat than considering how best to impose his plans and his will on a badly shaken enemy. None of Frederick's by now familiar sarcasm served to move Henry from his decision to remain in place, and to devastate by requisitions the territory between the Iser

46 W.H. Bruford, *Germany in the Eighteenth Century: The Social Background of the Literary Revival* (Cambridge, 1935), p. 117.

47 Beales, *Joseph I*, pp. 410 ff., is a solid analysis of Austria's ambivalent diplomacy.

48 Frederick to Prince Henry, 11 Aug. 1778, *PC*, XLI, 349.

and the Bohemian frontier. This would serve both to warn Austria of the consequences of continuing a useless war, and to protect Prussia against an invasion from that sector for another year.[49]

A disgruntled Frederick sought to reshape the campaign by moving his army on 16 August to a new entrenched camp a few miles distant, on the site of the Battle of Soor. The King may well have remembered more fortunate days when he discovered the Austrians had not only kept pace with him, but were also well entrenched in front of him. Frederick briefly considered storming the new Habsburg positions, then abandoned the idea in favour of imitating his brother by staging an eating withdrawal to his own frontiers, stripping Moravia of supplies as Henry proposed to do in Bohemia.[50]

As in 1744, the King was frustrated by the weather. On 31 August it turned cold and began to rain. A supply system already overstrained collapsed completely. An army already too large by far for its foraging areas compensated for hunger by eating everything available, including the by now rotten potatoes which gave the war its name. Dysentery and desertion stalked Prussian bivouacs to the point where Frederick described the wastage as 'enormous'.[51] Horses fared even worse than men as officers of once-proud cavalry regiments sold their mounts' hay and pocketed the proceeds.[52] Artillery teams, already at the bottom of the equine pecking order, could not begin to move the guns, except in easy stages and by double-, even triple-teaming. Austrian light troops harassed Frederick's retreat with successes unknown since the Silesian wars.

Frederick nevertheless refused to give up. By mid-October, with his main army safely back in Silesia, the King began making plans for the next year's campaign. He would have to fight without his brother. Henry, who had managed to withdraw his corps in relatively good order, resigned. His replacement was Prince Charles of Brunswick, a captain perfectly adequate to the demands of manoeuvre warfare. The problem lay in the tools available – or perhaps better expressed, in the quality of the tools available to the Austrians. The Habsburg

49 Joseph to Maria Theresa, 14 and 24 Aug. 1778, in Arneth, *Maria Theresia und Joseph II*, vol. III, pp. 48–9, 63 ff.; Prince Henry to Frederick, 22 and 27 Aug. 1778, *PC*, XL, 384–5, 393–4.

50 Frederick to Prince Henry, 26 Aug. 1778, *PC*, XLI, 387 ff.

51 Typically he referred to Henry's losses rather than his own. Frederick to Prince Henry, 3 Oct. 1778, *PC*, XLI, 453–94.

52 Duffy, *Army of Frederick the Great*, p. 205.

army continued to take the measure of the Prussians in the 'little war' waged along the frontiers once the weather moderated.

The Prussian army's structure and mission as developed after 1763 left almost no room for light troops of any kind. Frederick had insisted that the hussars be used primarily as battle cavalry, executing scouting and raiding missions only when nothing more important was required. He attempted to create most of his light infantry *ad hoc*, along the lines of the 'Free Battalions' of the Seven Years War. As suggested earlier in this chapter, the social and political climates in central Europe were significantly unfavourable for recruiting the kind of adventurous free-lancers such units required. The few that saw action achieved nothing except disgrace – assuming that either their officers or their men understood the concept. Efforts to convert second-line garrison battalions to free-ranging skirmishers met the expected results. As for the *Jäger*, Frederick took no more than six companies of them to war – and began by replacing three-fourths of their rifles with standard-issue muskets. The intention seems to have been to decrease their vulnerability to cavalry: an important point as Europe's terrain grew increasingly open. The results were demoralization and desertion on a massive scale.[53]

Operationally, the Prussian army found itself in the embarrassing position of being nibbled to death by ducks. Austrian battle groups, by now often including regular light infantry as well as the familiar Croats and hussars, found easy meat against Prussian foraging parties, patrols, and detachments. It was not so much that Frederick's light troops were outmatched – there simply were none available. The heavy units, infantry and cavalry alike, faced situations completely outside their training, and beyond the experience of all but their most senior officers.

With the turn of the year the whitecoats grew bolder. On 18 January two battalions of Prussian infantry, reduced in numbers by desertion and in energy by sickness, were cut off in the God-forsaken Silesian hamlet of Habelschwert. Some of them put up a hard fight, surrendering only when shelled out of their improvised blockhouse. Others scattered or threw down their muskets. Relief forces arrived too late; pursuit was ineffective; the Austrians made a clean break with more than 200 prisoners.

Similar events, albeit on a smaller scale, took place everywhere

53 Peter Paret, *Yorck and the Era of Prussian Reform* (Princeton, NJ, 1966), pp. 226 *passim*; and generally Johannes Kunisch, *Der kleine Krieg. Studien zum Heerwesen des Absolutismus* (Wiesbaden, 1973), *passim*.

in the theatre of war in the first weeks of 1779. On one level they should have surprised no one. The Prussian army had seldom been at its best in outpost fighting. Had the large-scale battles Frederick expected later in the spring actually taken place, Habelschwert and its counterparts would have been no more than footnotes in some general staff history. As it was, without grander events to balance them, they stood out in bold relief – much like the ambush of the US Rangers in Mogadishu in the autumn of 1993. Yet as his proud regulars rediscovered their military limitations, Frederick's army was winning Frederick's last war – by fulfilling its deterrent function.[54]

THE LAST VICTORY

In order to match the numbers Prussia and Saxony were able to field, Austria once again strained its financial resources and its administrative system to the point of self-destruction. On paper at least, 300,000 men stood under Habsburg colours ready for the 1779 campaigning season. The numbers actually under arms were lower. The numbers that could be effectively supported for any reasonable length of time were lower still. Maria Theresa had been unenthusiastic about the war from its inception. Joseph's dreams of martial glory had been tempered, if not entirely dissipated, by a season in the field, dealing with events and men who stubbornly defied the rational and enlightened principles that shaped the future monarch's thinking.[55] Operationally the Habsburg generals were confident enough that they could defeat the Prussians even in pitched battle, as long as they could choose the ground. Offensive operations seemed another story. Frederick's physical vigour had declined and his moral force diminished, but no one in the Austrian high command was seriously enthusiastic about the prospects for invading either Saxony or Silesia. Lacy was cautious and Loudan ill; even without the excuse of diarrhoea he was no longer the hard-driving battle captain of 1759. The situation from a Habsburg perspective, in short, was best described as '*déjà vu* all over again': Marshal Daun *redivivus*.

---

54 Frederick Wilhelm Carl Graf von Schmettau, *Über den Feldzug der preussischen Armee in Böhmen im Jahre 1778* (Berlin, 1789), remains the war's most detailed account from a Prussian operational perspective. The Austrian side is presented in the official history, Oscar Criste, *Kriege unter Kaiser Josef II* (Vienna, 1904).

55 Cf., for example, Joseph to Leopold, 18 July 1778, and to Maria Theresa, 27(?) Aug. 1778, in Arneth, *Maria Theresia und Joseph*, vol. II, pp. 351–3; and vol. III, pp. 68–9.

Diplomatic paradigms as well had changed since the 1760s. Breaking Prussia's power, returning it to the ranks of secondary states, was no longer a viable option – not least because Frederick had spent fifteen years demonstrating his new-found preference for cooperation rather than confrontation. From a general European perspective, Austria could legitimately be described as seeking to achieve in Bavaria what Prussia had desired in Silesia four decades earlier: a permanent alteration of the balance of power in its favour[56]. It was small wonder that the great powers viewed the situation in their midst with increasing alarm. Initially, Catherine of Russia had refused to live up to the letter of the Russo-Prussian alliance, denying both cash and soldiers. Increasingly, however, the young and restless Joseph seemed from the perspective of St Petersburg a greater long-term threat than a Prussian king who insisted he wished only to spend his last days in peace.

Nor did Frederick rely only on words. The French foreign ministry faced an empty treasury, a collapsing revenue structure, and growing internal challenges to a weak monarch. In spite of these weaknesses France was well engaged in the process of supporting the American rebels. To concentrate on the colonial war and to prevent Britain from exploiting a Continental war in its own interests, the government was desperately concerned with maintaining Europe's peace at almost any price that did not include *louis d'or* and fighting men. Frederick encouraged France to use instead its diplomatic credit – specifically, its still favourable position with the Sublime Porte. French good offices played a major role in securing agreement between Russia and Turkey to at least put on the back-burner a set of differences that had remained unresolved by the 1774 Peace of Kutchuk Kainardji.[57]

Catherine, encouraged by advisers influenced by Prussian ideas and Prussian gold, responded by informing Vienna in November that if the war was not settled satisfactorily Russia would honour its treaty and support Frederick with an expeditionary force. Words were cheap, but 15,000 Russian troops on the march to the Austrian frontier were impossible to ignore. Their looming presence gave

56 See Paul W. Schroeder, *The Transformation of European Politics 1763–1848* (Oxford, 1994), pp. 5 ff. and 28–9, for an analysis of the international system generally and in the context of the Potato War.

57 Cf. M.S. Anderson, *The Eastern Question 1774–1923* (London, 1966), pp. 6–7; and more generally, A. Fisher, *The Russian Annexation of the Crimea 1772–1783* (Cambridge, 1970).

weight to Maria Theresa's insistence on opening negotiations. France and Russia were willing. Frederick was eager – particularly when Catherine declared her intention to oppose any significant changes in the Holy Roman Empire.[58]

After two months of squabbling, the powers agreed to terms. An armistice in March became the Peace of Teschen in May. Bavaria went to the Elector Palatine and his heirs, except for a small strip, the Innviertel, ceded to Austria. Prussia's rights in Ansbach and Bayreuth were upheld: twelve years later both entities would come under the black eagle.[59] As much to the point, Prussia's status among the lesser states of Germany underwent a sea change. From the disturber of the Empire's peace, Frederick's kingdom had emerged as the defender of the sovereign rights established by the Peace of Westphalia in 1648 against Austrian aggrandizement. Austria's position in central Europe was not as secure as it seemed to contemporaries. The Habsburg Empire's financial and administrative structures were not those of a hegemonial power. The size of the army Joseph and Maria Theresa had been able to field was, however, carefully noted in capitals from Dresden to Hanover. No conceivable coalition of German states would have a remote chance of standing against the Habsburgs without the wholehearted support of a great power. France and Russia might seek the diplomatic advantages accruing to a protector at any acceptable price. It was, however, questionable whether either would intervene to protect those liberties. Britain was far away – more distant diplomatically from German affairs than at any time in over a century. As for the remaining contender, Frederick was old. His heir was inconsequential. It was highly unlikely that Prussia would take in the foreseeable future the kind of risks it had so blithely assumed in 1740. The upstart kingdom might not have entirely completed the transition from goat to gardener; nevertheless, especially after Maria Theresa's death in 1780, the King appeared a more than preferable alternative to the Emperor.[60]

58 Stribrny, *Russlandpolitik*, pp. 98 ff.; and Wiliam C. Fuller, *Strategy and Power in Russia, 1600–1914* (New York, 1992) p. 122 *passim*, survey Russia's diplomatic and strategic situation.

59 Adolf Unzer, *Der Friede von Teschen. Ein Beitrag zur Geschichte des bayerischen Erbfolgestreites* (Kiel, 1903), remains useful for both the treaty's details and its diplomatic background.

60 Schroeder, *Transformation of European Politics*, pp. 29 ff; Aretin, *Heiliges Römisches Reich*, vol. I, pp. 117 ff.; and H.M. Scott, *British Foreign Policy in the Age of the American Revolution* (Oxford, 1990).

The Potato War, in short, was far from the débâcle or the farce often presented in narrowly focused military histories. It provided instead the kind of diplomatic/political triumph Frederick had always hoped for from the army he had spent his life building. The costs had been acceptable relative to the gains. The 30,000 men who died or deserted included large numbers of foreigners enlisted expressly for the purpose of being expended. Expenses had been met from current revenues, with the war chest remaining essentially untouched. And, far from shrugging off the operational shortcomings of his army, Frederick took comprehensive pains to shave off the worst of the rust that had spread beneath fifteen years of paint and polish.

Foremost in this category was the King's attention to developing an effective force of light troops. Despite their poor performance, the *Jäger* were increased to a full regiment of ten companies. The King also developed a series of instructions and directives for the use of light troops, and in 1786 began raising cadres for three specialized regiments of light infantry. Some idea of his approach is suggested in the name he proposed for these units – 'Free Regiments' – recalling the irregular *Freibataillonen* of his earlier wars. Far from procuring light troops as the possible nucleus of a new tactical approach, Frederick saw them as primarily useful for outpost and picket duties with a secondary mission as first line of attack in a pitched battle. Advancing at the run and in open order – open at least by the standards of the line regiments – the *Jäger* and Free Regiments would at least draw the enemy's fire, and at best close with him in a hand-to-hand mêlée that would prepare the way for the line regiments. Marksmanship took a distant second place to *élan*; the King expected his light troops to employ as a matter of course the same system of volley fire used by the regular infantry.[61]

Frederick's instructions can hardly be interpreted as directly prefiguring the light infantry tactics of the French Revolution. He remained convinced that skirmishers could play no more than a secondary tactical role in modern war. The King's focus was operational: providing an effective counter to the Austrian light troops that had proved such a handicap to the movement and supply of his main forces. On the other hand, the fusiliers who grew out of the experimental Free Regiments proved a good match for the best

61 Frederick II, 'Instruction für die Frei-Regimenter, oder leichten Infanterie-Regimenter', 5 Dec. 1783, *Œuvres de Frédéric le Grand*, ed. J.D.E. Preuss, 30 vols (Berlin, 1846–56), vol. XXX, pp. 431 *passim*; Jany, *Preussische Armee*, vol. III, p. 131.

voltigeurs of France in the 1790s, while the *Jäger* regiment became one of the best in Prussian service.[62]

Arguably more significant for the Prussian army's future was Frederick's continued reluctance to modify its centralized command structure and task-force/battle-group organization. Much of the operational inflexibility characterizing the Potato War was a consequence of the field armies having grown too large to be controlled in the fashion of those in the Seven Years War. The Austrians had faced a similar problem, but their defensive stance made it less obvious. The lesson was not overlooked in France, where it seemed to confirm the system of permanent infantry brigades assigned to territorially based infantry divisions established in 1776.[63] Prussia, however, went on as before – and would pay the price twenty years later.

Frederick's advancing age and declining physical and mental vigour precluded in any case the inauguration of further military reforms during the half-dozen years of life that remained to him. The King lived increasingly in the past, remembering Hohenfriedberg, Leuthen, and Torgau as he watched his regiments pass before him. In January 1786, Ziethen died, last of the great captains of the army's golden years. Frederick's response is well-known: 'In wartime he always commanded the advance guard, and now he has taken the lead in death. I always led the main army, and now I shall follow after him just as on campaign.'[64] Seven months later, on 17 August 1786, Frederick the Great was dead.

---

62 Dennis E. Showalter, 'Hubertusberg to Auerstädt: The Prussian Army in Decline?' *German History*, XII (1994), 308–33.

63 Steven T. Ross, 'The Development of the Combat Division in Eighteenth-Century French Armies', *French Historical Studies*, IV (1965), pp. 84–94.

64 Quoted in Duffy, *Army of Frederick the Great*, p. 207.

REFLECTIONS

In 1937, the *Infantry Journal* published 'An All-Time Command Team' for a then state-of-the-art army corps. The author chose as his commanding general Frederick the Great, praising him as a strategist able to tell the difference between good and bad advice, a strong disciplinarian, and successful in sustaining domestic political support.[1] This minor *jeu d'esprit* by an obscure field officer may be extreme, but it is hardly unique. Frederick's reputation as soldier and statesman endures at the end of the twentieth century. One recent work goes so far as to describe him as one of the early modern world's 'invincible generals.'[2] Yet recent scholarship has also produced its share of revisionists. As a general, Frederick emerges from their pages as obsessed with the *fata morgana* of decisive battle. As a statesman he is presented as the first in a long line of Prussian/German rulers and captains whose reach exceeded their grasp, whose visions of grandeur excluded recognizing or willing the means to achieve the ends. It was Frederick, according to these interpreters, who established the matrix for the belief that the security of the Prussian kingdom and the German Reich depended on the application of military power in a specific way. It was Frederick whose career, and the myths surrounding it, led generations of diplomats and soldiers to insist, against all contrary evidence, that Germany could not only fight and win short wars against exponentially superior adversaries, but convince her erstwhile enemies to accept the outcome of those wars without further challenge.[3]

---

1 Lt.-Col. George L. Simpson, 'An All-Time Command Team', reprinted in *The Infantry Journal Reader*, ed. Col. J.L. Greene (Garden City, NY, 1943), pp. 338–41.

2 Philip Haythornthwaite, *Invincible Generals* (Bloomington, Ind., 1992).

3 Cf. the discussion of this issue in Dennis E. Showalter, 'German Grand Strategy: A Contradiction in Terms?' *Militärgeschichtliche Mitteilungen*, XLVIII (1990), 65–102.

Understanding the wars of Frederick the Great depends on understanding two general points. The first is that at operational levels, deadlock is war's normal condition. Armed forces tend to learn from each other, copying and adopting behaviours and techniques to suit their own dynamics. Napoleon's achievements from Marengo to Aspern, the panzers' string of victories between 1939 and 1941, even the triumph of the NVA over the U.S. expeditionary forces in Vietnam – all are exceptions reflecting the exploitation of windows of opportunity, that close more or less rapidly, depending on how vital a given conflict's stakes are to the participants.

Nothing essential to Frederick's way of war was inherently unique to Prussia. The Austrians, the Russians, even the French were able between 1740 and 1763 to overhaul their military systems to a point where even Frederick's skills as strategist and commander could do no more than force a long end-game. States and statesmen rolled the iron dice of battle as a means of improving negotiating positions, but also for the game's own sake. War can be intoxicating at all its levels from the front line to the council chamber. Victory offers at least the promise of cutting the Gordian knot of agreements, expectations, and premises that sustain any system involving sovereign powers. Mutually-enhanced proficiency, however, tends to confirm stasis at higher levels of intensity – a point highlighted by the Seven Years War. Prussia was ultimately saved from defeat, perhaps destruction, not by the military genius of its ruler, but by the death of Russia's Empress Elizabeth and her temporary replacement by an extreme Prussophile. Once Russia left the war the remaining combatants collapsed from mutual exhaustion, as much relieved to have found an excuse to stop fighting as frustrated by the war's outcome.

War's tendency towards stasis enhances the importance of politics as a means of resolving conflict – not as a second-best solution, but a desirable norm. Before 1740 and after 1763 Europe faced a continuing series of diplomatic crises and small wars, all constantly threatening to escalate out of control.[4] The statesmen of the eighteenth century, and the soldiers as well, genuinely desired balance. That concept is the second crucial issue underlying the

---

4 Cf. the essays in Jeremy Black, 'Mid-Eighteenth-Century Conflicts with Particular Reference to the War of the Polish and Austrian Successions', in *The Origins of War in Early Modern Europe*, ed. J. Black (Edinburgh, 1987); and the discussion in Paul W. Schroeder, *The Transformation of European Politics, 1763–1848*, (Oxford, 1994), pp. 5 ff.

wars of Frederick. The term has a meaning far broader than the power relations of states. It involved correlating ends and means, risks and gains, aspirations and possibilities.[5] One of the taproots of balance was intellectual. The Age of Reason informed by *l'ésprit géometrique* discouraged heroic vitalisms of all kinds. A second taproot was historical. The experience of two bitter centuries showed that even the most powerful states neither controlled sufficient surplus resources nor possessed sufficient capacity to mobilize the resources at their disposal to sustain a position as primary power, let alone that of hegemon. Overstressed internal structures resulted in domestic gridlocks just as detrimental to vaulting ambition as were the hostile international coalitions such ambitions tended to produce.

This state of affairs did not exclude the possibility of the significant aggrandizement of particular states. It did mean that such aggrandizement was best sought in the context of existing systems. From his earliest days on the throne Frederick sought not to overthrow the balance of Europe, but to adjust that balance in Prussia's favour. But how could that outcome be best secured? States are like bridge players. They tend to lead from strength, or perceived strength. Prussia's history was that of a minor power. Prussia's economy illustrated at best the capacity to make bricks with a minimum of straw. Prussia's society was highly regimented in a Europe where daily life was virtually libertarian by twentieth-century standards. Prospects, in short, for generating a bandwagon effect scarcely existed. Instead, developing Prussia as a model for other ambitious states meant a risk on one hand of generating a hostile coalition against a paradigmatic threat, and on the other of destabilizing the very great powerful system Frederick sought to join as a full member.

The challenge for Prussia's King, therefore, involved pushing the envelope: adjusting Europe's structure without denying its principles. In this context Frederick's demonstrated disinterest in creating new military paradigms represents less a failure of vision than a conscious decision. His army was designed to maximize the war-making potential of Prussia's social contract. The state's government, economy, and society were placed at the service of a military machine intended to strain the kingdom's resources, but not exhaust them. The army was structured to maximize its efficiency under existing conditions of warfare. Its training, its discipline, and its tactics were refinements

---

5 This concept was originally presented in a different context in Walter A. McDougall, 'Oh Henry! Kissinger and His Critics', *Orbis*, XXXVIII (1994), 665.

rather than innovations. In an age when battles were decided by the firepower of linear formations and victory was completed by cavalry charges, Prussian infantry could deliver more rounds per minute than any of their European counterparts. Prussian cavalry could strike harder, rally more completely, and appear more quickly where needed than any other horsemen on the continent. In an age when manoeuvre in the face of an enemy risked disruption by counterattacks, Frederick's battalions could change from columns of march into lines of battle so rapidly that the process seemed almost magical. The famous oblique order, with one flank of the army weighted heavily and echeloned forward to roll up the enemy, depended as much on quickness of deployment on the field as on pre-battle planning.

Balance was intended to prevent empire rather than preserve peace. Nor did it guarantee the position of lesser players. Alliances were intended for expansion and acquisition as well as for security.[6] Prussian territory was spread in fragments from the Rhine to the Memel. Prussia was a correspondingly obvious target in an international system that by 1740 was clearly suffering from multiple tensions likely to destabilize it in the near future.

The death of Austrian Emperor Charles VI was, for Frederick, a catalyst. The Prussian King legitimately expected the Habsburg Empire, now ruled by a young and inexperienced woman, to be challenged on all of its frontiers by all of its neighbours. In such a context Prussia must be either hammer or anvil. To stand aside was to invite Brandenburg's fate in the Thirty Years' War: ravaged by all, respected by none. War, moreover, offered a tempting prize. The Austrian province of Silesia offered human and material resources that, properly utilized, would enable Prussia to become a European power of the first rank. The Prussian army, ready for war from a standing start, should be able to secure Silesia and hold it against all comers while Frederick legitimized the new order by negotiations.

This calculation determined the course of Prussian policy for over two decades because it was such a spectacular miscalculation. From Mollwitz in 1741 to Hohenfriedberg in 1745, the Prussian army established itself as the new master of Europe's battlefields. Frederick displayed the diplomatic virtuosity of a riverboat gambler, making and abrogating treaties, concluding and abandoning alliances, with breathtaking audacity. Yet Austria and its Empress Maria Theresa

6 Schroeder, *The Transformation of European Politics*, p. 7.

remained unreconciled to the new *status quo*, while the King's behaviour created enough mistrust among his neighbours that by 1756 France, Russia, and Austria formed a grand alliance whose major aim was, if not to destroy Prussia completely, then to reduce it definitively and permanently to the status of a middle-ranking German state. By 1756 Frederick stood alone in a sea of enemies, his only support an English connection that never became more than a relationship of convenience.

Frederick initiated the Seven Years War with exactly the same assumptions that had shaped his behaviour in 1740. By attacking first he hoped to win victories decisive enough to encourage his adversaries to negotiate a durable peace. The history of the war itself is the history of that strategy's failure. From Kolin in 1757 to Torgau in 1760 the Prussian army was never outfought. It was defeated often enough to keep the anti-Prussian coalition in the field despite its increasing internal conflicts. And it was victorious often enough to keep Frederick from seeking the best terms he could get. In gambler's terms, the army was a hole card high enough to encourage another round of betting even when the King was beaten on the board. The resulting escalation of the stakes made exiting the game impossible: a classic double bind.

Taken in the long run, however, Prussia's waging of the Seven Years War was a marked success. Frederick had secured his state's place at the continent's head table. Prussia in 1763 was by no means a satiated power. But during the second half of his reign Frederick sought aggrandizement in the context of the great-power relationships established after the Peace of Hubertusberg in 1763. By the Bavarian succession crisis of 1778–79, indeed, Prussia as ruler emerged as the continent's elder statesman, sustaining a German and European order apparently threatened by the vaulting ambitions of Austria's young Emperor Joseph II.

For Frederick, Prussia's army was as much a deterrent as a war-fighting instrument. Its purpose was first to win victories, then to demonstrate the state's readiness and capacity to defend its interests. The parades, the manoeuvres, even the mythology that ultimately developed around Rossbach, Leuthen, and Zorndorf – all were designed to highlight the risks of trying conclusions with a dangerous enemy. It took a quarter-century to establish the deterrent's credibility. Once in place it endured for twenty years after its creator's death – a long time in an environment that unquestionably accepted war as a normal consequence of diplomacy. Even then it required the ambition and the genius of Napoleon to challenge Frederick's legacy systematically.

Frederick the Great did not transcend his milieu either as soldier or as statesman. Nevertheless, by establishing Prussia as a European power, and by encouraging the definition of that status in primarily military terms, he decisively shaped the next two centuries of Europe's history. As for his status as a commander, one could do worse than repeat the challenge made in the article cited at the beginning of these comments: 'Trot out your corps and name your ground. If, at the conclusion of hostilities, my politicians are not showing your politicians where to sign on the dotted line, I'll buy a round of drinks.'[7] Even at long odds, one could do worse than bet on Old Fritz when the shooting started.

7 Simpson, 'An All-Time Command Team', p. 340.

FURTHER READING

The Wars of Frederick the Great stands on the shoulders of two distinguished scholars. Jeremy Black has almost single-handedly made the study of eighteenth-century international relations intellectually respectable. His demonstration of the importance of obscure and long-forgotten negotiations, his ability to combine seemingly discrete evidence into coherent and compelling analyses of the mentality underlying diplomacy, have 'recovered' an aspect of history as completely 'lost' as the daily lives of women in the remotest Sussex village. Christopher Duffy, has brilliantly applied the principles of the 'new military history' to the study of eighteenth-century armed forces. His ability to dissect the military institutions of Europe and present their internal dynamics is matched by his skill at showing armies at their work of war-making. Steering a course between these giants is like passing between Scylla and Charybdis.

The reference apparatus of this work is designed to be user-friendly – no small task given the immense body of material at the disposal of even a casual student of Frederick's wars. I decided to keep chapter footnotes at the minimum consistent with scholarly standards. Contemporary works are as a rule cited only for direct quotations or to confirm a specialized point of information. That left the problem of dealing with literally hundreds of secondary sources. As a beginning, I chose to limit direct references to major standard works, utilizing them instead to construct the general narrative and mentioning those most important in this essay.

To begin with personalities, the standard general biography of Frederick II remains Reinhold Koser's four-volume *Geschichte Friedrichs des Grossen*. Originally published in 1893–95, the standard revised edition appeared at Stuttgart in four volumes between 1921 and 1925; there is now a reprint edition (Darmstadt, 1963). Alfred Ritter von Arneth, *Geschichte Maria Theresias*, 10 vols. (Vienna, 1863–79), is Koser's counterpart: a detailed study of the Austrian Empress and her reign: a mine of detail of diplomatic and military issues. Theodor Schieder's *Friedrich der Grosse: Ein Königtum der Widersprüche* (Frankfurt, 1983), is the best modern analysis of the King's personality. Ingrid Mittenzwei, *Friedrich II, von Preussen Eine Biographie* (Berlin, 1979), heads the list of a large body of East German research on a monarch whose image changed constantly with the politics of the East German state. Christopher Duffy, *Frederick the Great: A Military Life* (London, 1985) remains the definitive analysis of Frederick as a soldier.

For the operational side of Frederick's wars, an indispensable source remains the massive General Staff history: *Die Kriege Friedrichs des Grossen*, Part I: *Der Erste Schlesische Kriege 1740–1742, Vols. I–III*. Part II: *Der Zweite Schlesische Kriege, 1744–1745, Vols. I–III*. Part III: *Der Siebenjährige Kriege, 1756–1763, I–XII*. Published between 1890 and 1913, they take the story only to the end of 1759. Often and legitimately criticized for their present-minded intellectual framework, the volumes are nevertheless a mine of detail of troop movements and an endless source of anecdotes. Even better is the Austrian official history, *Geschichte der Kämpfe Österreichs. Kriege unter der Regierung der Kaiserin-Königin Maria Theresia: Österreichischen Erbfolge-Kriege 1740–1748*, 9 vols (Vienna, 1896–1914). Unfortunately uncompleted, it was even more unfortunately not carried forward to the greater conflict that began in 1756. R. Waddington's *La Guerre de Sept Ans. Histoire Diplomatique et Militaire*, 5 vols (Paris, 1899–1914), has a French perspective but incorporates much information from French officers attached to the Austrian army. For readers blind of their Russian eye, D.F. Masslowski, *Der siebenjährige Krieg nach russischer Darstellung*, tr. A. von Drygalski, 3 vols (Berlin, 1889–1893), is excellent.

Put together these works provided the raw material for most of the battle descriptions in the present text. For specifically military information, readers need go no further than Christopher Duffy's magisterial treatments of *The Army of Frederick the Great* (Newton Abbot, 1974); *The Army of Maria Theresa: the Armed Forces of Imperial Austria, 1740–1780* (London, 1977); and *Russia's Military Way to the West: Origins and Nature of Russian Military Power 1700–1800* (London, 1981); while for France there are Lee Kennett, *The French Armies in the Seven Years' War* (Durham, N.C., 1967) and André Corvisier's two-part *L'armée française de la fin du XVIIe siècle au ministère de Choiseul: le soldat* (Paris, 1964). Volume II of Curt Jany's *Geschichte der Königlich Preussischen Armee von 15. Jahrhundert bis zum Jahre 1807*, 2nd ed. rev., 4 vols (Osnabrück,

1967) is a solid shortcut for anyone lacking the months necessary to peruse the larger General Staff history.

As a rule the chapter footnotes refer to specialized modern works on a particular subject, be it diplomatic, economic, or operational. Around the turn of the century, however, German and Austrian scholars published a large number of campaign and battle histories for the years from 1740 to 1763. Many of these are quite brief. Most are stronger on narrative than analysis. Much of their important material was integrated into the later, larger works mentioned above. I nevertheless chose to incorporate them into the footnotes along with more recent battle studies, both as guides to the perplexed and as makeweights to my own interpretations of the complex and confusing fields on which Europe's destiny was decided between 1740 and 1763.

NORTH SEA

BALT

BRAND
P

Berlin

HANNOVER

Elbe R.

† Hastenbeck (1757)

Magdeburg

Minden (1759) †

† Torgau (1760)

SAXONY

Weser R.

† Rossbach (1757)

Dresden

Lobositz (1756) †

GERMAN STATES

Pragu

BOHE

Main R.

Molau

FRANCE

Rhine R.

Danu

The Wars of Frederick the Great

EA

Konigsberg
† Gross-Jagersdorf (1757)
EAST PRUSSIA

RG-
A

Zorndorf (1758)

Kunersdorf (1759)

Vistula R.

KINGDOM OF POLAND

Breslau
† Liegnitz (1760)
† Leuthen (1757)
ochkirch (1758)
† Hohenfriedberg (1745)
† Mollwitz (1741)
† Soor (1745)

Oder R.

ague (1757) † Chotusitz (1742)
† Kolin (1757)

† Olmütz (1758)

AUSTRIA

MORAVIA

HUNGARY

March R.

| 0 | | 100 mls |

Vienna

INDEX

administration of Prussian state under Frederick William I, 27–8

agriculture under Frederick William I, 17

Aix-la-Chapelle, Peace of (1748), 89, 90

allotment system, 20–1

America, North, French and British rivalry in, 90, 119, 120, 123, 126, 258, 298

annexation as means of Prussian expansion, 32

Ansbach-Bayreuth, 94, 342

Apraksin, Field-Marshal S., 178–9

armies,
Austrian, 43–4, 136, 137–9, 322–3
battle drill, 25, 67–9, 109, 110, 114
British, 121–2
enlistment into, 11–12, 169, 170
French, 12, 168–71, 173–5
Prussian, 231–4, 260–4, 300–1, 326–37, 351–2, 355–6, 357
artillery, 34–6, 70–1, 72, 332–3
battle drill, 67–9, 109, 110, 114
Cadet Corps, 8, 233
cantonists, 21–3, 101–4, 105
cavalry, 51, 71–3, 113–15
death rates, 23
desertion, 23, 101–2, 143, 144–5, 335
discipline, 24–7, 77, 331–2
under Frederick William I, 18, 19–27, 71, 110
infantry, 33–4, 35–6, 68–9, 232–3
nobility integrated into, 104–5
officer corps, 9, 105, 233, 261, 336–7
recruitment, 20–3
right of leave, 23–4
structure of, 33–4, 106
tactics and operational methods, 105–16

weapon systems, 34–6, 70–1, 332–3
recruitment, 11–12, 20–3, 169–70
Russian, 21, 122–3
size of, 10, 12
standing, 12
structure of, 6–9, 33–4, 106
Swedish, 20–1
training, 24, 109–10, 111
weapon systems, 6–7, 34–6, 70–1, 72, 332–3

arms production, 98–101
see also weapons systems

artillery, 7, 34–6, 70–1, 232, 261–2

Austria, 178, 338, 339, 356–7
administrative reform, 137, 297
army, 43–4, 136, 137–9, 322–3
victory at Breslau, 193
and Britain, 61, 62, 91–2, 118, 119, 121, 123, 314
Court War Council, 137
economic crisis, 317–18
and France, 117, 118, 127, 129–30, 266
war with France, 31, 62–3
General War Commissary, 137
Imperial Election Scheme, 119
and Russia, 93, 117, 122, 124, 208, 266–7, 312
alliance with Saxony, 74
and Seven Years' War, 135–6, 139–42, 148–65, 181, 183–206 *passim*, 221–7, 235, 236, 242–56 *passim*, 267–81, 285–99, 305–6, 318–20
first Silesian war, 39–61
second Silesian war, 73–89, 90
and Treaty of Worms, 64
War of the Austrian Succession, 38–91 *passim*
and War of the Bavarian Succession, 341–51

Austrian Netherlands, 74, 124, 341

365